A BIRDER'S GUIDE
TO THE
RIO GRANDE VALLEY

MARK W. LOCKWOOD

WILLIAM B. MCKINNEY

JAMES N. PATON

BARRY R. ZIMMER

AmericanBirding
ASSOCIATION

Library of Congress Control Number: 2008037158

ISBN: 1-878788-49-3

Fourth Edition
1   2   3   4   5   6   7   8

Printed in the United States of America

Publisher
American Birding Association, Inc.

Editor
Paul E. Lehman

Maps
Cindy Lippincott and Virginia Maynard

Production
Virginia Maynard

Front Cover Photograph
Green Jay
Kevin Karlson

Back Cover Photographs
Hooded Oriole
Brad McKinney

Lucifer Hummingbird
Barry Zimmer

Other Photographs
Mark W. Lockwood, Brad McKinney, Michael O'Brien, Barry Zimmer

Illustrations
Jen Brumfield, Shawneen Finnegan, Michael O'Brien, Louise Zemaitis

Distributed by
American Birding Association Sales
115 Fairview Road, Asheville, NC 28803
toll-free 800-634-7736 (in USA and Canada)
or 828-274-5575 (international)
fax 800-590-2473 (in USA and Canada) or 719-578-9705 (international)
email: abasales@abasales.com
website: www.americanbirding.org/abasales

DEDICATIONS

From Brad:
For Janette and Will

From Mark to Amy and Paul:
Thank you for being there for me
when I needed you most

From Jim:
Thanks to Rita, Grant, and Andrew
for your love and support

From Barry to Yvonne and Alex:
Thanks for being my everything

ACKNOWLEDGMENTS

A *Birder's Guide to the Rio Grande Valley* has a long history; it found roots in 1971 as a modest 72-page book, part of the Lane Guide Series authored by the late Jim Lane. The first Lane Guides revolutionized birdfinding by providing a simple but effective means of assisting the traveling birder to find the best birding spots and most of a region's avian specialties, along with suggesting strategies for seeing the greatest number of species. The guide was updated in 1978 and 1988 by Jim, and in 1992 by the late Harold Holt. Harold had taken on the task of updating the Lane Guides upon Jim Lane's death. We all owe a debt of gratitude to Jim and Harold for their tireless work and devotion to the formative years of this guide. In 1999, the current team of authors and long-time Texas birders, Mark W. Lockwood, William B. McKinney, James N. Paton, and Barry R. Zimmer, worked together to publish a definitive new edition of the book.

Several sections of the draft text were reviewed by Mary Gustafson. Cindy Lippincott contributed editing and proofreading advice for the entire guide. Martin Hagne wrote the short section discussing potential impacts of the "border wall." Other helpful input was received from Michael O'Brien, Father Tom Pincelli, and Pat Sutton.

Mark W. Lockwood was responsible for the Del Rio/Amistad area, central Trans-Pecos (Big Bend National Park, Big Bend Ranch State Park, Alpine, Fort Davis, and Balmorhea), and the Edwards Plateau. Mark acknowledges important contributions by Doug Booher, who reviewed the Edwards Plateau section; Chuck Sexton, who provided details for Balcones Canyonlands National Wildlife Refuge; Mark Flippo, who reviewed the Big Bend National Park section; Nick Jackson, who reviewed the Kerrville section and checked several other sites; Kelly Bryan, who provided details and text for the Big Bend Ranch State Park and Devils River State Natural Area segments; and Junie Sorola, who reviewed the Del Rio text.

William B. McKinney tackled the popular Lower Rio Grande Valley from the coast upriver to San Ygnacio. Brad wishes to thank the following people for their important contributions to the text: Tim Brush reviewed the

Santa Ana National Wildlife Refuge, Anzalduas County Park, and Edinburg area text; Mike Carlo reviewed the Roma Bluffs and Santa Ana National Wildlife Refuge text; Kim Eckert reviewed the text for Starr and Zapata Counties; Martin Hagne reviewed the Weslaco and Harlingen area text; Jim Hailey wrote the Laredo text; Jennifer Owen-White reviewed the text for Estero Llano Grande State Park; Joshua Rose reviewed the Hidalgo and Bentsen State Park text; Ruben Zamora reviewed the Edinburg area text. Brad also thanks Jim Bangma, Colleen Hook, Jane Kittleman, and Marisa Oliva for reviewing parts of the manuscript. Special thanks to Janette McKinney for her encouragement throughout the project.

James N. Paton revised and added to the text covering the Pecos Valley, El Paso, El Paso Valley, Guadalupe Mountains, and New Mexico sites in Las Cruces, the Organ Mountains, and Carlsbad Caverns, in addition to writing a number of the species accounts in the Annotated Checklist. Jim thanks John Sproul for information on Feather Lake and Rio Bosque Wetlands Park, and JoBeth Holub and John Karges for providing information on the Chandler Ranch/Independence Creek Preserve. Carl Lundblad, Marcy Scott, and Jimmy Zabriskie were helpful in providing information for the Las Cruces area. Jerry Oldenettel helped with information on Washington Ranch. Jim is grateful to his wife, Rita, for her support and understanding.

Barry R. Zimmer worked with Jim Paton on the Trans-Pecos text and on many of the species accounts. Barry is grateful to Jim Peterson, John Sproul, and Kevin Zimmer for their contributions to Trans-Pecos birding knowledge and for their help with his section of the guide. He is also grateful to his wife, Yvonne, for her constant support and encouragement.

TABLE OF CONTENTS

Ferruginous Pygmy-Owl

Jen Brumfield

INTRODUCTION

Texas birdlife is strongly influenced by the incredible diversity of habitats found within its borders. The Rio Grande corridor is a great example of this diversity. From El Paso to Brownsville, this once-majestic river forms the 1,569-mile southern and western borders of Texas. At El Paso, the average rainfall is only nine inches per year compared to the 26-inch annual rainfall of the subtropical Lower Rio Grande Valley. In between can be found the magnificent Chihuahuan Desert with its mountain islands, the Stockton and Edwards Plateaus, and the brush-covered plains of South Texas.

The Rio Grande begins near the Continental Divide in the San Juan Mountains of Colorado. It starts as a clear spring-fed and snow-fed stream at about 12,000 feet above sea level. It is one of the major drainage systems of the southwestern United States. The 1,896-mile course of the river makes it the fifth-longest river in North America. Once bordered by riparian woodlands through New Mexico and West Texas and vast stands of Sabal Palms at the Delta, the Rio Grande has suffered greatly at the hands of humans. Most of the woodlands have long since been cut down, and there are five major reservoirs along the river's length. At Presidio, it is often just a trickle before meeting the Rio Conchos coming out of Mexico. Here and at other locations, the river is choked by salt cedar. Despite these problems, the Rio Grande corridor still provides habitat for a wide variety of birds, butterflies, mammals, amphibians, and reptiles, and the river itself can be breathtakingly beautiful.

The fact that the Rio Grande forms the boundary between Texas and Mexico adds further to its mystique. Many subtropical species reach the northern limits of their ranges along the border. The Lower Rio Grande Valley is known as one of the premier places to look for Mexican birds during the winter. Species are routinely added to the Texas state list from this area. The river also crosses the 100th meridian of longitude, which is often thought of as a dividing line between eastern and western species. El Paso is 10 degrees of longitude, or 500 miles, west of Brownsville, and the differences between their plants and animals are extreme.

Much of the region along the Rio Grande is arid, and, as a result, thorny shrubs often dominate the landscape. These similar-looking plant communities often have vastly different avifaunas, however. There is little overlap in the avian communities of the brush country of the South Texas Plains and the thorn scrub of the Chihuahuan Desert. There are, in fact, several distinct regions in Texas and each has a wide variety of habitats, some of which are limited in scope within a particular region.

REGIONS OF TEXAS

Texas is divided into 10 ecological or physiographic regions. The area covered by this guide lies within three of these regions: the South Texas Plains, the Edwards Plateau, and the Trans-Pecos. The extreme southern tip of South Texas is further separated as the Lower Rio Grande Valley. Many Texans refer to the area from Falcon Dam to the Gulf simply as "The Valley."

Texas is a large state, and good birding opportunities can be found throughout. However, each ecological region has its own specialties and these areas are often very far apart. The spectacular trans-Gulf migrations take place, for the most part, along the coast. Most of the tropical species that reach Texas are limited to the Lower Valley or Big Bend. A few Rocky Mountain species can be found in Texas only in the Guadalupe and Davis Mountains. Two of the state specialties are restricted to the Edwards Plateau. Needless to say, most visiting birders will have to make several trips to Texas in order to visit most or all of the premier birding locations.

WHEN TO COME

Many out-of-state birders center their plans to visit Texas around spring migration on the Upper Texas Coast. This usually means a visit between mid-April and early May, a good time to visit most of the major birding areas of the state. A mid-winter visit to South Texas is almost a must; the weather is generally pleasant and the potential for vagrant birds from Mexico is at its peak. Unfortunately, not all of the South Texas specialties can be found in winter.

During the summer, it is not uncommon to find temperatures of 100°F or more from the Lower Valley to El Paso. If you can withstand these high temperatures, the late summer is an excellent time to visit Big Bend National Park and bird the Chisos Mountains. The temperatures in the mountains are usually in the upper 80s to low 90s°F. This is a great time to see the spectacular fall hummingbird migration and is also the time to look for post-breeding wanderers from nearby mountain ranges in Mexico.

In general, fall migration starts with shorebirds in mid-July and reaches its peak in September and October. In the Trans-Pecos, fall is often better than spring for observing passerine migrants. Large concentrations of birds are not as common as in spring, but your chances of finding rare and out-of-place species are greater.

WHERE TO STAY

Hotels are available in most of the towns along the Rio Grande. The problem is that there are very few towns in some of the areas covered in this guide. This is particularly true in the Trans-Pecos. Reservations are highly recommended in the Lower Valley during the winter and spring break, particularly between Christmas and mid-March. The same is true for Big Bend and Guadalupe Mountains National Parks at all times of the year. Near Big Bend, there are small hotels in Lajitas and Study Butte. If those are unavailable, Alpine and Marathon are the next closest towns, 110 and 60 miles from Panther Junction, respectively. Whites City, New Mexico, is 20 miles north of Guadalupe Mountains National Park and has the only motels within 55 miles of the park. The Edwards Plateau is an area where motels and campgrounds are numerous.

Campgrounds are available at almost all state parks in Texas as well as at the national parks. At national parks, the general rule is first-come first-served; at Texas state parks, however, there is a central reservation system at the Austin headquarters. Campground reservations can be made by calling 512-389-8900. At a few state parks, there are other facilities available for rent, such as cabins at Garner State Park. There is also a campground at Aguirre Springs National Recreation Area east of Las Cruces that is first-come first-served.

Two of the parks have lodges and both are in excellent birding areas. The Basin Lodge at Big Bend (National Parks Concessions, Inc., Big Bend National Park, TX 79834; phone 915-477-2291) has fairly good food and accommodations. Indian Lodge in the Davis Mountains (Davis Mountains State Park, Fort Davis, TX 79734; phone 915-426-3254) is a beautiful spot to spend a vacation. Reservations are required at both.

Private RV parks are plentiful in the Lower Valley and on the Edwards Plateau, but there are very few in the Trans-Pecos. The national and state parks in that part of the state are the best bet for RV sites with hook-ups.

A list of the state parks can be obtained from the Texas Parks and Wildlife Department, 4200 Smith School Road, Austin, TX 78744, or online at *www.tpwd.state.tx.us/*. Bird checklists are available for a small fee at most of the state parks described in this guide. Maps and other tourist information are available from the Texas Highway Department, Austin, TX 78763, or from the Tourism Division of the Texas Department of Commerce, Box 12728, Austin, TX 78711. Detailed county maps can be purchased for a small fee from the Texas Highway Department, Planning Survey Division, Box 5051, Austin, TX 78763.

BIRDING BEHAVIOR

In the appendices to this book is a copy of the American Birding Association's *Code of Birding Ethics*. Generally, the code indicates that birders must:

1. Always act in ways that do not endanger the welfare of birds or other wildlife;
2. Always act in ways that do not harm the natural environment;
3. Always respect the rights of others;
4. Assume special responsibilities when birding in groups.

For the region covered in this book, it is important to emphasize two aspects of birding ethics. First, birders should always, but especially in Texas, respect the private property of others. Trespassing in Texas is a major offense and birders should be especially sensitive to this fact. This particularly applies to birders and naturalists. Many landowners consider birders and naturalists to be a threat because they may report rare or endangered species from private lands. The sites described in this book are usually public ones. For those that are not, the text usually indicates how to obtain permission to bird. Second, the use of tapes on public property is generally against regulations. Using tapes to attract endangered birds is inappropriate.

ORGANIZATIONS

Audubon Society chapters and independent birding clubs are active in El Paso, Alpine, Austin, San Antonio, and the Lower Valley (Arroyo Colorado, Frontera, and Rio Grande Delta Audubon Societies).

The **Texas Ornithological Society** (6338 N. New Braunfels Avenue, PMB # 189, San Antonio, TX 78209; $25 per year; *www.texasbirds.org*) has three publications: *TOS News, Texas Birds Annual*, and *The Bulletin of the Texas Ornithological Society*. The *Bulletin* publishes scientific papers dealing with birds in Texas. The TOS also holds spring and fall meetings at various locations around the state. Attending one of these meetings can introduce you to birders from all over the state and provide the opportunity to participate in field trips and other activities.

The statewide **Rare Bird Alert** is an Internet-only service and can be checked through the TexBirds archive at *http://listserv.uh.edu/archives/texbirds. html*. There are also RBAs for the Lower Rio Grande Valley (956-584-2731), the Austin area (Internet only, can be checked through the TexBirds archive as well), and the San Antonio area (210-308-6788). These numbers may change from time to time.

Green Kingfisher Brad McKinney

HAZARDS

Mosquitoes can be a problem in Texas in the spring and summer. At a variety of seasons—depending on temperature and rainfall—chiggers and ticks are frequently encountered. All of these arthropods are more common in wet years. Insect repellents are effective and sold widely. Liquid types, such as DEET, are very effective against mosquitoes, biting flies, and gnats. **Chiggers** are tiny red mites that are found in grassy areas. Their bites leave raised welts that itch like crazy. The welts usually appear within a few hours and generally last for weeks. Chiggers attack wherever clothes fit tightly, such as around the waistline and under socks. Soaking affected areas in a mixture of water and bleach is reputed to help shorten the period of itching. **Ticks** prefer brushy places and are fairly common in South Texas and on the Edwards Plateau. Ticks and chiggers are generally not much of a problem in the Trans-Pecos. Do not remove ticks by pulling. The proboscis will break off and form a sore. Usually they can be made to let go by applying a hot instrument such as a recently burnt match. External applications of alcohol are also effective. There are primarily three species of ticks found in the area covered in this guide. The incidence of Lyme and other diseases in Texas is very low, but it is always best to take precautions to discourage bites. Check yourself often. Applying insect repellent to your pants and socks can help dissuade chiggers and ticks. Applying sulphur powder to these areas is also effective. The best advice is to try to avoid areas of grass or weeds, or walk rapidly when crossing them. In Texas, never lie down in the grass in spring.

Fire Ants are a problem in the more eastern regions covered by this guide.

Africanized bees arrived in South Texas in 1990. They are now well established in many of the regions covered in this guide. All indications are that they will continue to spread. Stay away from bee swarms. The only known protection when you are being attacked is to out-run the bees.

Several species of **venomous snakes** are found in southern and western Texas. Do not handle them.

Lastly, do not undestimate the dangers posed by excessive exposure to **high temperatures**, mostly between April and October.

HOW TO USE THIS BOOK

The main purpose of this guide is to help in finding the special birds of the region. If a specific location is considered an outstanding birding spot, it is shown in bold-faced type. Most of the birds can be found by stopping just at these excellent sites.

Mileages listed in the text, often in parentheses—for example: (11.6 miles)—indicate the mileage *from the last spot so listed*.

This guide follows the Rio Grande from Brownsville upriver to El Paso and Las Cruces, New Mexico. There are also detours to the Edwards Plateau, the Pecos and Devils River drainages, and Guadalupe Mountains National Park. It is over 800 miles between Brownsville and El Paso. For most birders, this means that several trips will be needed to visit the area covered in this guide. A trip to South Texas or to Big Bend would probably be first on the list of places to visit. On an extended trip along the Rio Grande, you will probably find that beginning in the Lower Valley and working northward is more productive. Many of the migrant birds return to the Lower Valley in late March and April, which allows you to start your trip slightly earlier than if you started farther north or west. Migration is much more pronounced in the Lower Valley, so the major objectives for the remainder of the trip will be summer residents, which will be present later in the spring. It is important to consider the general arrival time of any species that you are particularly interested in seeing. For example, the breeding populations of Painted and Varied Buntings usually arrive about 20 April. Such facts may alter the timing of your trip.

If you have only a limited amount of time to visit, it is probably best to research the various areas and choose one. As was mentioned before, the distances between the primary birding areas covered in this guide can be considerable. It is possible to bird in the Lower Valley for three or four days—visiting places such as Laguna Atascosa and Santa Ana National Wildlife Refuges, Bentsen-Rio Grande Valley State Park, and the Falcon Dam area—and then spend a day or so on the Edwards Plateau. Getting to Big Bend takes almost a full day, and you will need at least two to three days to quickly cover several of the best birding locations in the park. The reservoirs in the Trans-Pecos, particularly Balmorhea Lake, Imperial Reservoir, and all of those in the El Paso area are well worth a trip by themselves. The El Paso/Las Cruces area offers great birding in a variety of habitats all close to an airport. The Davis Mountains are well worth a visit and can easily be added to a trip to Big Bend if time allows. This mountain range offers opportunities to see Montezuma Quail and nesting Common Black-Hawk.

CURRENT BIRD NAMES

Since the last edition of the guide in 1999, the American Ornithologists' Union (AOU) has published eight supplements to its *Check-list of North American Birds*. These supplements, numbers 42 through 49, outline changes resulting from actions of the AOU's Committee on Classification and Nomenclature. The bird names used here are those adopted by the AOU and, in turn, which are always then adopted by the American Birding Association Checklist Committee and used in the American Birding Association's *ABA Checklist: Birds of the Continental United States and Canada*, 7th edition (2008).

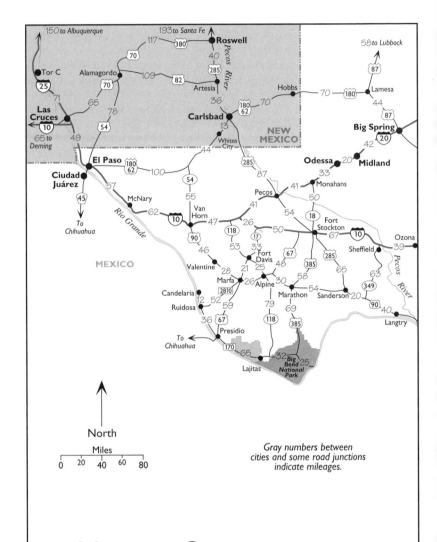

North

Miles

0   20   40   60   80

*Gray numbers between
cities and some road junctions
indicate mileages.*

MILEAGE CHARTS FOR THE
RIO GRANDE VALLEY
OF TEXAS AND
SOUTHEASTERN NEW MEXICO

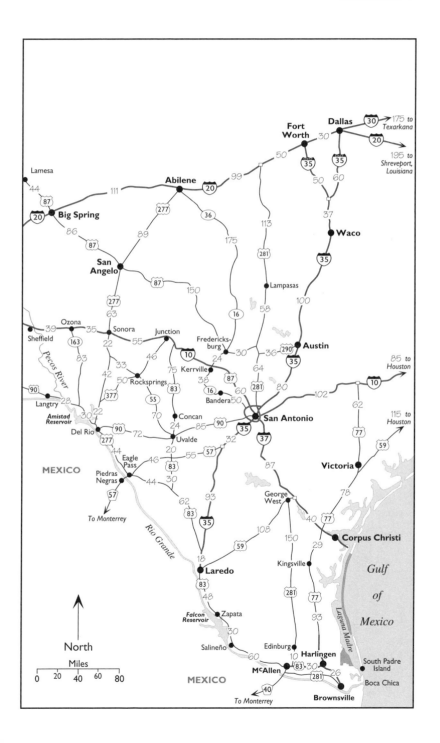

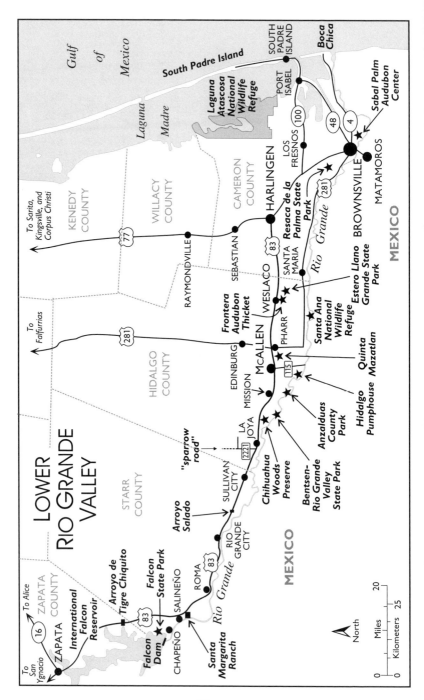

LOWER RIO GRANDE VALLEY

Gulf of Mexico

Laguna Madre

Laguna Atascosa National Wildlife Refuge

South Padre Island

SOUTH PADRE ISLAND

Boca Chica

PORT ISABEL

100

48

4

Sabal Palm Audubon Center

MATAMOROS

BROWNSVILLE

LOS FRESNOS

281

Rio Grande

Resaca de la Palma State Park

HARLINGEN

Estero Llano Grande State Park

To Sarita, Kingsville, and Corpus Christi

KENEDY COUNTY

WILLACY COUNTY

CAMERON COUNTY

77

RAYMONDVILLE

SEBASTIAN

SANTA MARIA

WESLACO

83

Frontera Audubon Thicket

Santa Ana National Wildlife Refuge

Quinta Mazatlan

MEXICO

To Falfurrias

281

HIDALGO COUNTY

EDINBURG

MCALLEN

PHARR

115

Hidalgo Pumphouse

Anzalduas County Park

MISSION

"sparrow road"

LA JOYA

2221

Chihuahua Woods Preserve

Bentsen-Rio Grande Valley State Park

STARR COUNTY

Arroyo Salado

SULLIVAN CITY

RIO GRANDE CITY

Rio Grande

ROMA

83

SALINEÑO

Arroyo de Tigre Chiquito

Falcon State Park

International Falcon Reservoir

ZAPATA COUNTY

16

To Alice

To San Ygnacio

Falcon Dam

CHAPEÑO

Santa Margarita Ranch

MEXICO

North

0 — Miles — 20

0 — Kilometers — 25

LOWER
RIO GRANDE VALLEY

Weaving its way from the snowmelt of southwestern Colorado, the Rio Grande winds through mountains and deserts of the Southwest, bringing life to an arid land before reaching the Gulf of Mexico. From its Colorado headwaters in the San Juan Mountains, the river flows through New Mexico and into Texas, forming an international boundary between the United States and Mexico. Coursing through the delta floodplain, the Rio Grande makes its final stretch to the sea in southernmost Texas, nourishing plant and animal life on both sides of the river.

In the year 1519, after months of sailing the coastal waters searching for a direct route to the Orient, Spanish explorers finally made landfall at a river mouth known today as Boca Chica. Alonso Alvarez de Piñeda, the first European to set eyes on this river, was so impressed that he named it Río de las Palmas, after the towering Sabal Palms lining its banks. Various names have been given to the river in the years since: those from the south called it Río del Norte, the Indians referred to it as Río Bravo (wild river), and others labeled it Río Turbio (muddy river). The final choice—the Rio Grande—signifies its continuing importance in the natural history of the Southwest.

The palm forests that so impressed Alvarez de Piñeda once flourished in the Rio Grande delta, covering nearly 40,000 acres on both sides of the river. In this semitropical arid climate, thorn-scrub forests thrived on rich alluvial deposits from the Rio Grande, whose banks once flooded seasonally. From the river's edge towered Montezuma Bald Cypresses, their massive trunks and spreading roots offering a sense of permanence amidst the moving water. This was the realm of the Gray Hawk, and sounds of tropical birds echoed through every bend in the river.

Land-clearing of the area for crops and cattle by European settlers in the latter part of the 18th century began the large-scale destruction of this highly diverse and delicate habitat. By the time Dr. James C. Merrill explored the region beginning in 1876, there were few Jaguars roaming north of the border.

11

Tropical Kingbird   Michael O'Brien

Still, the diversity of birds was amazing, as detailed in Dr. Merrill's *Notes on the Ornithology of Southern Texas,* in which 252 species were documented from the Brownsville area between February 1876 and June 1878.

Today, with over 95 percent of its lands converted to agriculture and other developments, the delta's diverse assemblage of birds is dependent not only upon state and federal wildlife refuges such as Bentsen-Rio Grande Valley State Park (Bentsen State Park) and Santa Ana National Wildlife Refuge, but also on private ranches, Audubon centers, local wildlife sanctuaries, and urban parks. To protect—and even create—more habitat for the myriad of animal life found here—from Malachite butterflies and Red-tailed Pennant dragonflies to Long-billed Thrashers and endangered Ocelots—additional forest tracts were needed to connect the existing natural areas along the Rio Grande. Because most of the land in Texas is privately owned, the landowners would play a critical role in restoring this biological oasis.

Collaborating closely with the Texas Parks and Wildlife Department, the U.S. Fish & Wildlife Service really got the ball rolling with the initiation of the Wildlife Corridor project in 1979. Through the joint efforts of groups both public and private, 90,000 acres have now been acquired along the river, which is a sizable chunk toward the project's goal of 132,500 acres. The 1998 acquisition of the Boca Chica Tract, which added 12,000 acres to the Lower Rio Grande Valley National Wildlife Refuge, was one of the most important land-preservation actions in recent memory. Another addition to the wildlife corridor is Chihuahua Woods, a 243-acre preserve within earshot of Bentsen State Park near Mission.

The recent creation of the **World Birding Center** (WBC) has further expanded nature tourism along the southern border of Texas. As a partnership with Texas Parks and Wildlife, the U.S. Fish & Wildlife Service, and several Valley communities, the WBC is a network of nine birding sites dotted along the Rio Grande from South Padre Island to Roma, with habitats ranging from coastal wetlands and freshwater marshes to dry brushlands and verdant river thickets. In addition to renovating existing properties such as Bentsen State Park and Hugh Ramsey Nature Park (in Harlingen), the WBC has opened new birding areas in Roma, McAllen, Hidalgo, Edinburg, Weslaco, Brownsville, and South Padre Island. Each of these sites will be featured in this Lower Rio Grande Valley section.

Although dams have long since tamed the once mighty Rio Grande, there is an amazing diversity of birds that has flourished in the region's wildlife sanctuaries. Birders traveling from the coast at Boca Chica to the upstream woodlands of the Falcon Dam area can expect to see many of the region's two dozen specialty birds, including Plain Chachalaca, Least Grebe, Gray Hawk, White-tipped Dove, Green Parakeet, Red-crowned Parrot, Buff-bellied Hummingbird, Ringed Kingfisher, Northern Beardless-Tyrannulet, Great Kiskadee, Tropical and Couch's Kingbirds, Green Jay, Clay-colored Thrush, Long-billed Thrasher, Olive Sparrow, and Altamira and Audubon's Orioles. More challenging Lower Valley species include Muscovy Duck, Hook-billed Kite, Red-billed Pigeon, Ferruginous Pygmy-Owl, Tropical Parula, and White-collared Seedeater. Tamaulipas Crows and Brown Jays have declined dramatically in recent years, both with very tenuous footholds north of the Mexican border. On the positive side, two former Texas rarities—Tropical Kingbird and Clay-colored Thrush—are both on the increase and are fairly easy to find in appropriate habitat.

As of early 2008, 513 species had been recorded in the four-county area of southernmost Texas. In addition to recent first U.S. records arriving from south of the border, such as Social Flycatcher (Bentsen State Park, 2005), White-crested Elaenia (South Padre Island, 2008), and Black-headed Nightingale-Thrush (Hidalgo County, 2004), the Lower Valley occasionally turns up wayward species from the north and west, including Yellow-billed Loon (Laguna Madre, 2001), Little Gull (Boca Chica, 2006), and Snow Bunting (South Padre Island, 2006). Because of the popularity of Texas pelagic birding trips, the Lower Coast has added a number of rare pelagic species to the Valley list, including Manx Shearwater (September 2002) and South Polar Skua (October 2004). What may show up next is anyone's guess!

POSSIBLE IMPACT TO
BIRDING SITES BY THE "BORDER WALL"

A ny time a book such as this birdfinding guide is written, there is a good chance that sites will change over time, making some information in the book outdated. Many of the birding sites along the Mexico and U.S. border in the Rio Grande Valley, especially in the Lower Rio Grande Valley area, face uncertain futures as this book goes to press. A very real threat to access for birders to a number of sites, as well as possible destruction of habitat and disruption to the wildlife corridor system, will begin in 2008.

Many of the most favored birding sites are located immediately along the Rio Grande. The Department of Homeland Security (DHS) and the U.S. Border Patrol (USBP) have been mandated by Congress to build solid barriers along some 370 miles of the Texas border with Mexico. As of mid-2008, DHS has not released firm plans as to the exact locations and design of these walls. Preliminary maps show sections of wall blocking such sites as the Sabal Palm Audubon Center and The Nature Conservancy's Southmost Preserve. About 80 percent of the tracts managed by the Lower Rio Grande Valley National Wildlife Refuge will be affected in some way. Many of Texas Parks and Wildlife's Wildlife Management Areas will also be behind the wall, dissected by some level of habitat destruction and/or abutted to wall structures. Wildlife corridors used by many animals, as well as water access, will also be affected.

DHS and USBP have not fully answered questions as to how, or if, visitor access will be allowed to such sites. Several factors could (but are unlikely to) change the outcome of all these plans, including pending legal challenges, legislative changes, and protest. It is obvious that the future of these sites is in question, both in terms of site access and habitat loss and disruption.

> ABA will post updates on its web site if there are changes in access to any of the sites described in this book.

CLIMATE

F or most of the year, the Lower Valley's climate could be summed up in three words: warm, humid, and windy. Except for narrow corridors along the region's two rivers (the Rio Grande and Arroyo Colorado) and oxbow lakes, plants and animals are adapted to semi-arid conditions. Much of the 26 inches of average annual rainfall occurs during the tropical cyclone season in August, September, and October. Farmers and residents alike welcome these life-giving rains of late summer, for this is when crops are quenched, reservoirs are filled, and the parched desert brushland is given new life. Precipitation generally decreases from east to west, so that by the time one moves upriver from Roma, some noticeable changes in the vegetation may be seen.

Due to its southern location and the moderating influences of the Gulf of Mexico, Valley temperatures rarely drop below freezing during the winter months. However, strong cold fronts occasionally reach the Valley, so winter travelers should pack a warm coat just to be safe. After a cold front pushes through, it's usually not long before the Gulf-blown cumulus clouds return to the skies, once again wrapping a warm and humid blanket over the Valley.

WHEN TO COME

Although there is good birding throughout the year in the Lower Valley, most birders choose to come during the relatively milder months from November through April. Regardless of the season, birders can expect to see many of the resident Lower Valley specialties: Plain Chachalaca, Least Grebe, White-tipped Dove, Buff-bellied Hummingbird, Ringed Kingfisher, Great Kiskadee, Couch's Kingbird, Green Jay, Long-billed Thrasher, Olive Sparrow, and Altamira Oriole. November is a great time to visit; most of the winter birds have arrived and the **Rio Grande Valley Birding Festival**, one of the country's premier birding extravaganzas, takes place during this time in Harlingen. Your chances of locating several normally hard-to-find birds, including Muscovy Duck, Hook-billed Kite, and Red-billed Pigeon, are slightly better in November than during the other winter months. This is also the greenest time of the year, and the butterflies can be spectacular.

Many birders arrive in winter when overwintering species are at their peak and mosquitoes are at a low ebb. Although Mexican rarities can show up in any season, they tend to occur more often in winter. By December, birders often flock to bird-feeding stations at Bentsen State Park, Santa Ana National Wildlife Refuge (NWR), Frontera Audubon Thicket, and Sabal Palm Audubon Center for great looks at Plain Chachalacas, White-tipped Doves, Green Jays, Altamira Orioles, and other Lower Valley specialties. December is also a good time to participate in one of the **Christmas Bird Counts** in the Valley. January and February are usually the coldest months, yet this can be the best time for waterfowl, gulls, large parrot flocks, and mixed-species flocks (which sometimes hold Black-throated Gray Warbler and Tropical Parula). Although Groove-billed Anis don't usually show up until late April, they often can be found somewhere in the Lower Valley during winter. The **Brownsville Birding Festival** usually takes place in February.

If your goal is to see as many species as possible, then the spring season would be a great time to visit. Huge flights of soaring raptors can be seen from the hawk towers at Santa Ana NWR and Bentsen State Park (late March through mid-April is peak), providing one of nature's grand spectacles. Depending on local weather conditions, the coastal migrant traps of South Padre Island and Boca Chica can support large numbers of passerines (April–early May), including many warblers, tanagers, buntings, and orioles. This is also the season when Red-billed Pigeon, Elf Owl, Northern Beardless-Tyrannulet, and

Tropical Parula are most vocal, and Muscovy Ducks are more regularly seen along the Rio Grande. Hook-billed Kites are more likely to be circling overhead within their breeding territories. McAllen's **Texas Tropics Nature Festival** is usually held in late March.

When a local birder mentions the "dog days of summer," it is more a reference to the heat than to the lack of birds. If you can tolerate the heat, then summer can be an exciting time along the Rio Grande. However, it's always best to get started early. The resident specialties, including Tamaulipas Crow (very rare) and Botteri's Sparrow, are on breeding territories, Magnificent Frigatebirds are seen regularly along the coast, Groove-billed Anis are usually easy to find Valley-wide, and it is peak time for the local-but-annual Yellow-green Vireo to show up at Sabal Palm or elsewhere along the Rio Grande. Summer is also the best time to take a pelagic birding trip off South Padre Island, where expected species include Cory's and Audubon's Shearwaters, Band-rumped Storm-Petrel, Masked Booby, and Sooty and Bridled Terns. Although summer is generally thought of as the off-season for rarities, there have been many great finds during this season, including Red-billed Tropicbird, Brown Booby, Jabiru, Northern Jacana, Green-breasted Mango, Green Violetear, Gray-crowned Yellowthroat, and Yellow-faced Grassquit.

Fall is wonderful time to bird in the Lower Valley; however, traveling birders should keep an eye on tropical weather systems in the Gulf of Mexico during this season. Fall migration starts with shorebirds in mid-July and reaches its peak in late September. Large concentrations of migrant passerines are not so common as in spring, but your chances of finding rare or vagrant species are greater. During mid-October, hawk migration is in full swing at places like Santa Ana NWR and Bentsen State Park. By early November, the honking of geese overhead announces the coming of winter as several hundred thousand waterfowl splash down in the numerous freshwater ponds and vast saltwater expanses of Laguna Atascosa NWR and elsewhere.

So regardless of the season, you should find many good birds on your visit to the Lower Rio Grande Valley.

BROWNSVILLE AREA

L ocated 25 miles inland from the Gulf of Mexico, Brownsville has a rich history dating back over 300 years. To this once remote place came men and women under five national banners: Spain, the Republic of Mexico, the Confederate States of America, the Republic of Texas, and the United States of America. Here lived hundreds of Indian groups that were collectively known as the Coahuiltecan Groups, including the fierce Karankawa tribes, now extinct.

Texas's southernmost city was named after Major Jacob Brown, who died in defense of Fort Texas during the Mexican War in 1846. Old Fort Brown was

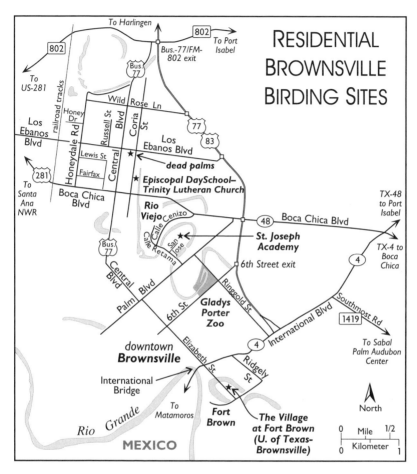

RESIDENTIAL
BROWNSVILLE
BIRDING SITES

located near the foot of today's International Bridge leading across to Matamoros, Mexico. During the Civil War, the Brownsville/Matamoros connection became the "backdoor to the Confederacy," the main exporter of cotton to Europe and a major importer of materials and supplies for the South. Brownsville, now with over 150,000 inhabitants, has long outgrown its frontier character, yet it is still connected economically and culturally with Matamoros, its sister city across the border.

The intersection of US-77 and FM-802 in Brownsville is the starting point for birding instructions in the Brownsville area. From this point you are only five minutes from Red-crowned Parrot roosts off Central Boulevard, 10 minutes from Green Parakeet roosts at Fort Brown, 15 minutes from the Brownsville Sanitary Landfill and its wintering gulls, and 20 minutes from the Sabal Palm Audubon Center with resident Buff-bellied Hummingbirds and other regional specialties. The Brownsville birding areas from Residential Brownsville through Fort Brown can all be done in one day.

RESIDENTIAL BROWNSVILLE

B rownsville is famous for its *resacas* (the Spanish name for oxbow lakes). These crescent-shaped former river channels were pinched off long ago when the Rio Grande changed its course. Most of the city's resacas are kept at a constant level, although a few of them are seasonal and may dry up completely during the hot summer months. The most productive birding is found at resacas that are lined extensively with native trees. This section of the book describes several of these prime birding sites. Each has the potential for Green Parakeets, Red-crowned Parrots, and Lower Valley specialties, including Buff-bellied Hummingbird, Ringed Kingfisher, Great Kiskadee, and Tropical and Couch's Kingbirds.

Birding the sites in residential Brownsville, as outlined below, can take anywhere from two to three hours; however, if you are stopping by just to find Red-crowned Parrots, you can be on your way again in 30 minutes.

Residential Brownsville can produce such species as White-winged Dove, Green Parakeet, Red-crowned Parrot, Buff-bellied Hummingbird, Great Kiskadee, Vermilion (winter) and Brown-crested (summer) Flycatchers, Tropical and Couch's Kingbirds, Scissor-tailed Flycatcher (summer), Yellow-green Vireo (rare, late spring and summer), Green Jay, Tropical Parula (rare, winter), Black-throated Gray (rare, winter) and Yellow-throated Warblers, Hooded (summer) and Altamira Orioles, and migrant passerines. You might also find Plain Chachalaca, White-tipped Dove, Long-billed Thrasher, Olive Sparrow, Bronzed Cowbird, and Altamira Oriole. Rarities that have turned up over the years include White-collared Swift, Black-whiskered Vireo, and Golden-crowned Warbler.

RED-CROWNED PARROT WINTER ROOST

A lthough parrots tend to favor certain urban locales, they are unpredictable, often traveling several miles in search of food sources (pecans, hackberries, and anacua berries are their preferred fruit). During the winter months, parrots travel in flocks ranging from a few individuals to over 100. Traditionally, a good spot for **Red-crowned Parrots** has been near the intersection of Honeydale Road and Los Ebanos Boulevard. Green Parakeets also occur in the area, but they are best seen at Fort Brown (see Fort Brown section below). It is best to get to the neighborhood sites before dawn and listen for their calls to direct you to their locations. With luck you will get more than fly-by views. Another strategy is to catch the birds in late afternoon. This works well for birders who want to bird elsewhere during the early morning hours.

Red-crowned Parrots   Brad McKinney

With the onset of the nesting season in March, Red-crowned Parrots begin to form pairs as they search for nesting sites. It is during the spring when birds may become difficult to find. Fortunately for birders, parrots tend to favor long established roost- and nest-sites. In past years, breeding pairs have been seen on nearby streets (Honey Drive and Fairfax), both off Honeydale Road.

To reach the Honeydale Road/Los Ebanos Boulevard area from southbound US-77, exit at Business US-77/FM-802 and get into the right lane as you approach the traffic light at FM-802 (street sign says Ruben M. Torres). Turn right at the light; you immediately come to another traffic light at Central Boulevard/Old US-77 (also marked as Business-77/83). Get into either of the two left-turn lanes, turning left onto Central Boulevard. For the next half-mile, watch for parrots on both sides of the street—they are sporadically seen flying at dawn in the general vicinity. The resaca (0.2 mile) on the left usually holds good numbers of Black-bellied Whistling-Ducks and, on rare occasions, a Fulvous Whistling-Duck.

Continue south on Central Boulevard to a traffic light at Wild Rose Lane (0.6 mile) and turn right. A serious search for parrots can now begin as you drive along Wild Rose Lane. The road makes a dogleg left turn (0.4 mile) and becomes Honeydale Road, a good street for finding both Green Parakeets and Red-crowned Parrots. The best strategy is to roll your windows down and follow their raucous *cree-cree-craw-craw* calls. To listen to audio files of both Red-crowned Parrot and Green Parakeet, visit: *www.world birdingcenter.org/bird_info*. On rare occasions, Red-crowneds have even been seen perched on the utility lines at sunup. If you haven't heard parrots by the time you reach the four-way stop at Honeydale Road and Los Ebanos Boulevard (0.5 mile), you have three options:

1. Proceed straight through the stop sign for a few blocks, turn left at either Lewis or Fairfax Streets, and wind around the neighborhood listening for the birds. From November to March, it is possible to see parrots here between about 6:45–7:15AM, and again in the late afternoon before dusk. Be aware that mixed in with the Red-crowned Parrots are the occasional White-fronted, Lilac-crowned, Red-lored, and Yellow-headed Parrots. These other parrots are all presumed escapees.

2. A left turn onto Los Ebanos Boulevard can also be good for parrots. Drive slowly to Russell Street (0.3 mile), turn left, and park on the right. You can walk back along Los Ebanos toward Honeydale to listen for parrots overhead. In the wooded areas along Los Ebanos, look for Plain Chachalaca, White-winged and White-tipped Doves, Brown-crested Flycatcher (summer), Great Kiskadee, Green Jay, Long-billed and Curve-billed Thrashers, Olive Sparrow, Hooded Oriole (summer), and neotropical migrants (spring). Such western rarities as Western Tanager, Black-headed Grosbeak, Lazuli Bunting, and Bullock's Oriole have been recorded in this general area, primarily between February and May.

3. Possibly the best parrot spot in the area is at the intersection of Coria and Los Ebanos Streets. To get to this spot, continue driving east on Los Ebanos Boulevard to the traffic light at Central Boulevard (0.1 mile). Go straight, to another traffic light at Coria Street (0.1 mile). Before reaching Coria Street notice the tall, dead Washingtonian Palms on the right side of Los Ebanos. There is usually parking at Tony's Nursery, located on the left of the Los Ebanos/Coria intersection. These palms are riddled with nesting holes, some of which might be occupied by Green Parakeets during the nesting season (April–July). Both parakeets and parrots are often seen in this area during the winter.

EPISCOPAL DAY SCHOOL, TRINITY LUTHERAN CHURCH

Turn right onto Coria Street and continue south to the **Episcopal Day School/Trinity Lutheran Church** (0.3 mile) on the left. The wooded area near the resaca behind the church can produce Anhinga (winter), White-winged Dove, Green Parakeet, Red-crowned Parrot, Ringed and Green Kingfishers, Brown-crested Flycatcher (summer), Great Kiskadee, Couch's Kingbird, Hermit Thrush (winter), Long-billed Thrasher, and Olive

Sparrow. There is usually ample parking at the rear of the church parking lot (next to the school).

In past years, Tropical Parula has been found in winter in the back woodlot, moving with mixed-species flocks, but this species is not to be expected. More often you will see Blue-headed Vireo, Black-crested Titmouse, Ruby-crowned Kinglet, Blue-gray Gnatcatcher, Orange-crowned, Yellow-rumped, Black-throated Green, Yellow-throated, and Wilson's Warblers, and sometimes Black-throated Gray (rare), Nashville, Yellow (rare), and Black-and-white Warblers. The first modern ABA-Area record of Golden-crowned Warbler (December 1979) occurred not far from here. Since then, three more Golden-crowned Warblers have been discovered in the Brownsville area.

RIO VIEJO AND SAINT JOSEPH ACADEMY

Once back on Coria Street, you immediately come to Boca Chica Boulevard, one of the city's busiest streets. Turn left here to Calle Cenizo (0.6 mile) and turn right to drive through **Rio Viejo**, one of Brownsville's oldest and most beautiful neighborhoods. Continue on Calle Cenizo, bearing left at the fork (0.3 mile) to a stop sign at Calle Retama (0.3 mile).

In winter, this entire neighborhood can be good for Lower Valley specialties and winter flocks. It is also a pretty good spot for Green Parakeets and occasionally Red-crowned Parrots in the late afternoon. It is best to park at the Saint Joseph Academy student parking lot (see below for directions) and walk back through the neighborhood. Look for Green Parakeet, Red-crowned Parrot, White-winged Dove, Buff-bellied Hummingbird, Vermilion Flycatcher (winter), Tropical and Couch's Kingbirds, Yellow-throated Warbler (winter), and Hooded Oriole (summer). Occasionally, Nashville, Black-throated Green, Pine, and Wilson's Warblers can be spotted in mixed-species flocks. Although not to be expected, Red-naped Sapsucker, Tropical Parula, Black-throated Gray Warbler, and Bullock's Oriole have been found here. Chimney Swift is found locally in summer. The swifts often are seen soaring in late afternoon with Purple Martins and Cliff and Cave Swallows.

To get to **Saint Joseph Academy**, turn left onto Calle Retama to Calle San Jose (0.1-0.2 mile) on the left. Turn left onto Calle San Jose; the school is straight ahead. Off to the left is a student parking lot, a good place to park.

For many years, the area around the football field has been a good spot for both Tropical and Couch's Kingbirds. Look for them perched on utility wires, fences, or any of the surrounding vegetation. Because these species are virtually identical in appearance, it is very helpful to learn their calls. To listen to audio files of both kingbird species, visit: *www.worldbirdingcenter.org/bird_info*. The wooded area down by the resaca harbors many of the region's specialties, including Black-bellied Whistling-Duck, Neotropic Cormorant, Anhinga,

Black-bellied Whistling-Ducks   Brad McKinney

White-tipped and White-winged Doves, Ringed and Green Kingfishers, Great Kiskadee, Cave Swallow, Long-billed Thrasher, and Olive Sparrow. In winter, Vermilion Flycatcher and the occasional Eastern Bluebird can be seen on the utility wires. At this season, you may get to compare the smaller Neotropic Cormorants with the more numerous and larger Double-crested Cormorants. In summer, you may also find Yellow-billed Cuckoo, Groove-billed Ani, and Brown-crested and Scissor-tailed Flycatchers. During school hours, birders should request permission to bird the school grounds. Birders wanting to telephone ahead should call **956-542-3581**; a map can be obtained at: *www.sja.us*.

To get back to the expressway (US-77) after birding Saint Joseph Academy, turn left at Calle Retama and go to the traffic light at Palm Boulevard (0.2 mile), turn left, drive to Boca Chica Boulevard (0.7 mile), and turn right. The expressway is one-half block ahead.

GLADYS PORTER ZOO

If you have extra time in Brownsville, the **Gladys Porter Zoo** is definitely worth a visit. This zoo has been widely recognized for its diversified collection of birds, reptiles, and mammals, and for its collection of endangered species. A variety of native birds is on display in the Audubon Aviary and Walk-through Aviary. On the grounds you might see wild birds, including Neotropic Cormorant, Green Heron, Common Moorhen, Great Kiskadee, and mixed-species flocks in winter. Buff-bellied Hummingbirds are found on the grounds at any time of year, though they are more likely in spring, summer, and early fall. Red-crowned Parrots and Green Parakeets are sometimes seen in late afternoon at Dean Porter Park (no fee), located across from the zoo. The park sits along a resaca that has many of the Lower Valley specialties. The zoo (see map on page 17) is located at 500 Ringgold Street; follow the signs from the 6th Street exit off US-77). For maps or more information on Gladys Porter Zoo please visit: *www.gpz.org*.

UNIVERSITY OF TEXAS–BROWNSVILLE WETLAND AND FORT BROWN

Fort Brown is an area near the Brownsville/Matamoros International Bridge now occupied by University of Texas–Brownsville dormitories (The Village at Fort Brown). The primary reason for going here is to see the impressive Green Parakeet roost, but there is also a very productive resaca along the southeastern boundary of the university. The best viewing opportunities are from the boardwalk behind the Education and Business Complex, but the resaca can also be accessed from University Boulevard (see Visitors Map at: *www.utb.edu*).

This resaca can hold Least Grebe, Anhinga, Neotropic Cormorant, Ringed and Green Kingfishers, Great Kiskadee, and Tropical and Couch's Kingbirds. In winter, the tree-lined wetland may have several warbler species, including Orange-crowned, Yellow (uncommon), Black-throated Green, Black-throated Gray (rare), Wilson's, and Tropical Parula (rare). This spot can also be good for migrant passerines in spring and fall. It is also one of the few places in the Lower Valley where you can see House Finch (rare, spring). A Golden-crowned Warbler was found in this general area in early 2005.

The Green Parakeets begin squawking and circling overhead about 90 minutes before sundown, which would still allow you plenty of time for a late afternoon shot at the Red-crowned Parrots (in residential Brownsville). From FM-802, take US-77 south through Brownsville to International Boulevard (3.4 miles). Exit right onto International Boulevard (toward the University of Texas at Brownsville). Get into the left lane, because sometimes the large trucks destined for Mexico will be in the slow-moving right lane. After about a mile, exit left onto Ridgely Street. This is also called the Fort Brown Alternate Route because it keeps you away from the congestion of the international bridge. Proceed down Ridgely Street and you will see the college on your right. There could be Green Parakeets anywhere along this road. You will come to a sharp right turn (0.5 mile), then a baseball field on your left. Turn

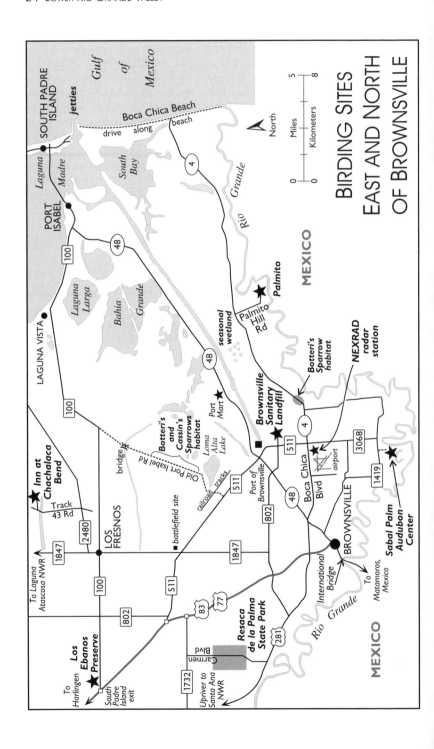

BIRDING SITES
EAST AND NORTH
OF BROWNSVILLE

right at Elizabeth Street (0.3 mile); the Village at Fort Brown is on your right (0.2 mile). Pull into one of the parking lots and begin searching the tops of the Washingtonian Palms for parakeets. There can be well over 100 birds flying overhead at any one time, providing quite a spectacle. Although the numbers are greater in winter, Green Parakeets can be found year-round at Fort Brown. You also may hear the rich chip note of a wintering Yellow-throated Warbler in the palm crowns. A variety of Lower Valley specialties could show up in the area, including Neotropic Cormorant, Red-crowned Parrot, Green Kingfisher, Great Kiskadee, and Tropical Kingbird. On 18 May 1997, a visiting birder found and photographed a White-collared Swift soaring with Cliff Swallows at Fort Brown. This sighting was a Valley first and provided only the second photographically documented record for Texas.

In late afternoon, you can have great looks at the parakeets and be on your way in less than fifteen minutes. Of course, you are within walking distance of several Mexico bars, which could delay you for several hours. For those wanting to walk across to Matamoros, Mexico, there is parking available along Elizabeth Street. To get back to US-77 from here, turn right onto Elizabeth Street and proceed to International Boulevard (0.4 mile). Turn right and continue for about a mile until you see the sign for US-77/83 North (Harlingen).

BIRDING EAST OF BROWNSVILLE

Several longer birding trips take you east toward or to the Gulf of Mexico. The starting point for all of these trips is the US-77/FM-802 intersection on the north side of Brownsville. You might want to visit Sabal Palm Audubon Center early in the morning, then stop at the Brownsville Sanitary Landfill to search for winter gulls, and wind up the day at Boca Chica Beach or South Padre Island, or head out to Laguna Atascosa National Wildlife Refuge (featured in ABA's *A Birder's Guide to the Texas Coast* by Cooksey and Weeks, 2006).

SABAL PALM AUDUBON CENTER

Surrounded by agricultural lands, **Sabal Palm Audubon Center** lies cradled in a bend of the Rio Grande just six miles southeast of Brownsville. With its majestic palms and dense jungle-like habitat, this 527-acre refuge is the most unique of the Lower Rio Grande Valley's natural areas. After the September rains, watch for tropical butterflies such as Blue Metalmark amidst the many blooms. Other striking butterflies found in the palm forest are Zebra and Gulf Fritillary, both passion-flower specialists. The sanctuary is also one of the last places where you could encounter endangered amphibians and reptiles, such as Rio Grande Lesser Siren and Speckled Racer.

The sanctuary bird list stands at over 300 species, boasting many of the Lower Valley specialties and several Mexican rarities. You are likely to find

Plain Chachalaca, Least Grebe, White-tipped Dove, Groove-billed Ani, Common Pauraque, Buff-bellied Hummingbird, Great Kiskadee, Green Jay, Clay-colored Thrush (rare), Long-billed Thrasher, Tropical Parula (rare), Black-throated Gray (rare) and Yellow-throated Warblers, Olive Sparrow, Hooded Oriole (summer), and Lesser Goldfinch. In addition to the Lower Valley specialties, Sabal Palm is good for wetland species, winter warblers, and migrant passerines. The sanctuary has seen its share of rare birds over the years, including Masked Duck, Short-tailed Hawk, Dusky-capped Flycatcher, Rose-throated Becard, Yellow-green Vireo, Gray-crowned Yellowthroat, Golden-crowned Warbler, Crimson-collared Grosbeak, and Blue Bunting.

Sabal Palm Audubon Center (P.O. Box 5052, Brownsville, TX 78523, phone 956-541-8034) is open year-round daily, 7:00AM to 5:00PM, with the exception of Thanksgiving, Christmas, and New Year's Days. The visitor center opens at 9:00AM. The daily entrance fee is $5/adults, $3/children, $2/age 6 and under. Annual membership is $20/individual or $30/family. For more information, visit the Sabal Palm website: *www.audubon.org/local/sanctuary/sabal.*

Allow at least two to three hours to walk the Forest and Resaca Loop Trails, scan the oxbow lake, and observe the feeders near the visitor center. If you visit the butterfly garden or explore the nature trail that leads to the river (Native Trail), you could easily spend more time here. Although mosquitoes are seasonal, you may find insect repellent to be indispensable. You may want to carry water as well; there is no drinking water beyond the visitor center.

To reach Sabal Palm Audubon Center from the US-77/FM-802 junction, drive east on FM-802 to FM-511 (6.4 miles). (The entrance to the Brownsville Sanitary Landfill is straight ahead.) Turn right (south) onto FM-511, staying on this road as it becomes FM-3068 (3.5 miles). FM-3068 ends at FM-1419 (1.5 miles). Turn right; the entrance road to Sabal Palm Audubon Center is on the left (0.6 mile). Follow this dirt road a little over a mile to the visitor center parking lot.

If you are driving this road before sunup or after sundown, look for the red eyeshine of Common Pauraques, which may be sitting in the middle of the road. During the day, White-tailed Kite, Red-tailed Hawk (winter), American Kestrel (winter), and other raptors might be working the fields or perched on utility poles. In spring and summer, check the wires for Couch's Kingbird and Scissor-tailed Flycatcher. In the sunflower fields during spring migration, look for Blue Grosbeak, Indigo Bunting, Dickcissel, and Bobolink (rare). As you near the parking lot, you will see historic Casa de Colores Museum, built in 1876. This grand old house was once part of the Rabb Plantation, which originally occupied 20,000 acres.

A little farther along on the left is the **Native Trail**, which crosses successional forest on its way to the Rio Grande. This is a good trail for spotting raptors, such as Swallow-tailed (rare, spring) and White-tailed Kites,

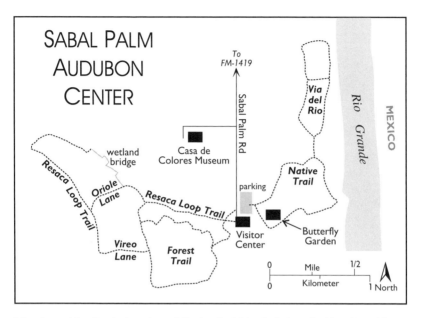

SABAL PALM AUDUBON CENTER

To FM-1419

Via del Rio

Rio Grande

MEXICO

Sabal Palm Rd

wetland bridge

Casa de Colores Museum

parking

Native Trail

Resaca Loop Trail

Oriole Lane

Resaca Loop Trail

Vireo Lane

Forest Trail

Visitor Center

Butterfly Garden

0   Mile   1/2
0   Kilometer   1   North

Northern Harrier (winter), and Red-tailed Hawk (winter). Also found here are Ladder-backed Woodpecker, Couch's Kingbird (summer), and migrants in both spring and fall. From the weedy margins along the Rio Grande, single Gray-crowned Yellowthroats (accidental) have delighted hundreds of birders on several occasions between 1988 and 2005. Although Gray-crowned Yellowthroats were locally common in the Brownsville area before the turn of the 20th century, they are extremely rare today. Beware possible confusion between this species and Common Yellowthroat, and the existence of probable hybrids.

Before stepping onto the **Forest Trail**, be sure to check in and pay the fee at the visitor center. Here you can scan the bird-sightings logbook and pick up a trail map. It's worth spending a few minutes at the bird feeders located just outside the visitor center. Although Buff-bellied Hummingbirds become scarce in much of the Valley during the winter months, you may find one here at the feeders. Surrounded by the pleasant sounds of rustling palm fronds and the cooing of White-tipped Doves, this is a very peaceful setting. The bird feeders and water feature attract Plain Chachalacas, White-tipped Doves, Green Jays, and Black-crested Titmice. Hooded Orioles begin showing up by early April and will remain through October.

The heart and soul of the refuge is the *boscaje de la palma*, a 32-acre relict forest of old-growth Sabal Palms. The lush vegetation along the beautiful Forest Trail provides many hiding places for Plain Chachalaca, White-tipped Dove, Yellow-billed Cuckoo (summer), Buff-bellied Hummingbird, Ladder-backed Woodpecker, Brown-crested Flycatcher (summer), Couch's King-

Boardwalk at Sabal Palm Audubon Center   Brad McKinney

bird, White-eyed and Yellow-green (rare, summer) Vireos, Green Jay, Carolina and House (winter) Wrens, Long-billed Thrasher, Olive Sparrow, and Hooded Oriole (summer). In winter, Yellow-throated Warblers often can be located by their loud, rich chips high in the palm-tree crowns. In the canopy of Texas Ebony, look for mixed-species flocks that may include Blue-headed Vireo, Black-crested Titmouse, Ruby-crowned Kinglet, Blue-gray Gnatcatcher, and Orange-crowned, Nashville, Black-throated Green, Yellow-rumped, and Wilson's Warblers. Tropical Parula and Black-throated Gray Warblers are rare but found every other winter or so. The open-deck platform near Forest Trail marker #12 is a good spot for winter warblers and Lesser Goldfinch (summer). Although very local in winter, Groove-billed Ani is found most winters somewhere in the sanctuary. In some winters, temperate species such as American Woodcock, Carolina Chickadee, and Winter Wren show up at the sanctuary, but they are rare. In spring, check the trailhead fork for migrant passerines, especially after the passage of a cold front. Some of the more typical migrants include Ruby-throated Hummingbird, Warbling Vireo, Swainson's Thrush, a variety of warblers, Summer and Scarlet Tanagers, Indigo and Painted Buntings, and Baltimore Oriole.

The resaca holds a variety of winter waterfowl, usually a few Least Grebes, Black-crowned Night-Herons and other waders, Ringed and Green Kingfishers, and the occasional raptor on a high perch. Other birds to look for include Mottled Duck, Cinnamon Teal (rare, winter), Anhinga (winter), Purple Gallinule (rare, summer), Spotted and Solitary Sandpipers, Groove-billed Ani (late spring and summer), Great Kiskadee, and Couch's Kingbird. The composition of birds can change rapidly at the resaca, depending on water level and season. Although somewhat cumbersome on the narrow Forest Trail, a spotting scope is handy for viewing waterbirds that are feeding or resting on the far side of the lake. The photo blind at the resaca provides good photography opportunities.

Another good birding spot is the boardwalk along the **Resaca Loop Trail**. Here one can usually find Least Grebe, Solitary Sandpiper (winter), Ringed and Green Kingfishers, Eastern Phoebe (winter), Great Kiskadee, Tropical (rare) and Couch's Kingbirds, Long-billed Thrasher, and a good assortment of winter warblers, including Orange-crowned, Nashville, Yellow-rumped, Black-throated Green, and Wilson's, and Common Yellowthroat. Some winters, American Robin, Clay-colored Thrush (rare), and Brown Thrasher (very rare) are found along the water's edge. This is also a good spot for viewing raptors. Resident Harris's Hawk and White-tailed Kite may be seen as flybys, as may winter raptors such as Cooper's, Sharp-shinned, Red-tailed, and Red-shouldered Hawks. Birders are fortunate to spot rare species like Zone-tailed (winter) and Short-tailed (summer) Hawks and Swallow-tailed Kite (spring and fall).

Beyond the boardwalk, you will shortly reach **Vireo Trail**. Here you can loop back toward the visitor center via the **Oriole** or **Forest Trails**. On a typical winter day, you can easily spend a couple of hours walking the boardwalk and nature trails in search of resident specialties and mixed-species flocks. After the winds die down in late afternoon, it is not long before Great Horned Owls and Common Pauraques signal the coming of nightfall. During this waning light of day is your best chance of seeing an Ocelot, one of South Texas's rare and endangered cats.

BROWNSVILLE SANITARY LANDFILL AND BROWNSVILLE INTERNATIONAL AIRPORT

Although Tamaulipas Crows are no longer found here, the **Brownsville Sanitary Landfill** can still be a worthwhile stop because of its concentration of gulls. Birding the landfill is best from January through March, when gull numbers are at their peak. It may take between one to two hours to sort through the many hundreds of gulls in search of something interesting. In winter, birders occasionally find Lesser Black-backed and, even more rarely, California and Thayer's Gulls among the many Laughing, Ring-billed, and Herring Gulls present. In spring, Franklin's Gulls are fairly common. All told, a dozen gull species have been recorded at the landfill, with such notables as Black-tailed, Slaty-backed, Glaucous, and Great Black-backed. In addition to gulls, this appealing locale is a good place to look for Zone-tailed Hawk (rare, winter), Crested Caracara, re-introduced Aplomado Falcon, and Chihuahuan Raven.

Many birders like to add on a trip to the city landfill after visiting Sabal Palm Audubon Center because the two spots are relatively close to each other. Don't wait too long, because the landfill officially closes at 3:30PM (and begging doesn't help). The landfill hours are from 9:00AM–3:30PM (closed Sundays).

To reach the Brownsville Sanitary Landfill from Sabal Palm Audubon Center, simply use directions to Sabal Palm in reverse: after driving north on the entrance road from the sanctuary, turn right onto FM-1419 (Southmost Road) and proceed until you reach FM-3068 (0.6 mile). Turn left (north) at FM-3068 (Indiana Road) and go straight until you reach FM-802 (5.0 miles). Turn right at FM-802, which is the entrance road to the landfill. At the stop sign (0.8 mile), turn right to the landfill office. Drive around the left side (not up on the scales) of the office building and show your binoculars to the landfill staff. The landfill staff will then alert you to specific areas where birding is permitted. Birders are not allowed to venture anywhere near heavy machinery.

To return to US-77 from the landfill, simply head back out the entrance road to FM-511 (0.8 mile from the office). Go straight (onto FM-802) and stay on this road until you intersect US-77 (6.4 miles).

Tamaulipas Crows are no longer found at the landfill in winter, as their U.S. population has plummeted in recent years. The best chance of spotting this elusive species is during the breeding season (April through June) in the vicinity of the NEXRAD radar dome and along adjoining streets near the Brownsville International Airport (along Boca Chica Boulevard). Upland and Buff-breasted Sandpipers (spring and fall) are sometimes found in the nearby grassy field that borders the airport and Boca Chica Boulevard.

Birders should become familiar with the crow's soft, frog-like *cahrr, crawr, creow* calls. To listen to a recording of Tamaulipas Crow calls, visit: *http://whatbird.wildbird.com/obj/785/_/target.aspx*. Tamaulipas Crows are distinguished from Chihuahuan Ravens by their call, smaller size, slimmer bill, glossier plumage, and rounder head. In flight, the crow's deeper wingbeats and square tail are distinctive.

BOCA CHICA BEACH

Allow at least three hours for the 18-mile drive to **Boca Chica Beach** from the FM-511/TX-4 intersection in east Brownsville. On the way, you encounter a variety of habitat types, including thorn-scrub forest edge, wetlands, coastal prairie, bayshore tidal flats, sandy beach, and open ocean waters. Target birds are Fulvous Whistling-Duck (summer), Mottled Duck, Northern Gannet (late fall through early spring), Brown Pelican, Magnificent

Frigatebird (late spring and summer), Roseate Spoonbill, Peregrine Falcon (winter), Snowy, Wilson's, and Piping Plovers, Groove-billed Ani (summer), Couch's Kingbird, Scissor-tailed Flycatcher (summer), and Botteri's Sparrow (summer).

To get to Boca Chica Beach from US-77, go east on FM-802 to FM-511 (6.4 miles) (the entrance to the Brownsville Sanitary Landfill is straight ahead). Turn right onto FM-511 and continue to TX-4 (1.5 miles). Turn left.

Note the *sacahuiste* (bunch grass) on both sides of the road (2.0 miles), which is the nesting habitat of Botteri's Sparrows. Birds should be on territory by mid- or late April. A search for this shy and local songster should begin in the early hours when it is most vocal. Its song is a varied series of chips that break into a bouncing-ball trill. To hear a recording of the bird, visit: www.world birdingcenter.org/bird_info/botteris_sparrow.phtml. Most Botteri's Sparrows withdraw into Mexico by early September.

Well off the highway on the left is a seasonal wetland (2.2 miles) that holds water most of the year, making it attractive to many species of waterbirds. A spotting scope is a must here. Check for Fulvous Whistling-Duck (summer), lots of other waterfowl, Eared Grebe, White and White-faced Ibises, Solitary Sandpiper, Wilson's Phalarope, and other shorebirds. Take time to check along a small dirt road bordered by native trees leading to the right. Many of the resident specialties can be found here. In spring, look for Groove-billed Ani, Brown-crested Flycatcher, Couch's Kingbird, and Scissor-tailed Flycatcher.

TX-4 is usually good for Chihuahuan Ravens and several species of raptors. You can't miss seeing the large raven nests built on the cross-beams of some of the utility poles. As you head toward the coast, you might see White-tailed Kite, Harris's Hawk, and, in winter, Osprey, Northern Harrier, White-tailed and Red-tailed Hawks, American Kestrel, and Peregrine Falcon. During spring, look for kettles of migrating Mississippi Kites and Broad-winged and Swainson's Hawks streaming northbound. On rare occasions, a Ferruginous Hawk (winter) or a banded Aplomado Falcon is spotted somewhere in the area.

You will notice that much of TX-4 has posted U.S. Fish & Wildlife signs. In the 1990s, the U.S. Fish & Wildlife Service purchased 12,000 acres of this critical coastal habitat. According to wildlife experts, the **Boca Chica Tract** has been one of the most important land acquisitions in the entire Wildlife Corridor project.

Look for Palmito Hill Road on your right (3.3 miles), which winds for 2.5 miles through a variety of habitats. The vegetation here is somewhat fragmented, but there are still good hedgerows that can attract warblers and other migrant passerines. If you are in the exploring mood, this rarely birded area is worth checking out. Being so close to the Rio Grande, you just never

Masked Booby   Brad McKinney

know what Mexican rarity may be lurking nearby. You will likely need to turn around at a locked gate and backtrack to TX-4.

Continuing east on TX-4, you come to an historical marker on the right (0.2 mile). The Battle of Palmito Ranch, which took place at this site, was the last engagement of the Civil War. The Confederates forces won this battle 24 days after Robert E. Lee surrendered at Appomattox.

You will also notice clay dune lomas (low hills) that are vegetated by stunted mesquites, ebonies, and other native trees. During April, these islands of brush are magnets for neotropical migrants. There are also numerous seasonal (dry in summer) mudflats along the way, which might hold shorebirds. In early May, it is possible to see White-rumped, Baird's, and Pectoral Sandpipers together with other peeps. You may see Gull-billed and Black (summer) Terns feeding for insects over the grassy fields before you get to the open Gulf. Although rare in winter, check for Burrowing Owl sitting atop man-made structures such as the concrete rubble (on the north side of the highway) in the last mile or so before reaching the Gulf (10.3 miles).

You can drive the sandy beach for miles; two-wheel drive is usually all that is necessary. However, in rare instances spring tides or high surf can make the beach road virtually impassable (with or without four-wheel drive). Probably the worst spot is the soft sand at the end of TX-4, so proceed here with caution. Along the open beach, look for Snowy, Wilson's, and Piping (winter) Plovers amongst the numerous Sanderlings. Also fairly common during the non-breeding season are Black-bellied Plover, Willet, and Ruddy Turnstone. Large flocks of Red Knots may be present along the beach during migration, but this species can be tough to find in winter. Most of the year, you will see Caspian, Royal, Sandwich, and Forster's Terns feeding along the surf line. Common, Least, and Black Terns do not arrive until spring. Resident Laughing Gulls share the beach with wintering Ring-billed, Herring, and the rare Lesser Black-backed. This stretch of coastline has turned up several rare gull species, including Glaucous and Great Black-backed.

Going right (south) takes you to the mouth of the Rio Grande (2.5 miles). There are usually large concentrations of birds in the shallow river delta on both sides of the river. This is a great place to add many species to your Mexico list. Look for American White and Brown Pelicans, Roseate Spoonbill, American Avocet, American Oystercatcher, Black Skimmer, and a variety of gulls, terns, and other waterbirds. While looking for Clapper Rail and Seaside Sparrow in the Black Mangrove trees, you may flush nearly 100 Black-crowned (and occasionally Yellow-crowned) Night-Herons from their daytime roost. With the passage of cool fronts in spring, the mangroves can be very good for migrant warblers. In March 1990, a "Mangrove" Yellow Warbler was found in this stand of Black Mangroves, providing the second record of this distinct subspecies for Texas and the United States. Since 2004, these birds have become locally uncommon permanent residents in Black Mangrove habitat in the Lower Laguna Madre near South Padre Island and Port Isabel.

Going left (north) on the beach from TX-4 takes you to the jetties (5 miles). Occasionally a Peregrine Falcon will be seen soaring or perched atop the high dunes. At the jetties, look for many of the same birds previously mentioned for the beach and the river mouth, as well as Common Loon, Eared Grebe, and Northern Gannet in winter and early spring, and Magnificent Frigatebird in summer. In February 1991, a Purple Sandpiper was found amongst a flock of Ruddy Turnstones on the jetties, providing the southernmost record for this species in the United States. Other rare or accidental species that have been seen on or near the jetties include Brown Booby (summer, fall), Sabine's (fall) and Little (winter) Gulls, Black-legged Kittiwake (winter), and Brown Noddy (summer). On the Lower Coast, pelagic species are rarely seen from land, but they could turn up at any time of year. Cory's Shearwater, Masked Booby, and Pomarine Jaeger have been seen just offshore from the jetties; a Sooty Shearwater was found along the beach in January 1992. Bridled and Sooty Terns are most likely to show up following tropical-storm activity in the Gulf.

If you should encounter a beached dolphin or whale while driving on Boca Chica Beach, please call the Coastal Study Lab (partnership of University of Texas-Brownsville and University of Texas–Pan American at Edinburg) at

South Padre Island (956-761-2644) during normal business hours, or the Texas Marine Mammal Stranding Network at 800-962-6625 (day or night).

OLD PORT ISABEL ROAD, LOMA ALTA LAKE

In this low-lying region of impermeable clay soils, Old Port Isabel Road can be a real adventure if it's wet. After a rain, it is four-wheel drive only. Fortunately, it is dry most of the time. All birding on this 7-mile stretch is done from the car. This is wide-open country that is exposed to wind, so it's advisable to get out early in the morning.

Old Port Isabel Road is best in spring when Cassin's and Botteri's Sparrows are on territory. As a bonus, re-introduced Aplomado Falcons are occasionally seen in the area. In 1995, an Aplomado Falcon pair nested in the vicinity, representing the first nesting of the species in Texas in over 50 years. Since 1995, Aplomado Falcons have become annual nesters in the area.

Target birds on this trip include Fulvous Whistling-Duck (summer), White-tailed Kite, Osprey, Harris's and White-tailed Hawks, Aplomado Falcon, Peregrine Falcon (fall, winter), Whimbrel, Brown-crested and Scissor-tailed Flycatchers (summer), Verdin, Cactus Wren, Curve-billed Thrasher, Sprague's Pipit (winter), Cassin's and Botteri's (summer) Sparrows, and Pyrrhuloxia.

To reach Old Port Isabel Road from US-77/FM-511, go east on FM-511 as though you were heading to the Port of Brownsville. Keep an eye out for several species of raptors, including White-tailed Kite, White-tailed Hawk, and Harris's Hawk. At the intersection with FM-1847 is the Palo Alto Battlefield National Historic Site (3.4 miles), marking the first battle of the Mexican-American War. The large tracts of native brush are off-limits to the general public, yet birding can still be done along the fence.

As you approach Old Port Isabel Road (3.3 miles), turn left onto a dirt road at the Loma Alta Skeet and Trap sign. **Loma Alta Lake** can be scanned for waterbirds from the railroad tracks (0.6 mile) with a spotting scope, but you will get only distant views. A little farther down the road a seasonal wetland provides much closer viewing (1.6 miles). Birds found here include Fulvous Whistling-Duck (summer), Mottled Duck, White and White-faced Ibises, Whimbrel (spring), Long-billed Curlew, Gull-billed Tern, Chihuahuan Raven, Eastern Meadowlark, and many other wetland species.

In spring and summer, check for Cassin's and Botteri's Sparrows singing on territory (0.3 mile, for about the next 2.5 miles). Although both occupy the same general area, they prefer different habitats: Botteri's is found near the *sacahuiste* (bunchgrass), whereas Cassin's prefers scrubby areas and can sometimes be spotted skylarking from Prickly Pear or mesquite. Sprague's

Pipits are sometimes seen in winter as they walk in the open grassy fields on the east side of the road (0.8 mile). Also in the area, look for Say's Phoebe (rare, winter), Brown-crested and Scissor-tailed Flycatchers (summer), Bewick's Wren, Sage (rare, winter) and Curve-billed Thrashers, and Pyrrhuloxia. It is possible to see Peregrine or Aplomado Falcons fly by anywhere along this stretch of road.

Old Port Isabel Road reaches a small bridge (2.7 miles) that is often closed. If the bridge is open, you can drive through until the road intersects TX-100 (1.4 miles). It was in this vicinity that a Snail Kite (third Texas record) was discovered in July 2007. Going right (east) on TX-100 takes you to Port Isabel and South Padre Island. Going left takes you to Los Fresnos and then to US-77. If the bridge is closed, just turn around and go back to FM-511. Turning right onto FM-511 will get you back to Brownsville. Turning left will take you to the Port of Brownsville. Before reaching the Port of Brownsville, you will pass several grain elevators on the left (1.8 miles), where occasionally a Yellow-headed Blackbird can be picked out from the hundreds of other blackbirds (mostly Red-wingeds). Look also for Crested Caracara, Common Ground-Dove, and Chihuahuan Raven in the area.

Just ahead at the junction of TX-48 is the Port of Brownsville (0.2 mile). Turning left onto TX-48 takes you to Port Isabel and South Padre Island. On the way to the island, look for Aplomado Falcons near the Port Mart (3.6 miles) on the left side of TX-48, across from the Amfels shipyard.

PORT ISABEL, SOUTH PADRE ISLAND

Only a 30-minute drive from Brownsville is the resort town of South Padre Island. South Padre Island occupies the southern end of Padre Island, which at 113 miles in length is the world's longest barrier island. South Padre has good shorebird habitat (Black Mangrove bayshore) and several wooded areas that provide critical stopovers for neotropical migrants. In summer, pelagic birding trips venture to offshore waters in search of shearwaters, storm-petrels, and other pelagic species. From Port Isabel, the deep water off the continental shelf occurs at only 45–50 miles offshore, the closest point along the entire Texas coast.

Expected species on South Padre Island for much of the year (although some are absent during summer) include Red-breasted Merganser, Common Loon, Eared Grebe, Northern Gannet, Brown Pelican, Reddish Egret, Roseate Spoonbill, Osprey, Peregrine Falcon, Clapper and Virginia Rails, Sora, Black-bellied, Snowy, Wilson's, and Piping Plovers, American Oystercatcher, Whimbrel, Long-billed Curlew, Marbled Godwit, and a variety of other shorebirds, terns, and migrant passerines. Migrant landbirds are best seen in spring (early April to mid-May) and fall (September to mid-November).

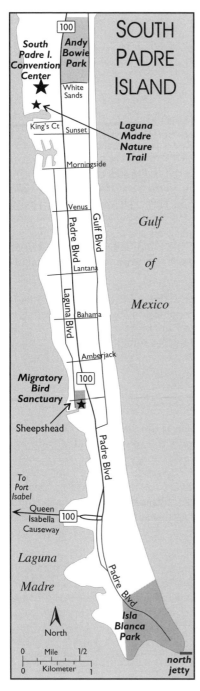

To get to South Padre Island from Brownsville, drive east on FM-802 (from US-77) to TX-48 (5.0 miles). Turn left onto TX-48, which takes you to Port Isabel. For the next 10 miles, watch for the occasional Horned Lark flying low across the highway or Gull-billed Terns swooping down for insects.

In winter, Ospreys are often found in the vicinity of the shrimp basin (6.0 miles), while Northern Harriers and Chihuahuan Ravens can usually be seen soaring over the flat floodplain. The Brownsville Ship Channel boat ramp (3.1 miles) usually has a variety of herons, shorebirds, gulls, and terns nearby. Look here in spring for Whimbrel and Long-billed Curlew. For the next several miles, the road traverses Bahía Grande—the Great Tidal Flat. The Bahía Grande is now a 6,000-plus-acre shallow lagoon thanks to the U.S. Fish & Wildlife Service Restoration Project. The wetland is attracting numerous ducks, herons, and shorebirds. Bringing attention to this newly created wetland, the Lower Valley's first American Flamingo was found feeding in these waters during the summer of 2004. A spotting scope is recommended here. For safety, pull as far off the road as possible and watch for fast-moving vehicles if you are crossing the highway.

Once you pass a sharp left curve (3.6 miles), watch for Harris's Hawks, which are sometimes seen in small family groups along the highway, particularly near mesquite-covered lomas. As you approach the intersection of TX-100 (2.6 miles), it is possible to see Reddish Egret, Roseate Spoonbill, American Avocet, Long-billed Curlew, and a variety of other waterbirds feeding in the seasonal tidal flats on both sides of the highway. If filled with water, these tidal flats can be good for a variety of shorebirds in spring and fall.

Note: Many birders may be traveling from US-77 to Port Isabel via TX-100 instead of TX-48. After passing through Los Fresnos on the way to Laguna Vista, you will pass through stretches of good birding habitat where White-tailed Hawk may be seen. Seasonal wetlands can be good for a variety of waterbirds, and, in spring, Botteri's Sparrows are often singing in the bunch-grass/mesquite habitats. Aplomado Falcons are sometimes seen on utility poles or fences two to four miles west of the town of Laguna Vista.

Turn right at the intersection of TX-100 (0.7 mile) and travel through **Port Isabel**. The old Port Isabel Lighthouse (1.4 mile) still stands as a monument to 19th-century coastal trade and commerce. Constructed in 1852, it was built to protect and guide ships through Brazos Santiago and the barrier islands. The light was extinguished during the Civil War (becoming permanently so in 1905), but is now maintained as a Texas State Historical Structure by the Texas Parks and Wildlife Department. A century later in 1952, the 72-foot-tall lighthouse was opened as a state park and remains the only lighthouse on the Texas coast open to the public.

There are several museums in Port Isabel that are open year-round. The Lighthouse and the Keeper's Cottage along with the Treasures of the Gulf Museum and the Port Isabel Historic Museum make up the Museums of Port Isabel complex, all of which are within walking distance of each other. The Port Isabel Historic Museum is located on 314 E. Railroad Street. The museum displays many artifacts, including those from a 1554 Spanish galleon that once sailed along the Texas coast, as well as from the Mexican-American War, the last battle of the Civil War, and other events that shaped the Laguna Madre area. You can get to the museum by turning right onto Tarnava Street (opposite the lighthouse). One block later turn right at E. Railroad Street, and less than a block away you will see the restored home of Charles Champion (founder of the town) on the right. Hours vary, but most sites are open Tuesday–Saturday, 10:00AM to 4:00PM. Individual site fees are $3/adults, $2/seniors, $1/children, and free for children four and under. There are also three-site combination tickets available. For more information, call 956-943-7602 or visit: *www.portisabelmuseums.com*.

Tropical Kingbirds were first recorded in Port Isabel in 1994 and are now locally common. They are fairly easy to find in several places around town. One of the better spots is along the bayshore near the intersection of Garcia and Adams Streets, where a pair has nested for many years.

At 2.6 miles in length, the Queen Isabella Memorial Causeway is the longest bridge in Texas. Connecting Port Isabel with **South Padre Island**, the causeway passes over the shallow yet expansive Laguna Madre, providing a high vantage point to see cormorants, pelicans, gulls, and terns. There are, however, no pullouts on the causeway. Commonly seen species in the Laguna Madre include Redhead, Red-breasted Merganser, Brown Pelican, Double-crested Cormorant, Eared and Pied-billed Grebes, Laughing, Ring-billed, and Herring Gulls, and Forster's, Royal, and Sandwich Terns. It takes a sharp eye to spot a high-soaring Magnificent Frigatebird, an occasional visitor from late spring through early fall. Unusual species that have been recorded in these waters include Harlequin Duck, Surf Scoter, Pacific and Yellow-billed Loons, Horned and Western Grebes, Manx Shearwater, Brown Booby, and Neotropic Cormorant.

Just as the causeway ends at South Padre Island, you can pull over to scan the Black Mangrove tidal flat to the right (south) that frequently has Reddish Egret, Black-crowned and Yellow-crowned Night-Herons, Clapper Rail, Black-bellied Plover, American Oystercatcher, Willet, Marbled Godwit, Black Skimmer, and a variety of shorebirds and terns. During spring, Snowy, Wilson's, and Piping Plovers, Whimbrel, and Hudsonian Godwit (rare) have turned up along this stretch of bayshore.

Similarly productive mudflats, best at low tide, are scattered all along the bayshore. Driving north on Padre Boulevard, look for a tidal flat (behind the miniature golf course at 0.9 mile) that sometimes has Snowy and Piping (fall through spring) Plovers, as well as a variety of other shorebirds, herons, and terns. Another good bayshore spot is at the Bahía Grande (about 3 miles north of the miniature golf course), just south of the South Padre Island Convention Center.

The small woodlots and landscaped yards on the island are especially attractive to migrants in spring and fall during fallout conditions, i.e., north winds in spring and tropical-storm activity in fall. One of the best migrant traps on the island is Valley Land Fund's **South Padre Island Migratory Bird Sanctuary**, consisting of six residential lots that have been landscaped with native vegetation. The best public site is located along Sheepshead, toward the bayshore from Padre Boulevard. It offers refuge to many migrant species, including such commonly seen species as Yellow-billed Cuckoo, Ruby-throated Hummingbird, Eastern Wood-Pewee, Great Crested Flycatcher, Western and Eastern Kingbirds, Scissor-tailed Flycatcher, Warbling and Red-eyed Vireos, Swainson's Thrush, Summer and Scarlet Tanagers, Chipping and Lark Sparrows, Rose-breasted and Blue Grosbeaks, Indigo and Painted Buntings, Baltimore Oriole, and many warblers. During migration, 39 warbler species have been recorded in the island woodlots, though a good day yields between 18 and 22 species. Although spring migration begins in late March (peaking in late April), migrants may be found through the end of May. Mid-May is usually the best time to see a variety of *Empidonax* flycatchers. Virtually all the eastern empids can be found on a good day in May, including Yellow-bellied, Acadian, Alder, Willow (rare), and Least Flycatchers.

Although the composition of migrants is dominated by eastern species, western species show up from time to time: Ash-throated Flycatcher, Yellow-headed Blackbird, and Bullock's Oriole may be found in spring, and Townsend's Warbler, Western Tanager, Black-headed Grosbeak, and Lazuli and Varied Buntings make appearances most years. Groove-billed Anis can also be found in island woodlots during migration but seem to be more numerous in fall. During migration, birders often see Franklin's Gulls, Chimney Swifts, and a variety of swallows streaming by overhead. Although rare, Swallow-tailed and Mississippi Kites and Zone-tailed Hawk have made appearances here. There have been several very rare species found during migration at the SPI woodlots, including Green Violetear, Gray Kingbird, Yellow-green Vireo, Flame-colored Tanager, and Cassin's Finch. The first ABA-Area White-crested Elaenia was found here in February 2008.

Another must stop is the **South Padre Island Convention Center**, located about 4 miles north of the causeway on Padre Boulevard. Just follow the signs to the brightly colored convention center (on the left) as you reach the end of development. There are several different habitats found here, including freshwater marsh, salt marsh, shallow bayshore, and native landscaping. An impressively landscaped Warbler Rest Stop, complete with water baths and misters, is located along the "whale wall" on the south side of the building, near the entrance to the **Laguna Madre Nature Trail**. This is often the premier landbird migrant site on the island. Rare and unusual species that have been found at the Warbler Rest Stop include Sulphur-bellied Flycatcher, Black-whiskered Vireo, Violet-green Swallow, Brown and Curve-billed Thrashers, Song and Harris's Sparrows, and Pyrrhuloxia. Tropical and Couch's Kingbirds are seen sporadically on fence-lines near the water-treatment plant adjacent to the Convention Center.

In winter, the boardwalk nature trail is a good spot for seeing rails; birders can often find Clapper Rail and Sora, and occasionally Virginia Rails. Black Rails have been heard irregularly in the marsh yet are seldom seen. In the cattails, look for Least Bittern, Black-crowned and Yellow-crowned Night-Herons, Common Yellowthroat, Savannah, Seaside (rare), Lincoln's, and Swamp Sparrows, as well as Sedge and Marsh Wrens. Purple Gallinule is best seen here during April and May. Throughout much of the winter, a Peregrine Falcon sits atop the water-tower railing watching over the wetland below. West and north of the Convention Center is a tidal mudflat that is a good spot for Reddish Egret and a variety of shorebirds, including Snowy, Wilson's, Semipalmated, and Piping Plovers, Pectoral Sandpiper, Dunlin, and Stilt Sandpiper. During winter, look for Red-breasted Merganser, Common Loon, Eared Grebe, and a variety of other waterfowl in the bay waters.

To drive along the open coast, you can enter Andy Bowie Park, located across the street from the Convention Center ($4/day fee). (You can also drive several miles north along Padre Boulevard until you see a passable road

Groove-billed Ani   Brad McKinney

leading toward the beach.) Four-wheel drive is highly recommended here. In winter, you will see Ring-billed, Herring, and occasionally Bonaparte's or even possibly a Lesser Black-backed amongst the numerous Laughing Gulls and shorebirds. Rare gulls that have been recorded along the open beach include Iceland, Glaucous, and Great Black-backed. In spring, you will likely see Black-bellied Plover, Ruddy Turnstone, Sanderling, Red Knot, and Caspian, Royal, Sandwich, Forster's, and Least Terns. Also look for Snowy and Piping Plovers, and for Black and Common Terns (more common in May). During a spring fallout, neotropical migrants often seek sand-dune vegetation in which to forage and shelter. In fall, South Padre Island is a major staging area for migrant Peregrine Falcons. There is no telling what could show up along the beach at South Padre Island.

Common Loon and Northern Gannet often can be spotted offshore in winter and spring, as are Magnificent Frigatebirds occasionally in summer. The best spot from which to look seems to be the rock jetties on the south tip of the island. Birding the jetties at **Isla Blanca Park** will cost you $4/day. From the jetties, birders will be able to see numerous coastal species depending on the season. Rare species that have been seen from the jetties include Surf and White-winged Scoters, Cory's Shearwater, Masked and Brown Boobies, Sabine's Gull, Black-legged Kittiwake, and Brown Noddy. On rare occasions in spring and summer, Sooty Terns have been seen in late afternoon flying from their Laguna Madre nesting sites toward the open Gulf.

From June through September, offshore Texas waters have been good for many pelagic species. Although individual numbers are low (compared to those off the East and, especially, West Coasts), birders can expect to see between six to nine pelagic species on a summer pelagic trip. Such trips are infrequent but usually occur at least twice a year (between June and September) from South Padre Island. Seabirds recorded on these trips include Yellow-nosed Albatross (accidental), Cory's and Audubon's Shearwaters, Leach's (accidental) and Band-rumped Storm-Petrels, Red-billed Tropicbird (accidental), Masked and Brown (rare) Boobies, Northern Gannet (late fall only), Magnificent Frigatebird, Bridled and Sooty Terns, South Polar Skua (accidental), and Pomarine, Parasitic, and Long-tailed (rare, fall) Jaegers. Also seen are pelagic Bottlenose and Spotted Dolphins, and occasionally sea turtles and Sperm Whales. For further information on Texas deep-water pelagic trips, check the web site, *www.texaspelagics.com*. Lower Laguna Madre boat tours that specialize in waterbirds and nature photography depart Sea Ranch Marina on South Padre Island. Departures are scheduled at your convenience. Frequently encountered wildlife includes Reddish Egret, Roseate Spoonbill, American Oystercatcher, "Mangrove" Yellow Warbler, and a variety of herons, shorebirds, gulls, terns, and Bottlenose Dolphins. Contact George or Scarlet Colley at 956-299-1957 (cell) or 956-761-7178 (office); *www.fin2feather.com*.

BIRDING NORTH AND
WEST OF BROWNSVILLE

Just north of our coverage area is Laguna Atascosa National Wildlife Refuge, a must visit for birders at any season. Another ABA/Lane Birdfinding Guide, *A Birder's Guide to the Texas Coast*, examines the birding possibilities at this exciting refuge in great detail. Several other sites close to Brownsville can be covered in a few hours as short excursions (see map on page 24).

FISH HATCHERY ROAD
AND CAMP LULA SAMS

The Texas Parks and Wildlife Department Coastal Fisheries Field Station, aka "Fish Hatchery" (95 Fish Hatchery Road) is a series of ponds in north Brownsville that attracts a variety of waterbirds. The numerous hedgerows on Fish Hatchery Road can be good for Couch's Kingbirds and other resident specialties. You can expect to see Black-bellied Whistling-Duck, Mottled Duck, Least Grebe, White-faced Ibis, Ringed Kingfisher, Scissor-tailed Fly-

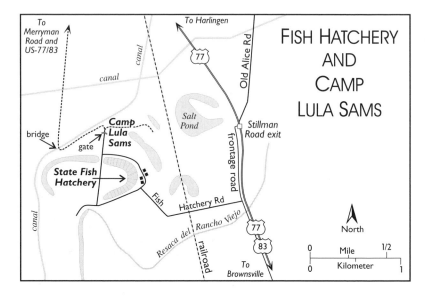

catcher (summer), and several Lower Valley specialties. Tropical Kingbird is also a possibility in the general vicinity.

To find **Fish Hatchery Road** from Brownsville at the US-77/FM-802 intersection, drive north on US-77 to the Stillman Road exit (3.0 miles). Exit right and then turn left (west) at the stop (Stillman Road). Turn left (south) again, now on the southbound frontage road, and continue until you see Fish Hatchery Road on the right (0.4 mile). Turn right to the ponds (0.7 mile). You can see the office straight ahead. Park in the spaces beyond the headquarters. There is sometimes an Eastern Screech-Owl visible in the large ash tree adjacent to the headquarters. Scan the ponds for Mottled Duck, Least Grebe, Anhinga (winter), Least Bittern (summer), White-faced Ibis, and Ringed Kingfisher. Also check the woodland edges for Vermilion (winter) and Brown-crested (summer) Flycatchers, Couch's and Tropical Kingbirds, Scissor-tailed Flycatcher (summer), and Altamira Oriole as you continue toward the Camp Lula Sams gate (0. 4 mile). For more information about the TPWD Coastal Fisheries Field Station, call **956-350-4490**.

Surrounded by native brushlands, **Camp Lula Sams** (280 North Fish Hatchery Road) offers birders an alternative to standard motels. This 87-acre private wildlife refuge has many of the regional specialties, including Plain Chachalaca, Buff-bellied Hummingbird, Brown-crested and Scissor-tailed Flycatchers (summer), Great Kiskadee, Green Jay, and Long-billed Thrasher. A Crimson-collared Grosbeak was recorded here in December 2004. The site also has a five-acre resaca that attracts many wetland species. Camp Lula Sams has overnight accommodations; home-style meals are available by special arrangement only. For reservations, call **956-350-9093** for a recorded message; your call will be returned.

If you continue past the gate, you will come to a bridge that is often not passable. This is usually the turnaround point. If you are able to cross the bridge, the road winds around pastureland, eventually coming to Merryman Road, which is very close to US-77. If you choose not to cross the bridge, you can backtrack toward the Texas Parks and Wildlife office to scan the other ponds.

RESACA DE LA PALMA STATE PARK

At the time of this writing, Brownsville's **Resaca de la Palma State Park** is open by appointment and reservation only. At 1,700 acres in size, Resaca de la Palma State Park is the largest of the World Birding Center complex and will soon be accessible to the general public. Habitats vary from Tamaulipan thorn-scrub woodlands and mesquite thickets to open fields. The heart of the sanctuary is the wooded oxbow lake, which is home to most of the Lower Valley specialties, including Plain Chachalaca, White-tipped Dove, Groove-billed Ani (summer), Common Pauraque, Great Kiskadee, Couch's Kingbird, Green Jay, Long-billed Thrasher, Olive Sparrow, and Altamira Oriole. The tree-lined resaca also attracts many species of migrant and overwintering passerines. When full, the resaca attracts a variety of waterbirds. Birds found in the scattered mesquite thickets include Common Ground-Dove, Brown-crested and Scissor-tailed Flycatchers (summer), Verdin, Carolina and Bewick's Wrens, and Lesser Goldfinch. The more open habitats attract numerous raptors and Eastern Meadowlark.

Currently (by appointment only), the main entrance to Resaca de la Palma State Park is off the US-77 exit for FM-1732. Go straight on FM-1732 to Carmen Boulevard and take a left on Carmen. Go straight until you see the entrance to the park on your left. For an online map, see: *www.worldbirdingcenter.org/sites/brownsville/brownsville_map.phtml*.

For more information about Resaca de la Palma State Park, 1000 New Carmen Boulevard, Olmito, TX 78575, 956-350-2920 (phone) or 956-350-3814 (fax), or visit: *www.worldbirdingcenter.org/sites/brownsville*.

LOS EBANOS PRESERVE

The **Los Ebanos Preserve** is a private 82-acre nature park located nine miles north of Brownsville on TX-100. A wide variety of birds and butterflies can be seen year-round. Blue Metalmark and Mexican Bluewing butterflies are often found here, sometimes in large numbers. Many of the Lower Valley's avian specialties can be seen here as well, including Plain Chachalaca, Least Grebe, White-tipped Dove, Groove-billed Ani (summer), Common

Pauraque, Buff-bellied Hummingbird, Ringed Kingfisher, Great Kiskadee, Couch's Kingbird, Green Jay, Long-billed Thrasher, Clay-colored Thrush, Olive Sparrow, and Altamira Oriole. Birders can wander the half-mile self-guided trails that cut through native woodlands in search of resident birds, winter flocks, or spring migrants. Visitors can also relax while watching feeder birds or scan the large lake for waterbirds and kingfishers. Some winters, Tropical Parula, Northern Beardless-Tyrannulet, and *Empidonax* flycatchers are seen along the trails. A Golden-crowned Warbler was found at Los Ebanos Preserve in January 2005.

The preserve is open from September to June. General admission is $5, group rate (five-plus) $4, children (ages 5–15) $3, and children under 5 free. To get to Los Ebanos Preserve from US-77/83, take the South Padre Island exit (TX-100) and go east 100 yards to the entrance on the left. The South Padre Island exit is 9.7 miles north of Brownsville's FM-802/US-77 intersection. Contact information: Los Ebanos Preserve, 27715 State Highway 100, San Benito, TX 78586; phone 956-399-9097. To read more about the rich history of Los Ebanos Preserve or its bird and butterfly lists, see: *www.los ebanospreserve.com*.

INN AT CHACHALACA BEND

Located near Los Fresnos, the Inn at Chachalaca Bend is a bed-and-breakfast for birding enthusiasts. Not only are the accommodations superb (President Jimmy Carter stayed here during his Lower Valley birding trip in April 2004), but the birding can also be quite good. Within its 40 acres, birders can choose to walk the half-mile nature trail that winds through native thorn-scrub forest, observe birds at the photo blind, scan the resaca for kingfishers and waterbirds, or watch hummingbirds from the back patio. Birders need not stay at the inn in order to bird the grounds, but please check in at the front office. The inn maintains numerous hummingbird feeders around the grounds that attract not only resident Buff-bellied Hummingbirds, but also migrant Ruby-throated and Rufous (winter) Hummingbirds. Broad-billed Hummingbird (August 1999) and Green-breasted Mango (May 1999) have appeared here. In addition to the hummingbirds, many landbirds are seen, including Plain Chachalaca, White-tipped Dove, Groove-billed Ani (summer), Ringed Kingfisher, Great Kiskadee, Couch's Kingbird, Green Jay, Long-billed Thrasher, Olive Sparrow, and Hooded (summer) and Altamira Orioles. Despite its small size, the Inn at Chachalaca Bend has recorded such notable birds as Rose-throated Becard and White-throated Thrush.

To get to the inn from US-77, take the South Padre Island exit (TX-100), proceed east toward Los Fresnos (7 miles), and turn left at the city's only stoplight onto Arroyo Boulevard (FM-1847). Go one-quarter mile and turn right (east) on FM-2480 (Old Port Road). Ramirez Supermarket is on the corner. Go exactly 2.0 miles and turn left (north) on Track 43 Road. Go across the resaca (which may hold a few wetland species) and turn right at Chachalaca Bend Drive. Continue straight toward the iron gate. If the gate is closed, follow instructions on the security keypad. Continue straight to the inn. The Inn at Chachalaca Bend, 200 Chachalaca Bend, P.O. Box 197, Los Fresnos, TX 78566; phone 956-233-1180, 888-612-6800; email: *inn@ chachalaca.com*; website: *www.chachalaca.com*.

HARLINGEN AREA

H arlingen is more than just the home of the **Rio Grande Valley Birding Festival** in November. It also has a variety of city parks along the Arroyo Colorado river where the birding can be quite good. If you are staying in Harlingen or you have extra time in the Valley, you may want to check out these sites. Many of the Rio Grande specialties can be found here, including Buff-bellied Hummingbird, Green Kingfisher, and Northern Beardless-Tyrannulet (rare). You can also find Red-crowned Parrots flying around various residential areas at dusk and dawn. Although rare, look for Tropical Parula in winter in patches of tall trees where you might encounter mixed-species flocks.

Tropical Kingbirds have been found in the vicinity of the Municipal Auditorium at 1204 Fair Park Road. This is also the headquarters of the annual birding festival. To get to the auditorium from northbound US-77, take the Tyler exit (right) and drive north on the frontage road, through two traffic lights, before coming to Fair Park Road. Turn right on Fair Park Road and follow it to the auditorium. See the Harlington area map on the next page.

HARLINGEN CITY PARKS
ALONG THE ARROYO COLORADO

H arlingen **Arroyo Colorado** (Hugh Ramsey Nature Park)—A gateway to the World Birding Center network, this 55-acre park has been transformed by extensive native landscaping projects into an urban oasis. Trails, ponds, water features, and photo blinds allow birders to enjoy a variety of species on a leisurely one-hour stroll. There is often a pair of Green Kingfishers near the pond on the 5/16 trail. If you miss the kingfishers here, there are other opportunities down along the Arroyo Colorado. Great Kiskadees are common throughout the park and Buff-bellied Hummingbirds are often found near nectar-rich flowers and hummingbird feeders. Listen for their buzzy rattle or high-pitched squeaks. Couch's Kingbirds can be found here year-round, and they are especially easy to find along the Arroyo Colorado (March–October). Many other Lower Valley or regional specialties can be found here, including Plain Chachalaca, Common Ground-Dove, White-tipped Dove, Common Pauraque, Brown-crested and Scissor-tailed Fly-

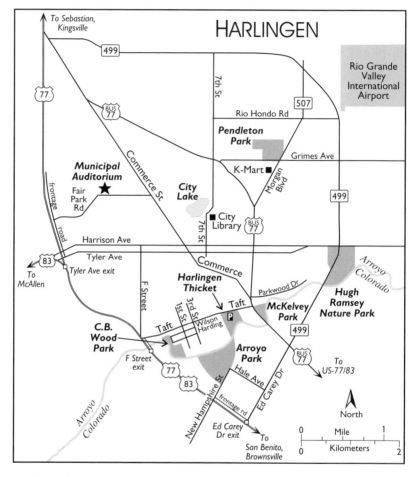

catchers (summer), Green Jay, Verdin, Long-billed and Curve-billed Thrashers, Olive Sparrow, Hooded Oriole (summer), and Lesser Goldfinch. In winter, look for all three kingfishers and Yellow-crowned Night-Herons down along the river. Northern Beardless-Tyrannulet, very rare outside Hidalgo County, has occurred here. The park can also be good for passerines in migration. Occasionally, Red-crowned Parrots are spotted flying to and from roost sites in the early morning and late afternoon.

To get to **Arroyo Colorado** and **Hugh Ramsey Nature Park** from northbound US-77, exit at Ed Carey Drive. Head east on Ed Carey Drive to the traffic light at Business US-77 (1.0 mile). Continue straight at the traffic light (you are now on 499 North) and look for the entrance to the park on your right (1.0 mile). Physical address is: 1001 S. Loop 499, Harlingen. Nature trails are open seven days a week, sunrise to sunset. Admission is free. For more information, contact the Harlingen Parks and Recreation Office, 900 Fairpark Boulevard, Harlingen, TX 78550; phone 956-427-8873, fax 956-412-0147; or visit: *www.worldbirdingcenter.org/sites/harlingen/index.phtml.*

Harlingen's hike-and-bike trail along the Arroyo Colorado connects the four city parks (below). It is easiest to access this trail from McKelvey Park. For a detailed map see: *www.riodeltawild.com.*

Arroyo Park: To reach Arroyo Park from US-77, exit at Ed Carey Drive. Continue north on the frontage road to New Hampshire Street (0.5 mile). Turn right at New Hampshire and continue until you see the Arroyo Park parking lot on your left (0.5 mile). Walk along the main sidewalk in the direction of the native vegetation. The sidewalk trail allows an overlook of the river. The best birding is to the left (south). You can get off the sidewalk to explore on the walking trails, but the trails are not marked or maintained so caution is advised. The birds here are similar to those at Hugh Ramsey Nature Park. Black-chinned Hummingbird and Verdin have been found nesting occasionally in the scrubby vegetation. Northern Beardless-Tyrannulet also has been spotted in these woods.

C. B. Wood Park: Exit US-77 at F Street and continue north. Reset your odometer at the first traffic light (you will continue straight through the light). Proceed to Taft Avenue (0.2 mile) and turn right. At First Street (0.5 mile), turn right. At Harding Street (0.2 mile), again turn right. Continue to C.B. Wood Park (0.1 mile) where you will see the parking lot off to your right. The best birding is to the east (or left, if you are approaching the Arroyo Colorado). Follow a primitive walking trail toward the thick vegetation. There are some good vantage points from which you can view the river.

Most of the Rio Grande specialties can be found in these woods, including Plain Chachalaca, White-tipped Dove, Great Kiskadee, Green Jay, Long-billed Thrasher, and Olive Sparrow. Also look for Verdin, Bewick's Wren, Curve-billed Thrasher, and Pyrrhuloxia. In spring, listen for the *puh-whEEer* calls of Common Pauraque at sundown or before dawn.

Harlingen Thicket: The Harlingen Thicket may be the most extensive birding habitat within the city, but it currently has only a makeshift parking lot. The birds found here are similar to those at the other city parks. This is the best spot in Harlingen to find Verdin, Cactus and Bewick's Wrens, and Pyrrhuloxia. To get to this site from C. B. Wood Park, continue on around the parking lot (street becomes Wilson Street) to First Street (0.2 mile). Turn left at First Street and proceed to Taft Street (less than 0.1 mile). Turn right at Taft and continue to the makeshift parking lot on the right (0.5 mile). Trails lead down to the Arroyo Colorado.

McKelvey Park: McKelvey Park is located on the east side of Business US-77 (77 Sunshine Strip) less than 1 mile north of Ed Carey. You can also get there from the Harlingen Thicket by crossing Commerce and Business US-77

Olive Sparrow   Jen Brumfield

(the two parks are just a few blocks away from each other). The vegetation at McKelvey Park is not as extensive as at the above-mentioned parks, but there is a nice hedgerow of tall native trees in the back. Many of the Rio Grande specialties can be found here. It is also a good spot for mixed-species flocks in winter and passerines in migration. Red-crowned Parrots are seen occasionally on the edge of the park at dawn and dusk. A pair of Great Horned Owls can sometimes be heard in the trees.

Red-crowned Parrot Roosts: Parrots wander around many areas of Harlingen, including McKelvey Park, Parkwood Street (off Business US-77), and City Lake (76 Drive). Recently, the best spot for parrots has been near Pendleton Park and at the K-Mart near the intersection of Morgan Street and Grimes Avenue. Both Green Parakeets and Red-crowned Parrots have been found nesting in the palms behind the Wal-Mart in nearby San Benito.

City Lake: To get to City Lake from northbound US-77, exit at Tyler Avenue. Turn right (east) and drive to 7th Street, where you turn left. Soon, 7th Street turns into 76 Drive and it won't be far until you see the City Library and Cultural Arts Center. Park on the street nearby and walk across the street to the lake. Tropical Kingbird is regular in the general vicinity of the library. In spring, you may see Purple Martins in the martin houses and Black-bellied Whistling-Ducks in the duck boxes around the lake. You are likely to see Green Heron, a resident flock of Laughing Gulls, and Gull-billed (uncommon),

Caspian, and Forster's Terns. Occasionally, Bonaparte's Gull can be found at the lake. Migrating raptors tend to soar across this area in spring and fall.

On the opposite side of the lake are some large trees, known locally as Boggus Woods. These trees can be good for Great Kiskadee, Green Jay, and other Lower Valley specialties, mixed-species flocks in winter, and migrant passerines in spring and fall. Occasionally, both Red-crowned and Yellow-headed Parrots can be seen here. Athough rare, both Spotted Towhee and Tropical Parula have been found here in winter.

Upland and Buff-breasted Sandpipers at Harlingen International Airport: For brief periods during spring and fall migrations, it may be possible to see large concentrations of Upland and Buff-breasted Sandpipers in grassy habitats in the Harlingen area. One of the better fields lies near the south end of the Harlingen International Airport, on Rio Hondo Road. This road dead-ends at the south end of the airport, allowing birders to easily scan the field for sandpipers.

Mountain Plovers north of Harlingen: In recent winters, there have been up to 35 Mountain Plovers in the plowed fields east of the town of Sebastian (about 10 miles north of Harlingen). To search for these birds, go to the town of Sebastian on US-77 and take route FM-1018 east. Turn north on paved road 2099 at the flashing amber light. Go 2 miles north and look for the green "street sign" on the right (east) that reads *Mesquite CR*. Turn right and proceed into the field on the dirt road. The plovers are sometimes seen in the plowed fields from about one-half to one mile down this road. This is also one of the only places in the Lower Valley where you might spot a Prairie Falcon.

UPRIVER ON OLD MILITARY HIGHWAY (US-281)

From Brownsville west to Rio Grande City, the fertile floodplain of the Rio Grande was once covered by dense thickets and subtropical woodlands. Most of this habitat has been replaced by cities, farms, and citrus groves, restricting many of the native species to the remaining patches of natural vegetation. Several wildlife refuges are located on Old Military Highway (US-281), the most notable being Santa Ana National Wildlife Refuge, about 45 miles west of Brownsville.

From the junction of US-77/FM-802 in Brownsville, go west on FM-802 to US-281 (2.2 miles). Turn right (west) onto US-281 and start watching for an irrigation canal that crosses the highway (1.7 miles). If it has not recently rained, you can turn right onto the dirt road on the west bank. This road takes you to **La Paloma Reservoir** (0.7 mile), which can be good for ducks in winter, shorebirds in migration, and Neotropic Cormorants during most of the year.

Continue west on US-281 to River Bend Country Club (0.3 mile), where you might find Wood Storks in late summer/early fall and Fulvous Whistling-Ducks in summer. Actually, Wood Storks could show up anywhere on this road between Brownsville and Santa Ana refuge from late June through September. As you drive west on Old Military Highway, look for Ringed Kingfisher, Couch's Kingbird, and Scissor-tailed Flycatcher (summer) perched on utility wires above canals or other wet areas. In winter, American Kestrel and Loggerhead Shrike are easily seen en route. It is easy to stop along the highway, so pull over to investigate some of the little ponds along both sides of the road.

The abundance of Least Grebes in the Valley is unpredictable; some years they are fairly common, but normally they can be hard to find. In those scarce years, they sometimes can be seen on **Old Cannon Pond**. Continue up the highway, watching on the right for a roadside rest area with a cannon (19.0 miles). Just beyond the cannon a dirt road leads right to the pond (1.4 miles), which is located on the Resaca del Rancho Viejo tract of the Lower Rio Grande Valley National Wildlife Refuge. The tract is not open to the public; do not leave the road to cross the fence here. Because of the thick vegetation, you might need to wait a while for the grebes to paddle into view. This area also attracts Black-bellied Whistling-Duck, Neotropic Cormorant, White-tailed Kite, and a variety of shorebirds, raptors, and landbirds. Continue up the dirt road to the electrical station (0.5 mile). It is here that Tropical Kingbirds have nested for many years. With a little patience you will usually be able to hear their twittering calls. Also nesting in the area are both Couch's and Western Kingbirds. After you reach the electrical station, turn left and you can continue driving along the tree-lined road. You will see some of the

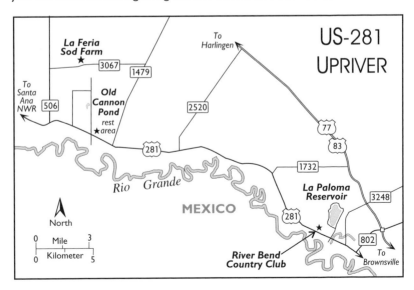

Lower Valley specialties along this road, and mixed-species flocks in winter, possibly including Tropical Parula (rare). It is also a good spot to see several raptor species. It was along this road that a Roadside Hawk was spotted in February 2005. The road reaches a T at the levee, where you will turn left and continue back to US-281. It was along this stretch of road that Dusky-capped Flycatcher, Rose-throated Becard, and White-throated Thrush were seen during the winter in early 2005.

Return to US-281 and continue west. To visit the **La Feria Sod Farm**, turn right at FM-506 (2.5 miles). Turn right again at FM-3067 (2.9 miles). The sod farm is on the left side of the highway (1.3 miles). During migration, check the fields in the area for American Golden-Plover, Upland and Buff-breasted Sandpipers, Horned Lark, and Sprague's Pipit.

Continue west on US-281 to a sign reading **El Zacatal**. The resacas on both sides of the highway here can be good for ducks, grebes, herons, and shorebirds. In spring, look for Wilson's Phalaropes and a variety of sandpipers. You might even find a Least Grebe or a Ringed Kingfisher.

WESLACO

L ocated near the headwaters of the Arroyo Colorado, **Llano Grande Lake** is an expanse of shallow water that attracts a variety of waterfowl and shorebirds (see map on next page). Llano Grande Lake is not to be confused with Estero Llano Grande State Park, a wonderful state park just down the highway on FM-1015 (described below). To reach Llano Grande Lake, continue west on US-281 to FM-1015 (4.9 miles) in the small community of Progreso. Turn right (north) on FM-1015 for 2.3 miles until you come to a dirt road leading right. By driving along the levee, you have a great vantage point for studying ducks, herons, and shorebirds. It is helpful to bring a spotting scope, as some birds may be at a considerable distance. In winter, look for Mottled Duck, Cinnamon Teal (uncommon), Least and Pied-billed Grebes, American White Pelican, Neotropic Cormorant, Yellow-crowned Night-Heron, White and White-faced Ibises, Roseate Spoonbill, Black-necked Stilt, and American Avocet. In migration, birders can usually find Greater and Lesser Yellowlegs, Solitary, Semipalmated, Western, Least, White-rumped, Pectoral, and Stilt Sandpipers, Long-billed Dowitcher, and Wilson's Phalarope. Look for Black Phoebe (winter) at the bridge on FM-1015, as well as Cave and Cliff Swallows (spring through fall).

Just a little farther north on FM-1015 is the **Methodist Camp Thicket** (0.4 mile). With tall specimens of ash, cedar, Black Willow, and hackberry, this area is prime bird habitat. Many of the Lower Valley specialties can be found in the woods year-round. Just stop by at the office to ask permission to bird, or call in advance: 956-565-6006.

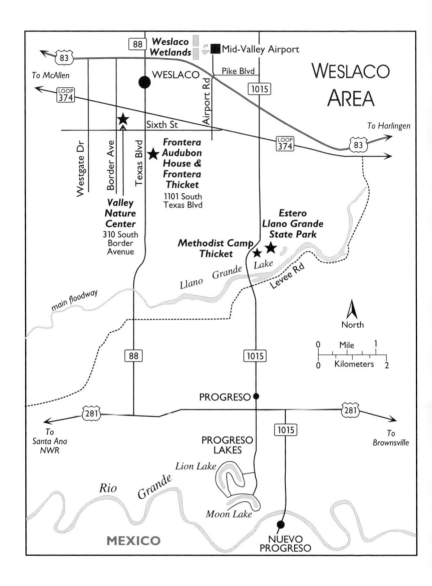

Estero Llano Grande State Park

As you continue north on FM-1015, you quickly will see the **Estero Llano Grande State Park/WBC** entrance sign on the right. If you are traveling from the north on US-83, exit FM-1015 and head south for 2.2 miles (WBC entrance sign). Turn left onto the entrance road (be careful of fast-moving traffic in the northbound lane) and pull into the parking lot.

Although this 200-acre park contains extensive woodland habitat, it is the wetlands that are its heart and soul. The conversion of agricultural fields into a complex series of ponds has drawn a vast array of waterfowl, waders, and shorebirds to the park. Birds often seen at Estero Llano Grande include Black-bellied and Fulvous (spring and summer) Whistling-Ducks, Mottled Duck, Least Grebe, American White Pelican, White and White-faced Ibises, Roseate Spoonbill, Sora, Black-necked Stilt, American Avocet, and Spotted and Least Sandpipers. Purple Gallinule occurs in spring, and there are usually concentrations of Wood Storks throughout summer.

The path to the visitor center is lined with native flowering shrubs that attract numerous butterfly species. Here you will see numerous White-tipped and Inca Doves, Common Ground-Dove, and maybe Lesser Goldfinch. Be sure to check in at the visitor center to pay the fee, check the wildlife sightings in the logbook, and get a trail map. With several hummingbird feeders scattered around the visitor center grounds, birders can usually find Buff-bellied (year-round), Ruby-throated and Black-chinned (migration), and Rufous (uncommon, winter). There are also seed feeders that attract the occasional Olive Sparrow. Adjacent to the visitor center is the observation deck, which looks out over two of the seven large ponds. Birders can scan the ponds from here or walk the boardwalks and nature trails around the ponds. The ponds

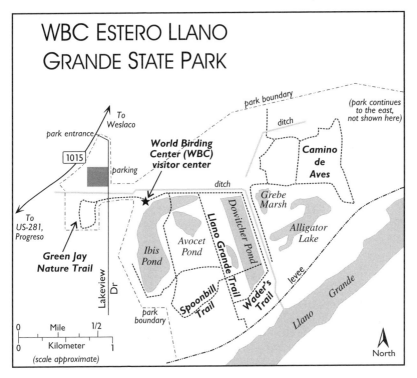

may hold Cinnamon Teal (uncommon), Least Bittern (summer), American Bittern (rare), and all three kingfishers. A Northern Jacana (accidental) was spotted at several of the ponds in the park during 2006.

The Lower Valley specialties are concentrated near the Green Jay Nature Trail located near the entrance to the park. The one-quarter-mile trail winds through four acres of native upland habitat that is continuous with the Methodist Thicket. It is here that birders can usually find Plain Chachalaca, White-tipped Dove, Great Kiskadee, Couch's Kingbird, Green Jay, Olive Sparrow, and Altamira Oriole. Red-crowned Parrots occasionally make dawn or dusk appearances here. Check with staff for the latest parrot information.

Those wanting a little more adventure can hike out to the levee that overlooks the Llano Grande (part of the Arroyo Colorado river system) and continue to Alligator Lake. Access the levee via Spoonbill Trail or the Llano Grande Hiking Trail. Llano Grande can be excellent for a variety of waterbirds. Tropical Kingbirds are sometimes seen on the hike to Alligator Lake, especially near the levee. In winter, Savannah Sparrows and Eastern Meadowlarks are common in the nearby fields. In addition to the large American Alligators, birders likely may find Least Grebe, Neotropic Cormorant, Anhinga, a variety of herons, and Great Kiskadee. Alligator Lake is a rookery for Great and Snowy Egrets, Little Blue and Tricolored Herons, and Black-crowned Night-Heron. Groove-billed Ani is a local nester here, as well as an irregular winter visitor. The refurbished historical pavilion near Alligator Lake has a water feature that may attract mixed-species flocks in winter as well as migrant passerines.

Although this park does not conduct formal hawkwatches, its close proximity to Santa Ana Refuge shows potential for decent numbers of migrating raptors. Most of the resident and wintering raptors can be spotted from the park, including Harris's, Red-shouldered (winter), and Red-tailed Hawks, and Crested Caracara.

The park is open daily, 8:00AM–5:00PM. For extended summer hours check with park staff. Admission: Adults $4, Children 12 and under free. Estero Llano Grande State Park, 3301 S. International Boulevard (FM-1015), Weslaco, TX 78596; phone: 956-565-3919, fax: 956-565-2864. For more information on the schedule of bird walks and other activities, visit: *www.worldbirdingcenter.org/sites/weslaco/index.phtml*

FRONTERA AUDUBON THICKET

Frontera Audubon Thicket is a wonderful urban park that is a must stop for birders at any season. Most of the Lower Valley specialties can be seen easily along the trails or from the observation blind, including Plain Chachalaca, White-tipped Dove, Buff-bellied Hummingbird, Green Kingfisher, Great Kiskadee, Green Jay, Clay-colored Thrush, Long-billed

Thrasher, Olive Sparrow, Altamira Oriole, and Lesser Goldfinch. Most winters this 22-acre park holds a number of warblers, including Orange-crowned, Yellow-rumped, Black-throated Green, Black-and-white, and Wilson's, Ovenbird, Northern Parula, Tropical Parula (rare), American Redstart (rare), and Northern Waterthrush. Other overwintering passerines include Hermit Thrush, American Robin, Gray Catbird, and Cedar Waxwing. The thicket is probably the easternmost locale where Gray Hawk is regularly seen. In summer, look for the rare Yellow-green Vireo amongst the resident birds.

Frontera Thicket can be a good inland migrant trap in spring and fall. It is also a good place to look for Green Parakeet and Red-crowned Parrot flocks, especially in late afternoon. The native landscaping, water features, and bird-feeding stations that attract many of the resident and migrant species have also attracted, over the years, an impressive array of Mexican rarities, including Mangrove Cuckoo, Violet-crowned Hummingbird, Elegant Trogon, Dusky-capped Flycatcher, White-throated Thrush, Blue Mockingbird, and Crimson-collared Grosbeak. The thicket and Audubon House are located at 1101 South Texas Boulevard (FM-88). Admission is $3 adults and $1 children. Hours and days vary with season, usually Sunday through Friday 8:00AM– 4:00PM and Saturday 7:00AM–7:00PM. Closed on major holidays. For more information call the Frontera Audubon Society office at 956-968-3275, 956-968-1388 (fax); email: *fronteraaudubon@yahoo.com;* or visit: *www.frontera audubon.org.*

Directions to Frontera Audubon Center: From US-83, exit on TX-88 (South Texas Boulevard), turn south, and proceed 1.7 miles on TX-88, through downtown Weslaco. Frontera Audubon Center is on the left (1101 South Texas Boulevard). Coming from the other direction on Old Military Highway (US-281) you can reach Frontera Audubon by driving 4.4 miles north on TX-88. The center will be on your right.

VALLEY NATURE CENTER

The **Valley Nature Center** is a six-acre urban park that contains a wonderful diversity of native plants, many of which were transplanted from areas that were slated for development. The local flora attracts several hummingbirds to the park, including Buff-bellied, Ruby-throated, Black-chinned, Anna's (casual), and Rufous (winter). While strolling the three-quarter-mile trail, birders may find a nice sampling of Lower Valley and regional specialties, including Green Parakeet and Red-crowned Parrot, Great Kiskadee, Tropical and Couch's Kingbirds, Groove-billed Ani, Clay-colored Thrush, Green Jay, Long-billed Thrasher, Olive Sparrow, and Lesser Goldfinch. The Valley Nature Center has been a good spot for migrant passerines and wintering warblers. This urban sanctuary has produced some interesting finds over the years, such as Bell's Vireo (spring) and an overwintering Wood Thrush. With its many flowers, the sanctuary boasts an impressive butterfly list, including such specialties as Malachite and the rare Erato Heliconian.

Altamira Oriole   Brad McKinney

Valley Nature Center is located in Gibson Park at 310 South Border Avenue, P.O. Box 8125, Weslaco, TX 78599-8125. phone 956-969-2475, fax 956-969-9915. To find Gibson Park, go one block south of Business 83 on Border Street in Weslaco. Go through the parking lot to the back and look for the tan-colored nature center building. The park is open Tuesday–Friday from 9:00AM–5:00PM, Saturday 8:00AM–5:00PM, Sunday 1:00–5:00PM, closed Mondays and all major holidays. The daily entrance fee is $3/adults, $1/children, $2.50/seniors. For more information visit: *www.valleynaturecenter.org*.

WESLACO WETLANDS

Weslaco Wetlands are a series of wastewater impoundments for the Weslaco wastewater-treatment plant. They can hold a variety of waterfowl and other waterbirds, including Black-bellied and Fulvous Whistling-Ducks, Least Grebe, Neotropic Cormorant, and Anhinga. The vegetated levees may host an assortment of landbirds such as Groove-billed Ani (summer), Vermilion Flycatcher (winter), Great Kiskadee, and Couch's and Tropical Kingbirds, and may also be good for passerines during migration. The area can be accessed most weekdays from the end of Airport Drive after it goes under US-83 (heading north), past the police/fire department. Parking is available at the end of Airport Drive (please do not block the gate). Always check in at the office and there should be no problem with access. The gate can sometimes be locked on weekends, so this site may be best visited on weekdays. Weslaco is in the process of developing the area for wildlife watching.

WESLACO PARROTS

Parrots and parakeets are seen almost daily from October through April flying over Weslaco neighborhoods in the vicinity of Sixth Street and Border Avenue. They roost in large trees near Sixth Street between Westgate Drive and Border Avenue. The main flock roosts at the Audubon House/ Frontera Thicket. For the latest on Weslaco parrot sightings, contact Valley Nature Center, 956-969-2475; or Frontera Audubon Society, 956-968-3275.

PROGRESO LAKES

If you want to try another spot for Tropical Kingbirds, stop at Progreso Lakes, a small community south of Weslaco on FM-1015. The birds have been found in the vicinity of the two resacas. To reach Progreso Lakes, travel south on FM-1015 past the town of Progreso. At the intersection with US-281 continue south to Progreso Lakes. The resaca is straight ahead about 1.5 miles. The birds have been found perched on tall trees and wires. Red-crowned Parrots have nested in this area. There is also a recent winter record of Greater Pewee here.

SANTA ANA
NATIONAL WILDLIFE REFUGE

Santa Ana National Wildlife Refuge offers some of the best birding in South Texas. More than 400 species of birds and over 250 species of butterflies have been recorded on the refuge. Virtually all of the Lower Valley specialties can be found here, including Hook-billed Kite, Northern Beardless-Tyrannulet, Clay-colored Thrush, and Tropical Parula. There is usually a good assortment of wintering waterfowl and other waterbirds on Willow, Pintail, and Cattail Lakes, and migrant raptors funnel past the refuge in large numbers during spring and fall. Mixed-species passerine flocks are present in winter, and you'll find an assortment of landbirds in migration. A number of Mexican rarities have been recorded here over the years.

At Santa Ana you will be looking for Least Grebe, Hook-billed Kite, Gray Hawk, Plain Chachalaca, White-tipped Dove, Groove-billed Ani (summer), Common Pauraque, Buff-bellied Hummingbird, Ringed and Green Kingfishers, Northern Beardless-Tyrannulet, Great Kiskadee, Couch's Kingbird, Green Jay, Clay-colored Thrush, Long-billed Thrasher, Tropical Parula (rare), Black-throated Gray Warbler (rare), Olive Sparrow, and Altamira Oriole.

Santa Ana NWR consists of 2,088 acres of riparian forest, the largest block of such habitat on the Rio Grande between Falcon Dam and the Gulf of Mexico. The refuge is covered by a tangle of brush and subtropical trees similar to those found in northeastern Mexico. This native vegetation harbors many unusual plants, mammals, reptiles, birds, and insects. A few of the plants around the visitor center are labeled, but the rest of the flora and fauna offers a real challenge in identification. The refuge was originally part of a 15-square-mile land grant awarded by Mexico to Benigno Leal in 1834. Between 1910 and 1930, this ranch was combined with adjacent lands to form the Alamo Tract, an area that was largely converted to farmland. The southern section, though, retained its natural riverine forest environment and in 1943 was acquired by the U.S. government to form Santa Ana NWR.

Both Santa Ana NWR and Bentsen State Park have substantial forest tracts along the Rio Grande attracting a number of rarities over the years. A list of Texas Review Species that have occurred at Santa Ana includes Masked Duck, Crane Hawk, Roadside Hawk, Short-tailed Hawk, Northern Jacana, Curlew Sandpiper, Ruddy Ground-Dove, Mangrove Cuckoo, Green-breasted Mango, Rose-throated Becard, White-throated Thrush, Rufous-backed Robin, Golden-crowned Warbler, Yellow-faced Grassquit, Crimson-collared Grosbeak, and Blue Bunting. Although many of these birds have appeared during winter, rarities are possible at any season.

To reach the refuge from the previous stop, continue west on US-281 (from its intersection with FM-1015) to FM-493 (6.9 miles). Start watching for the sign for Santa Ana National Wildlife Refuge, turning left onto the entrance road (4.6 miles). [To reach Santa Ana NWR from McAllen, drive east on US-83 for about 10 miles to the FM-907 exit in Alamo. Go south on FM-907 for about 7.5 miles to US-281, where you jog left for 0.3 mile to the Santa Ana NWR entrance road.] Entrance fees: $3/car/visit or $10/annual pass. Access is free on the first Sunday of each month. Fees may be paid at a pay station or in the visitor center. Stop in at the visitor center for maps of the refuge's trail system, checklists of birds, vertebrates, and butterflies, an as-

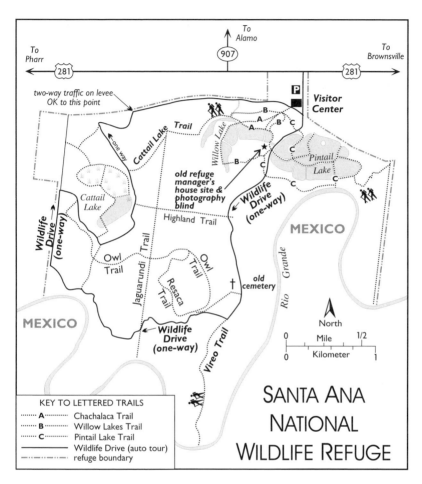

To
Alamo

To
Pharr

To
Brownsville

907

281

281

two-way traffic on levee
OK to this point

P

Visitor
Center

Cattail Lake Trail

one way

Willow Lake

old refuge
manager's
house site &
photography
blind

Cattail
Lake

Wildlife
Drive
(one-way)

Pintail
Lake

MEXICO

Highland Trail

Wildlife
Drive
(one-way)

Owl
Trail

Jaguarundi Trail

Owl
Trail

Resaca
Trail

Rio Grande

old
cemetery

MEXICO

Wildlife
Drive
(one-way)

Vireo Trail

North

0   Mile   1/2

0   Kilometer   1

KEY TO LETTERED TRAILS
A .... Chachalaca Trail
B .... Willow Lakes Trail
C .... Pintail Lake Trail
————— Wildlife Drive (auto tour)
-·-·-·-·-·- refuge boundary

SANTA ANA
NATIONAL
WILDLIFE REFUGE

sortment of natural history books, and to take a look at the log book for information on recent sightings. The visitor center is open 8:00AM–4:00PM, seven days a week, except Thanksgiving, Christmas, and New Year's Day. Scheduled programs about Santa Ana NWR and the Wildlife Corridor are shown in the auditorium. The refuge offers guided birding walking tours regularly throughout the fall and winter seasons. These tours are free; call 956-784-7500 for current schedules. For more information: Santa Ana National Wildlife Refuge, Route 2, Box 202A, Alamo, TX 78516; phone 956-784-7500; or visit: *www.fws.gov/southwest/refuges/texas/santana.html*

The 7-mile **Wildlife Drive**, open to private vehicles on weekends during the summer, provides excellent opportunities for exploring the more remote areas of Santa Ana. The drive can be driven from 8:30AM to 3:30PM, Saturdays and Sundays from May through October. Please call the visitor center at

Chachalaca Trail, Santa Ana NWR   Brad McKinney

956-784-7500 before arrival to confirm that the drive will be open. When the drive is closed, you must either walk in (sunrise to sunset daily) or take an interpretive tram tour. The 1.5-hour tram tours usually operate three times a day from November through April; please call the visitor center at 956-784-7500 before arrival to confirm that the tram is running; cost is $4/adults and $1/children 12 and under. Bicycles are welcome on the Wildlife Drive daily from sunrise to sunset. Keep bicycles off the walking trails, park them off the refuge drive, and do not travel the wrong way on the one-way road. Hiking off the trails is not permitted; there are picnic facilities outside the visitor center. Pets are permitted only in the main parking lot and visitor center area.

Some of the best birding is from the walking trails along the five impoundments at **Willow Lake**. The first three impoundments (Willow 1, 2, and 3) are not far from the visitor center. Before heading out to the trails, be sure to get a trail map. On the way out, check the bird-feeding station at the visitor center for Plain Chachalaca, Buff-bellied Hummingbird, Green Jay, Golden-fronted Woodpecker and White-tipped Dove. Keep alert to the possibility of vagrant hummingbirds: Green Violetear (summer), Green-breasted Mango (fall), and Broad-billed Hummingbird (winter) have been recorded in the area. The visitor center parking lots and adjacent gardens and picnic areas are among the best places to find several South Texas specialty birds, such as Great Kiskadee, Clay-colored Thrush, Olive Sparrow, and Altamira Oriole.

Most of the trails offer short walks that can be completed in less than one hour. When crossing the irrigation canal on the way to the trailhead and the start of the popular **Chachalaca, Willow Lake, and Pintail Lake Trails**, watch for Green Kingfisher. At the trailhead, many people choose the universally accessible, 0.5-mile Chachalaca Trail, which passes through beautiful patches of moss-draped forest of Sugar Hackberry and Cedar Elm on the way to Willow Lake. In winter, Mottled Duck, Cinnamon Teal (uncommon), Ring-necked Duck, Least Grebe, Neotropic Cormorant, Anhinga, White-faced Ibis, Ringed and Green Kingfishers, and other waterbirds may be found at the lake.

In spring and summer, Black-bellied and Fulvous Whistling-Ducks are often observed in Willow Lake 3, and the cattails usually harbor Least Bitterns. Wood Storks usually arrive at Santa Ana by late June (especially on Pintail Lake) and are also occasionally seen soaring overhead. Although Masked Ducks have occurred on Willow Lake in all seasons, your best chance of spotting one is in summer. Masked Duck is an erratic Mexican vagrant, often absent for many years from South Texas before finally reappearing. Its presence in the Valley often coincides with wet years. There are perhaps a half-dozen refuge records in the past 20 years.

In spring, scan the overhanging brush around the lake for flycatchers and warblers. Santa Ana is one of the Valley's best spots for finding MacGillivray's Warbler during migration. Listen for the "bouncing-ball" call of Olive Sparrow or the melodic song of Long-billed Thrasher along the forest trail. Both species can be found in the leaf litter or in the thick tangles. Also listen for White-tipped Doves —their soft resonant cooing resembles the sound made by blowing across a bottle mouth. As you walk along the lakeshore, you come to three observation points (two open decks and one that is semi-enclosed). Look and listen for Clay-colored Thrush and Northern Beardless-Tyrannulet near the lake, as they have nested there in recent years. Online recordings of Clay-colored Thrush and other Lower Valley specialties can be heard at: *www.worldbirdingcenter.org/bird_info.*

Birds you might have seen along Chachalaca Trail up to this point include Plain Chachalaca, Common Ground-Dove, Golden-fronted and Ladder-backed Woodpeckers, Brown-crested Flycatcher (summer), Couch's Kingbird, Green Jay, Carolina and House (winter) Wrens, and Hooded (summer) and Altamira Orioles. In winter, the tall trees periodically come alive with sounds of mixed-species flocks consisting of Blue-headed Vireo, Black-crested Titmouse, Ruby-crowned Kinglet, Blue-gray Gnatcatcher, and Orange-crowned Warbler. You might also find Eastern Phoebes working the forest edge. Occasionally, Tropical Parula and Black-throated Gray Warbler can be found as well.

Each of the three lake-observation points provides excellent views of the water and shoreline. Just past the third observation point (deck), Chachalaca Trail turns away from the lake and returns to the trailhead, but you will notice an unimproved trail to the right (notice the small gap in the concrete curb). This connects with Willow Lake and Pintail Lake Trails, past two reedy sections of Willow Lake with variable water levels. As you come to a small pond called "Willow 1" on the left, you will be approaching the area where the old manager's residence formerly stood. Willow 1 is good for Green Kingfisher, Groove-billed Ani (summer), Clay-colored Thrush, and Altamira Oriole. Keep an eye open for Rose-throated Becard (on average this species has made appearances every other year for the past 20 years). In recent years, the becard has attempted to nest (unsuccessfully) in the vicinity of Willow 1 and also at the visitor center parking lot. The soccer-ball shaped nest is usually conspicuous. Check with refuge staff for the latest information. If you are fortunate enough to observe an active nest, please maintain a respectable distance.

The old manager's residence and related buildings have long since been torn down, but the parking lot remains. When walking along the narrow concrete path through the flowering shrubs, you may notice a plaque commemorating the former site as a registered natural landmark. The blooming plants near the plaque often draw Buff-bellied Hummingbirds year-round, Ruby-throated Hummingbirds in migration, and sometimes Rufous Hummingbirds in winter. Long-billed Thrashers and Olive Sparrows often can be heard scratching about the leaf litter here.

Some years Groove-billed Anis and Altamira Orioles have nested in trees surrounding the parking lot. Tucked in behind some tall trees south of the parking lot is the impressive 43-foot Tree Tower. With an unbroken canopy below, the view from the tower is spectacular. Here birders have actually looked down on singing Altamira Orioles and Northern Beardless-Tyrannulets! This area of tall trees is good for mixed-species flocks in winter, warblers and other passerines in migration, and occasionally a Clay-colored Thrush. Tropical Parulas have nested in the moss-draped Texas Ebony and Cedar Elms; they are most easily located when singing during the breeding season. The best spots to find them in spring and summer seem to be on Resaca Trail and the north end of Vireo Trail. Tropical Parulas can show up at any season, especially in winter, when they quietly move with mixed-species flocks. Some winters, temperate species such as Carolina Chickadee, Red-breasted Nuthatch, and Golden-crowned Kinglet have made rare appearances. Also, look for Winter Wren (rare) along nearby walking trails during the winter months.

The area around the parking lot can be good for birds of prey, including such migrants and winter visitors as Sharp-shinned, Cooper's, Harris's (year-round), Red-shouldered, and Red-tailed Hawks, and Merlin. Hook-billed Kites and Gray Hawks occasionally are seen soaring overhead. During hawk migration, which peaks in late March/early April and in early October, look for kettles of Broad-winged and Swainson's Hawks, as well as Mississippi Kites. You may even see some dark-morph Broad-wingeds in the large kettles. Other raptors seen in migration include Osprey, Swallow-tailed Kite (rare),

Northern Harrier, Zone-tailed Hawk (rare), Golden Eagle (very rare), and Peregrine Falcon.

Birders visiting Santa Ana in April or October should try to get out to the Tree Tower in the late afternoon, when you may witness one of nature's magnificent spectacles: watching hundreds of soaring Broad-winged Hawks or Mississippi Kites abruptly descend upon the forest canopy to roost for the night. Observers wishing to participate in the seasonal hawkwatches should check with refuge staff.

The route to the site of the old manager's residence will have led you through a selection of fine birding areas. From this site, you have several options: The shortest way back to the visitor center is along the Wildlife Drive which returns to the levee. Many of the woodland species seen previously on the walking trail can be found along the way. Also check the wires for Couch's Kingbird and Scissor-tailed Flycatcher, especially from March through September.

The levee road is also a good vantage point for viewing migrating hawks. This is a good spot to see Harris's Hawk and to look for resident specialties such as Hook-billed Kite and Gray Hawk. Undoubtedly, the rarest raptor seen from the levee (and on the refuge) was Crane Hawk, a first ABA-Area re-

Golden-fronted Woodpecker   Louise Zemaitis

cord that delighted (and occasionally frustrated) hundreds of birders from December 1987 to April 1988.

From the old manager's residence, you can reach the photography blind by taking the Willow Lakes Trail south of the parking lot. The refuge puts bird seed out and provides water at this blind from November through March, and photographers can get close to several species of doves, Golden-fronted Woodpeckers, Green Jays, and several species of songbirds using the water feature. White-tipped Doves are also found out on the trails, where they prefer to walk rather than fly. When these chunky birds do take to the air, they usually fly low through the forest. On the other hand, a Red-billed Pigeon flashes across at tree-top level, resembling a dark falcon. Red-billed Pigeons are very rarely seen at Santa Ana except in late spring and summer. The best place to look for them is along Vireo Trail toward the river. Many birders choose to walk out to nearby Pintail Lake, where the birding is usually good, and a variety of ducks, wading birds, shorebirds, and passerines can be seen.

Pintail Lake Trail, found directly across the road, leads to the Pintail Lakes wetland complex. While walking the trail, you may hear the raucous cries of Great Kiskadees or the quiet rattle of a low-perching Green Kingfisher. Green Kingfishers can be seen in several areas around the lake, especially at the eastern end of the complex. Also look for Eastern Phoebe (winter), Vermilion Flycatcher (winter), Loggerhead Shrike (winter), and Couch's Kingbird on exposed perches bordering the lake. Although Tropical Kingbirds generally prefer more open habitats, there have been sightings at Pintail Lake.

Spring is the best time to look for breeding-plumaged Glossy Ibis (rare) amidst the many White-faced Ibises at Pintail Lake. The surrounding vegetation is also a likely spot for Groove-billed Anis during the breeding season. Several rarities have been discovered here in recent years, including Northern Jacana, Curlew Sandpiper (two spring records), Red-naped Sapsucker, and Gray-crowned Yellowthroat. Least Grebes usually can be located on the main impoundment at Pintail Lake; however, in some years they can be hard to come by. Look for Least Bittern (summer), Sora, Purple Gallinule (rare, summer), Sedge (rare) and Marsh Wrens (winter), and Common Yellowthroat in the cattails. Depending on season and water levels, you can find a variety of ducks, waders, and shorebirds.

The open area around the lake provides a good vantage point for viewing soaring Hook-billed Kites or Gray Hawks. If you happen to chance upon either of these raptors, consider yourself very fortunate, for these birds are notoriously difficult to find—unless, of course, you are not looking for them. One is more likely to see a White-tailed Kite or a Harris's Hawk. While birding in the old manager's residence/Pintail Lake area, keep an eye out for Short-tailed Hawk, a rare Mexican visitor to South Texas. This species was first documented in Texas in July 1989 (Santa Margarita Ranch), yet it has been found in the Lower Valley almost every spring or summer since. Although there is one February record for the refuge, that was likely an early migrant, as most sightings are concentrated between April and June.

If time allows, you should attempt walking all of the **Chachalaca and Willow Lakes Trails** (0.5 mile and 1.6 miles respectively). One of the best spots for Clay-colored Thrush in recent years has been on Willow Lakes Trail, between the two small bridges overlooking a narrow water channel that is usually dry. Before reaching the bridges, the trail passes through large stands of Prickly Pear cactus where Pyrrhuloxia and Altamira Oriole are seen occasionally. There have been at least four winter records for Golden-crowned Warbler at Santa Ana since 1984 and most have come from along Willow Lakes Trail. A first U.S. record for Yellow-faced Grassquit also occurred in this general area in late January 1990.

Willow Lakes Trail joins the **Cattail Lakes Trail**, which leads to Cattail Lake. It is a nice hike—but a fairly long one. Many people choose to drive there (when the main road is open to vehicles). Least Grebes and, on very rare occasions, Northern Jacana (August 2006) and Masked Duck have shown up at the lake. In summer, look for Least Bittern and Purple Gallinule along the banks. Common Pauraques sometimes flush from the shaded thickets at the south corner of the pond, where you might also encounter a Giant Toad. Hook-billed Kites and Gray Hawks are occasionally spotted in the area, especially in summer.

Keep a look out for wild Muscovy Ducks at Cattail, Willow, or Pintail Lakes during late spring and summer. Although very rare in the mid-Valley, this bird seems to be turning up more frequently in recent years.

After spring and summer rains, frogs and toads are abundant about the lakes. Most will be Rio Grande Leopard Frogs, Giant Toads, and Gulf Coast Toads; however, you could find Great Plains Narrowmouth Toad, Sheep Frogs, and Mexican Tree Frogs as well. The most common turtle at the refuge is the Red-eared Slider of mud-bottomed ponds and sluggish streams. It can be identified by a bright red stripe behind the eye, which is easily seen because these large turtles often crawl out on rocks and logs to bask. However, the red stripe fades in older individuals. There are two other turtles here. Yellow Mud Turtle is uncommon in ponds, canals, and streams with mud bottoms, but it may be missed because it is mainly nocturnal and it does not crawl out of the water to bask. The large pancake-like Spiny Softshell may be found in refuge lakes and along the Rio Grande. You also may find an endangered Texas Tortoise, which was once fairly common throughout the dry, brushy areas of South Texas. It has clubfeet and a high rounded shell. Young tortoises have a yellow square in the center of each large scute.

The only venomous snake at Santa Ana is the non-aggressive Texas Coral Snake, which should not be handled. One of the most commonly seen snakes is the endangered Texas Indigo Snake, often referred to as a Black Snake. This is the longest snake in North America, occasionally exceeding eight feet. Other commonly encountered snakes include Southwestern Rat Snake, Diamondback Water Snake, Bull Snake, Texas Patch-nose Snake, and Gulf Coast Ribbon Snake.

To explore the refuge further you should drive the one-way, 7-mile **Wildlife Drive** (when it is open for vehicles). Bicycles are allowed year-round and are a good way to cover the entire road. In late spring and early summer, look for Hook-billed Kite, Gray Hawk, Northern Beardless-Tyrannulet, and Tropical Parula, as well as a few Greater Roadrunners. There are many places to stop along the road, nearly all of them worthwhile. The cactus patch behind the Old Cemetery may attract a handful of species such as Ladder-backed Woodpecker, White-eyed Vireo, Verdin, and Curve-billed Thrasher, and may even hide a Greater Roadrunner. From the cemetery, periodically look up to see if there is any raptor activity. Depending on the season, look for large kettles of Turkey and Black Vultures (year-round), Cooper's, Sharp-shinned, Swainson's, and Broad-winged Hawks during migration, and Harris's Hawk (year-round). A Short-tailed Hawk stayed in this area for the spring and summer in 2004.

Much of the refuge is covered by jungle-like thickets, which can be difficult to bird by car. To get a feel for the refuge, try hiking some of the trails, such as Vireo Trail. From the head of Vireo Trail along the Wildlife Drive, it is a one-mile hike to the Rio Grande. The closest parking lot is at the Old Cemetery (0.2 mile). Be sure to take along a trail map and plenty of water.

One of the hardest-to-find of the permanent residents is Northern Beardless-Tyrannulet. This bird definitely follows the rule that the longer the name, the smaller the bird. And what a nondescript little bird it is! It is best located by voice, a plaintive *dee-dee-dee*. The bird forages at all tree levels and is usually seen in an upright posture. Summer is the best season to find tyrannulets, though males may begin singing on territory as early as March. This bird has been found in thickets all over the refuge: along the Vireo Trail, the Owl Trail, the Highland Trail, and near the old manager's residence. In winter, it may be seen in mixed-species flocks.

Half-day canoe trips on the Rio Grande are offered several times per week in winter (additional fee charged, reservations required). There is a very good chance that canoe trip participants will see all three U.S. kingfishers—Ringed, Green, and Belted—and many other species, plus you can build life lists in Mexico and the U.S. at the same time.

With an exciting mix of Rio Grande specialties, migrants, and potential rarities from Mexico, Santa Ana National Wildlife Refuge is a must stop on any birder's visit to the Valley.

MCALLEN AREA

The city of McAllen is named after rancher John McAllen, a Scot who arrived in the Valley in the early 1850s. The town itself was unofficially founded in 1904, when John McAllen donated land to establish a new railroad stop. At that time, commerce began to grow around citrus and vegetable crops. Today, McAllen has a population of 125,000 and an international airport, plenty of hotels and restaurants, and is a quick drive from either Santa Ana NWR or Bentsen State Park. In addition to the surrounding hotspots, there is good birding in town at Quinta Mazatlan, a wing of the World Birding Center, and at the McAllen sewage ponds. McAllen is home to the **Texas Tropics Nature Festival**, held each spring at the Holiday Inn Civic Center off US-83.

Target birds in the vicinity may include Black-bellied and Fulvous Whistling-Ducks, Cinnamon Teal, Least Grebe, White-faced Ibis, White-rumped and Baird's Sandpipers, Green Parakeet, Red-crowned Parrot, Burrowing Owl, Buff-bellied Hummingbird, Scissor-tailed Flycatcher, Couch's Kingbird, Sprague's Pipit, Clay-colored Thrush, Tropical Parula, Hooded Oriole, and Lesser Goldfinch.

MCALLEN SEWAGE PONDS

When you drive out the entrance road at Santa Ana refuge, turn left (west) onto US-281 to its junction with FM-2557 (1.8 miles). A Burrowing Owl has been seen in the area in past winters; to look for it, turn right onto FM-2557, then left onto dirt Anaya Street (1.0 mile). Begin scanning the crop fields and dirt mounds for the owl. You may find Sprague's Pipits in these fields during winter. Burrowing Owls are very hard to find in South Texas, though they are occasionally found along lesser-traveled roads throughout the Lower Valley. These owls have been seen in past years near the intersection of FM-88 and FM-1422 north of Edcouch-Elsa (Hidalgo County; see map on page 83) and more recently near the town of Granjeno (see map on next page). For the latest on Burrowing Owl status, check with staff at Santa Ana or Bentsen.

Back on US-281, you will soon see where the highway heads north (right) to Pharr (2.1 miles). Instead of turning right to Pharr, however, go straight ahead on US-281 West toward Hidalgo and Reynosa. Go past FM-336 (3.2 miles) to the end of the road (1.1 mile) in Hidalgo. Turn right onto Spur 115. (If you turn left, you wind up in Reynosa, Mexico.) To get to the **McAllen sewage ponds**, pass FM-1016 (2.8 miles) and turn left at the first signal (1.0 mile) onto Idela Drive. The ponds begin at South 37th (1.3 miles), where you will find water-filled impounds off the dikes on the left. Drive up onto the

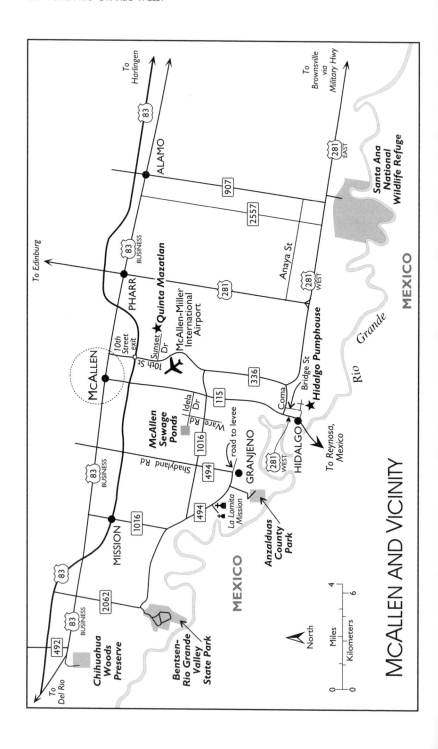

MCALLEN AND VICINITY

levee that encircles the ponds on your left, where the sign welcoming birders is located. (Avoid driving the levee after heavy rains.)

Depending on water levels, the ponds can be productive at times for ducks, waders, and shorebirds. Least Grebes are sometimes found here, especially in winter and spring. If water levels are high enough, there will usually be a few Black-bellied Whistling-Ducks around. The ponds are best in spring and fall when shorebirds are moving through. This is a good spot to find Black-necked Stilt, American Avocet, American Golden-Plover, Hudsonian Godwit (rare), Semipalmated, Western, Least, White-rumped (spring only), Baird's, Pectoral, and Stilt Sandpipers, and Wilson's Phalarope. Occasionally Fulvous Whistling-Duck (spring) and Cinnamon Teal (winter) are found; there are also at least two spring sightings of Glossy Ibis (April and May). Water levels and season are important factors affecting the abundance and diversity of birds here. The willow trees that border the impoundments can be good for passerines, and can be especially productive during migration. In some winters, Say's Phoebe (rare) is found in the open areas around the impoundments.

QUINTA MAZATLAN

Just minutes from the McAllen-Miller International Airport is **Quinta Mazatlan**, the McAllen wing of the World Birding Center complex. An historic adobe hacienda forms the centerpiece of this 15-acre urban sanctuary, which is surrounded by lush tropical landscaping and native woodland that attracts numerous bird species. Quinta Mazatlan offers nature enthusiasts a broad range of birding experiences, from nature programs to guided bird walks to relaxing at bird feeders. The winding half-mile nature trail, complete with five water features, about 25 hummingbird feeders, and bird feeding stations, holds many of the Lower Valley specialties. Quinta Mazatlan is also one of the easiest spots to see Clay-colored Thrush, as multiple birds often are seen while you walk the trails. Birders can also stroll through the historic mansion built in the 1930s and which includes a carved bird exhibit featuring 22 Lower Valley specialties, a nature art gallery with changing shows, and a nature gift store with a great selection of books.

To get to Quinta Mazatlan, take US-83 to the 10th Street Exit in McAllen. Travel south on 10th Street. Turn east on Sunset (across the street from McCreery Aviation). Proceed along Sunset to the Quinta Mazatlan gates; parking is out front. Hours: Tuesday–Saturday, 8:00AM–5:00PM; minimal admission fee. Please call ahead for program and group tour rates.

Birds seen at Quinta Mazatlan include White-tipped Dove, Eastern Screech-Owl, Common Pauraque, Buff-bellied Hummingbird, Great Kiskadee, Couch's Kingbird, Green Jay, Clay-colored Thrush, Long-billed and Curve-billed Thrashers, Tropical Parula (rare), Black-throated Gray Warbler

Eastern Screech-Owl, McCall's race   Barry Zimmer

(rare), Olive Sparrow, and Lesser Goldfinch. It is possible to see Tropical Kingbirds while walking in from the parking area, although they are somewhat irregular here; they are more likely to be found along the adjacent golf course, to the south toward the airport. They may be found in all seasons but are generally easier to see in the winter months, when most Couch's Kingbirds have moved southward into eastern Mexico.

In addition to easy viewing of many of the Lower Valley specialties, Quinta Mazatlan is a good place to view overwintering warblers such as Orange-crowned, Northern and Tropical (rare) Parulas, Black-throated Gray (rare), Black-throated Green, Yellow-throated (often seen in the palms), and Black-and-white. During winter, you may also find Black-chinned Hummingbird (rare), American Robin, Gray Catbird, Cedar Waxwing, Black-headed Grosbeak (rare), and Summer Tanager (uncommon). As an urban sanctuary that happens to be the highest point in McAllen (27 feet above sea level), Quinta Mazatlan is a welcome stopover for migrant songbirds passing through the mid-Valley. From mid-April to mid-May, a variety of migrants may be found not only in the tall shade trees but also in the dense tangle of vegetation and at the many water features and bird feeding stations. The hummingbird feeders attract Buff-bellied Hummingbirds year-round, Ruby-throated and Black-chinned Hummingbirds in migration, and Rufous Hummingbirds in winter. Although not to be expected, a Broad-tailed Hummingbird (rare) has been recorded on the property.

While walking the nature trail, you may encounter an Eastern Screech-Owl poking its head out of a palm cavity roost. Be sure to ask sanctuary staff for the latest on the owl's roosting site. Green Parakeets often nest on the property in the palm trees, and Red-crowned Parrots are frequently seen as flybys both early and late in the day. As of yet, there is no documented nesting of Red-crowneds on the property.

Although not yet known as a hawkwatching destination, Quinta Mazatlan has ample open areas from which to view soaring Broad-winged and Swainson's Hawks during spring (April) and fall (September) migrations. Gray Hawk is an irregular winter visitor.

A printable checklist can be downloaded at: *www.quintamazatlan. com/docs/BirdChecklist.pdf.* Quinta Mazatlan is under the stewardship of the City of McAllen Parks and Recreation Department, and is located on 600 Sunset, in the heart of McAllen. Mailing address is P.O. Box 220, McAllen, TX 78505-0220. For more information call 956-688-3370 or visit: *www. quintamazatlan.com.*

RESIDENTIAL MCALLEN

Like Brownsville, Harlingen, and Weslaco, McAllen also hosts parrot roost-sites. Large winter congregations of Green Parakeets are consistently found in late afternoon along 10th Street at Violet and Robin Streets, and they roost in varying spots to the east. Some past roost-sites for Red-crowned Parrots have been on the east end of Dallas Avenue (in the vicinity of Mockingbird Street) and on the north side of town on Wisteria Avenue just west of 10th Street. Some birders drive up and down North Main Street, north of LaVista, with their car windows open for one hour after sunrise or one hour before sunset to listen for flocks of roosting parrots.

Being the nomadic creatures that they are, Red-crowned Parrots are prone to wander from season to season and from year to year. For the latest parrot information you may want to check with several sources, including the staff at Bentsen State Park (956-584-9156), Quinta Mazatlan (956-688-3370), or Valley Nature Center (956-969-2475). It might also be helpful to check the Lower Rio Grande Rare Bird Alert (956-969-2731) or the TexBird archives at: *http://listserv.uh.edu/archives/texbirds.html.*

Other birds found in McAllen's residential areas include Black-bellied Whistling-Duck, Plain Chachalaca, White-tipped Dove, Buff-bellied Hummingbird (summer), Great Kiskadee, Couch's Kingbird (summer), Scissor-tailed Flycatcher, Green Jay, Long-billed and Curve-billed Thrashers, Bronzed Cowbird, Hooded Oriole (summer), and Lesser Goldfinch (uncommon).

During winter, you can usually find mixed-species flocks and winter warblers, including Orange-crowned, Nashville (uncommon), Northern and Tropical (rare) Parulas, Yellow-rumped, Black-throated Green, Yellow-throated, and Black-and-white (uncommon). In migration, a fair number of neotropical migrants can be found throughout the city (though typically far fewer than at sites closer to the coast), and migrating raptors may be seen soaring in large numbers during April and September. Some years, Clay-colored Thrushes show up in scattered residential locations, including the intersection of Fresno and 1st Streets; however, it is best to go to Quinta Mazatlan when searching for this species. Rarities such as Green-breasted Mango, Broad-billed Hummingbird, Acorn Woodpecker, and Crimson-collared Grosbeak have been found in residential McAllen.

HIDALGO PUMPHOUSE

The Hidalgo wing of the World Birding Center is a beautiful site along the Rio Grande that offers a nice blend of history and nature. Here birders can wander in native butterfly gardens, relax on the platform overlook, or venture along the paved hiking trail through a 600-acre U.S. Fish & Wildlife tract along the Rio Grande. Hidalgo Pumphouse offers both natural and cultural history tours on which one can see the local birds and the impressive steam-driven irrigation pumps that transformed Hidalgo County into a year-round farming phenomenon.

To get to the **Hidalgo Pumphouse**, take 10th Street in McAllen south for about 7 miles and curve west into US-281 (Coma Street), continuing west to Bridge Street (first traffic light). Follow Hidalgo Pumphouse signs left on Bridge Street and continue six short blocks to Flora Avenue. Turn left onto Flora to 2nd Street and turn right into the WBC-Hidalgo Pumphouse grounds. Nature trails are open seven days a week and are free to the public. Museum hours are Monday–Friday, 10:00AM–5:00PM; Sunday, 1:00PM–5:00PM; closed Saturday. Admission to the museum is Adults $3, Seniors $2, and Children $1.

Lying along the forested banks of the Rio Grande, Hidalgo Pumphouse contains varied habitats that attract a nice mix of waterbirds and upland species. Birds seen here include Neotropic Cormorant, Groove-billed Ani (summer), Buff-bellied Hummingbird, Ringed and Green Kingfishers, Black Phoebe, Great Kiskadee, Couch's Kingbird, Clay-colored Thrush, Long-billed Thrasher, Olive Sparrow, Hooded Oriole (summer), House Finch (rare), and Lesser Goldfinch. Like most access points along the Rio Grande, it is possible to see Ringed and Green Kingfishers along the river, along with a variety of waterbirds. Many waterbirds can be seen in or around the Carlson Settling Basin, a large wetland that borders the Hidalgo Hike and Bike Trail a short distance east from the parking area.

In the forested U.S. Fish & Wildlife tract, you are likely to see many of the Lower Valley specialties, including Great Kiskadee and Couch's Kingbird. The best spot to see Black Phoebe is from the platform overlooking the channel that connects the old pumphouse to the Rio Grande. The unobstructed view at the amphitheater makes it a natural spot from which to watch migrant raptors soaring overhead. Large flights of Broad-winged and Swainson's Hawks and Mississippi Kites funnel through the area during the peak hawkwatching seasons in April and September.

Old Hidalgo Pumphouse, 902 S. Second Street, Hidalgo, TX 78557. Reservations and phone information: phone 956-843-8686, fax 956-8430-6519. For more information visit: *www.worldbirdingcenter.org/sites/hidalgo/index.phtml.*

ANZALDUAS COUNTY PARK

A s you exit the McAllen Sewage Ponds, you will be at the west end of Idela Drive. Head back (east) on Idela Drive to Ware Road (0.5 mile). Turn right (south) and proceed to West Military Highway (FM-1016). Turn right (west) and continue to FM-494 (1.5 miles). Turn left onto FM-494 and drive through Granjeno. In past winters, there have been as many as six Short-eared Owls (rare) hunting at dusk over the grassy floodway at Granjeno. Burrowing Owl has also been spotted atop concrete culverts in the vicinity. To search for the owls, slow down when FM-494 curves sharply to the right (1.4 miles) as you are approaching Granjeno. Watch for a paved road that heads in the opposite direction and over a steep floodway levee. Park on the levee, making sure not to block the gates or otherwise hinder traffic. The owls have been observed hunting over the tall grass in the floodway from about 5:30PM until dark.

To get to **Anzalduas County Park**, proceed from the sharp right curve on FM-494 past the cemetery, turning left at the Anzalduas County Park and Dam sign (1.5 miles). Proceed to the entrance of the park (0.6 mile). (This entrance road has some sharp, winding curves before it reaches the office.) The daily fee is $4/car on Saturday and Sunday; no fee is charged on weekdays. The park gates are open from 8:00AM–7:00PM every day except some holidays. The park often gets crowded on weekends, so get there early.

The best time to visit Anzalduas is on weekdays, when there is no entrance fee and it is less crowded. In winter, check the short, grassy field between the office and the Rio Grande for Sprague's Pipits. You should see plenty of meadowlarks—the tricky part is trying to tell the Easterns from the Westerns. The vast majority of meadowlarks found in large winter flocks (especially in shortgrass habitats) are Westerns.

Tall trees around the picnic grounds and restrooms can hold Inca Dove, Common Ground-Dove, Golden-fronted and Ladder-backed Woodpeckers, Scissor-tailed Flycatcher, Black-crested Titmouse, Clay-colored Thrush, and Altamira Oriole. In winter, look for Vermilion Flycatcher and mixed-species flocks, which may include Black-throated Gray, Black-throated Green, Townsend's (rare), Hermit (accidental), and Pine Warblers and Tropical Parula. It might be worth giving each Yellow-bellied Sapsucker a second look, as Red-naped Sapsucker has made rare winter appearances at Anzalduas. Although migrant passerines are not nearly as concentrated at Anzalduas as

Long-billed Thrasher   Brad McKinney

along the immediate coast, there can still be a good variety in the tall shade-trees during spring and fall migration. Northern Beardless-Tyrannulet, Brown-crested Flycatcher, Couch's Kingbird, and Tropical Parula (some years) are a few of the summer residents found at Anzalduas. Both Northern Beardless-Tyrannulet and Tropical Parula may be easiest to find during spring, when males are singing.

Ringed and Green Kingfishers can be found at several spots along the river, from the boat ramp (near the restrooms) to the clear waters below the dam. Most winters Eastern Bluebirds are seen in open areas of the park, espe-cially as one approaches the dam. When scanning the waters above and below the dam, look for Black Phoebe perched on exposed rocks (the species has nested in the park). When birding along the Rio Grande in winter, it is worth sorting through American Wigeon flocks in search of Eurasian Wigeon; there are several Lower Valley records. The lone Anzalduas sighting of Eurasian Wigeon came in February 1997.

You can get to the dam from the office by turning left at the stop sign (0.2 mile) and crossing over the levee to the area below the dam (0.7 mile). North-ern Beardless-Tyrannulet has turned up in this section of the park. The wooded area along the fence is the Gabrielson Tract of the Lower Rio Grande Valley National Wildlife Refuge, currently not open to the public. The air-space over the Gabrielson Tract is a good spot to look for soaring Hook-billed Kites at any time of day and in any season, but especially in spring. Look for their distinctive silhouette (paddle-shaped wings), long banded tail, and large bill.

Like Santa Ana NWR (to the east) and Bentsen State Park (to the west), Anzalduas County Park gets good numbers of migrating raptors in spring and fall. In migration, look for kettles of Mississippi Kites and Broad-winged and Swainson's Hawks, along with an assortment of other buteos, accipiters, and falcons. Occasionally, Zone-tailed Hawks will turn up in winter or in migra-tion, frequently in the company of Turkey Vultures. Although accidental in the Lower Valley, Bald Eagle has been recorded along the Rio Grande at Anzalduas during winter, so keep your eyes peeled whenever you encounter large concentrations of vultures. Rare sightings at Anzalduas include Ruddy Ground-Dove (November 1986, January 2008), Greater Pewee (December 2002–April 2003), Social Flycatcher (March–April 1990), and Rose-throated Becard (three records from winter, spring, and summer; has nested in the park within the last decade).

If you go back to the park entrance and walk left (west) down the levee, you will soon come to another section of the refuge, the Madero Tract. This area is not open either, but you can scan it from the road.

Return to FM-494 and turn left. As soon as you pass the big Oblate Monas-tery (currently a seminary; 0.8 mile), cross the tracks and turn left onto the first road over the levee (0.2 mile) to tiny La Lomita Mission, founded in 1865 and rebuilt in 1899. It abuts the west end of the refuge tract and has a pleasant little picnic ground.

Bentsen-Rio Grande Valley State Park

Well known to birders as one of the country's premier birding destinations, the 760-acre **Bentsen-Rio Grande Valley State Park** (Bentsen State Park) is home to a splendid array of Lower Valley specialties, including Hook-billed Kite and the elusive Ferruginous Pygmy-Owl. The land was donated in 1944 to the state by the late Senator Lloyd Bentsen's family. Much of the original subtropical vegetation has been preserved, and it abounds with birds. As headquarters of the World Birding Center complex, Bentsen State Park has upgraded its facilities with new buildings, a tram, a state-of-the-art hawk tower, and two new photo blinds. More importantly, the park has stepped up its habitat restoration efforts in several areas of the park, including the headquarters, where farmland has been transformed into viable birding and butterfly habitat. The road and trail names have all been changed to reflect the local flora and fauna. For a downloadable park map, check either of these two websites: *www.worldbirdingcenter.org/sites/mission/index.phtml* or *www.tpwd.state.tx.us/publications/pwdpubs/media/park_maps/pwd_mp_ p4502_058m.pdf*.

Birds to look for here include Plain Chachalaca, Least Grebe, Hook-billed Kite, Gray Hawk, White-tipped Dove, Groove-billed Ani (summer), Ferruginous Pygmy-Owl, Elf Owl (spring and summer), Common Pauraque, Buff-bellied Hummingbird, Northern Beardless-Tyrannulet, Brown-crested Flycatcher (summer), Great Kiskadee, Couch's Kingbird, Scissor-tailed Flycatcher (summer), Green Jay, Clay-colored Thrush, Long-billed Thrasher, Tropical Parula (rare), Black-throated Gray Warbler (winter), Olive Sparrow, and Altamira Oriole.

To reach Bentsen-Rio Grande Valley State Park from the previous stop—La Lomita Mission—continue west on FM-494 and FM-1016 (also signed as Military Road) to the curve (0.8 mile). Instead of going right with FM-1016, take the unmarked road straight ahead as you cross the railroad tracks. You might check the little pond (1.7 miles) on the left at the stop sign for Least Grebes. Look for soaring Hook-billed Kites on this stretch of road. Continue on to the next stop sign (1.6 miles) at FM-2062 (Bentsen-Palm Drive). You will see the large parking area to the right.

For those arriving from US-83, exit at Bentsen-Palm Drive and travel south to the World Birding Center Headquarters at Bentsen State Park.

Only primitive camping is allowed within the park. Adjacent to the headquarters is Bentsen Palm Village RV Resort with daily, weekly, monthly, and seasonal spaces. For reservation information, call 877-247-3727 or visit: *www.bentsenpalmvillage.com/rvpark.html*.

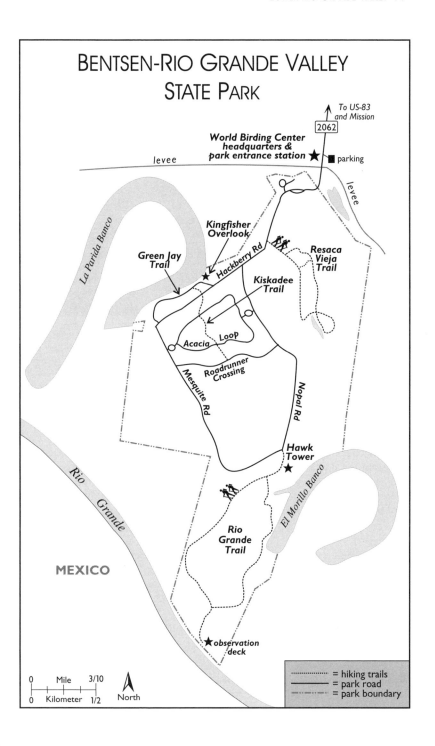

BENTSEN-RIO GRANDE VALLEY STATE PARK

To US-83 and Mission

2062

World Birding Center headquarters & park entrance station ★ ■ parking

levee

levee

La Parida Banco

Kingfisher Overlook

Green Jay Trail

Hackberry Rd

Resaca Vieja Trail

Kiskadee Trail

Acacia Loop

Roadrunner Crossing

Mesquite Rd

Nopal Rd

Hawk Tower ★

El Morillo Banco

Rio Grande

Rio Grande Trail

MEXICO

★ observation deck

| 0 | Mile | 3/10 |
| 0 | Kilometer | 1/2 |

North

.... = hiking trails
——— = park road
—··—··— = park boundary

Buff-bellied Hummingbird   Michael O'Brien

Park hours are 6:00AM–10:00PM seven days a week. Gift Shop and Cafe hours are 8:00AM–5:00PM daily (closed Monday and Tuesday during the summer). Check with refuge staff for summer hours. Admission is adults $5, seniors (Texas residents age 65-plus) $3, children (under 12) free; free for Parklands Pass and Texas State Parks Pass holders.

After checking in at headquarters and paying the fee, birders may catch a tram (no cost), which runs every 30 minutes to an hour from 8:30AM–4:30PM, or you can just walk or bicycle into the park. The main loop is now broken down into three named stretches: Hackberry Road, Mesquite Road, and Nopal Road. Near the entrance interpretive center is the first of several bird-feeding stations, where you will often get splendid looks at Plain Chachalaca, White-tipped Dove, Green Jay, Long-billed Thrasher, and Altamira Oriole. It is a nice leisurely 30-minute walk along Hackberry Road to Kingfisher Overlook. On the way there you can stop at bird-feeding stations, hike along Resaca Vieja Trail in search of Ferruginous Pygmy-Owl and Northern Beardless-Tyrannulet, or continue to Kingfisher Overlook, which offers nice views of the oxbow lake (La Parida Banco). Greater Roadrunner may be seen anywhere along the park roads, especially from the park entrance to Resaca Vieja Trail.

The **Resaca Vieja Trail** (1-mile loop) traverses thorn-scrub woodlands (also called chaparral or matorral). Although the birds are shyer and less numerous here compared to those frequenting Acacia Loop, you might see

Hook-billed Kite (rare), Harris's Hawk, Common Ground-Dove, Groove-billed Ani (summer), Northern Beardless-Tyrannulet, Ash-throated (spring) and Brown-crested (summer) Flycatchers, White-eyed Vireo, Black-tailed Gnatcatcher (rare), Hermit Thrush (winter), Long-billed Thrasher, Yellow-rumped Warbler (winter), and mixed-species flocks (winter). At Kingfisher Overlook, there are not usually many birds on the open water of La Parida Banco, but you will likely see a Pied-billed Grebe, a handful of other waterbirds, Spotted Sandpiper, Green (uncommon) and Ringed Kingfishers, Ladder-backed Woodpecker, Great Kiskadee, Couch's Kingbird, and a variety of passerines in the tall trees along the bank. A Northern Jacana was found in this area in August 2006. Kingfisher Overlook is a nice meeting point, with nearby butterfly gardens, bird feeding stations, and bathrooms, and it is a short walk from here to both the Green Jay Trail and bird-rich Acacia Loop.

Many birders like to first walk along the one-quarter-mile **Green Jay Trail** in search of Clay-colored Thrush and mixed-species flocks that may hold Blue-headed Vireo, Black-crested Titmouse, Ruby-crowned Kinglet, Blue-gray Gnatcatcher, and a variety of warblers, including Black-throated Gray and Tropical Parula (rare). Groove-billed Ani (summer) and Northern Beardless-Tyrannulet can be found in many areas of the park, including along Green Jay Trail.

Most birders choose to access Acacia Loop via Kiskadee Trail. **Acacia Loop** is a wonderful birding spot, as birders often get extended views of many of the Lower Valley specialties, including Clay-colored Thrush and Altamira Oriole. Birds commonly seen at the feeding stations include Plain Chachalaca, White-tipped Dove, Ladder-backed Woodpecker, Green Jay, Clay-colored Thrush, Long-billed Thrasher, Olive Sparrow, and Altamira Oriole. In winter, the tall trees along Acacia Loop are good places to see mixed-species flocks, which may include Northern Beardless-Tyrannulet, Black-throated Gray Warbler, and Tropical Parula. There are occasionally small numbers of Cave Swallows soaring high overhead. While walking Acacia Loop, you may even see one of Bentsen's hybrid (Altamira X Audubon's) orioles, which resemble an Altamira Oriole but with varying amounts of black color in the face. Over the years, local birders have given these unique birds names like "Smudgy" and "Son of Smudgy." Because Audubon's Oriole is only a very rare winter visitor to the park, it is little wonder that these hybrid birds sing classic Altamira Oriole songs.

Acacia Loop is the most likely spot to chance upon a Ferruginous Pygmy-Owl sitting quietly by day. Check with park staff about "Creatures of the Night" tours that target Ferruginous Pygmy-Owl, Elf Owl (in spring), and Common Pauraque. Online recordings of Ferruginous Pygmy-Owl and Common Pauraque can be heard at: *www.worldbirdingcenter.org/bird_info*. Other nocturnal species seen on these night tours include Barn Owl, Eastern Screech-Owl, Great Horned Owl, and Lesser Nighthawk. There are also a handful of rare owls that have been documented in the park, including

Long-eared, Stygian (two records), and Short-eared. Somewhere in the park there is usually an Eastern Screech-Owl that is visible at a daytime roost hole; check with park staff for current locations.

Acacia Loop is also the best spot for finding a rare Blue Bunting, a Mexican species that has shown up a dozen times in the past 25 years. Virtually all sightings of Blue Buntings have come from the feeding stations along Acacia Loop in winter. A number of additional Mexican species have made appearances along Acacia Loop, including Roadside and Short-tailed Hawks, Collared Forest-Falcon, Ruddy Quail-Dove, Dusky-capped, Piratic, and Social Flycatchers, Rose-throated Becard, Masked Tityra, and White-throated Thrush.

Just a five-minute tram ride away is the entrance to the **Rio Grande Trail** and the **Hawk Tower**. The entrance to the Rio Grande Trail is yet another spot where birders may hear the plaintive *dee-dee-dee* calls of Northern Beardless-Tyrannulet. From March through May, Elf Owls may be found in the area at dusk. The area from the entrance of Rio Grande Trail to the Hawk Tower is one of the better spots to search for Hook-billed Kite and Gray Hawk. Both raptors can be seen anywhere in the park and at any season, but they tend to be more regular in occurrence around the entrance to the Rio Grande Trail. Gray Hawk is a local nester in the park, whereas Hook-billed Kite is locally uncommon to rare, more common from spring through fall. This species is often unpredictable and its movements may vary as a result of changing abundance of land snails. Online recordings of Gray Hawk and Hook-billed Kite may be heard at: *www.worldbirdingcenter.org/bird_info*.

The view from the Hawk Tower is impressive, providing a great vantage point for observing migrating raptors from late March through April and from September through October. There are seven records of Short-tailed Hawk from Bentsen State Park. Although extreme dates for Short-tailed Hawk are 15 February and 4 October, most sightings occur between April and June. The Hawk Tower also provides great views of the seasonal wetland (El Morillo Banco) below, where a variety of waterfowl, rails, shorebirds, and other waterbirds can be found. When there is water in El Morillo Banco, listen for King (rare) and Virginia (uncommon) Rails and Sora (fairly common).

You can spend a full day or more birding these sites; however, committed birders can see most of the resident specialties from dawn to midday. Those with more time may want to hike the two-mile Rio Grande Trail, which reaches an observation deck along the Rio Grande before circling back. This trail winds through a variety of habitats, from slightly elevated areas of dry, sandy soil where you will see Prickly Pear cactus and mesquite, to the lower marshy areas along the resaca (when wet) and the Rio Grande where willows and cattails grow. Along most of the trail, you are more likely to encounter species associated with drier environs such as Bewick's and Cactus Wrens, Verdin, and Curve-billed Thrasher. Although rarely seen, both Lazuli and Varied Buntings have been sighted along this trail in past years. It was along the

Rio Grande Trail that a Yellow-faced Grassquit (accidental) was discovered in June 2002.

Contact information: Bentsen-Rio Grande Valley State Park, 2800 S. Bentsen-Palm Drive, Mission, TX 78572. Reservations and phone information: 956-585-1107; fax: 956-585-3448. For more information, visit: www.worldbirding center.org/sites/mission/index.phtml.

CHIHUAHUA WOODS PRESERVE

This Nature Conservancy of Texas, 243-acre wildlife preserve is located 2.5 miles from Bentsen State Park. The preserve is open only during daylight hours and access is walk-in only. You are welcome to explore, but please stay on obvious roads or trails. A one-mile self-guided nature trail leads through Tamaulipan thorn-scrub vegetation that is so typical of the Valley. Be aware that cactus and thorns are abundant; sturdy leather shoes or boots are advised. No restroom facilities are available. No camping or overnighting is allowed.

Although the birds found at **Chihuahua Woods Preserve** are similar to those found at Bentsen State Park, they are generally harder to find. On an early-morning walk in the preserve, you should see Plain Chachalaca, Common Ground-Dove, White-tipped Dove, Great Kiskadee, Green Jay, Olive Sparrow, and Altamira Oriole. Notable sightings include Hook-billed Kite, White-tailed Hawk, Peregrine Falcon (winter), Red-billed Pigeon (summer), Groove-billed Ani (summer), Northern Beardless-Tyrannulet, Clay-colored Thrush, and Tropical Parula. This park contains a desert component (like Falcon Dam), which is reflected by western species such as Ash-throated Flycatcher, Black-tailed Gnatcatcher, Sage Thrasher (winter), and Black-throated Sparrow.

To get to Chihuahua Woods Preserve from Bentsen State Park, drive north on FM-2062 to Business US-83 (2.7 miles). Turn left (west) and proceed to where the highway curves right (2.0 miles). At the curve, go straight onto the blacktop road that parallels the railroad tracks for approximately 0.1 mile. Where the blacktop crosses the tracks, the preserve entrance is on your left.

Directions to Chihuahua Woods from McAllen: Take US-83 west of Mission to FM-492 (at stop light). Turn left (south) onto FM-492 and go about 1 mile to Business US-83 (at blinking light). Turn right (west) and go to the point where Business US-83 curves right (0.8 mile). Follow the above directions.

Walk-in access (parties are limited to six adults) is permitted during daylight hours only. Any other access must be requested from TNC's South Texas Land Steward. For more information, contact The Nature Conservancy's South Texas Office in Corpus Christi; phone: 361-882-3584.

EDINBURG AND VICINITY

dinburg Scenic Wetlands: As one of the World Birding Center satellite sites, this 40-acre urban sanctuary offers refuge to a diverse assemblage of birds, butterflies, and dragonflies. Like Estero Llano Grande State Park, the feature attraction of the Edinburg Scenic Wetlands is its complex of shallow ponds that draw a variety of waterfowl, shorebirds, other waterbirds, and kingfishers. Least Grebe, Buff-bellied Hummingbird, and Green Kingfisher are regular here. In addition to its wetlands, the site also contains over three acres of native shrubs surrounding its interpretive center, which attract Buff-bellied, Ruby-throated, Black-chinned, and Rufous (winter) Hummingbirds and numerous butterflies. Several of the Lower Valley specialties are found along the woodland edges bordering the ponds.

Birds seen at Edinburg Scenic Wetlands include Black-bellied Whistling-Duck, Least Grebe, American White Pelican (winter), Neotropic Cormorant, Anhinga (winter), Black-crowned Night-Heron, Roseate Spoonbill (spring), Wood Stork (irregular, summer), Buff-bellied Hummingbird, Groove-billed Ani (summer), Green Kingfisher, Vermilion Flycatcher (winter), Great Kiskadee, Tropical and Couch's Kingbirds, Scissor-tailed Flycatcher (summer), Long-billed Thrasher, and Lesser Goldfinch.

The ponds are attractive to numerous waterfowl and other waterbirds in winter. A sampling of species found includes Black-bellied Whistling-Duck, Blue-winged Teal, Northern Shoveler, Green-winged Teal, Lesser Scaup, Ruddy Duck, Least and Pied-billed Grebes, American White Pelican, Neotropic and Double-crested Cormorants, Anhinga, and Tricolored Heron. The receding water levels in spring attract a variety of shorebirds, including Black-necked Stilt, Greater and Lesser Yellowlegs, Semipalmated, Western, Least, and Pectoral Sandpipers, and Long-billed Dowitcher. In past years, both Least and Gull-billed (uncommon) Terns have nested within the park. Green Kingfisher frequents various spots within the park, yet it is most often seen flying low over the wood-fringed ponds or perched on low-hanging branches over the water. Ringed Kingfisher is seen most regularly during the winter months due to a lack of local nest sites.

The magnificent butterfly gardens attract hummingbirds and Lesser Goldfinch (at sunflowers). A variety of sparrows can be found here in migration and winter. Groove-billed Ani (summer), Great Kiskadee, and Couch's Kingbird may be seen along woodland edges, while Vermilion Flycatcher (winter), Scissor-tailed Flycatcher (summer), and Tropical Kingbird are often found in more open areas. Several raptor species may be seen in the park, including resident White-tailed Kite, Harris's and White-tailed (rare) Hawks, wintering Sharp-shinned, Cooper's, and Red-tailed Hawks, and migrant Broad-winged and Swainson's Hawks.

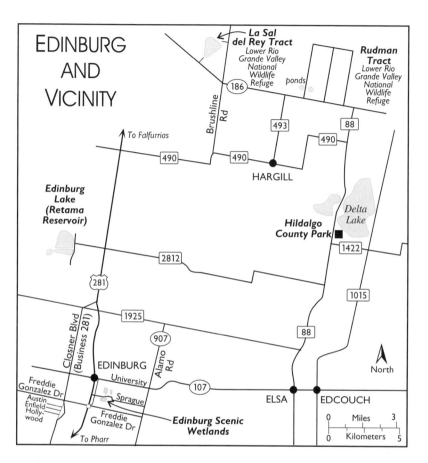

EDINBURG AND VICINITY

To get to the Edinburg Scenic Wetlands, take US-83 west to US-281 north. Travel north on US-281 to the Freddy Gonzalez exit (6.4 miles). Continue north on the frontage road for one block and you will reach Sprague Street. Turn right (east) onto Sprague and continue until you reach the entrance to the wetlands. An alternate route to the site involves taking the University Drive exit (7.3 miles). Travel east on University Drive to Raul Longoria Road. Head south on Raul Longoria to Sprague Street and turn east onto Sprague into the Edinburg Municipal Park. Turn into the first parking lot on the left. The Interpretive Center will be just to the north.

Contact information: WBC–Edinburg Scenic Wetlands, 714 S. Raul Longoria, Edinburg, TX 78539; phone: 956-381-9922; fax: 956-381-0715. Hours: Monday–Thursday, 8:00AM–5:00PM, Friday–Saturday, 8:00AM–6:00PM; closed Sunday. Grounds open sunrise to sunset. Check with center staff for summer hours. Admission: adults $2, seniors and children $1. For information on the interpretive center, upcoming nature programs, or other information, call 956-381-9922 or visit the WBC website: *www.worldbirding center.org/sites/edinburg/index.phtml.*

For those birders with extra time, a trip to the farmlands north and east of Edinburg might produce a different list of birds. In winter, there may be Sandhill Crane, Ross's Goose and other waterfowl, White-tailed Hawk, Crested Caracara, Green Kingfisher, Vermilion Flycatcher, Couch's Kingbird, Curve-billed Thrasher, Pyrrhuloxia, and a variety of sparrows.

From TX-107 in Edinburg, go north on US-281. Opposite FM-2812 (6.3 miles) you can reach **Edinburg Lake (Retama Reservoir)** by turning left onto a road which soon (0.3 mile) turns to gravel and leads to a T-intersection (1.0 mile). Turn left and go up the bank on the right (0.3 mile). This lake is at its best in winter, when you may find ducks and shorebirds. Waterfowl and waders also use the canal network to and from the reservoir. Despite the signs, birders can walk the dikes during daylight hours. Or, you can continue on the road as it swings right to a parking lot at the road's end (0.2 mile). From here you can walk up onto the dike.

A Northern Jacana lingered along the road to the right (north) at the T in November–December 1981. The cattail-lined slough here is spring-fed. Masked Duck (casual) also has been found here; check these areas for Green Kingfishers. Continuing up US-281 to FM-490 (4.3 miles), turn right toward Hargill. The patches of mesquite can offer Vermilion (winter) and Ash-throated (spring) Flycatchers, Curve-billed Thrasher, Pyrrhuloxia, and Painted Bunting (summer). A few small ponds in the area may be good for shorebirds depending on the season and water levels.

Follow FM-490 until it makes a sharp turn left. At the zigzag there is a caliche road (Brushline Road) that runs north to TX-186. The fields here may hold Sandhill Cranes (winter) and White-tailed Hawk (year-round). Continuing on Brushline Road past TX-186 will take you to the east entrance of **La Sal del Rey**, a 5,000-acre tract of the Lower Rio Grande Valley National Wildlife Refuge (LRGVNWR). There is pedestrian access for this tract, with at least two entrances and parking areas on the south side (off TX-186) and on the east side (off Brushline Road, 2 miles north, there is a signed parking lot on your left). La Sal del Rey is a good spot during winter and migration. In winter, these inland salt lakes attract concentrations of ducks, Eared Grebes, Sandhill Cranes, and a variety of shorebirds, including Snowy Plover, Sanderling, and Wilson's Phalarope (the only regular wintering site for this species in the U.S.). In migration, you might see American Golden-Plover, Semipalmated, Western, Least, and Stilt Sandpipers, and Wilson's and Red-necked (rare) Phalaropes. Also during winter, several raptor species can be seen, including Sharp-shinned, Cooper's, White-tailed, and Red-tailed Hawks; in migration, additional species include Mississippi and Swallow-tailed (rare) Kites and Broad-winged and Swainson's Hawks. During migration, the weedy fields can hold Blue Grosbeak, Indigo Bunting, Dickcissel, and a variety of other birds.

Rarities at La Sal del Rey have included Whooping Crane (winter 2005–2006) and Western Gull (November 2004).

You can also follow FM-490 as it zigzags across the area, watching for ponds as you go. At Hargill (8.0 miles), turn left onto FM-493 until it reaches TX-186. Turn right here and then to a dirt road on the left (1.0 mile), where you turn. Bird the pasture on the left to the small pond (0.5 mile); another pond is just across the road. Both are good for ducks and Vermilion Flycatchers in winter; Crested Caracaras frequent the fields nearby. Continue a total of 3 miles, then turn right and continue a mile. You are now birding in the **Rudman Tract** of the LRGVNWR.

There are three county roads here, each 3 miles long and a mile apart, with a county road along the north, and TX-186 along the south. The Rudman Tract is excellent for hawks, Northern Bobwhite, Verdin, Cactus and Bewick's Wrens, winter sparrows such as Cassin's, Lark, and Lincoln's, and Pyrrhuloxia. Among the raptors, look for White-tailed Kite and Harris's Hawks and Crested Caracara. Also found in the area are Great Kiskadee, Couch's Kingbird, Scissor-tailed Flycatcher (summer), Loggerhead Shrike (winter), and White-eyed Vireo. The easternmost road in this complex is just one-half mile west of FM-88. Continuing west on TX-186, you will pass the Tres Corrales Ranch ponds. These and other nearby ponds can have a Ross's Goose hidden among the numerous Snow Geese.

To reach **Delta Lake**, backtrack on TX-186 (heading east) to FM-88. Turn right and proceed to Delta Lake (4.5 miles). The lake can be good for ducks and shorebirds. Continue 0.4 mile and turn left into Hidalgo County Park, open dawn to dusk, for more ducks and migrant passerines. An Elegant Trogon was observed here for a week in January 1990.

At FM-2812 (3.7 miles), turn right (west) to check more fields and ponds. At US-281 (11.5 miles), turn left and return to Edinburg (6.0 miles).

Within the city of Edinburg you can find some of the resident specialties in wooded or brushy areas. In summer, you might see Chimney Swifts (uncommon nesters) and Couch's and Western Kingbirds. Blue Jay, which is accidental in the Valley, has also been found in town. The best birding area in town is the well-vegetated residential area near the Echo Hotel (1903 S. Closner Boulevard, one block south of Freddy Gonzalez Drive). Just south of the hotel, take a right off Business 281 (S. Closner Boulevard) onto Tourist Drive. Take any of the next three right turns (W. Austin Boulevard, W. Enfield Road, and W. Hollywood Drive), each of which leads west into an area with older homes and many Lower Valley specialties. Plain Chachalaca, Great Kiskadee, and Couch's Kingbird seem particularly numerous; Clay-colored Thrush has nested in recent years; and a variety of raptors can be seen during migration and winter. As for rarities, Edinburg was the site of the second state record of Fork-tailed Flycatcher (February 1961) and, more recently, a

Golden-crowned Warbler at the University of Texas–Pan American University campus in 2002. Amazingly, three Band-rumped Storm-Petrels were found in Edinburg in June 1954, surely the result of major tropical-storm activity in the Gulf of Mexico.

UPRIVER TO SAN YGNACIO

After leaving the citrus groves of the coastal plain at Mission, you may hardly notice the rise in elevation except for the increasingly scrubby vegetation and the ridge-forming Goliad sandstone. The hard, pebbly, gray sandstone and pinkish claystones continue to Falcon Dam, where the ridges and mesas become rather prominent, especially on the side of the highway away from the river. In this more arid land, you'll be looking for a new suite of birds: Scaled Quail, Crested Caracara, Cave Swallow, Verdin, Cactus Wren, Cassin's, Black-throated, and White-crowned Sparrows, and Pyrrhuloxia.

Depart McAllen on westbound US-83. By the time you reach **La Joya** (11 miles from Mission, and an infamous speed-trap), you will have entered the arid, hilly brushlands—or chaparral country—which cover much of the coastal plains south of the Edwards Plateau. For over 200 miles to the north and west, the land is poor, alkaline, and marginal in productivity. Previously overgrazed, the region recently has been converted to pastures and irrigated fields.

For birders who do not plan to travel much farther west than the McAllen/Mission area, it is still possible to see some of the desert birds fairly close at hand. While driving through the town of La Joya, watch for Scissor-tailed Flycatchers perched on utility lines. La Joya is one of the few places where this species can be found in the dead of winter. As you leave La Joya (see map on page 10), the road curves to the left and goes down a slight grade. In the middle of the curve, FM-2221 heads north, which leads to "sparrow road." At a stop sign, this road turns right (6.0 miles from US-83). Instead of turning right, continue straight down a caliche (and very dusty) road, which goes on for another 2 miles before you need to turn around. This 2-mile stretch of caliche is know to local birders as "sparrow road." Although Mountain Plovers are best found in agricultural fields north of Harlingen in the eastern Valley during winter (see Harlingen section), you may want to scan the field on your right for this rare and irregular species in this section of the Lower Valley. Although sparrow road can be productive in winter, many of the species below are more easily found farther west in the Falcon Dam region. Sparrows found along this road in winter include Cassin's, Chipping, Clay-colored, Vesper, Lark, Black-throated, Savannah, Grasshopper, Lincoln's, and White-crowned. In the thickets of mesquite, acacia, and cactus look for Scaled Quail (rare), Northern Bobwhite, Common Ground-Dove, Greater Roadrunner, Verdin, Cactus Wren, Curve-billed Thrasher, Lark

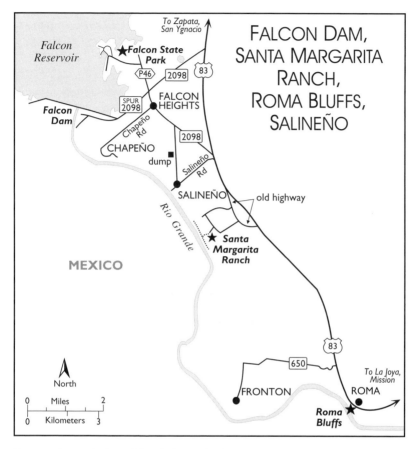

FALCON DAM, SANTA MARGARITA RANCH, ROMA BLUFFS, SALINEÑO

Bunting (irregular), and Pyrrhuloxia. Birding is best in the early morning. In warm seasons, you might encounter a rattlesnake if you decide to wander into the brush.

Farther west on US-83 is the small town of Sullivan City. Watch for a sign for a wash called Arroyo Salado (9.6 miles from FM-2221; see map on page 10). Cave Swallows nest under the culvert here; they may be seen in the area throughout the year.

Many of the towns along the highway west of Mission date back to the 1750s, when Spanish General José de Escandón established settlements along the Rio Grande such as Carnestolendas, located on the north bank of the river near present-day Rio Grande City. Later, both Rio Grande City and Roma-Los Saenz were busy steamboat ports. For much of the last half of the 19th century, this area (and much of the Rio Grande Valley as well) was the scene of cattle raids and land disputes comparable to the classic days of the

Wild West. Modern-day civilization has slowly crept into the region, yet much of the frontier character remains to this day.

As you continue west into Starr County, you will notice an increase in the number of hawks, yet ravens are somewhat scarce until you reach Zapata County. American Crows do not occur in this area or anywhere in the Lower Valley, so any crow-sized bird is certainly a Chihuahuan Raven. Harris's Hawk is the most common buteo during much of the year, but you also may see lots of Red-taileds in winter. Also, keep an eye out for Northern Harrier, Sharp-shinned, Cooper's, and White-tailed Hawks, Crested Caracara, and American Kestrel. Although rarely seen in the area, Ferruginous Hawk should be watched for; some winters they move into South Texas in higher numbers. This region is on the main migration route for Mississippi Kites and Broad-winged and Swainson's Hawks. Broad-wingeds roost in trees or thickets, while Swainson's roost on the ground, preferring newly plowed fields. If your timing is just right, and you arrive in the morning before the thermals get established, you could possibly find hundreds of Swainson's Hawks standing around in the fields.

Ringed, Belted, and Green Kingfishers are found at various places along the river. They become more numerous when there is extensive riparian vegetation lining the river together with clear water for fishing. About the only areas where clear water can be found is below the dams, which slow the water and allow the suspended particles to settle. One of the clearest sections is the 15-mile stretch below Falcon Dam, and kingfishers are common here. Upon reaching Roma, you have reached a section of the Rio Grande where Muscovy Duck, Hook-billed Kite, Red-billed Pigeon, Brown Jay (very rare), and Audubon's Oriole are found. It usually takes at least a couple of days of birding the following Starr County sites to see most of these specialties.

ROMA BLUFFS

Roma is among the most historic cities in Texas, and it is being restored to reflect its glory days as a steamboat port on the Rio Grande. As the westernmost site of the World Birding Center complex, the scenic Roma Bluffs offer a fine vista over the woodlands along the Rio Grande. In Starr County, the Rio Grande runs shallow and clear, sometimes rising several feet with releases from Falcon Dam about 20 miles upstream. The WBC Roma Bluffs includes a riparian nature area of three acres, containing an observation deck, feeding stations, native plant gardens, outdoor amphitheater, and a one-quarter-mile nature trail below the bluffs along the river.

To get to the **Roma Bluffs**, continue west on US-83 to Roma. Go west (left) onto Lincoln Avenue, then travel to the intersection of Lincoln and Portscheller. Take a left onto Portscheller to Convent. The World Birding Center is located on the southeast corner of the intersection of Portscheller

Ringed Kingfisher   Jen Brumfield

and Convent. The Roma Bluffs and wildlife viewing area are at the west end and one block north of the Plaza.

Birds to look for at the Roma Bluffs include Muscovy Duck (rare), Plain Chachalaca, Red-billed Pigeon (spring and summer), Groove-billed Ani (summer), Black-chinned Hummingbird (summer), Ringed and Green Kingfishers, Yellow-billed Cuckoo (spring and summer), Black Phoebe, Brown-crested Flycatcher (summer), Great Kiskadee, Couch's Kingbird, Scissor-tailed Flycatcher (summer), Clay-colored Thrush, Hooded (summer), Altamira, and Audubon's Orioles, and Lesser Goldfinch (grassy fields). From the observation deck, birders can sometimes spot a Red-billed Pigeon or an Audubon's Oriole amongst the trees below the bluffs and immediately upriver on the island, or several species of swallows soaring above the river. A spotting scope is strongly recommended here.

The narrow band of river woodlands below the bluffs harbors many of the Lower Valley specialties, as well as mixed-species flocks in winter and a number of migrant passerines in spring and fall. There is potential access to recently acquired tracts of the Lower Rio Grande Valley National Wildlife Refuge upstream along the Rio Grande. These large river tracts contain Texas Ebony, Rio Grande Ash, Black Willow, Sugar Hackberry, and occasionally the majestic Montezuma Bald Cypress; drier upland sites feature colorful mesquite-Prickly Pear associations. The riparian forests hold many of the Starr County specialties, and sometimes a rarity such as a Common Black-Hawk.

Staff working in the visitor center provide current information on recent bird sightings and other nearby birding opportunities. Volunteers offer birding walks and other interpretive programs during the late fall, winter, and early spring seasons, including half-day canoe trips on the Rio Grande (fee, reservations required). Contact information: WBC–Roma Bluffs, 77 Convent Street, P.O. Box 947, Roma, TX 78584; reservations: phone 956-849-4930, fax 956-849-3963. Hours: November–April, open daily 8:00AM–4:00PM; call the visitor center for summer hours. Nature trails and Rio Grande Observation Deck are open seven days a week and are free. For a downloadable checklist, hours, and program schedule, visit the WBC website: *www.worldbirdingcenter. org/sites/roma/index.phtml.*

SANTA MARGARITA RANCH

The caliche road into **Santa Margarita Ranch** crosses through desert brushland on its way to a productive stretch of riparian woodland along the river. This is a good spot for both desert and water birds, as well as many Lower Valley specialties.

This private ranch can be reached by driving west on US-83 from the Fronton Road (FM-650). After 5.7 miles, the highway curves right but you should bear left onto the old highway (old US-83). After crossing a little bridge, turn left onto an unmarked dirt road (0.7 mile), following it as it bends right and tops a hill overlooking the ranch buildings. Turn left at the entrance road (1.1 miles) and proceed to the second house on the left. *Because of the loose, unpredictable dogs, stay in your car and beep your horn.* Someone will come out to collect the small fee. If no one comes, go to the second house on the right. The residents want to make sure that they will not be held liable for an injury or accident—snakebites included—on the property and that visitors understand that they bird at their own risk.

Santa Margarita Ranch was deeded to the Gonzalez family in an old Spanish Land Grant and is situated on a sandstone bluff overlooking the Rio Grande. Many unique cacti and shrubs inhabit this desert-like terrain. You may encounter desert birds such as Scaled Quail, Lesser Nighthawk (summer), Common Poorwill (uncommon), Ash-throated Flycatcher (summer), Verdin, Cactus Wren, Curve-billed Thrasher, Black-tailed Gnatcatcher (rare), Black-throated Sparrow, and Pyrrhuloxia in this habitat. Resident species found in the river woodlands include Muscovy Duck, "Mexican Duck" ("Mexican Mallard"), Plain Chachalaca, Hook-billed Kite (rare), Gray Hawk (rare), White-tipped Dove, Common Pauraque, Ringed and Green Kingfishers, Great Kiskadee, Green Jay, Clay-colored Thrush, Long-billed Thrasher,

Olive Sparrow, and Altamira and Audubon's Orioles. Also along the Rio Grande from spring through summer, you may find Red-billed Pigeon, Groove-billed Ani, Brown-crested Flycatcher, Couch's Kingbird, Scissor-tailed Flycatcher, Bell's Vireo (uncommon), Blue Grosbeak, and Varied (rare) and Painted Buntings. Rarely seen but possible along the river are Common Black-Hawk, Zone-tailed Hawk, and Brown Jay (formerly a rare resident).

The road to the river is gated and often locked, so you will likely need to walk rather than drive. Park near the gate but do not block the road. The ranch road crosses through an area of mesquite trees, and ends in verdant riparian woodlands bordering the Rio Grande. For years, birders visited Santa Margarita to see the small flock of Brown Jays that inhabited this area, although the jays have been absent here since the mid-1990s. All three kingfishers are fairly common along the Rio Grande, and most of the Lower Valley specialties may be seen while walking the woodland edge along the river.

Some rarities seen over the years at Santa Margarita Ranch include Eurasian Wigeon (December 1989–January 1990), Roadside Hawk (January 1979), Short-tailed Hawk (July 1989), Sulphur-bellied Flycatcher (May–August 1975 and a nesting pair that also returned the following two summers), and Rufous-backed Robin (December 1975).

If you do not find the kingfishers at the ranch, try farther upriver at Salineño (*sah-lih-NAYN-yo*) or Chapeño (*chah-PAYN-yo*). As you leave the ranch, turn left (west) onto the gravel road. Follow it around until it returns to the old highway (1.6 miles). Here, you can turn left to reach US-83 (0.4 mile). Along the way check the arid brushlands for Scaled Quail, Greater Roadrunner, Vermilion (winter) and Ash-throated (summer) Flycatchers, Cactus Wren, Black-tailed Gnatcatcher, Cassin's and Black-throated Sparrows, Pyrrhuloxia, and Bullock's Oriole (summer).

SALINEÑO

For many years now, **Salineño** has been *the* birding hotspot of the Falcon Dam area. There is a good view of the river, and bird feeders nearby are maintained during the winter months, formerly by the gracious Pat and Gail Dewind but now by caretakers of the Valley Land Fund property. Several other habitats in the area are worth checking, including riparian woodland, arid thorn-scrub forest, a water-treatment pond, and the dump road.

Go west on US-83 to the sign for Salineño (1.2 miles). Turn left; this road can be good for a variety of birds in winter and spring. Some winters, Say's Phoebe and Sage Thrasher are found in the area. One spot to check for Say's is the fence on the right side next to some concrete picnic tables (0.4 mile). The brushy areas a little farther on can produce Cassin's, Chipping, Clay-colored, Vesper, Lark, Black-throated, Grasshopper, and White-crowned Sparrows and Lark Bunting. Watch for Scaled Quail, Greater Roadrunner, Bell's Vireo (summer), Verdin, Bewick's Wren, and winter warblers.

One thing you are sure to notice are the brightly colored wreaths at the town cemetery. In the adjacent fields in winter, you are likely to see both Eastern and, primarily, Western Meadowlarks. As the road forks, bear right and watch for three speed bumps before the town square. Continue straight through to the Rio Grande. When the river is low, or at least at "normal" levels, the lookout provides good views for many birds, both on the water and in the trees lining the bank. A spotting scope is recommended.

Birds seen from the lookout in winter include Least (rare) and Pied-billed Grebes, American White Pelican, Neotropic and Double-crested Cormorants, Anhinga (rare), several herons, Greater White-fronted and Snow Geese (rare), many species of other waterfowl, and often all three kingfishers. Occasionally, Black Phoebe can be found along the river.

Ringed and Green Kingfishers may be found anywhere along the river. The large, massive-billed Ringed Kingfisher is often seen flying high above the river with strong sweeping wingbeats. It can be located by its loud, deep kak-kak-kak calls. You may find a Green Kingfisher out in the open near the middle of the river, but it is more likely to be hidden among the willows along the shore. The way to find this secretive little bird is to walk quietly downriver along the trail, checking branches overhanging the water. Those with sharp ears may hear the kingfisher's dry rattle (given while perched) or a rough zchurrk as it takes flight low over the water. This small bird needs shallow water for fishing, preferring isolated pools that remain when the river is low. The depth of the river fluctuates greatly depending upon release of water from the dam; the lowest water levels usually occur early in the morning. Online recordings of both kingfishers can be heard at: www.worldbirdingcenter. org/bird_info.

Salineño is one of the best spots in the region for Muscovy Ducks, but they are generally difficult to find. Your chances of spotting one are much better during the early-morning hours. And although Muscovies are found along this stretch of the Rio Grande in all seasons, your chances are better from April through November. These large birds are wary, preferring sheltered waters on tree-lined banks of the river. Muscovies are rarely spotted in roost trees, yet they are occasionally seen flying along the river, having been flushed by motorboats or other disturbances. Common winter waterfowl on the Rio Grande here include American Wigeon, Gadwall, Mottled Duck, Blue-winged Teal, Northern Shoveler, Northern Pintail, Green-winged Teal, Ring-necked Duck, Lesser Scaup, Bufflehead, and Ruddy Duck. Occasionally, Wood Duck, "Mexican Duck," Cinnamon Teal, Canvasback, and Redhead are seen as well.

Along the shore (if there is any), look for Greater Yellowlegs, Spotted and Least Sandpipers, and American Pipits. In the morning, the tall trees along the bank can come alive with bird song. Usually seen in the woodlands or flying

Mottled Duck   Louise Zemaitis

back and forth across the river are Golden-fronted and Ladder-backed Woodpeckers, Great Kiskadee, Couch's Kingbird, Green Jay, Clay-colored Thrush (uncommon), and Altamira and Audubon's Orioles. Also look for Osprey and Gray (rare), Harris's, and Red-shouldered Hawks perched on snags on both sides of the river. Although Red-billed Pigeons are seen flying across the river throughout the year, they are more likely in spring and summer. Though rarely encountered, Hook-billed Kite, Common Black-Hawk, Zone-tailed Hawk, Rose-throated Becard, and Blue Bunting have visited the area.

One of the biggest attractions at Salineño are bird feeders, which if being stocked, may attract Inca and White-tipped Doves, Golden-fronted and Ladder-backed Woodpeckers, Great Kiskadee, Green and Brown (very rare) Jays, Bewick's Wren, Black-crested Titmouse, Clay-colored Thrush, Long-billed and Curve-billed Thrashers, Orange-crowned and Yellow-rumped Warblers, Olive and Lincoln's Sparrows, Northern Cardinal, Altamira and Audubon's Orioles, Lesser (uncommon) and American Gold-finches, and others. Although Brown Jays have been sporadic at the feeders in recent years, there were times in the not-so-distant past when they were fairly regular here. With or without Brown Jays, the Salineño feeders are a must stop on any birder's itinerary.

On the way to the water-treatment pond (just up the road), check the thorn scrub for Bell's Vireo (rare, summer), Verdin, Cactus Wren, Black-tailed Gnatcatcher (rare), and Chipping Sparrow. At the water-treatment pond, you can usually find Sora, Common Moorhen, Common Yellowthroat, and occasionally Green Kingfisher, Groove-billed Ani, or Altamira Oriole. Every now and then, some lucky birder will spot a Gray Hawk, Clay-colored Thrush, or White-collared Seedeater in the area. As you leave the Salineño bird feeders, you can either return straight to US-83 or try the Salineño dump road. To get to the dump road, turn left at the first street (0.2 mile). This road is hard-topped for 0.4 mile but turns to dirt, which can be slick and impassable after a rain. Slow down for speed-bumps. Where the road begins to bear right, you should be able to spot Bank Swallow burrows in the exposed bank to the left. The road passes the Salineño dump and continues on to FM-2098, and can be good for sparrows and other birds in winter. You might find Scaled Quail, Greater Roadrunner, Chihuahuan Raven, Verdin, Cactus Wren, Sage (rare) and Curve-billed Thrashers, Cassin's, Black-throated, and White-crowned Sparrows, and Pyrrhuloxia. Seldom seen but possible are Black-chinned Hummingbird (summer), Rock Wren (winter), Green-tailed Towhee (winter), and Lesser Goldfinch.

CHAPEÑO

Chapeño is another spot along the river worth checking for Muscovy Duck, Hook-billed Kite, Gray Hawk, Red-billed Pigeon, and Audubon's Oriole. It and Salineño are the only two spots in the United States where you might still find Brown Jay. Although widespread and common in Mexico, the species has declined during the past two decades in Texas, having withdrawn from its former haunts at Santa Margarita Ranch and the woodlands below Falcon Dam. Although no more than three individuals have been sighted at Chapeño in recent years, the fact that juveniles are still being seen among the small flock brings some hope of their continued toehold here.

To reach the former settlement of **Chapeño**, go a quarter-mile beyond (west of) the Salineño Road on US-83 and turn left onto FM-2098, which leads to Falcon Dam. As you enter the town of Falcon Heights, watch on the left for Chapeño Road (2.8 miles) opposite the Catholic Church. Although there is no longer an "RV Park" sign marking Chapeño Road, there is both a green road sign before the Catholic Church and a brown Great Texas Birding Trail sign number 081. (If you took the Salineño dump-road detour through to FM-2098, that intersection would leave you about 1.5 miles from the turnoff by the church.) Turn left onto Chapeño Road and continue until the road bends left (2.5 miles). After that, take the second dirt road to the right and stop in front of the concrete block house. Watch for dogs. Pay the small fee to bird the property.

The bird feeders, which may attract Brown Jays, are regularly maintained. Check with the owners for parking locations. For years, birders were able to park near the feeders, but you may need to take the fourth dirt road (right after the bend in the paved road) for public access. This road runs steeply down to the river, where there is ample parking. The edge is soft and muddy, but it offers good views up and down and across to a close island that obscures most of the view of Mexico. The road is currently in good condition, but be careful after heavy rain, when it washes into deep ruts; low-clearance cars should be parked at the top after heavy rain.

Brown Jays are most frequently seen around the feeders in the early morning, but they are occasionally seen flying along the mesquite thickets up and down the river. Although the jays can be found at all seasons, they may be slightly more regular during winter, when they travel in small, noisy flocks. When not vocalizing, these large birds are shy and difficult to see, so it's best to get out early. Listen for their harsh, screaming *kyeeaah! kyaah!,* which is similar to the call of Red-shouldered Hawk. Online recordings of Brown Jay can be heard at: *www.worldbirdingcenter.org/bird_info.*

All three kingfishers can be found along this broad sweep of the river. As with other nearby spots, Muscovy Ducks are difficult to find but may be seen perching in trees overhanging the water, swimming in the river, or flying across the water. Also look for Wood Duck, "Mexican Duck," and Least Grebe on the river and Black Phoebe on shoreline perches. Also found in the riparian areas are many of the Lower Valley specialties, including Hook-billed Kite, Gray Hawk, Red-billed Pigeon (spring and summer), Golden-fronted and Ladder-backed Woodpeckers, Great Kiskadee, Couch's Kingbird, Green Jay, and Altamira and Audubon's Orioles. A dirt road nearby leads to a boat ramp with cattails on both sides of the small clearing. In these cattails, White-collared Seedeaters have been reported sporadically.

After backtracking on Chapeño Road to FM-2098, turn left (west). At the western edge of Falcon Heights, there is a major intersection (0.5 mile). From this point, FM-2098 goes northeast for 2.5 miles to rejoin US-83. Drive east on FM-2098 and you will find a lake on the left (north) side (1.7 miles), which in winter may have Least Grebe, Greater White-fronted Goose, Hooded Merganser, and Ruddy Duck.

Back at the intersection, Park Road 46 goes north 1.0 mile into Falcon State Park, and Spur Road 2098 goes west for 2.0 miles to the dam. On both sides of this latter road is Starr County Park, offering limited facilities on the north side of the road. This park is good for Vermilion Flycatcher, Cactus Wren, Curve-billed Thrasher, a variety of wintering sparrows, and Pyrrhuloxia. Sometimes Red-billed Pigeon (spring and summer), Groove-billed Ani (spring), Black-tailed Gnatcatcher, Spotted Towhee (winter), and Brewer's Sparrow (winter) are seen in the county park.

FALCON STATE PARK

Falcon State Park (573 acres) is located at the south end of the 98,960-acre International Falcon Reservoir. Like much of the surrounding area, the park's gently rolling hills are covered with patches of thorny brushland, consisting mostly of mesquite, Huisache, Mexican Olive, Texas Ebony, and a variety of cacti and grasses. Although the vegetation looks sparse, there is a good variety of birds and reptiles here, especially desert species. If you are camping, this is a good spot from which to base your birding in the area. The entrance fee is $2/ person (children under 12 free), plus a fee for camping, hot showers, hook-ups, or screened shelters. For more information, contact Falcon State Park, P.O. Box 2, Falcon Heights, TX 78545; phone 956-848-5327.

In the brushy thorn scrub along the road and around the campgrounds, you should see Harris's Hawk, Common Ground-Dove, Greater Roadrunner, Golden-fronted and Ladder-backed Woodpeckers, Vermilion Flycatcher, Cactus and Bewick's Wrens, Northern Mockingbird, Curve-billed Thrasher, Green-tailed Towhee (uncommon, winter), Cassin's, Lark, and Black-throated Sparrows, Northern Cardinal, Pyrrhuloxia, Brewer's Blackbird (uncommon), and Bronzed and Brown-headed Cowbirds. Also look for Northern Bobwhites and Scaled Quail running around the campsites or park roads during the day. You may hear Great Horned Owl at night, or, if you are lucky, see one on a late-afternoon perch.

In spring and summer, expect Ash-throated Flycatcher, Blue Grosbeak, Painted Bunting, Dickcissel, Bullock's Oriole, and Lesser Goldfinch. In winter, look for American Kestrel, Say's Phoebe (rare), Vermilion Flycatcher, Loggerhead Shrike, Eastern Bluebird, Sage Thrasher (rare most years), Lark Bunting, Cassin's, Chipping, Clay-colored, Brewer's (rare), Field, Vesper, Lark, Savannah, Grasshopper, and White-crowned Sparrows, and Brewer's Blackbird (uncommon). Hooded Orioles usually can be found in summer around the office. Hooded and Altamira Orioles occasionally visit the camping areas if someone has put out sugar-water feeders. A wayward Scott's Oriole was found here during the winter of 2007–2008.

The best area for active feeders is in the RV section. This is a good spot for Northern Bobwhite, Greater Roadrunner, and sparrows. If you have not seen Black-throated Sparrow by now, try searching down the hill (toward the lake) in the scrubby vegetation. You could also find Bell's Vireo (summer) and Verdin in the taller mesquites along the bottom of the wash.

As a rule, the lakeshore is not very productive, but you can scope for Common Loon (rare), Neotropic and Double-crested (winter) Cormorants, American White Pelican, ducks, a few coots, and Gull-billed Tern (uncommon breeder). Scan the lake for vagrant gulls in winter: Thayer's and Glaucous Gulls and Black-legged Kittiwake have been recorded in the Falcon Dam area.

A small sheltered bay full of dead snags can yield Spotted Sandpiper, Green Kingfisher, and American Pipit. To reach it, go to the far end of the loop in the area of screened shelters. Here you will find a path leading to the beach, where you turn left and follow the shore until you come to the bay.

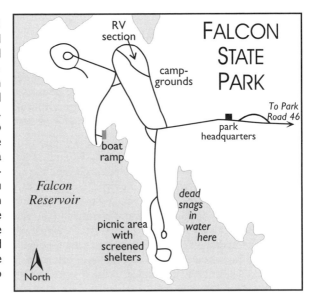

FALCON STATE PARK

RV section

camp-grounds

To Park Road 46

park headquarters

boat ramp

Falcon Reservoir

dead snags in water here

picnic area with screened shelters

North

Since the lake has been established, the number of frogs and toads has increased considerably. They may be abundant after heavy rains in spring and summer. Rio Grande Leopard Frog and Gulf Coast Toad are usually most common, but you may find others such as Blanchard's Cricket Frog, Mexican Burrowing Toad, and Sheep Frog.

With the abundance of food, the snake population has increased, too. By driving the back roads at night, you may find Eastern Checkered Garter Snake, Western Ribbon Snake, Mexican Hognose Snake, Western Coachwhip, Schott's Whipsnake, Western Rough Green Snake, Texas Indigo Snake, Texas Patchnose Snake, Great Plains Rat Snake, Texas Glossy Snake, Bull Snake, Desert Kingsnake, Texas Longnose Snake, Ground Snake, Western Hooknose Snake, Texas Night Snake, Northern Cat-eyed Snake, Flathead Snake, Texas Blackhead Snake, Massasauga, and Western Diamondback Rattlesnake. Despite the potential, on most nights you would be lucky to find a single snake.

For more information on Falcon State Park visit: *www.tpwd.state. tx.us/spdest/findadest/parks/falcon.*

FALCON DAM

Since 2001, access to Falcon Dam (and the woodlands below Falcon Dam) has been restricted because of federal security concerns. Because these birding areas may open up again in the future, the Falcon Dam section (with only minor edits from the previous edition of this guide) is reproduced below.

Falcon Dam—built for water conservation, irrigation, power, flood control, and recreation purposes and dedicated in October 1953—trapped the waters of the Rio Grande to form a 60-mile-long lake. From the spillway, scan the river for ducks, cormorants, kingfishers, and other birds before heading to the riparian woodland below the dam. From a viewpoint near the middle of the dam, you can survey the lake for ducks, gulls, and terns. Once in a great while, a vagrant gull will turn up here in winter. You must pass through U.S. Customs on the way back, however, and that can be a real inconvenience if your car is packed with gear. It's easiest to ask if you can park at customs and walk out on the dam road.

The area below the dam is much better—but, again, it is currently inaccessible. If this area is ever reopened, go west (toward Falcon Dam) on Spur Road 2098 for 1.0 mile and veer left onto a small, paved road. (This road is reached well before you come abreast of the customs station.) Drive to the spillway parking area (1.8 miles). Check the utility poles for Great Horned Owls at dawn. (There is a gate near customs that is locked from 6:00PM to 6:00AM, and all day on holidays.)

From the top of the wall, you can scan the concrete spillway below, where Neotropic and Double-crested Cormorants can be compared. When there is a trickle of water, shorebirds can be common, particularly during migration. The most common winter shorebirds in the area are Spotted and Least Sandpipers. Baird's Sandpiper and others pass through in migration. Rare shorebird species are certainly possible, as both Purple Sandpiper (December 1975) and Northern Jacana (November 1992–April 1993) have been recorded here. In winter, Cave Swallows may be soaring overhead; Ringed and Green Kingfishers often are seen fishing at water's edge; and, in summer, Red-billed Pigeons may be perched in the tall trees along the bank. In summer, some Cliff Swallows nest on the dam face.

Although Zone-tailed Hawks are rare in the Valley, they seem to turn up with more regularity at the Falcon Dam spillway, usually with Turkey Vultures. A number of dabbling ducks winter on the river below the spillway, including Mottled and "Mexican." Also look for Black Phoebe at the base of the spillway and, in winter, Rock Wren on the rock mound below. Look also among the rocks for Blue Spiny Lizards

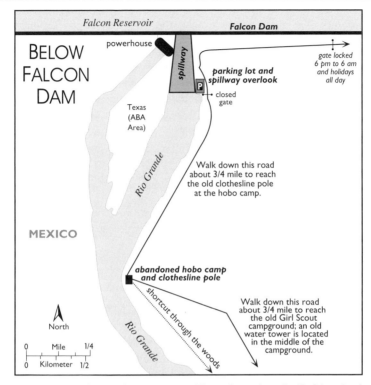

Falcon Reservoir

Falcon Dam

BELOW FALCON DAM

powerhouse

spillway

gate locked
6 pm to 6 am
and holidays
all day

**parking lot and
spillway overlook**

P

closed
gate

Texas
(ABA
Area)

Rio Grande

Walk down this road
about 3/4 mile to reach
the old clothesline pole
at the hobo camp.

MEXICO

**abandoned hobo camp
and clothesline pole**

shortcut through the woods

Walk down this road
about 3/4 mile to reach
the old Girl Scout
campground; an old
water tower is located
in the middle of the
campground.

North

0   Mile   1/4

0   Kilometer   1/2

Rio Grande

sunning themselves in late morning. These large lizards (5–14 inches) with black collars are endemic to south Texas and northeastern Mexico.

Walk past the gate on the dirt road leading downriver. In about three-quarters of a mile you reach the old "hobo camp" and clothesline pole in a grove of Texas Ebony trees. (Alternately, you may choose to follow a rough trail, which starts just beyond the rock mound and follows the riverbank.) The grove attracts about the same species found at Santa Margarita Ranch and Salineño, including most of the Lower Valley specialties.

At the west end of the abandoned campsite by the old clothesline pole, there is access to the riverbank. This is an excellent vantage point for spotting soaring Hook-billed Kite or Gray Hawk. You may also see Red-billed Pigeon (spring and summer) and Ringed Kingfisher as they fly up and down the river. Of course, you could just sit here and watch the river go by.

You may explore the area further by one of two routes that end up at the same place, an old Girl Scout campground farther downriver. If you take the road to the left, the distance is approximately three-quarters of a mile to where it meets the river. Sometimes Red-billed Pigeons are seen in the area, especially in spring and summer. Before you actually reach the river, a trail goes off the right to the old Girl Scout campground (an old water tower sits in the middle of the site). Although Ferruginous Pygmy-Owl and Brown Jay have not been present for several years, they were both former residents in these woodlands. Audubon's Orioles are still fairly reliable in the vicinity of the river and the Girl Scout camp.

Rarities recorded from below Falcon Dam include Rufous-capped Warbler (February 1973). Although Tropical Kingbirds are now widespread across most of the Lower Valley, a 1991 sighting at Falcon Dam was notable.

It is advisable not to bird alone here in remote areas because of the proximity of known routes used by drug runners in the vicinity of Falcon Dam and other parts of Starr County.

ZAPATA AND SAN YGNACIO

Zapata and San Ygnacio are two towns along the Rio Grande where you have a reasonable chance of seeing White-collared Seedeaters. You might also find Red-billed Pigeons in spring and summer along the river.

Between Falcon Dam and Big Bend, the land is arid, thinly vegetated, and relatively unproductive. There are still a few places to stop, however. About 7.3 miles from the intersection of US-83 and Spur Road 2098 at Falcon Dam, check a culvert at a creek called Tigre Chiquito (see map on page 10) for Cave Swallows, especially if you missed them at Arroyo Salado or other culverts on US-83. If a lot of water is backed up from Falcon Dam, look for waterbirds and ducks here. You may also see Crested Caracaras along this stretch of highway.

White-collared Seedeaters are sometimes spotted at the City Park in **Zapata** (27.0 miles from US-83 and Spur Road 2098). The park is two blocks west of US-83 on 9th Avenue. Search the cattail pond and surrounding area (including the grassy fence-line behind the library) for the seedeaters. Online recordings of White-collared Seedeater can be heard at: *www.world birdingcenter.org/bird_info*.

Also at City Park, you can expect some of the Rio Grande specialties, such as Green Jay and Altamira Oriole year-round, Say's Phoebe and Vermilion Flycatcher in winter, a few migrant passerines in migration, and Couch's Kingbird in summer. House Finch, very rare in the Lower Valley, has shown up at

Zapata City Park. Hopelessly lost, a Red-billed Tropicbird was found along the river at Zapata in April 1989.

Continue upriver on US-83 toward San Ygnacio. Some 2 miles west of Zapata turn right at the sign for the hamlet of Las Palmas. This road winds through open desert scrub, which can be good for Black-throated Sparrows and, occasionally, Scaled Quail. Check the largest trees on the western horizon in the afternoon for Red-billed Pigeons. Return to US-83.

Continue upriver on US-83 to historic **San Ygnacio** (12.0 miles), a town that dates back to the late 1700s and the original Spanish settlements of General Jose de Escandon. White-collared Seedeaters have been fairly reliable here for a number of years. Currently the best area for the seedeaters is at the San Ygnacio Bird and Butterfly Park at the end of Washington Street. A small fee is required to bird the property. This private bird sanctuary, owned and maintained by curator Joel Ruíz (*datlax@sc2000.net*), contains a nature trail along the river with several feeding stations and water features. Although the seedeaters sometimes frequent the feeding stations, they are more often spotted in the nearby vegetation, especially the river reed-beds. A recent breeding survey along the Rio Grande found no fewer than fifteen singing males. Many Lower Valley specialties (both birds and butterflies) can be found at the San Ygnacio Bird and Butterfly Park.

Rarities that have turned up in San Ygnacio include Roadside Hawk (January–March 2005) and Lesser Black-backed Gull (April 1989). If you have no luck with the seedeaters at the traditional spots in Zapata or San Ygnacio, try the rest area along US-83 about 3 miles north of San Ygnacio (in the long grass and reeds behind and below the rest stop), or continue to Laredo. The rest stop also provides a good view of the river and might produce Muscovy Duck and Red-billed Pigeon.

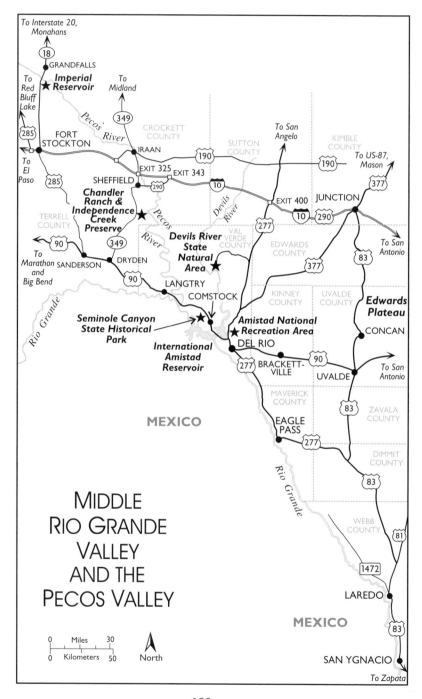

To Interstate 20, Monahans

18 GRANDFALLS

To Red Bluff Lake

Imperial Reservoir ★

To Midland

285

349

FORT STOCKTON

Pecos River

CROCKETT COUNTY

SUTTON COUNTY

KIMBLE COUNTY

To San Angelo

IRAAN 190 190

To US-87, Mason

377

To El Paso

285

SHEFFIELD

EXIT 325 EXIT 343

290 10 EXIT 400

JUNCTION

377

Chandler Ranch & Independence Creek Preserve ★

Pecos River

Devils River

10 290

TERRELL COUNTY

90

349

Devils River State Natural Area ★

VAL VERDE COUNTY

277

EDWARDS COUNTY

To San Antonio

To Marathon and Big Bend

SANDERSON DRYDEN

90

LANGTRY

COMSTOCK

377

83

KINNEY COUNTY

UVALDE COUNTY

Edwards Plateau

Rio Grande

Seminole Canyon State Historical Park

★ **Amistad National Recreation Area** ★

DEL RIO

CONCAN

International Amistad Reservoir

277 BRACKETT-VILLE

90

UVALDE

To San Antonio

MEXICO

MAVERICK COUNTY

83

ZAVALA COUNTY

EAGLE PASS

277

DIMMIT COUNTY

83

MIDDLE RIO GRANDE VALLEY AND THE PECOS VALLEY

Rio Grande

WEBB COUNTY

81

1472

LAREDO

0 Miles 30
0 Kilometers 50

North

MEXICO

SAN YGNACIO

83

To Zapata

MIDDLE
RIO GRANDE VALLEY
AND THE
PECOS VALLEY

As one follows the Rio Grande northward toward Laredo, the true character of the South Texas Brush Country becomes readily apparent. This
region of Texas is dominated by plains, with a few low rolling hills characterized by Tamaulipan thorn scrub. Many species of acacia are on display here. In
spring, the orangish flowers of Huisache (*Acacia smallii*) offer a visual spectacle;
they also attract migrant birds to feast on the many insects that feed on the
blooms. Many birds that are generally thought of as "Lower Valley specialties"
are found in this region. Some are widespread, such as Green Jay, Long-billed
Thrasher, and Olive Sparrow, whereas others are found in more specialized
habitats along the Rio Grande floodplain and tributaries. This region of the
state is poorly explored and undoubtedly offers many new discoveries, which
should continue to increase as more birding sites open to the public.

The area covered in this chapter extends northward to the Balcones Escarpment, and birding sites near Del Rio, Sheffield, and Fort Stockton offer an
opportunity to explore the avifauna of this underbirded region. About halfway between San Antonio and Big Bend, the Pecos River enters the Rio
Grande near Del Rio, having traveled south through the western portion of
the Stockton Plateau. The Pecos here is narrow and muddy, a far cry from its
beginnings in the Sangre de Cristo Mountains of northern New Mexico. For
most birders, this part of Texas is an obstacle to traverse on the way to more
famous birding locales. However, the Pecos Valley and the areas between Del
Rio and Laredo have much to offer. The rugged scenery is among the best in
Texas. Black-capped Vireo can be found easily at several locations. Many spots

103

offer a fascinating blend of species from the south, west, and east. Depending on the direction you are traveling, this area can provide your first glimpse of, or your last chance at, particular species. Birding pressure is light and the chances of interesting discoveries are high.

LAREDO

There are several fairly good spots for White-collared Seedeater along the Rio Grande in the city of **Laredo**. Here you also can find Audubon's and Altamira Orioles and a variety of Lower Valley specialties. If you have visited the sites south of Laredo (for instance San Ygnacio Bird Sanctuary) and remain on US-83, you will enter Laredo from the south. Follow US-83 past its intersection with TX-359. Just after this intersection, go under an overpass. Continue on this road until it becomes one-way heading west (Guadalupe Street). Guadalupe will become Matamoros Street after you cross Zacate Creek. Turn left on the first street after the bridge (San Leonardo) and continue south until you reach Water Street. This is a narrow one-way street passing through a very old Laredo neighborhood. At the Water Street intersection, take a right and follow it down to the sign on your left that says **Las Palmas Trail**. Park your vehicle in the pulloff to the left. Be sure valuables are out of sight and your vehicle is locked. This birding site is on the Rio Grande and you will probably get a visit from the Border Patrol. The trail leads toward the river, then travels downriver (left) ultimately passing under a bluff on your left. At the end of the trail, another trail goes to the left and follows Zacate Creek back toward Matamoros Street. This area can be very good in winter. Here you may find a variety of waterbirds, all three kingfishers, Green Jay, mixed-species flocks (Blue-headed Vireo, Ruby-crowned Kinglet, Blue-gray Gnatcatcher, and Orange-crowned and Black-throated Green Warblers), Audubon's and Altamira Orioles, and White-collared Seedeater. One of the better spots for seedeaters is along the cane (reeds) near the bluff under Water Street. Scarce species such as Long-eared Owl and Winter Wren have been sighted in the area; a male Blue Bunting was discovered on the Christmas Bird Count in 2005.

From here, you should continue straight ahead, passing over a small culvert with a track put there by the Border Patrol for crossing the indentation. Be careful as you walk over the culvert. Go across the large parking lot to a city park situated on the river. You can walk along the bank of the river looking for White-collared Seedeater. Birds seen along this stretch of river also include a variety of waterfowl (winter), Osprey, and Ringed and Green Kingfishers.

Another spot to look for seedeaters is at the **Lamar Bruni Vergara Environmental Science Center**. To get to the center, you must first backtrack up Water Street to San Enrique (just before the apartments begin) and take a left. Follow this narrow street, being careful at each intersection, all

the way back to Matamoros Street and make a left—this will take you to where US-83 intersects I-35. Take a right and stay in the access (frontage) lane to Washington Street, which crosses I-35 on an overpass. Follow this road all the way to a railroad overpass. After crossing the overpass, make a right at the light. On your right, you will see a group of wind turbines. Drive toward them to reach the Lamar Bruni Vergara Environmental Science Center. Here, take the Paso del Indio trail down to the river. If the Center is open, ask for directions. If not, from the base of the trail, you can go both upriver and downriver exploring the area. Downriver is an area the locals call the "Gravel Pits." You might see White-collared Seedeaters anywhere along this trail in the right habitat. This is a good spot for a variety of waterbirds, raptors, warblers, and sparrows, and at the right time of year butterflies are abundant as well.

Now that you have visited Laredo's hotspots, there are several other locations of interest. Take US-59 from I-35 east to Loop 20. At the light make a left onto Loop 20 and go about a half-mile to **Casa Blanca International Park**. This can be a good birding spot in winter for a variety of waterfowl. At the Boy

Green Jay   Barry Zimmer

Scout Camp at the rear of the park, you also will have the opportunity to look for species that prefer wooded or grassy habitats. From here, go back to Loop 20 and turn right (north). When you reach **Texas A&M International University**, turn right and explore the areas along the edge of the university grounds for grassland birds, including Scaled Quail, Northern Bobwhite, and several sparrow species. Head back to the Loop and make a right. Follow Loop 20 to Del Mar Boulevard, where you turn left. Go to the light at the intersection with Country Club Drive and take a left. The water here is called Susan's Ponds, where several duck species reside in winter, including Wood Duck (rare). This spot is worth a quick look.

If you have the time you should take **Old Mines Road** away from town to the north. Take FM-1472 from I-35. This is a heavily used area for trucks, so be careful. The road becomes a divided highway and can be driven all the way to Eagle Pass; however, the pavement ends about 40 miles out of town and becomes a gravel road. This is a good winter birding road. Just past the Columbia Solidarity Bridge about 20 miles from town, there is a pond on the left side of the road that is good to check. Farther up the road at El Chapote Ranch on your right (if you start at I-35 and US-83, this will be 28.4 miles), you can knock on the power pole just to the north of the gate and might have an Eastern Screech-Owl respond. Again using the I-35/US-83 intersection, at 38 miles there is a small pond on the left adjacent to some cattle pens. Black-tailed Gnatcatcher has been found here. In all, this is a nice road, with little traffic after the Columbia Bridge. Here you can find Scaled Quail, Northern Bobwhite, and a variety of hawks, doves, and sparrows. Explore and enjoy as far as you want. This road runs for over 100 miles.

DEL RIO

Del **Rio** is located along the Rio Grande in the northwesternmost point of the South Texas Plains. It is not as regularly birded as other areas in this book, but it does have great potential. As with the southwestern Edwards Plateau, the avifaunas of three physiographic regions come together and thus offer an interesting and sometimes unexpected assemblage of birds. In addition, the Serranias del Burro are only 50 miles to the west in Mexico. This small mountain range is believed to the be the origin of the recently discovered breeding population of Tropical Parulas in the Devils and Pecos River drainages, as well as the numerous Rufous-capped Warblers that have turned up in these areas over the years. Unfortunately, there is very little public land away from the shores of nearby Lake Amistad, and riparian zones along the Rio Grande are accessible only in a few locations. From Del Rio, you may travel eastward onto the Edwards Plateau or westward toward Big Bend.

One of the places in Del Rio worth checking is the area around **San Felipe Springs**. The springs are located at the end of San Felipe Springs Road, which is 1.6 miles east of the intersection of US-90 (Gibbs Street) and US-277 (Avenue F) in downtown. Upon reaching San Felipe Springs Road, turn left and drive to the end. The springs are the third-largest in Texas, with an outflow of about 90 million gallons of water per day into San Felipe Creek. The creek winds its way through the municipal golf course and several city parks. At the end of the road you pass through a gate (open from 7:00AM to 5:30PM) and on to the spring pumphouse. Park and bird around the spring. Back at the fork, walk across the bridge and bird along the west side of the creek, especially in the wooded area north of the maintenance shed. Before going up the creek behind the shed, be sure to get permission at the clubhouse on US-90. The property belongs to the San Felipe Country Club, which is happy to allow public access to this area for birdwatching. Birds found here

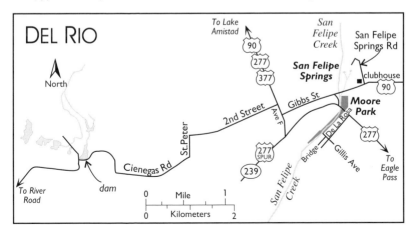

year-round include Green and Ringed Kingfishers, Great Kiskadee, Black Phoebe, Vermilion Flycatcher, Olive Sparrow, and Lesser Goldfinch. In summer, watch for Couch's and Western Kingbirds.

Return to US-90 and turn right. Almost immediately, you will see the beginning of Moore Park on your left. Green Kingfishers often are found near the railroad bridge or down near the park's swimming pool. Because of its small size and secretive habits, this bird is easy to overlook. This park can be very crowded on weekends and during the summer.

To check the rest of the park system along the creek on the south side of US-277, continue west on US-90 and turn left (south) onto US-277 (0.25 mile) to De La Rosa (0.3 mile), turn right (southwest) two blocks, and park at the Amphitheater Center. There is a paved trail following the creek that continues through the park for another half-mile. Or, continue to drive southwest on De La Rosa three blocks, turn right one block onto Gillis Avenue, and left onto Bridge to the creek, pond, and picnic area. The whole park is also good for spring and fall migrants such as Spotted Sandpiper, Hermit Thrush, Nashville, Orange-crowned, Yellow, Yellow-rumped, and Wilson's Warblers, and Spotted Towhee. Snowy Egrets can be found here throughout the year; also be sure to look carefully in the trees on the other side of the creek for Yellow-crowned Night-Herons.

Another good area is the roadside thicket between the Rio Grande and the railroad just west of the city. It is an avian meeting-spot for East and West, with a touch of the Lower Rio Grande thrown in. Here you should find Northern Bobwhite and Scaled Quail, Eastern, Black, and Say's Phoebes, Ash-throated and Brown-crested Flycatchers, Carolina, Canyon, and Cactus Wrens, Rufous-crowned Sparrow, Northern Cardinal, Pyrrhuloxia, and Orchard, Bullock's, and Hooded Orioles. Golden-fronted and Ladder-backed Woodpeckers are common. Bronzed and Brown-headed Cowbirds are common in summer. Olive Sparrows, although difficult to find, are actually present in good numbers; familiarity with their call-notes makes finding them much easier. White-tailed Kites also can be found hunting over the tree-lined fields.

To reach this area of thickets and other habitats from the downtown starting point of US-90 and US-277/377, go two blocks north and turn left (west) onto 2nd Street. Drive to the end (1.2 miles) at the cemetery, turn left onto St. Peter, and right onto Cienegas Road (0.2 mile) to a farm pond and dam (1.7 miles). Look over the ducks (some are domestic) and the cormorants. Neotropic Cormorants can be common here, especially in summer. Occasionally, Least Terns are found feeding over these ponds. At the corner, turn left under the railroad and check the ponds and thickets along the way to River Road, where you turn right (2.0 miles). Summer residents include Black-bellied Whistling-Duck and Groove-billed Ani, along with many of the above species. The road follows along the river north to a locked gate (5.0 miles). You can park here and walk farther up the road along the railroad

Scaled Quail   Mark Lockwood

tracks. Additional birds such as Great Kiskadee, Black Phoebe, Vermilion Fly-catcher, and Couch's Kingbird may be found.

AMISTAD NATIONAL RECREATION AREA

The building of Amistad Dam in 1969 and creation of Lake Amistad just northwest of Del Rio has attracted many species that were either absent from this area of the state or were previously rare. The reservoir is adminis-tered by both Mexico and the United States. When it is at "conservation-pool level" of 1,117 feet above sea level, it covers 64,860 acres and stores 3,505,439 acre-feet of water. The United States' shoreline is 851 miles long, while that of Mexico is 304 miles. The recreation area provides boating, fishing, swimming, hunting, and camping. (There are five small primitive, free camping areas with picnic tables under shelters and chemical toilets.) Birding opportunities are numerous on the water and along the shore, as well as in the dry scrub of higher ground, composed of Blackbrush, Guajillo, Ceniza, yucca, Sotol, mes-quite, Creosote Bush, Leatherplant, and various cacti.

To reach the recreation area, drive north from Del Rio on US-90/277/377 for about 4 miles to the National Park Service headquarters office on the right. Here you can pick up information, brochures, and books. At about one-quarter mile beyond, US-90 swings westward and US-277/377 continues north. There are two areas to visit along the lakeshore by taking US-277/377. The first is found after crossing over the east arm of the reservoir (6.0 miles). There is a small campground that offers a place to scan that part of the lake. In winter, look for waterfowl (including Cinnamon Teal), Double-crested and Neotropic Cormorants, Ring-billed and Bonaparte's Gulls, and Forster's Tern. Search the moist, open grassy areas along the shoreline for Le Conte's Sparrow. This area may produce several desert species, including Verdin, Cactus Wren, Curve-billed Thrasher, Canyon Towhee, Black-throated Sparrow, and Pyrrhuloxia. Savannah, Vesper, Lincoln's, and Song Sparrows and

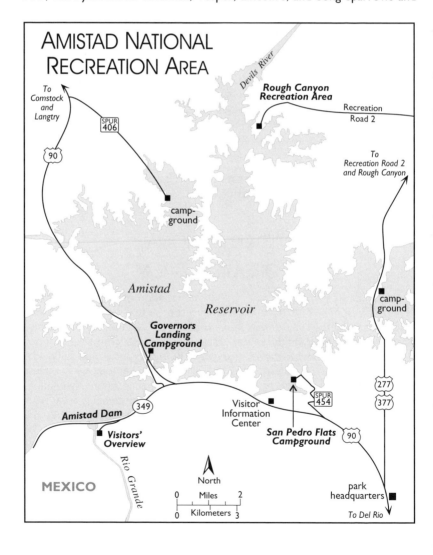

AMISTAD NATIONAL
RECREATION AREA

Devils River

To
Comstock
and
Langtry

SPUR
406

90

**Rough Canyon
Recreation Area**

Recreation
Road 2

To
*Recreation Road 2
and Rough Canyon*

camp-
ground

Amistad

Reservoir

camp-
ground

**Governors
Landing
Campground**

277

377

349

Visitor
Information
Center

SPUR
454

Amistad Dam

**Visitors'
Overview**

**San Pedro Flats
Campground**

90

Rio Grande

MEXICO

North

0   Miles   2

0   Kilometers   3

park
headquarters

To Del Rio

Lark Bunting can be found in this area during the winter. Scissor-tailed and Vermilion Flycatchers and Blue Grosbeak are common in spring and summer. Continue north on US-277/377 to the **Rough Canyon Recreation Area** turnoff (5.0 miles). Follow Recreation Road 2 to the marina (7.2 miles). Rough Canyon is on the Devils River arm of Lake Amistad. Many of the same species mentioned above can be found here.

Traveling west on US-90 from Del Rio, you may explore other areas of Lake Amistad. One of the best places to see waterbirds on the lake is at the **San Pedro Flats Campground**. To reach the campground, take Spur Road 454 (2.4 miles) and follow the signs. Resident species include Scaled Quail, Harris's Hawk, Green Kingfisher, Chihuahuan Raven, Cactus, Rock, and Canyon Wrens, Blue-gray Gnatcatcher, Verdin, and Pyrrhuloxia. In summer, look for Pied-billed Grebe, Black-necked Stilt, Snowy Egret (rare), Least Tern, Common and Lesser Nighthawks, and Hooded Oriole. Interior Least Tern and Snowy Plover nest at Amistad. There have even been nesting Laughing Gulls at this lake. In winter, watch for numerous dabbling ducks, Red-breasted Merganser, Horned Grebe, Say's Phoebe, Sage Thrasher, and Green-tailed and Canyon Towhees. Mountain Bluebirds sometimes can be seen in the grasslands. There is a record of Eurasian Wigeon from this area. In migration, look for American White Pelican, White-faced Ibis, Mississippi Kite, Snowy Plover (very rare), Long-billed Curlew, Solitary, Spotted, Upland, Pectoral, Least, and Western Sandpipers, and Forster's Tern. Bald and Golden Eagles occasionally are seen. Osprey is a regular winter resident and Peregrine Falcons are seen regularly during migration. At least 17 species of sparrows have been found here during migration and winter.

Continue west on US-90 to Road 349 (5.2 miles) and turn left (south) to the visitor center at the dam (2.5 miles). Turn around and go back to the road (0.4 mile) that leads to the **Visitors' Overview**, a short trail giving a good view of the river below the dam, as well as the downriver face of the dam. Ringed and Green Kingfishers prefer the clear, shallow water below dams. This is also a good location for observing White-throated Swifts and a variety of swallows during migration.

Return north on Road 349 to just north of the railroad and turn left to **Governors Landing Campground** (1.2 miles). Check for passerines along this road, and look in the small ponds for Least and Pied-billed Grebes and ducks. It is not unusual to find Canyon Wrens nesting in the roof supports of the picnic-table shelters. Continue on US-90 west across the long bridge over the Devils River arm of Amistad Reservoir to Spur Road 406 (10.1 miles) and turn right to the campground at the end (4.7 miles). This good birding area has most of the same species as San Pedro Flats, but it has larger bushes and trees.

This area of the state also has a tremendous diversity of reptiles. The common lizards in this rocky, thorny area of limestone between Del Rio and Big

Bend are Texas Banded Gecko (nocturnal), Collared Lizard, Greater Earless Lizard, Crevice Spiny and Texas Spiny Lizards, Canyon, Tree, Desert Side-blotched, Texas Horned, and Round-tailed Horned Lizards, and Texas Spot-ted Whiptail. The common snakes are Western Hognose Snake, Western Coachwhip, Central Texas and Schott's Whipsnakes, Mountain Patchnose Snake, Great Plains and Trans-Pecos Rat Snakes, Bullsnake, Gray-banded and Desert Kingsnakes, Texas Longnose Snake, Western Hooknose Snake (rare), Texas Night Snake, and Blacktail and Western Diamondback Rattlesnakes. Along the river and in other moist areas, look for Texas and Trans-Pecos Blind Snakes, Blotched Water Snake, Checkered and Black-necked Garter Snakes, Western Ribbon, Flat-headed, Plains, and Southwestern Black-headed Snakes, Copperhead, and even the very rare Devils River Black-headed Snake.

DEVILS RIVER
STATE NATURAL AREA

An option is to continue north on US-277 for 32 miles (approximately 3.6 miles north of Loma Alta), turn left onto Dolan Creek Road (gravel), and go 18.6 miles to **Devils River State Natural Area** ($3/person entrance fee). Dolan Creek Road is about 0.2 mile north of a covered picnic site located 3.4 miles north of Loma Alta (a store with basic supplies and gas, the last op-portunity for such). It is a well-maintained dirt road, but it includes numerous low water crossings; extreme caution is advised in rainy weather.

The park headquarters is located just off (east of) the main road 3.5 miles inside the park entrance. Shower facilities are available at the park headquar-ters. A lodge and bunkhouse also are located nearby and are available for pub-lic use (fee). Otherwise, primitive camping is the only other accommodation available. The park is very remote; the nearest medical facilities and major supplies are located in Del Rio, one and one-half hours away.

Devils River State Natural Area is wonderfully diverse, with a variety of upland and aquatic habitats and abundant birdlife. As with other areas in this region, a mix of eastern, western, and subtropical birds can be found here. The best birding is from the headquarters complex down to Dolan Creek Canyon to Dolan Springs and along the Devils River. Typical upland birds in-clude Scaled Quail, Northern Bobwhite, Greater Roadrunner, Ladder-backed Woodpecker, Say's Phoebe, Verdin, Bewick's, Rock, and Cactus Wrens, Curve-billed Thrasher, Canyon Towhee, Black-throated, Cassin's and Rufous-crowned Sparrows, Northern Cardinal, Pyrrhuloxia, and House Finch. In summer, look for Vermilion Flycatcher (common near water habi-tats), Ash-throated Flycatcher, Yellow-breasted Chat, Painted and Varied Buntings, Scott's and Hooded Orioles, Summer Tanager, and Blue Grosbeak.

NORTH AND WEST OF DEL RIO

To
Pandale

To
Ozona

Dolan Creek

To
Sonora,
Interstate 10

Dolan Creek Road

277

no vehicle
travel
beyond
here

■ Park HQ

LOMA
ALTA

Devils   River

**Devils River
State
Natural Area**

To
Langtry

Pecos
River

1024

163

Devils

River

To
Rocksprings

377

277
377

90

**Seminole
Canyon
State
Historical
Park**

COMSTOCK

Rio Grande

**Rough Canyon
Recreational
Area**

MEXICO

90

★

**Amistad National
Recreation Area**

To
Brackettville

**International
Amistad
Reservoir**

Rio Grande

DEL RIO

90

To
Eagle
Pass

277

North

0   Miles   8

0   Kilometers   12

MEXICO

Vertical cliffs in the limestone hills along Dolan Creek create habitat for such birds as Cliff Swallow and Canyon Wren. Occasionally, White-throated Swifts are encountered along these bluffs. Turkey Vultures, Golden Eagles, American Kestrels, and Common Ravens utilize shelves and crevices in the cliffs for nesting and roosting areas. In the larger live oaks at the base of these cliffs and elsewhere in the park, look for nesting Cooper's, Red-shouldered, and Zone-tailed Hawks.

Vireo diversity at the park is high, with six species represented as breeders and an additional four species as migrants. Black-capped Vireo is common from late March through early September, and occupies shrub thickets and oak mottes in the riparian corridors of the park. On mesa slopes and drier habitats with scattered trees and shrubs, Gray Vireo can usually be found without much difficulty. Look for Bell's Vireo in the drier riparian thickets and thorn-scrub habitats, especially in Huisache along the river. White-eyed Vireo prefers understory thickets, particularly those associated with the more mature riparian woodlands such as Plateau Live Oak and Pecan. This species overwinters in similar habitat and males can be in full song by late January. Finally, both Red-eyed and Yellow-throated Vireos occupy the mid-story and canopy of mature woodlands. At some locations within the park, all six nesting vireo species can be found in close proximity to each other. Migrants include Philadelphia (rare), Warbling, Cassin's, and Blue-headed Vireos.

Approximately one-half mile from the Devils River, the main public-access road ends. Park in the lot and continue your birding adventure on foot (or by bicycle), using the main road as a trail.

The portion of the park that lies along the river includes just the eastern bank from where the main road joins the riparian zone, north approximately 1.5 miles to the old fish camp. At the camp, one of the few remaining terrace woodlands can be found. During the spring and summer, Acadian and Great Crested Flycatchers, Eastern Wood-Pewee, Tropical Parula, Yellow-throated Warbler, Olive Sparrow, and Indigo Bunting are present. There are two or three territories of Tropical Parula in this area. Listen for singing males between late March and mid-June. These birds normally can be found fairly easily, but this woodland extends off the Natural Area, and thus sometimes parulas can only be heard from the state lands.

The properties to the south, north, and west are all privately owned and, therefore, off-limits to park visitors without special permission. A road leads north along the river inside the steep bluff and is available for use as a trail. If you desire to bird along this stretch, be prepared to walk through standing water and numerous springs. Be careful not to unduly damage the sensitive aquatic systems. The initial stretch of the river is a large section of standing water which appears to be lake-like. At the north end of this section is a series of rapids, islands, and marshy thickets. Look for Ringed Kingfisher flying up and down the river. In fact, all three kingfishers are often present.

Curve-billed Thrasher

Brad McKinney

Devils River State Natural Area is situated at a strategic location on the southwestern Edwards Plateau and is an excellent location for birding. The diversity of habitats and associated birdlife make the park an excellent destination for anyone looking for an out-of-the-way spot that has tremendous potential but is terribly underbirded. Rarities that have been recorded at the park include Flammulated Owl, Broad-billed Hummingbird, Acorn Woodpecker, Great Kiskadee, Hammond's Flycatcher, Golden-cheeked Warbler, and Rufous-capped Warbler.

SEMINOLE CANYON
STATE PARK AND HISTORIC SITE

Seminole Canyon State Park and Historic Site (P.O. Box 820, Comstock TX 78837; phone 512-292-4464) is located along US-90, 9 miles west of Comstock, and west of Amistad Reservoir. The primary function of this 2,173-acre park (entrance fee $3) is to protect the Indian rock art (picto- graphs) found within Seminole Canyon. Along the walls of the canyon are several deep overhangs that provided shelter for the pre-Columbian cultures that inhabited the area. Seminole Canyon contains some of the most spectacular examples of this pre-Columbian artwork. These pictographs are believed to be North America's oldest; some are thought to have been painted perhaps 8,000 years ago. The pictographs are accessible only by guided tours provided by the park staff. The Visitor Center contains exhibits depicting the lifestyle of early man based upon artifacts and rock art. While at the Visitor Center, pick up brochures and a preliminary bird checklist.

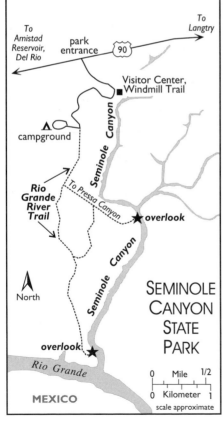

Windmill Trail starts from the Visitor Center and leads half a mile to Seminole Spring in a draw near Main Canyon. This is a fairly easy hike. Birds to look for here and along the way are Zone-tailed Hawk, Green Kingfisher, Black Phoebe, Varied Bunting, and Hooded Oriole.

The **Rio Grande Trail** (6 miles round-trip) leads from near the campground to a scenic overlook on the Rio Grande shores of Amistad Reservoir. About halfway is a cutoff trail to the Pressa Canyon overlook. At this upland area, watch for Scaled Quail, Verdin, Black-throated Sparrow, and Pyrrhuloxia. In winter, Lark Buntings are rather common, as are other wintering sparrows. During spring and fall migrations, watch for waterfowl and shorebirds at the river, and fly-catchers and warblers along the trail. White-throated Swifts nest on the canyon walls, as do Black and Turkey Vultures, Chihuahuan and Common Ravens, and Canyon Wrens.

On leaving the park, continue west on US-90 to the first road on the left (1.5 miles) and turn left (south) to the National Park Service's Pecos River District Headquarters (1.3 miles). The scenic view of the mouth of the Pecos River at the Rio Grande is great. What you see today has looked much the same for thousands of years. The water level, however, is now 50 feet deeper because of backwater from Amistad Dam. There is a self-guiding, quarter-mile nature trail and overlook.

LANGTRY

The Texas Department of Transportation maintains a travel information center at **Langtry** (17 miles). It is open during regular business hours seven days a week. The Judge Roy Bean Museum is located within this facility. When Roy Bean was made the justice of the peace in 1882, he changed the name of Eagle's Nest Spring to Langtry. He performed his official duties in the Jersey Lillie Saloon. Both the saloon and town were named after the English actress Emilie Charlotte (Lillie) Langtry, whom Bean greatly admired. Bean's colorful manner and unorthodox justice earned him great notoriety. He became known as "The Law West of the Pecos."

In the fall of 1976, a Rufous-backed Robin spent a week in the cactus garden at the information center. The beautiful garden has a large variety of plants, all labeled, including some 34 cacti, yuccas, and agaves, 19 species of trees, and 44 species of shrubs and others. Resident birds include Scaled Quail, Black-chinned Hummingbird (summer), Cactus and Rock Wrens, Curve-billed Thrasher, Black-throated Sparrow, Pyrrhuloxia, Hooded Oriole (summer), and House Finch.

From Langtry, travel west on US-90 toward the Big Bend country of West Texas. In the small town of Dryden (40 miles), you can either turn north on TX-349 to investigate the Pecos Valley, or continue on US-90 to Marathon and Big Bend National Park.

THE PECOS VALLEY

"The Pecos" is a name synonymous with the Old West. The Pecos River makes a 926-mile journey from the Sangre de Cristo Mountains of northern New Mexico to the Rio Grande northwest of Del Rio. It cuts a thin and muddy path through a section of West Texas that, to the birder traveling on Interstates 10 or 20, must look terribly bleak and unpromising. There are, however, a handful of good birding spots. Several of these offer a productive break on the long trek between the Edwards Plateau and Big Bend.

CHANDLER RANCH AND
INDEPENDENCE CREEK PRESERVE

The most varied birding in the Pecos Valley is around the small town of Sheffield, and the single best birding spot is Chandler Ranch/Independence Creek Preserve. To reach Chandler Ranch, exit Interstate 10 at exit 325 (TX-290/TX-349 for Iraan/Sheffield) and go south on TX-290 to the junction with TX-349 in Sheffield (4.9 miles). Turn right onto TX-349 (notice the sign for the Chandler Guest Ranch and Independence Creek Preserve), and proceed to Independence Creek Road (22.3 miles). If you are traveling US-90 between Del Rio and Big Bend, turn north onto TX-349 in Dryden and go about 38 miles to this intersection. Take Independence Creek Road (dirt) east to the Chandler Ranch (5.4 miles). The road crosses Independence Creek in another 1.3 miles. Some of the best habitat is to the right and left immediately after the creek crossing.

Chandler Ranch is a guest ranch offering hunting and fishing in addition to birding. It is open only to hunters from the beginning of October through December. The enclosed **Independence Creek Preserve** is a 702-acre conservation easement of The Nature Conservancy. The preserve was established primarily to protect breeding Black-capped Vireos, as well as rare fish of the Pecos watershed. The clear waters of Independence Creek flow past majestic oak groves to meet the Pecos River, banked on the east by impressive cliffs. The rocky hills are cloaked with junipers, and mesquite brushland dominates the intervening areas.

Prior arrangements are needed for any visit. For a day-visit, contact either Chandler Ranch (P.O. Box 10, Dryden, TX 78851; phone 915-753-2345) or the Trans-Pecos office of The Nature Conservancy (P.O. Box 2137, Alpine, TX 79831; phone 432-837-5954). Contact the TNC office at least two weeks in advance. They can send you a bird checklist, as well as maps of the easement and preserve instructions; in return, they would appreciate a list of the birds you find. There is a cabin on the property, but in recent years it has been on a continuous corporate lease and is not available for overnight stays. Camping on the easement is available only for researchers or TNC functions. It is not necessary to be a TNC member to visit the preserve.

The birdlife is a fascinating blend of east and west, with a number of species at the limits of their ranges. The oak groves act as an island for a handful of eastern breeders. April to June is perhaps the best time for a visit, and it is certainly the time to see Black-capped Vireos. The juniper-clad hillsides around the stream crossing and just to the east are good for this species. As with all Black-capped Vireo sites, *do not use tapes*. Look for breeders such as Scaled Quail, Zone-tailed Hawk, Common Ground-Dove, Common Poorwill, Black-chinned Hummingbird, Green Kingfisher, Golden-fronted Woodpecker,

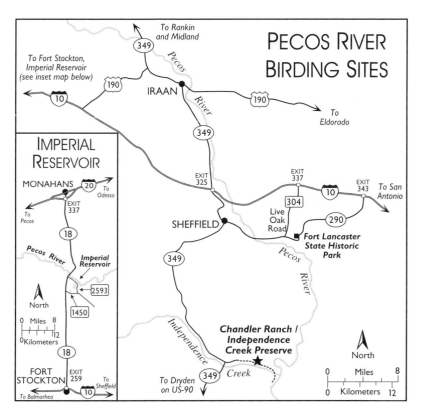

Say's Phoebe, Vermilion, Ash-throated, and Scissor-tailed Flycatchers, White-eyed, Bell's, and Yellow-throated Vireos, Common Raven, Black-crested Titmouse, Verdin, Bewick's Wren, Yellow-breasted Chat, Summer Tanager, Cassin's and Lark Sparrows, Northern Cardinal, Blue Grosbeak, Varied and Painted Buntings, and Orchard and Bullock's Orioles. Some of these species are resident. Northern Bobwhite, Red-shouldered Hawk, Eastern Wood-Pewee, Brown-crested Flycatcher, Red-eyed Vireo, and Carolina Wren have been seen and may breed at least sporadically. The ranch lies in the contact zone between Eastern and Western Screech-Owls; the Easterns are of the South Texas *mccallii* race. Ringed Kingfisher has been seen here at least twice, and you are close enough to South Texas to perhaps expect a stray such as Couch's Kingbird, Long-billed Thrasher, or Olive Sparrow. Nearly anything could drop in during migration. Look in the oaks for Eastern Fox Squirrels at the extreme western edge of their natural range.

Sheffield Area

Several locations closer to **Sheffield** deserve mention. Go east on US-290 from Sheffield to the Pecos River (4.0 miles). Look here for Cave Swallows with the Cliffs and Barns. Continue east to Live Oak Road (CR-304; 3.7 miles). A left turn here leads to some roadside oak groves good for Golden-fronted Woodpecker and Black-crested Titmouse. These isolated groves must look inviting to migrants as well. *Please stay on the roads.* It is possible to continue north on CR-304 to Interstate 10 exit 337 (Live Oak Road). Look for Green Kingfisher at any stream crossings with flowing water.

Continuing east on US-290 from the junction with CR-304, notice the entrance to Fort Lancaster State Historical Park (1.0 mile). The fort was established in 1855 to protect settlers traveling the road between San Antonio and El Paso. It was abandoned in 1861. Soon after the fort entrance, US-290 climbs a steep canyon to a picnic area (2.2 miles). In the canyon across from the picnic area, look from the roadside for Gray Vireo, a local breeder. Black-capped Vireo has occurred here. Listen for Canyon Wren. The view west is impressive. Interstate 10 exit 343 (TX-290 West) is reached by continuing east across barren flats for 8.8 miles. Detouring along TX-290 is a welcome reprieve for the interstate traveler.

Most of the 400-mile stretch of Interstate 10 between El Paso and the hard-earned trees along the North Llano River west of Junction is dull and monotonous. Birdlife is sparse. Smack-dab in the middle of this drive is Fort Stockton, on the creosote-covered bedrock of the Stockton Plateau. For the traveler looking for a change of pace, nearby Imperial Reservoir is well worth a visit at any season.

Imperial Reservoir

Imperial Reservoir is reached by taking Interstate 10 exit 259 (TX-18/FM-1053) in Fort Stockton. Head north on TX-18 to FM-1450 (23.3 miles). Take FM-1450 east to RR-2593 (3.2 miles), then north to the entrance on the left (2.9 miles). From Interstate 20, take exit 80 in Monahans and head south on TX-18 through Grandfalls. A $10 fee may be charged per car for boating, fishing, or picnicking; expect to pay for a birding visit if the gate is open. Access and visitation policies seem to change here without warning; you may be reduced to scoping the reservoir from outside the gate, putting you a considerable distance from the water.

Imperial Reservoir consistently has the best shorebird habitat in the Trans-Pecos. It is possible to drive along the east shore part way around the lake. A scope is necessary. Snowy Plovers breed, and recent observations suggest at least a few may be present year-round. Expect to see Least Terns in the summer—they breed at least sporadically. An assortment of shorebirds is likely, and numerous waterfowl winter on the lake. Western and Clark's Grebes have been seen but are not to be counted on, as they are at Balmorhea Lake or McNary Reservoir much farther to the west (see next chapter). Check for a stray loon between October and March, and look for odd herons and other waterbirds during the warmer months.

The potential of this isolated body of water is evidenced by the rare birds reported in recent years: Black-bellied Whistling-Duck, Red-throated and Pacific Loons, Brown Pelican, Reddish Egret, Roseate Spoonbill, American Golden-Plover, Whimbrel, Hudsonian Godwit, Dunlin, Laughing Gull, Sabine's Gull, and Black-legged Kittiwake. Part of the lake is surrounded by tamarisk, which may hold a few migrants; the surrounding desert has little to offer. If you have a few hours to spare and enjoy the thrill of finding the unexpected, then pay Imperial Reservoir a visit.

RED BLUFF LAKE

To the north, at the Texas/New Mexico border, the Pecos River has been dammed to create **Red Bluff Lake**, by far the largest body of water in the Trans-Pecos. Although reasonably accessible from Interstate 20, the Guadalupe Mountains, or Carlsbad, New Mexico, the lake has been very lightly birded and its birds are poorly known. The chances for a major find are good. Pacific Loon, Roseate Spoonbill, Black-legged Kittiwake, and Parasitic Jaeger have been reported in recent years, along with some sizable waterbird concentrations. The lake sits in some very stark oilfields; adjacent areas will hold few birds.

Exit Interstate 20 in Pecos (exit 42), and head north on US-285 to the tiny town of Orla (40 miles). (You may notice on maps what appears to be a large lake—Lake Toyah—just south of Pecos. This "lake" is now, and is generally, a dry alkali flat, but has had water in wet years.) Orla is practically deserted; do not count on any services. Carlsbad, New Mexico, is 45 miles to the north, and by taking FM-652 to the west, the Guadalupe Mountains are just over an hour away (see next chapter).

The land is nearly all private, and access to the lake is limited. Continue north from Orla on US-285 to FM-447 (2.7 miles). Turn right here to the dam (2.7 miles). As you approach the dam, look for a hand-painted sign for a "Sand Beach." A right turn here leads to a beach on the east side from which the southern end of the lake can be scoped. Another option is to head to the dam, then left through a gate to some picnic tables. You may be charged a nominal fee here, but the south end can be examined. A scope is essential for birding at this large lake.

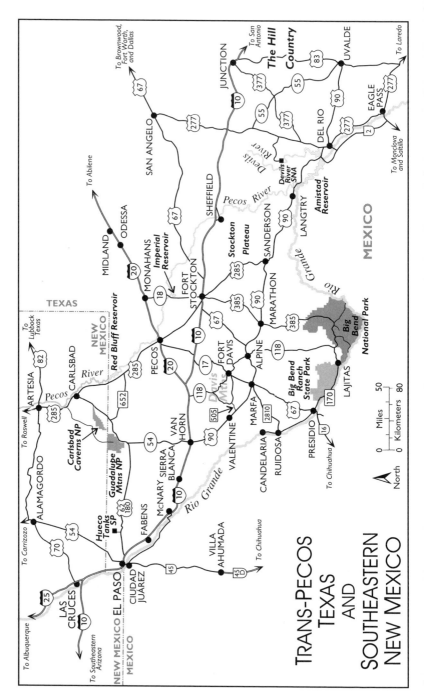

TRANS-PECOS
TEXAS
AND
SOUTHEASTERN
NEW MEXICO

THE TRANS-PECOS:
BIG BEND AND
DAVIS MOUNTAINS
PARKS

The region of Texas west of the Pecos River is called the Trans-Pecos. The Chihuahuan Desert encompasses most of this part of the state. Desert mountain ranges dominate the landscape down the center of the vast region. The mixture of desert, grasslands, and woodlands gives this part of Texas an incredible diversity of habitats and thus birdlife.

The Chihuahuan Desert can appear barren and hostile at first glance, but a closer look reveals a diverse avifauna. Much of the desert is dominated by open creosote flats that do not offer much in the way of bird diversity. But riparian corridors and the mixed desert scrub along arroyos and other protected areas offer excellent birding opportunities. The mid-elevation grasslands provide habitat to an entirely different suite of birds. There are no large tracts of this habitat open to the public, but roadside birding usually can provide the opportunity to observe most of the species found there. The mountains provide islands of woodland habitats, and each mountain range has a slightly different avifauna. Big Bend and Guadalupe Mountains National Parks provide access to these habitats. The climate is dry and temperate, with a rainy season from July to September. The amount of rainfall varies greatly from year to year and, obviously, affects the quality of birding through the year. Wet summers mean lush vegetation in the fall, the primary blooming period for most plants, which translates into a higher-quality winter food crop.

Many montane western species found in the Trans-Pecos are not found anywhere else in the state. Colima Warbler is the only species found in the

Montezuma Quail   Barry Zimmer

Trans-Pecos that cannot be found anywhere else in the United States. The Chisos Mountains in Big Bend National Park are home to the northernmost population of this species. Other montane species of interest include Montezuma Quail, Band-tailed Pigeon, Flammulated Owl, Whip-poor-will, Blue-throated and Broad-tailed Hummingbirds, Cordilleran Flycatcher, Plumbeous and Hutton's Vireos, Steller's and Mexican Jays, Mountain Chickadee, Pygmy Nuthatch, Western Bluebird, Grace's Warbler, Painted Redstart, Hepatic and Western Tanagers, Spotted Towhee, and Black-headed Grosbeak.

MARATHON

In the 1880s, settlers began moving into the expansive grasslands of the Marathon Basin. With the arrival of the railroad, a booming cattle industry sprang up. The community of **Marathon** became well established as a rail stop, and cattle from all over the Big Bend region passed through its stockyards. Cattle baron Alfred Gage built the Gage Hotel in 1927 as the headquarters for his 600-section ranch, the largest landholding in Texas at the time. Legend has it that over a million head of cattle were bought and sold in the lobby of the Gage Hotel. Today, the restored hotel offers a welcome rest and West Texas dining for visitors to the Big Bend area.

To visit a small county park (locally referred to as The Post), turn south on the paved road 0.5 mile west of the intersection of US-90 and US-385 and proceed to the entrance (5.0 miles). (Pavement gives way to dirt after about four miles.) Before reaching the park, the road crosses a creek. This area can be productive, particularly in winter; look for Ring-necked Duck, Sora, Eastern Phoebe, Marsh Wren, and Common Yellowthroat. Inside the park, the creek is dammed to form a small pond. There are numerous cottonwood trees as well as manicured grounds and a small amount of desert scrub. This site is worth checking during migration and winter. During the breeding season, look for Golden-fronted Woodpecker, Vermilion Flycatcher, Black Phoebe, Cactus Wren, and Lark and Black-throated Sparrows. In winter, Yellow-bellied and Red-naped Sapsuckers, Brown Creeper, Marsh Wren, and numerous sparrows can be found. There have even been documented records of Northern Jacana, Groove-billed Ani, Tropical Kingbird, and Lawrence's Goldfinch from this site.

Before leaving Marathon for Big Bend, make sure that you have plenty of gasoline. The park entrance at Persimmon Gap is 42 miles south on US-385. The Visitor Center (park headquarters) at Panther Junction is another 26 miles.

BIG BEND NATIONAL PARK

Halfway between El Paso and Laredo, the Rio Grande swings southward, forming a large bend that now holds Big Bend National Park. The park was established in 1944 and covers 801,163 acres, or about 1,252 square miles. The Chisos Mountains are the centerpiece of the park. The woodlands at the upper elevations give way to desert grasslands that in turn give way to the open desert. During much of the year, the desert can be extremely harsh and dry, but the summer rains transform the landscape into green hillsides covered with wildflowers. This flush of growth coincides with fall migration and is also the best time to search for vagrants dispersing from the nearby Sierra del Carmen and other mountain ranges farther into Mexico.

Despite this harshness, the park offers unforgettable scenery. The open desert is dissected by arroyos, and mountains stand majestically over the rocky terrain. The Rio Grande has carved magnificent canyons with walls towering hundreds of feet above the river. One cannot begin to experience this vast park on a single visit.

There is a $20 (per week) entrance fee. The first stop is the Visitor Center (open 8:00AM–6:00PM) at Panther Junction, which has exhibits and books. The park staff can be very helpful in getting you oriented. You may want to buy a few books, road and trail guides, topographic maps, and checklists of the rep-

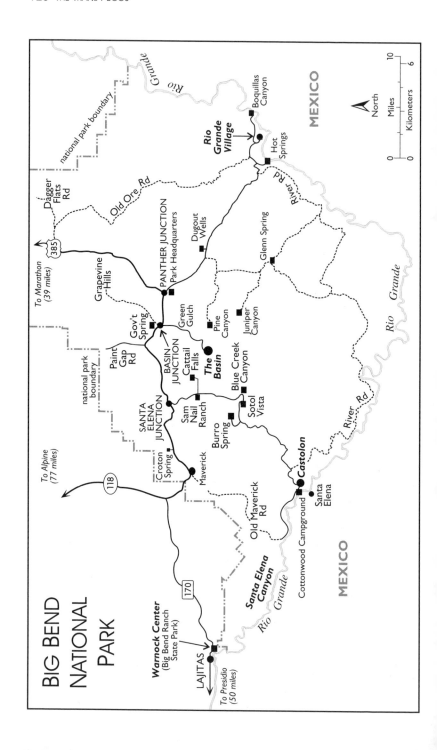

BIG BEND NATIONAL PARK

tiles, mammals, and birds. There is also a wildlife-sightings log at the front desk. You should contribute to the log by filling out sighting cards available from the personnel on duty. These cards are archived; the sightings log formed the backbone of Ro Wauer's *A Field Guide to Birds of the Big Bend.*

Gasoline is limited. There are gas stations just outside the park at Study Butte. There are only two service stations in the park, one at Panther Junction and the other at Rio Grande Village. They are open seven days a week, but normally only during regular business hours. There are campgrounds at Rio Grande Village, The Basin, and Castolon, as well as small stores. For non-campers, there is a modern lodge, dining room, and stone cottages in "The Basin;" advance reservations are required most of the year (phone 432-477-2291; web site: *www.chisosmountainslodge.com*).

Over 448 species of birds (57 of which are on the hypothetical list) have been found in the park, along with 75 species of mammals and 67 species of reptiles and amphibians. The best birding spots are widely scattered. A good strategy is to visit birding areas at various elevations. The avifauna of the mountains is very different from that of the desert. Get a map of the park and determine the areas that you are interested in visiting. There are dozens of little springs and canyons that may yield good birds. Some of the more regularly birded locations are listed below.

Rio Grande Village — This area usually provides good year-round birding. There are several sections to Rio Grande Village, and the best place to start is at the little store. Park here and walk into the cottonwood grove behind the store. Be sure to check the boat ramp at the river. This is also a camping area for groups.

Among the trees, you may find White-winged and Inca Doves, Common Ground-Dove, Western Screech-Owl (night), Great Horned Owl, Greater Roadrunner, Golden-fronted and Ladder-backed Woodpeckers, Vermilion Flycatcher, Black-tailed Gnatcatcher, Northern Mockingbird, Brown-headed Cowbird, House Finch, and Lesser Goldfinch. In summer, look for Gray Hawk, Yellow-billed Cuckoo, Elf Owl (night), Black-chinned Hummingbird, Western Kingbird, Summer Tanager, Blue Grosbeak, Painted Bunting, Orchard Oriole, and Bronzed Cowbird. In winter, watch for Northern (Red-shafted) Flicker, Yellow-bellied and Red-naped Sapsuckers, Blue-gray Gnatcatcher, Ruby-crowned Kinglet, American Robin, Orange-crowned and Yellow-rumped Warblers, Green-tailed and Spotted Towhees, Dark-eyed Junco, and American Goldfinch. During migration, an amazing variety of eastern and western species have been found. Yellow-green Vireo has turned up on three occasions. Many other rarities have made an appearance here, including Ruddy Ground-Dove, Tufted Flycatcher (first U.S. record), Thick-billed Kingbird, Tropical Parula, and Black-vented Oriole. The Sennett's race of the Hooded Oriole found here is almost red about the face; these birds are often hard to find, however.

The road to the right of the store goes past the RV campsites to the river (0.7 mile). Upon reaching the parking area, check the thickets along the river and surrounding the cottonwood stand. This area can be very productive. The species to be looked for here are the same as those listed above. This is usually the best location for Gray Hawk, and a pair of Common Black-Hawks has nested in this area for several years. Look especially in the large cottonwoods just west of the RV sites. Great Horned Owls are almost always present; keep an eye overhead for Zone-tailed Hawk. In winter, look for a variety of sparrows, including Swamp and White-throated. There is a small pond located behind the northwest corner of the cottonwood stand. Common Yellowthroat can be found here year-round; the resident subspecies is very bright and slightly larger than the various northern subspecies that winter in or migrate through the park. This is also a good place to look for Black Phoebe, swallows, and waterbirds such as Pied-billed Grebe and herons. Shorebirds (if mudflats are available) and Sora are often present during migration. Least Grebe has been found here on a couple of occasions. A common plant in this and other parts of the park is the Screwbean Mesquite (*Prosopis pubescens*); the tight corkscrew-shaped seed pods are among the most interesting fruit of any local plant.

The road to the left from the store also leads to the river. There is a small pond down a service road on the right just before the entrance to the campground. You may find Ring-necked Duck or Pied-billed Grebe on the pond, and this area can be very productive for passerines year-round. The pond is also the home of the world's native population of *Gambusia gaigei*, a tiny mosquitofish. Verdin, Pyrrhuloxia, and, in summer, Bell's Vireo can be found in the nearby mesquite thickets.

Go back and carefully check the campground. Elf Owls are sometimes found in holes in the utility poles, utilizing cavities made by Ladder-backed Woodpeckers. In general, you should find the same species here as mentioned for the area surrounding the store.

A short nature trail starts opposite campsite #18. From the boardwalk among the tangle of willows and Carrizo Cane, you may find Yellow-billed Cuckoo, Bell's Vireo, Carolina Wren (westernmost breeding area in the state), Painted Bunting, Orchard Oriole, and many migrants in season. The trail ends on a high point above the river. From this vantage point, you can scan the cattail-filled ponds and surroundings. Watch for Belted Kingfisher, Common Yellowthroat, and Yellow-breasted Chat. This is an excellent spot for migrants. Shorebirds sometimes can be found along the shoreline of the river, and, in summer, the air may be filled with Northern Rough-winged, Barn, and Cliff Swallows. Cave Swallows have been seen in this area, but they are fairly rare in the park.

Boquillas Canyon (*bow-KEY-yas*) — This canyon is a spectacular sight, but it is better for photography than for birds. White-throated Swift and Canyon Wren can be found along the cliffs, and Rock Wren and Black-throated Sparrow can usually be seen along the trail to the canyon. On summer nights, Common Poorwills are sometimes seen along the entrance road. Sage Thrashers are sporadic winter visitors in the park, but they can be found in the mesquite flats upcanyon during the fall and early winter.

Hot Springs — The Hot Springs is located toward Panther Junction from Rio Grande Village. A rather rough two-mile road leads to an abandoned village. From there, a one-mile hike is required to reach the springs, but it is one of the more picturesque spots along the river. Say's Phoebes have nested about the ruins of the old motel, and Hooded Orioles nest in the cottonwoods. Bell's Vireos and Verdins frequent the mesquite thickets, and Black-tailed Gnatcatchers can be found in the dry washes.

River Road — This very primitive road crosses the southern end of the park from Rio Grande Village to Castolon. A high-clearance vehicle is required. It takes less time to go by way of Panther Junction on the paved road, so do not take this road if your time is limited, and do not go at any time of year other than winter. It is a long, hot, dry, and rough route, but geologists and botanists will find it fascinating. The display of Big Bend Bluebonnets in February can be breathtaking.

Dugout Wells — There is a still-functioning windmill at this little oasis, which can be good during migration and early in the morning during dry periods. Resident species include Scaled Quail, Greater Roadrunner, Western Screech-Owl (night), Ladder-backed Woodpecker, Northern Mockingbird, and Black-throated Sparrow. Bell's Vireo nests. The surrounding creosote flats are good for Verdin and Black-tailed Gnatcatcher.

Pine Canyon — The turnoff for Pine Canyon is about 2.5 miles south of the main road along the graveled Glenn Spring Road. A primitive road goes up the canyon another 5 miles, but the last several are steep, rocky, and sometimes impassable. The road ends at the old Wade Ranch, from which a short trail leads to a waterfall. During the rainy season, the falls can be very impressive. The upper part of the canyon is well-wooded and full of birds. Among the Arizona Cypress, Arizona and Mexican Pinyon Pines, Douglas-fir, Texas Madrone, Big-toothed Maple, and Emory and Grave's Oaks, look in summer for Broad-tailed and Black-chinned Hummingbirds, Ash-throated Flycatcher, Hutton's Vireo, Mexican Jay, Black-crested Titmouse, Bushtit, Bewick's Wren, Blue-gray Gnatcatcher, Hepatic Tanager, Spotted Towhee, Rufous-crowned Sparrow, and Black-headed Grosbeak. In August and early September, many of the higher-elevation species can be found in the upper reaches of this canyon, including Colima Warbler. In recent years, the canyon has also produced some outstanding rarities, including Northern Pygmy-Owl, Sulphur-bellied Flycatcher, Dusky-capped Flycatcher, Red-faced Warbler, Fan-tailed Warbler, and Flame-colored Tanager (the latter two being first state records).

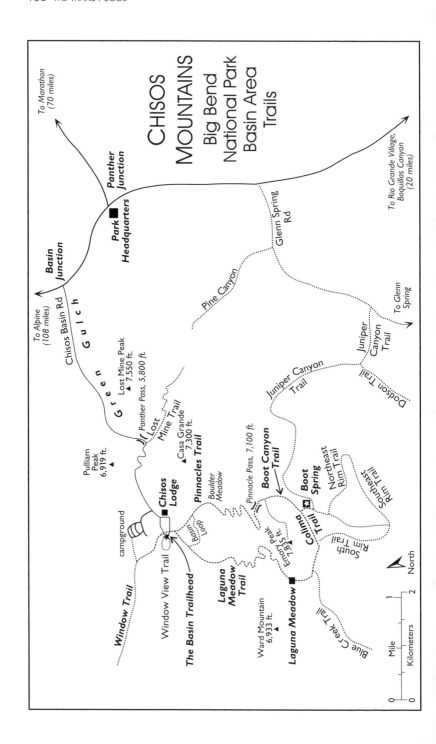

Juniper Canyon — This is a good birding area, but it is difficult to reach. The turnoff is another 4.4 miles down the Glenn Spring Road beyond the Pine Canyon road. From here a very rough and primitive road leads another 7.5 miles into the canyon. A 6.5-mile hiking-trail continues up the canyon to the cabin at Boot Spring. It is a rough hike, but you should see numerous birds.

Green Gulch — (3.3 miles west of US-385). The first 5 miles of the 7-mile road leading into The Basin go through Green Gulch. In the desert scrub at the bottom, you may find Scaled Quail, Greater Roadrunner, Curve-billed Thrasher, Verdin, Black-tailed Gnatcatcher, and Black-throated Sparrow. As the brush gets thicker, look for Ladder-backed Woodpecker, Bell's Vireo, Phainopepla, Pyrrhuloxia, and Varied Bunting. When you see the first Drooping Junipers, start watching for flowering agaves. Their tall, flowering stalks furnish a banquet for White-winged Dove, Lucifer and Black-chinned Hummingbirds, and Scott's Oriole. After the agaves quit blooming in the summer, the hummingbirds move higher up into the mountains as the late summer and fall blooming occurs there. There are pullouts for parking along this road.

Lost Mine Trail — The road up Green Gulch passes through Panther Pass (elevation 5,800 feet) on the way into The Basin. Here you will find the start of the Lost Mine Trail. The view into Juniper Canyon at the end of this 2-mile trail is one of the finest in the park, but most hikers settle for the magnificent view at the end of the first mile. Buy a pamphlet at the trailhead to follow the self-guiding tour; it will give you a better understanding of the area. During late summer and fall, this trail can be excellent for hummingbirds and other fall migrants. The oak woodlands also can produce Hutton's Vireo, Mexican Jay, Bushtit, Summer Tanager, and Black-headed Grosbeak, as well as other mid-elevation montane species.

The Basin — This large bowl-shaped valley sits in the very center of the Chisos Mountains at about 5,400 feet of elevation. The beauty of the surrounding peaks and the relatively cool, highland climate makes this a favorite spot for both birds and people in summer. The Chisos Lodge and a large campground (fee) are located here. Mexican Jays, Cactus Wrens, and Canyon Towhees are often abundant. The area surrounding the hotel and campground is very good for Black-chinned Sparrow and Lesser Goldfinch. Elf Owls and Common Poorwills can be heard on spring and summer nights. The best birding is along the trails that emanate from The Basin Trailhead. There are 32 hiking trails in the park, totaling more than 150 miles. These trails are listed in the hiker's guide, *Hiking Big Bend National Park*, available from the Big Bend Natural History Association and sold at park headquarters and at the ranger station in the Basin. Campers may stay up to 14 consecutive days.

The Window Trail — This 5.2-mile round-trip starts at The Basin Trailhead across the parking lot from the lodge, but it is a mile shorter if you catch it along the southwest edge of the campground. The trail crosses a brushy grassland interspersed with oaks, pinyon, and juniper. In the early morning, you should find Ladder-backed Woodpecker, Say's Phoebe, Canyon, Rock, Bewick's, and Cactus Wrens, Pyrrhuloxia, Canyon Towhee, Black-chinned and Rufous-crowned Sparrows, Blue Grosbeak, and Scott's Oriole. Black-capped and Gray Vireos breed in the scrub habitat below the sewage pond. This is also a good area to look for Lucifer Hummingbird and Varied Bunting. There is even a winter record of Elegant Trogon here.

Boot Spring — From mid-spring to late summer, this is often the most exciting area for birding in the park. The Colima Warbler is the main attraction, but there are other tantalizing possibilities. When you are this close to the border, who knows what may wander up from Mexico? Some of the rarities that have been documented here include Berylline Hummingbird, Elegant Trogon, Greater Pewee, Dusky-capped Flycatcher, Aztec Thrush, Red-faced Warbler, Slate-throated Redstart, Flame-colored Tanager, and Yellow-eyed Junco. Most of these birds have been found only once or twice, but the potential for vagrants from Mexico is readily apparent.

The hike to the spring is strenuous. All of the routes into Boot Canyon require long hikes. The most direct route is up the Pinnacles Trail via Boulder Meadow and Pinnacle Pass (elevation 7,100 feet). It is a steep 3.5-mile climb to the top of the pass, after which the trail descends another mile into Boot Canyon. The alternative, a 10-mile loop-route used by most birders, goes up the Laguna Meadow Trail from The Basin Trailhead, across the Colima Trail, and back down the Boot Canyon Trail and Pinnacles Trail through Boulder Meadow. Following this route, it is 5.5 miles to Boot Spring, but the hiking is much easier than on the Pinnacles Trail. (Also, Colima Warblers can be present all summer at Laguna Meadow. If this is your only target, you may not have to walk the entire loop-route, though the Boot Spring area itself is excellent for many other birds.)

There is no drinking water at Boot Spring. Be sure to take along plenty. This is usually a long, hot trip, but it is sometimes cool, particularly after the rainy season starts.

Mid-April through mid-June is the best time to find the breeding birds of the lower elevations, but some of the highland species do not start to nest until the summer rains begin in early July. By late June, many of the lowland birds have moved into the mountains, and by late August some post-breeders from the Rockies have arrived. As soon as you leave The Basin Trailhead, start watching for Ash-throated Flycatcher, Bewick's Wren, and Rufous-crowned Sparrow. Crissal Thrasher and Black-chinned Sparrow nest on the brushy hillsides at Laguna Meadow (3.5 miles). When the red-flowered Mountain Sage (*Salvia regla*) and the yellow-flowered Century Plant (*Agave* sp.) are in bloom, this meadow is a great spot for Black-chinned Hummingbird and Scott's Oriole. Watch for post-breeding Lucifer (June–September) and Rufous (July–October) Hummingbirds as well.

Above Laguna Meadow you will enter woodlands of deciduous oaks and maples that are preferred by the **Colima Warbler**. In early spring, the new leaves of the oaks stand out in sharp contrast to the surrounding vegetation, making it easy to pick out clumps where the warbler might be found. The birds can sometimes be found at lower elevations when they first arrive, normally between 10–15 April, or just before they leave in mid-September, but the nesting sites are all above 5,900 feet in elevation. (The nests are built on the ground.) The first arriving Colima Warblers in the breeding areas above Laguna Meadow (or above Boulder Meadow along the Pinnacles Trail) often can be found at this same time, but trips timed after 15 April have a higher probability of success. Although this warbler will respond to squeaks and pishes, it can be hard to see. The key to finding the territorial males is being familiar with its trilling song, which is reminiscent of a Pine or an Orange-crowned Warbler or a Chipping Sparrow. Luckily, the males are persistent singers from the time they arrive in April to about mid-June. The females often can be found by their sharp *psit* call-note. Trips in August through mid-September can also produce Colima Warbler sightings. Males will occasionally sing at this time, but the call-note is the normal vocalization. Many pairs still have dependent young well into August and are more vocal as a result. After about 10 September, Colimas become increasingly scarce and can be easily missed.

Colima Warbler   Mark Lockwood

At the start of the South Rim Trail, 0.5 mile above Laguna Meadow, there is a trail junction. The trail to the right continues along the rim and joins the Southeast Rim Trail, which eventually comes back to the Boot Canyon Trail after 3 miles. To the left is the Boot Canyon Trail; this portion of the trail is called the "Colima Trail." It is 1 mile to the cabin at the spring, which is located in about the middle of the canyon. Boot Canyon is well wooded with Arizona Cypress, Arizona Pine, Douglas-fir, Texas Madrone, Big-tooth Maple, and Emory and Grave Oaks, and it offers some of the best birding in the Chisos. Another area that should be carefully birded is the first few hundred yards of the South Rim Trail above Boot Spring. The mixture of maples and oaks makes this another prime birding area.

Colima Warblers are fairly common and can be found throughout this area, including in all of Boot Canyon and along all of the trails emanating from the cabin. Also watch for Band-tailed Pigeon and for Broad-tailed, Blue-throated, and Magnificent (rare) Hummingbirds. During fall migration, dozens of Rufous, Broad-tailed, and Black-chinned Hummingbirds can be seen daily. Keep a careful watch out for more uncommon species, such as Lucifer, Calliope, and Ruby-throated (rare) Hummingbirds. The male Calliopes move through in July, followed by females and immatures during August. It is not unusual to see seven species of hummingbirds during an August hike in the Chisos. Watch for Acorn Woodpecker, Cordilleran Flycatcher, Hutton's Vireo, Violet-green Swallow, Mexican Jay, Black-crested Titmouse, Bushtit, White-breasted Nuthatch, Painted Redstart (some springs and summers), and Hepatic Tanager. Warbler migration, particularly in the fall (mid-August to early September), can be fabulous. Townsend's is normally the most common, with Yellow, Yellow-rumped, Black-and-white, and Wilson's being fairly common. Usually there are also a few Virginia's, Black-throated Gray, and Hermit Warblers to be found. Nashville and MacGillivray's Warblers occasionally are seen as high as Boulder Meadow, but they are usually at lower elevations. Red-faced Warbler has been documented almost annually in the Chisos since the early 1990s. Most records are from August, and in most years only one bird has been found. Slate-throated Redstart has been seen here in late April or early May on three occasions. Another rarity that has been seen on a number of occasions in recent years is Dusky-capped Flycatcher, which has been present during the summer almost annually since 2001. If you camp here overnight, you should hear Western Screech-Owl, Flammulated Owl (late May and June), and Whip-poor-will (April–August).

About a half-mile below the cabin on your way back to The Basin, you will find the Boot, a volcanic spire shaped like an upside-down cowboy boot. In the same area, you will find the Emory Peak Trail, which goes one mile to the top of the highest peak (elevation 7,835 feet) in the park. There are not many birds on the mountain, but the view is terrific.

A half-mile below the Emory Peak Trail is Pinnacle Pass (elevation 7,100 feet), from which you can get a fine view of the Basin far below. From this high

"The Boot," Boot Canyon, Big Bend National Park   Mark Lockwood

vantage point, you can see Turkey Vultures, Red-tailed Hawks, White-throated Swifts, and an occasional Golden Eagle. This is also a great place to watch for Zone-tailed Hawk.

A 1.5-mile series of steep switchbacks will bring you to the floor of the Basin at Boulder Meadow only 1.5 miles from the lodge. Colima Warblers can be found along the upper half of this stretch. You may be too tired after the long walk to Boot Spring to bird this area, but if you take time to come back another day, you will find it a good spot. Lucifer Hummingbirds can be found in summer about the blooming agaves.

Government Spring — This spring is on the left side of the road to the Grapevine Hills (0.3 mile west of Basin Junction) about a half-mile north of the main road from Panther Junction to Maverick. When the springs are flowing, birds come here to drink. Look for Scaled Quail, Canyon Towhee, Black-throated Sparrow, Pyrrhuloxia, Varied Bunting, and migrants. Many wintering sparrows feed at the horse corral. Early in the morning or just at dusk, you can see Mule Deer, Collared Peccary, Coyote, and Desert Cottontail coming to the spring, and you might see a Gray Fox, a Bobcat, or even a Mountain Lion. Be on the lookout for rattlesnakes in the summer.

The remainder of the road to the Grapevine Hills is scenic, but it is usually not as productive as other areas in the park. There is good habitat for Lucifer Hummingbirds along the arroyos found throughout this grassland. The same may be said of the Paint Gap Road. Croton Spring can be good for mammals, but the spring is not so productive since it was "improved" a few years ago.

Sam Nail Ranch — The parking area for the ranch is 3.0 miles south of Santa Elena Junction. Most of the buildings are gone and the windmill no longer functions. The birds are concentrated in a very small area. Look for Yellow-breasted Chat, Summer Tanager, Black-throated Sparrow, Northern Cardinal, Pyrrhuloxia, Blue Grosbeak, and Scott's Oriole. Crissal Thrashers and Varied Buntings are fairly common here. By spending an hour or two in this peaceful spot (a bench in the shade is provided for your comfort), you also may see Yellow-billed Cuckoo, Lucifer and Black-chinned Hummingbirds, Bell's Vireo, and Painted Bunting. This area has the potential to be a good migrant trap. Orange-crowned, Nashville, Virginia's, Yellow, and Wilson's Warblers are found frequently during migration. There are also records of vagrant Blackburnian and Prairie Warblers. Other rarities such as Clay-colored Thrush and Long-billed Thrasher have been seen as well.

Cattail Falls — Cattail Creek starts on the north side of Ward Mountain and flows westward. During periods of heavy rain, it actually crosses the highway just north of the Sam Nail Ranch. To reach the falls, go east on Oak Canyon Road, which starts almost opposite the Sam Nail Ranch parking area. This dirt road soon bears left and crosses the dry bed of Cattail Creek. Park and walk up the creekbed. Most of the same birds mentioned for Sam Nail Ranch can be found here.

Blue Creek Canyon — On the left near the highest point on the Santa Elena Road, you will come to the Blue Creek Overlook, from which a trail drops into the canyon and goes 5.5 miles up (left) to Laguna Meadow. About a mile above the old Wilson Ranch and near a spectacular formation of red rock spires, a narrow canyon branches off to the north (right). A rare red oak (*Quercus graciliformis*) occurs far up the canyon. The canyon is particularly good for Lucifer Hummingbird, Gray Vireo, Canyon Wren, Crissal Thrasher, and Varied Bunting in April and May. Black-capped Vireo can be found here .

Sotol Vista — The view from this vista is terrific. The Sotol-dominated grassland surrounding the parking area is usually not very productive for birds, but wintering grassland sparrows can sometimes be found.

Burro Spring — This is one of the better springs in the desert areas of the park, and it attracts many animals. The 1-mile trail starts from the road that leads to the Burro Mesa Pour-off. There is another trail that goes to the pour-off, but the spring is the best birding area. The spring attracts the usual mammals, such as Mule Deer, Collared Peccary, and Coyote, but you may also see a Burro. Most of the Burros have wandered up from Mexico. They have adapted well to the hostile environment. The tourists may consider these hardy animals to be cute, but they can be very detrimental to the fragile habitat and to the native mammals.

Castolon (25.0 miles from Santa Elena Junction) — The weedy fields near Castolon are at their best in early winter when you can find great flocks of sparrows. The common species are Vesper, Brewer's, and White-crowned. With a little more effort, you may find Cassin's, Chipping, Clay-colored, Field, Savannah, Grasshopper, Lincoln's, Swamp, Song, and White-throated.

Cottonwood Campground (fee, primitive) is currently an excellent birding location, but this area is slowly undergoing change. The cottonwoods require regular watering and care by the park service personnel. As these cottonwoods die, they will be replaced with lower-maintenance, desert-adapted species. Greater Roadrunners are very tame here and White-winged Doves are abundant. Migrant warblers such as Yellow-rumped ("Audubon's") are common in spring. Other nesting species include Gray Hawk, Inca and Mourning Doves, Western Screech-Owl (common), Great Horned Owl, Common Poorwill, Ash-throated Flycatcher, Western Kingbird, Black-tailed Gnatcatcher, Summer Tanager, and Orchard and Hooded Orioles. Black Vultures can be seen in this section of the park. Thick-billed Kingbirds nested here from 1988 to 1991 and Tropical Kingbirds have nested here since 1996. Incredibly, in the summer of 2007 a pair of Couch's was present as well. This is one of the best places in Texas to see Lucy's Warbler; they are found in the mesquite woodlands surrounding the campground, and typically arrive in early March and remain through June.

The mesquite thickets and willows along the river may yield Ladder-backed Woodpecker, Vermilion Flycatcher, and Canyon Towhee. Other birds to be found in summer are Yellow-billed Cuckoo, Black-chinned Hummingbird, Bell's Vireo, Yellow-breasted Chat, Summer Tanager, Blue Grosbeak, Painted Bunting, and Orchard Oriole. Lucy's Warbler is also found in the mesquite thickets between Castolon and Santa Elena Canyon.

Between Castolon and Cottonwood Campground, a road to the left leads to the river-crossing for Santa Elena, Mexico. This maintained dirt road offers excellent birding. There are stands of cottonwoods along arroyos in several spots. All of the species listed for the campground can be found here. Gray Hawks have nested in the cottonwood stands.

Santa Elena Canyon (8.0 miles) — You might want to visit this very scenic spot, even though it is not particularly good for birds. You likely will be impressed, however, by the Peregrine Falcons and the White-throated Swifts that zoom up and down the canyon, and by the beautiful songs of Canyon Wrens that echo down from the cliffs. The 1.7-mile round-trip trail into the canyon has markers identifying the plants and other features. Be on the alert for rarities; on at least two occasions, Rufous-capped Warbler has made an appearance.

Old Maverick Road — This 14-mile gravel road leading from Santa Elena Canyon to Maverick (at the west entrance to the park) can be good for hawks at all seasons and nightjars on summer evenings. It also makes an interesting alternative to retracing your way back up the main road. At the turn of the century, this was prime grassland with cottonwood-lined streams. By the end of World War I, overgrazing and drought had reduced it to its present state.

Texas Highway 118 to Alpine — Of all the routes into the park, this one offers the best opportunities for birding. In winter, the grasslands along the way abound with sparrows and Lark Buntings. About midway, there is a wooded rest area that should be checked for migrants. Golden-fronted Woodpecker is resident. North of that, you will find Calamity Creek, which sometimes attracts a few birds. As the road climbs toward Alpine, it enters an open oak/juniper woodland. This is an excellent area in some winters for Townsend's Solitaires and Western and Mountain Bluebirds. The abundance of these species varies greatly from year to year.

The Lajitas–Big Bend Ranch State Park–Presidio Route — The route from the park to Marfa via TX-170 and TX-67 is longer and rougher, but offers a scenic trip along the river. The headquarters for the Big Bend Ranch State Park (16.0 miles) is on the south side of the road. Stop here at the Warnock Center for information on this new state park.

In the center of Lajitas (1.2 miles), turn south (toward the river) where there are signs advertising the trading post, golf course, and RV campground. Down this dirt road there are four ponds, two on each side of the road (0.1 mile). The two closest to the road are the least productive. The other two have vegetation all around them and are difficult to see; however, they are worth a check. A Ruddy Ground-Dove spent a month here in 1990. Resident species include "Mexican Duck," Inca and White-winged Doves, Lucifer Hummingbird (summer, rare), and Black-throated Sparrow. In winter, also look for Green Heron, Swamp Sparrow, and Lesser Goldfinch. Migrants include various western warblers, Grasshopper Sparrow, and Lazuli Bunting. Several unusual sightings include Swallow-tailed Kite and Common Grackle.

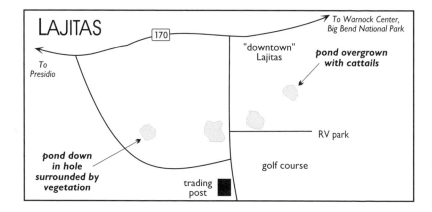

LAJITAS

To Warnock Center,
Big Bend National Park

170

To
Presidio

"downtown"
Lajitas

pond overgrown
with cattails

RV park

pond down
in hole
surrounded by
vegetation

golf course

trading
post

BIG BEND RANCH STATE PARK

Big **Bend Ranch State Park** (fee $3 per person) is the largest state park in Texas, and one of the largest in the U.S. Approximately 280,000 acres in size, it is more than 45 miles from its southeast corner to the northwest corner. The park can be divided up into several fairly distinct units, including the Barton Warnock Environmental Education Center near Lajitas, the river corridor (the area along TX-170 between Presidio and Lajitas), Fort Leaton State Historic Site near Presidio, and Sauceda in the interior of the park in an area accessible to the public (the Bofecillos Mountains/Plateau). Much of this vast park lacks the roads and other infrastructure to allow public access at this time. (See map on next page.)

Birds of the area are typical of those found in the general region and the northern portions of the Chihuahuan Desert. Habitats range from riparian woodlands and thickets to canyons, desert scrub, and desert grasslands. Elevations range from approximately 2,200 feet near Lajitas to 5,135 feet at the top of Oso Mountain. The river corridor is open to the general public, but permits are required to travel off the highway right-of-way. To access Sauceda in the interior, you must get a permit and gate combination from either Fort Leaton near the west entrance to the park or The Warnock Center at Lajitas near the east entrance. Day trips are permitted in the interior; overnight accommodations include primitive camping at one of ten designated areas, bunkhouse-style lodging, and lodging in the main ranch house. Shower facilities are available for campers at the Sauceda Ranger Station.

Conditions in the park may be extremely harsh at times. Temperatures over 100°F can occur during many months of the year. Most plants are armed with thorns, several species of animals can inflict painful bites/stings, and several species of snakes are venomous. Backcountry areas of the park are vast and remote, and getting lost would be a potential risk to one's life. If you are going to bird remote portions of the park, always consult the park staff in advance and advise them of your plans. At the Warnock Education Center near Lajitas, you can walk through a desert garden to become familiar with many of the desert plants. The garden has a pond and feeders that attract a variety of desert birds, as well as migrants.

Several areas along the river are good locations to begin your birding adventure at Big Bend Ranch State Park. Going west from Lajitas approximately 8 miles, you come to an area called **Grassy Banks**. Bird along the dirt roads and the river in mesquite and salt-cedar habitat. You can usually find Ladder-backed Woodpecker, Black and Say's Phoebe, Vermilion Flycatcher, Verdin, Black-tailed Gnatcatcher, Crissal Thrasher, and Pyrrhuloxia. This area can be very productive during spring and fall migrations. During winter, subsequent to a wet summer/fall season, the area can be especially good. Typical winter birds include White-throated Swift, Northern Rough-winged Swallow,

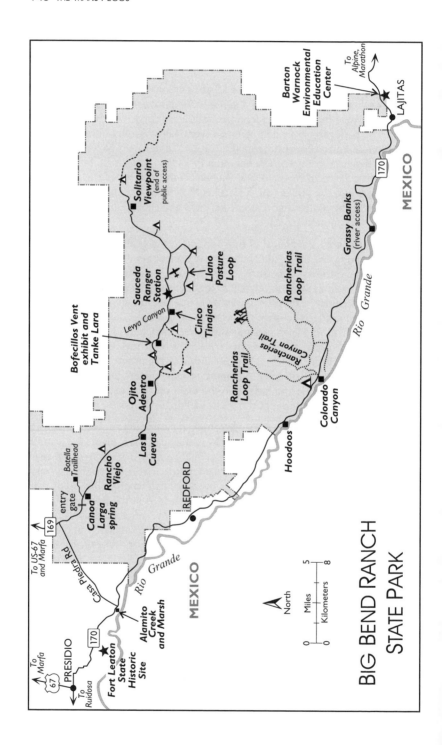

BIG BEND RANCH
STATE PARK

Ruby-crowned Kinglet, Blue-gray Gnatcatcher, Hermit Thrush, American Pipit, Orange-crowned and Yellow-rumped Warblers, Spotted and Green-tailed Towhees, Chipping, Brewer's, Savannah, Lincoln's, and White-crowned Sparrows, Dark-eyed Junco, and Lesser Goldfinch. Dusky, Gray, and Ash-throated Flycatchers, Townsend's Warbler, Blue Grosbeak, Varied Bunting, and Scott's Oriole have been observed in winter.

There are numerous other sites along the river road that provide birding opportunities in similar habitats and settings. Two major trails lead off the highway; one is the 18-mile Rancherias Loop and the other is the Rancherias Canyon trail, which is available for day hikes. Because summer seasons are excessively hot, the best time to visit the area is from October through April. On the steep bluffs of Colorado Canyon (and at one additional site upstream), look for Peregrine Falcon. Summer birds expected along this corridor are typical of those occupying riparian habitat zones throughout the region and include Turkey Vulture, White-winged Dove, Lesser Nighthawk, Black-chinned Hummingbird, Ash-throated Flycatcher, Western Kingbird, Bell's Vireo, Cliff Swallow, Yellow-breasted Chat, Summer Tanager, Blue Grosbeak, Varied and Painted Buntings, Orchard, Hooded, Bullock's, and Scott's Orioles, Bronzed Cowbird, and Lesser Goldfinch.

Fort Leaton State Historic Site, located 3 miles south of Presidio on FM-170, serves as the western visitor-services station for the park. The cottonwood trees and thorn-scrub/mesquite woodland located behind Fort Leaton are excellent to bird, especially during spring and fall migrations. To access the interior of the park (after obtaining proper permits), proceed south on FM-170 for 5 miles and take a left onto Casa Piedra Road. Although not within the park, this stretch of the highway includes a couple of birding stops, among them Alamito Marsh just west of and including the Alamito Creek bridge. The marsh can be good for Green Heron, various rails, Marsh Wren, and Swamp Sparrow.

Casa Piedra Road is a county-maintained dirt road that leads northeast away from the river and highway. From the highway, it is approximately 26.5 miles to the Sauceda Ranger Station. Approximately 6.5 miles down Casa Piedra Road, take the right fork and proceed 2.5 miles to the locked gate entrance to the park. A short distance into the park (just past the Botella turnoff where wayside exhibit #1 is located), you come to **Canoa Larga**. In the thickets on the right of the road is a spring that flows into a water trough. The combination of thick cover and water attracts a variety of typical low-desert birds and migrants; Gray Vireo has wintered at this location.

Wayside #2 near **Rancho Vieja** is 15 miles from the highway and is another opportunity to check out typical desert birds. Another 2.5 miles beyond is the Las Cuevas wayside exhibit (#3). The yellow bluffs of volcanic tuff located there offer a great photographic opportunity. The road then crosses

Common Nighthawk

Louise Zemaitis

woodland thickets along Bofecillos Creek, but you must confine your birding to the main road unless participating on a guided tour.

Two and one-half miles ahead (18.5 miles from the highway) is one of your best birding opportunities in the interior. Stop at the **Ojito Adentro** wayside (#4) and take the short trail (less than one-half mile) down to the beautiful woodland tucked into the head of the canyon. This area of cotton-woods, willows, and hackberry is typical of many such sites in the park where permanent surface-water exists. A 30-foot-high waterfall is located at the end of the trail at the head of the canyon. Find a spot where birds are coming to drink at the stream, sit quietly in the shade, and observe. This site can be particularly productive during migration and some winters. Anna's and Rufous Hummingbirds, Dusky Flycatcher, and Varied Bunting have been observed here in winter. Numerous species of flycatchers, vireos, warblers (including Painted Redstart), tanagers, and orioles occur during migration. Just over a mile ahead at the top of the steep hill is Cuesta Prima, which provides a scenic overlook of Bofecillos Canyon and, in the distance, Presidio and the Rio Grande.

Just past wayside exhibit #6 (Bofecillos Vent), approximately 25 miles from the highway, is **Tanke Lara**. The earthen tank can be productive when water is present. During winter, a number of waterfowl species utilize the pond. Look for shorebirds during migration. In summer, there is an evening flight of Common and Lesser Nighthawks, and the number of bat species can be spectacular. Almost 4 miles ahead is wayside exhibit #7 (Cinco Tinajas, "Five Waterholes"). Leyva Canyon cuts a narrow slot through the volcanic mountains, creating secluded pools of semi-permanent and permanent water. Black Phoebes are active at the pools; Canyon and Rock Wrens can be heard singing from the bluffs.

The **Sauceda Ranger Station** is only 1 mile ahead. At times, excellent birding opportunities exist around the buildings and along Levya Creek just west of the complex. In this typical desert habitat, summer birds include Elf Owl, Common Nighthawk, Common Poorwill, Golden-fronted Wood-pecker, Cliff, Cave, and Barn Swallows, Vermilion and Ash-throated Fly-catchers, Say's Phoebe, Cassin's Kingbird, Loggerhead Shrike, Cactus and Bewick's Wrens, Verdin, Curve-billed Thrasher, House Finch, and Lesser Goldfinch. During migration, Yellow-headed, Red-winged, and Brewer's Blackbirds, Brown-headed and Bronzed Cowbirds, and an occasional Great-tailed Grackle may be found in the corrals. Look for numbers of sparrows in winter.

From Sauceda, you can take a loop drive through the **Llano Pasture** (8.5 miles round trip). Go east past the airport and turn to the south 3 miles from Sauceda; the road will turn back to the west and then north, returning to the complex. Desert grassland habitats are found all along this route and can be very productive, especially after wet late summer/fall rainy periods. A high-clearance vehicle is recommended. Look for excellent sparrow diversity in winter: Black-throated Sparrow is a common resident, Sage Sparrow is usu-ally uncommon in winter, and Cassin's Sparrow can be abundant in spring and summer. These grassland flats also have harbored Gambel's Quail, Prairie Fal-con, Green-tailed Towhee (winter), and Chestnut-collared and McCown's Longspurs (winter). If you locate a desert waterhole (look behind the numer-ous erosion-control berms in the drainages), find a shady spot to sit and watch. You will be rewarded with good looks at almost every species of bird in the vicinity and perhaps other species of wildlife.

On the main road 9 miles east of Sauceda, the public access ends at the Fresno Canyon/Solitario overlook (wayside exhibit #10). Here you get a spec-tacular vista of Fresno Canyon and The Solitario (a volcanic collapsed dome 8–10 miles in diameter). Enjoy the view and the solitude; you are 35 miles from the highway via the route you followed.

PRESIDIO TO MARFA

Back along FM-170, continue toward Presidio; agricultural activities begin to increase as the floodplain of the Rio Grande widens near Redford (34 miles. In summer, there are Yellow-breasted Chats, Northern Cardinals, and

Painted and Varied Buntings. After the Alamito Creek crossing (9.0 miles), a small marshy area between the road and the Rio Grande can be loaded with migrant waterfowl and shorebirds. Most of the shorebirds are Least Sandpipers, but Westerns are also common and there may be a few Baird's.

Presidio (3.5 miles) is said to be the oldest settlement in the United States. The Indians inhabited this region long before Spaniards arrived in the 16th century. North of Presidio on US-67, you will find the ghost town of Shafter (19 miles), where some $18,000,000 worth of silver was mined. At Presidio you have a choice. You can turn north to Marfa on US-67 or continue northwest on River Road 170 to Ruidosa (36 miles). The road to Ruidosa is narrow and undulating. Drive carefully because loose cattle and other livestock are common. Along the way watch for Turkey Vulture, Greater Roadrunner, White-winged and Mourning Doves, Verdin, Cactus Wren, and Crissal Thrasher. Black Vultures are rather common. Harris's Hawk is resident in this area and you may begin to see Gambel's Quail.

The best birding is beyond Ruidosa along the road to **Candelaria** (12.0 miles; see map on page 122). Along this stretch, watch the skies carefully. Common Black-Hawk, Zone-tailed Hawk, and Peregrine and Prairie Falcons have all nested in this area. Golden Eagles are fairly common, especially in migration. Near Candelaria, an oxbow of the river can be alive with spring migrant waterfowl and shorebirds. In the sandy draws and in the trees, look for migrant warblers and Lazuli Bunting. In summer, such species as Ladder-backed Woodpecker, Bell's Vireo, Common Yellowthroat, Yellow-breasted Chat, Summer Tanager, Varied Bunting, and Hooded and Scott's Orioles may be present. From mid-March to early June, listen for the high-pitched trill of singing Lucy's Warbler; the area around Candelaria is one of the few reliable places in Texas where this species nests. In winter, numerous species of sparrows are found.

This road ends at Candelaria, so return to Ruidosa, and if you are really adventurous, take Ranch Road 2810 to the left over the Chinati Mountains (not recommended for low-clearance vehicles) to Marfa (52 miles). This road is dirt and narrow, but very scenic. (There are no bridges on 2810; if it is raining or has recently rained, be very careful at low-water crossings, which may be impassable.) After going over the pass (20 miles), the road is paved for the last 32 miles. (Alternately, you can go all the way back to Presidio before turning north onto US-67 to Marfa.) Western Scrub-Jays and Phainopeplas are rather common around cottonwoods and junipers. All land off the road is private; do not trespass.

If traveling north on US-67 to Marfa (40 miles), at one mile south of town and on the east side of the road you will find an area flooded with water from the sewage-treatment plant. In winter, you should see Snow Goose, "Mexican Duck", and other dabbling ducks, and Yellow-headed Blackbird; in migration, check for White-faced Ibis and shorebirds. There are usually Pronghorns present.

Upon reaching Marfa, there are several choices of routes: TX-17 north to the Davis Mountains and US-90/67 east to Alpine or northwest toward Valentine and Van Horn.

US-90, MARFA TO VALENTINE

A vast grassland extends from Marfa northward along US-90 (see map on page 122). This is an excellent area to look for raptors during the winter. Red-tailed and Ferruginous Hawks, American Kestrel, Merlin (scarce), and Prairie Falcon can be found. This is one of the areas where efforts to reintroduce the Aplomado Falcon in West Texas are taking place. The Peregrine Fund first released birds in this area in 2001, and now the species can be seen along this stretch of road and along the western half of FM-505. The western 3 miles of FM-505 from its intersection with US-90 (6.7 miles south of Valentine) pass through excellent grassland habitat and normally have very little traffic. Both of these roads offer the opportunity to study a wide variety of sparrows; Chestnut-collared and McCown's Longspurs can be numerous in winter as well. In recent years, Baird's Sparrow has been found here in late fall and early winter. Pronghorns are commonly seen along this route. FM-505 connects US-90 with the scenic loop around the Davis Mountains.

Ranch Road 2810 Southwest of Marfa: Ranch Road 2810 (see map on page 122) offers an excellent opportunity to study the grassland birds of the Marfa Plateau. This road is paved for 33 miles before becoming gravel and continuing through Pinto Canyon to Ruidosa and TX-170. The paved portion is on the Marfa Plateau and can be productive at any time of the year, but it probably has the most to offer in fall and early winter. Here can be found Scaled Quail, Long-billed Curlew, Horned Lark, Canyon Towhee, Cassin's, Brewer's, Vesper, Black-throated, Savannah, Grasshopper, and Baird's (rare) Sparrows, Chestnut-collared Longspur, and Eastern and Western Meadowlarks. The resident Eastern Meadowlarks are of the pale *lileanae* subspecies. This is another area that is excellent for wintering raptors such as Northern Harrier, Red-tailed and Ferruginous Hawks, Golden Eagle, Prairie Falcon, and the occasional Merlin. The reintroduced Aplomado Falcons are also seen along this road occasionally. During the summer, Swainson's Hawk, Scaled Quail, Horned Lark, Canyon Towhee, Cassin's and Black-throated Sparrows, and Eastern Meadowlark are present.

US-90, MARFA TO ALPINE

The grasslands along US-90 between Marfa and Alpine are good for Eastern and Western (winter only) Meadowlarks, an occasional Prairie Falcon or Golden Eagle, and, in winter, flocks of sparrows and McCown's and Chestnut-collared Longspurs. Occasionally, Swainson's Hawks nest on power poles along the way.

During World War II, the now-overgrown airport at Marfa was a busy military base. Some adventuresome airmen spent their spare time looking for what are now known as the Marfa Lights. On most nights, there are definitely unexplained lights on the horizon. The lights appear to be in the foothills of Chinati Peak some 20 miles away in a southwesterly direction. They look like a lantern or bonfire that brightens, flickers, fades, and brightens again, and even seem to move around. Some people think that they are the lights of a distant car, but there are no roads in that area. A hundred years ago, when the lights were first observed, there were no cars. Several explanations for the

Common Black-Hawk   Barry Zimmer

lights have been offered, but none verified. Unromantic and scientific types explain them away as a phosphate deposit that glows on dark nights after a rain, but they can be seen on moonlit nights in dry weather. Local legends say that they are the ghost of Alsate, an ancient Indian chief, looking for his lost wives. Next to the former entrance to the base, the State Highway Department has opened a sizable picnic area as the official Marfa Lights viewing position.

Alpine: You may think of Alpine (population 5,700, elevation 4,484 feet) as a small town, but it is the largest enclave in the largest county (5,935 square miles) in Texas. To most travelers, Alpine is only a rest stop, and it has been one for centuries because several old Indian trails passed this way. Cabeza de Vaca, the first European to cross Texas, camped about a mile north of the present town in 1532.

Going north from Alpine on TX-118 on the way to Fort Davis, you will find a large pond (16 miles) next to the road. View it from the stone wall and do not cross the fence. In winter, there will be various ducks, including Cinnamon Teal, "Mexican Duck," Northern Shoveler, Gadwall, Ring-necked Duck, Bufflehead, and others. Look also for Eastern Phoebes and Eastern Bluebirds. In summer, look for Black Phoebe, Vermilion and Ash-throated Flycatchers, Phainopepla, Summer Tanager, and Black-headed and Blue Grosbeaks. In migration, check for Osprey, *Empidonax* flycatchers, five species of swallows, House Wren, Western Tanager, Indigo Bunting, and warblers such as Yellow, Yellow-rumped, MacGillivray's, Wilson's, and Common Yellowthroat.

A picnic-area rest stop is just 1.5 miles up the road. A traveler can overnight here. Early in the morning or late in the evening, Wild Turkey, Mule Deer, and Collared Peccary (Javelina) can be seen in the large pasture along the right side of the highway. The turkeys can be seen strutting in this pasture during April.

DAVIS MOUNTAINS

Open grasslands surround the **Davis Mountains**. This range is much larger than the Chisos or Chinati Mountains and has a higher average rainfall. The foothills are rounded and well-vegetated in oak/juniper, not rugged and bare like those of the Chisos. Palisade rock formations are very evident around Fort Davis and in many of the surrounding canyons.

Mount Livermore (elevation 8,382 feet) is the highest peak, and the second-highest in Texas. In fact, there is not a higher mountain east of this point until one reaches the Alps in Europe. The upper elevations of the peak are privately owned and closed to public access. This is regrettable, because the forests of Gambel Oak, Ponderosa and Limber Pines, and aspen on top are a relic of another era when the climate was wetter and the flora of the Rocky Moun-

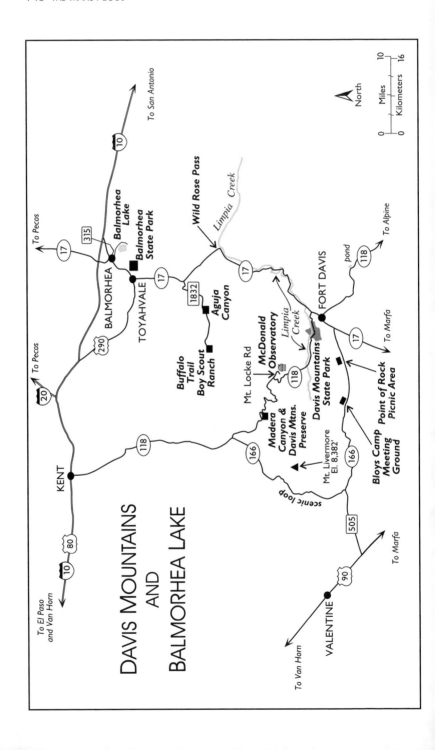

tains extended farther south. The rich birding areas around the lower parts of the mountain are accessible from the 74-mile scenic loop that encircles the peak. The starting point for this trip is 24 miles north of Alpine at Fort Davis, which has stores, motels, cafes, and service stations. This little town has only 900 people, but it is the largest in Jeff Davis County. The other town, Valentine, has a population of only 330. The entire county has a population of about one person for each of its 2,363 square miles. Cattle, sheep, deer, and Pronghorns far outnumber humans.

This area is off the beaten path today, but during the last half of the 19th century it was not. After the discovery of gold in California, thousands of people migrated west via the San Antonio/El Paso Trail, which passed this way, to take advantage of the abundance of grass and water. The wagon trains and cattle of the migrants were prime targets for the raiding Mescalero Apaches and Comanches. To provide protection, the United States Army in 1854 established Fort Davis, named after Jefferson Davis, then Secretary of War. The fort was used off and on until 1891. In 1963, it was made a National Historic Site. The site is open from 8:00AM to 5:00PM all year, except Christmas and New Year's Day. It encompasses 460 acres, has several miles of hiking trails, and a shaded picnic area.

Check the area by the gate or along the Tall Grass Nature Trail for Eastern and Western Meadowlarks (Western in winter only), Horned Lark, and Cassin's Sparrow. Look for Rock and Canyon Wrens, Canyon Towhee, and Rufous-crowned Sparrow by the rocky cliffs. In summer, Cassin's Kingbirds and Orchard Orioles nest in the trees along the highway.

There are three distinct birding areas in the Davis Mountains: the Scenic Loop around the mountains, Limpia Creek, and Aguja Canyon. Although many birds are common to all three areas, each has a few species that are not seen elsewhere in the mountains. Some 235 species of birds have been recorded in Jeff Davis County, and the Davis Mountains Christmas Bird Count averages over 100 species. All of these birds are seen from the roadsides, because West Texas birders make it a rule never to trespass on private property. Visitors should behave accordingly.

THE SCENIC LOOP

To follow this 74-mile loop, go north from Fort Davis on TX-17. Travel in a counterclockwise direction, turning left at both TX-118 (1.0 mile) and TX-166 (29 miles), then returning to Fort Davis. The first few miles of TX-118 follow Limpia Creek, which will be discussed later.

After leaving Limpia Creek behind, TX-118 traverses grassy hillsides with scattered clumps of Gray and Emory Oaks, Pinyon Pine, and Alligator and One-seeded Junipers. Especially note the Alligator Juniper with its conspicuous squarish bark-scales, which resemble the hide of an alligator. During June, another feature of this part of the loop is the 12-foot stalk of the yellow-blossomed Century Plants. When these are in bloom, watch for Black-chinned Hummingbirds and Scott's Orioles around the flowers. Another favorite of the hummingbirds is the Scarlet Bouvardia, which blooms most of the summer. It is an attractive shrub with neat foliage and clusters of bright red, honeysuckle-like flowers.

Davis Mountains State Park (1,869 acres; entrance fee $6 per person) is about 3 miles up TX-118 and located in the foothills between the grassland and the mountains. It has an excellent campground (fee). The Indian Lodge (Box 786, Fort Davis, TX 79734; phone 915-426-3254) has good food, comfortable rooms, a heated pool, and is a great spot to spend a few days; advance reservations are highly recommended. An elevation of 4,900 to 5,500 feet provides cool winters and mild summers, with an average annual rainfall of 19 inches. A 4.5-mile hiking trail connects the park with Fort Davis. A seasonal checklist of Jeff Davis County birds can be purchased at the park.

Campers are usually awakened by the noisy Cassin's Kingbirds and Western Scrub-Jays. Other birds to look for here and along the highway are White-winged Dove, Ladder-backed and Acorn Woodpeckers, Say's Phoebe, Black-crested Titmouse, Bushtit, Rock and Bewick's Wrens, Western Bluebird, Phainopepla, Chipping Sparrow, and House Finch. In summer, look for Common Poorwill, White-throated Swift, Western and Summer Tanagers, Canyon Towhee, Cassin's and Lark Sparrows, Pyrrhuloxia, Black-headed Grosbeak, and Orchard Oriole. In winter, you should be able to find Red-naped Sapsucker, Spotted and Green-tailed Towhees, and Dark-eyed Junco. There is one record of Williamson's Sapsucker in the park; the species is annual, however, at the upper elevations in the mountains.

The park is one of the best locations for seeing Montezuma Quail. They can be found anywhere and may take some patience to find. The park host in the campground operates a feeding station. Early in the morning and in the late afternoon, the quail sometimes visit the feeding station for seed and water. Check with park staff to see if the birds are currently visiting the feeding station. Watch for quail in and along the dry wash that runs through the middle of the campground, as well as along the road to Indian Lodge and in the canyon behind the lodge. They often sit motionless when cars drive near them along the highway; sharp-eyed birders may find them by driving slowly and watching closely. The best location is along TX-118 on either side of the Mount Locke Road during the two hours before dark. The quail seem to be most numerous during the year following a wet year.

Those interested in astronomy should take the trip up the steepest and highest road in the state of Texas, to the McDonald Observatory atop Mount Locke (elevation 6,802 feet). The facility is operated by the University of Texas. Tours are given each afternoon year-round (also in the mornings in summer), and the view from the top is excellent. In the residential area at the base of the mountain, you may find Montezuma Quail.

Canyon Wren   Mark Lockwood

Beyond the Mount Locke Road, the highway soon passes the mile-high marker and stays above that elevation for several miles. This higher country is more forested, and the birdlife changes. The best birding spot is the **Lawrence E. Wood Picnic Grounds** in Madera Canyon. Bushtits, White-breasted Nuthatches, and Western Bluebirds are found in the picnic area. Acorn Woodpeckers nest in the dead pines across the creek. Violet-green Swallows nest in the old woodpecker holes. Hepatic Tanagers and Black-headed Grosbeaks do so in the Ponderosa Pines. On June nights, Western Screech-Owls and Common Poorwills can be heard. Mountain Chickadees and Steller's Jays sometimes wander down from their homes on the slopes of Mount Livermore after the nesting season or during winter, when you can also find Townsend's Solitaire, Mountain Bluebird, and Dark-eyed Junco. In migration, Townsend's, Yellow-rumped, and Wilson's Warblers occur. If Pinyon Jays are in the neighborhood (rare), they will make themselves known by their raucous cries. Also watch in winter for Red-naped and Williamson's Sapsuckers; there is even a record of Red-breasted Sapsucker from this park. Look for Band-tailed Pigeons throughout the high country and for Golden Eagle overhead. The Nature Conservancy of Texas has acquired the land surrounding the picnic area and has constructed a 2.4-mile trail that allows wider birding opportunities. The trail passes primarily through more pinyon/juniper habitats, but it includes more grassy habitats as well. The birds to be expected along this trail are basically the same as those found in the picnic area, but there is a much higher probability of encountering Montezuma Quail and

Gray Flycatcher. There is a small pond along the trail where "Mexican Ducks" can be found at any time of the year.

The Nature Conservancy operates the **Davis Mountains Preserve** (32,000 acres), which includes much of Madera Canyon from Mount Livermore to well downstream of the Lawrence E. Wood picnic area. This fantastic area is open to the public at regular intervals during open weekends, open hiking days, and other scheduled events. These dates can be obtained from The Nature Conservancy office in Alpine (P.O. Box 2137, Alpine, TX 79831; phone 432-837-5954). Birding opportunities in the Davis Mountains Preserve center on **Madera Canyon**. The lower portion of the canyon is very similar to that of the Lawrence E. Wood Picnic Area; however, about 2.5 miles up the canyon there is a change of habitat, and stands of Ponderosa Pines become common. At this point, several species of birds become more numerous, including (in spring and summer) Montezuma Quail (uncommon), Zone-tailed Hawk, Band-tailed Pigeon, White-winged Dove, White-throated Swift, Broad-tailed Hummingbird, Acorn Woodpecker, Northern (Red-shafted) Flicker, Western Wood-Pewee, Gray Flycatcher, Hutton's, Plumbeous, and Warbling Vireos, Steller's Jay, Mountain Chickadee, White-breasted Nuthatch, Grace's Warbler, Hepatic and Western Tanagers, Black-headed Grosbeak, and Red Crossbill (rare). Since 1999, a very small population of Buff-breasted Flycatchers has been present in Madera Canyon. During winter, Williamson's (rare) and Red-naped Sapsuckers may be found.

The high elevations in the Davis Mountains Preserve offer different birding opportunities. The hike from the parking area at the Cat Tank turnoff to Mount Livermore is approximately 4 miles and includes some very steep sections of trail, particularly along the upper portions. This highest section passes through Southwestern White Pine woodlands and then into a more open oak/pine woodland where many of the same species found in Madera Canyon are found, and there are also Cordilleran Flycatchers and Virginia's and Yellow-rumped (Audubon's) Warblers in summer. In patches of dwarf oak, there are breeding Green-tailed Towhees and Black-chinned Sparrows. There are also a few pairs of Dusky Flycatchers during the summer. Watch the skies for Zone-tailed Hawk, Prairie Falcon, and the occasional Golden Eagle.

After a few more miles of high country, the scenic loop turns left onto TX-166 and drops into lower, more open country. Pronghorns are frequently seen. You also may see White-tailed and Mule Deer, Rock Squirrel, Black-tailed Jackrabbit, Eastern Cottontail, and Mexican and Spotted Ground Squirrels. At night, there may be Striped and Hog-nosed Skunks, Raccoon, Gray Fox, Coyote, Bobcat, and Porcupine. In winter, this open stretch is the best spot for seeing Ferruginous Hawk, Golden Eagle, and McCown's and Chestnut-collared Longspurs. Other birds include Prairie Falcon, Say's Phoebe, Cassin's Sparrow, and Western Meadowlark.

After several miles of open country, scattered oaks again appear. An excellent place to see birds of this habitat is the Bloys Camp Meeting Ground (ask permission). Montezuma Quail may stroll about the grounds, Acorn Woodpeckers are common, and Phainopeplas frequent the area in fall and winter.

At Point of Rock roadside picnic area (5.0 miles), you can hear the down-the-scale song of Canyon Wrens and may possibly be able to locate one with your binoculars. The grasslands along the way back to Fort Davis could be harboring a few Mountain Plovers (nesting records) and good numbers of McCown's and Chestnut-collared Longspurs in winter. Watch for Pronghorn.

LIMPIA CREEK

It is well worth the $1 picnicking fee to have the privilege of birding among the cottonwoods and willows about the private campground on **Limpia Creek** at the junction of TX-17 and TX-118. In winter, at least 40 species can be found in two hours, including Vermilion Flycatcher, Black Phoebe, Eastern, Western, and Mountain Bluebirds, Lincoln's, Swamp, Song, and White-throated Sparrows, and Lesser Goldfinch. In summer, Western Wood-Pewee and Summer Tanager are among the nesting birds. For several years, a pair of Common Black-Hawks has nested in the cottonwoods farther up the creek. After birding the campground, go northeast on TX-17, which follows Limpia Creek all the way to Wild Rose Pass. After 0.8 mile, stop at the litter barrel sign. The hawks nest in the tall cottonwood across Limpia Creek. *Do not cross the fence.* Continue up the road, stopping at each bridge and beside all oak groves and thickets. In summer, Cliff Swallows nest under the bridges, and in winter, Green-tailed and Spotted Towhees are common in the brush. Canyon Towhees and Rufous-crowned Sparrows are present all year. Inca Doves and Common Ground-Doves are seen occasionally in the fields. Some 15 species of sparrows winter in the grassy areas, and small flocks of Lark Buntings sometimes find their way this far into the mountains.

Where the canyon is narrow and the road approaches the palisade-like cliffs, Canyon Wrens may be heard singing at almost anytime of year. Great Horned Owls sit in crevices. Hawks soar above the cliffs; Red-tailed Hawk is the most common, but watch in winter for Ferruginous as well.

AGUJA CANYON

After crossing Wild Rose Pass (22.6 miles), continue north on TX-17 to the sign indicating Road 1832 to the Buffalo Trail Boy Scout Ranch (12.1 miles). Turn left (west) here through typical foothill brush country. This paved road has lots of room, so you can pull over to birdwatch. This is the habitat of such typical desert species as Greater Roadrunner, Western Kingbird,

Loggerhead Shrike   Louise Zemaitis

Ash-throated Flycatcher, Verdin, Cactus Wren, Curve-billed and Sage Thrashers, Pyrrhuloxia, and Black-throated and Brewer's Sparrows. After 8.5 miles, the road enters a wide-mouthed canyon and the scrub gives way to larger trees.

At the first place the road fords the creek, look in summer among the streamside thickets for White-winged Dove, Bell's Vireo, Summer Tanager, and Varied and Painted Buntings. Do not leave the highway; all of the land along this road is private. At the second ford, look in winter for Black-chinned Sparrow. At the entrance to the Boy Scout Ranch (12.0 miles), watch along the cliffs for White-throated Swifts, which are present year-round and may be seen even in winter on warm days.

The first few miles of this road are often one of the best places to study sparrows in the Davis Mountains. Lark Buntings, Chipping, Clay-colored, Brewer's, Field, Black-throated, Vesper, Savannah, and White-crowned Sparrows may be present. There are even several documented records of Baird's Sparrow from this area.

BALMORHEA STATE PARK

Return to TX-17, go north to the town of Toyahvale and US-290 (7.0 miles), and turn right. Just beyond is **Balmorhea State Park**, a fine place for birding (entrance fee $5 per person; camping and showers available; accommodations are also available at San Solomon Springs Courts: Box 15, Toyahvale, TX 78786; phone 915-375-2370). The park is noted for the 26 million-gallon-per-day artesian San Solomon Spring, around which is built a natural-looking swimming pool. These spring waters are home to two endangered desert fishes, the Comanche Spring Pupfish and the Pecos Mosquitofish. Cave Swallows nest under the eaves of the entrance station and other buildings, along with Barn and Cliff Swallows.

In 1996, Texas Parks and Wildlife, along with the Reeves County Water District and the Texas Department of Transportation, restored a ciénega, or desert wetland, within the park. The ciénega was constructed to preserve the endangered fish as well as to provide educational opportunities. The marsh also provides a great birding opportunity. The restoration project includes native plants around the marsh. The potential of this area for birds is not fully known, but Wood Duck, Greater Scaup, Hooded and Red-breasted Mergansers, American and Least Bitterns, Virginia Rail, and Sora have been noted. Marsh Wren and Swamp Sparrow are common in winter.

Resident birds in the remainder of the park include Scaled Quail, Eurasian Collared-Dove, White-winged and Inca Doves, Greater Roadrunner, Ladder-backed Woodpecker, Black and Say's Phoebes, Loggerhead Shrike, Cactus Wren, Curve-billed Thrasher, Canyon Towhee, Black-throated Sparrow, Pyrrhuloxia, Eastern Meadowlark, Great-tailed and Common (uncommon) Grackles, and House Finch. Other nesters include Black-chinned Hummingbird, Cassin's and Western Kingbirds, Bewick's Wren, and Blue Grosbeak. In winter, look for Northern Flicker, Ruby-crowned Kinglet, Hermit Thrush, Cedar Waxwing, Yellow-rumped Warbler, Green-tailed and Spotted Towhees, Chipping, Clay-colored, Brewer's, Vesper, Savannah, Song, Lincoln's, and White-crowned Sparrows, Lark Bunting, Dark-eyed Junco, and Western Meadowlark. Migration should bring Wilson's Warbler, Summer Tanager (spring), and Orchard and Bullock's (uncommon) Orioles.

BALMORHEA LAKE

In the town of Balmorhea (4 miles), turn right at the sign for **Balmorhea Lake** onto Houston Street and drive to the lake (2.6 miles). Check in at the store; there is a charge of $4 per day for birdwatching, fishing, and primitive camping at this private lake. The lake acts as a storage area for irrigation projects, with the water coming from San Solomon Springs at the Balmorhea State Park. Balmorhea Lake is one of the premier places in all of the Trans-Pecos for waterbirds, particularly during migration and winter.

Some 40 species of waterbirds winter here, including Ross's Goose and "Mexican Duck." The duck is most common in the irrigation canals leading into or out of the lake, but is present on the lake as well. Western and Clark's Grebes winter here in large numbers. In recent years, individuals of both species have begun summering on the lake. There are great fluctuations in water levels in the summer, sometimes leaving the prime nesting areas unavailable during that time of the year; however, *Aechmophorus* grebes will also nest during the spring, fall, and even early winter. Many shorebirds can be seen in spring and fall migrations, including American Avocet, Long-billed Curlew, Pectoral, White-rumped (May only), and Stilt Sandpipers, Wilson's Snipe (also winters), and Wilson's and Red-necked Phalaropes (the latter is rare and found primarily in fall). The lake is well known for its nesting Snowy Plovers. Black-necked Stilts also breed in good numbers. Neotropic Cormorants have become regular in fall. Rarities found here include all three scoters, Red-throated, Pacific, and Yellow-billed (two records) Loons, Brown Pelican, Tricolored Heron, Reddish Egret, Sabine's Gull, Pomarine Jaeger, and Arctic and Elegant Terns. The lake is not large (573 acres), but it is large enough to require a scope. It is not uncommon to encounter windy conditions that create waves large enough to make birds in the center of the lake difficult to see. The dirt roads around the lake can be rough driving and are often impassable after rains.

Many raptors can be found wintering around the lake or migrating through, including Osprey, Northern Harrier, Ferruginous and Rough-legged (rare) Hawks, Golden Eagle (rare), American Kestrel, and Prairie Falcon. A checklist available at the state park includes the lake and town. Lesser and Common (rare) Nighthawks and Common Poorwill can be found around the lake in spring and summer. Ash-throated and Scissor-tailed (rare) Flycatchers breed in the area. Western Wood-Pewee and Willow, Least, and Dusky Flycatchers are rare but regular migrants. Common Ravens are resident. American Pipit is common in winter. Verdins are resident in the surrounding fields.

Return to Balmorhea via Houston Street; upon reaching TX-17, turn north (right), and continue 1.9 miles to County Road 315. Turn left and follow it under Interstate 10 (at a very low bridge that RVs probably cannot travel under) for about 1.6 miles to open range. This open desert grassland can appear very barren in drought years, but it offers excellent sparrow habitat during the winter; this is a consistent location for Sage Sparrow, Lark Bunting, and many other species.

EL PASO VALLEY

To continue west after your visit to Balmorhea Lake and the Davis Mountains, take Interstate 10 to Van Horn (68 miles). At the junction with TX-54, you have a choice of continuing west to El Paso or driving north to the Guadalupe Mountains. If you opt for El Paso, continue west on Interstate 10 to

Sierra Blanca (33 miles). About 28 miles west of Sierra Blanca, you can leave I-10 at McNary (exit 78) to follow old TX-20 through the farmlands of the El Paso Valley. Most of the little towns along the way are practically deserted now, but the road is in good shape and there's little traffic. There are a few good birding spots in this oasis, and you're likely to find the green cotton fields to be a pleasant relief from the desert.

The first missionaries came through the valley in 1581, but the first mission was not established until 1659. On Socorro Road (FM-258) near Clint, you can see San Elizario Mission and several other historic buildings. One is the original El Paso County Courthouse, and another is reported to be the oldest building in Texas. This is also the site of the first introduction by Europeans of domestic animals into the United States. They were brought here in 1598 when Don Juan de Onate established the first military garrison.

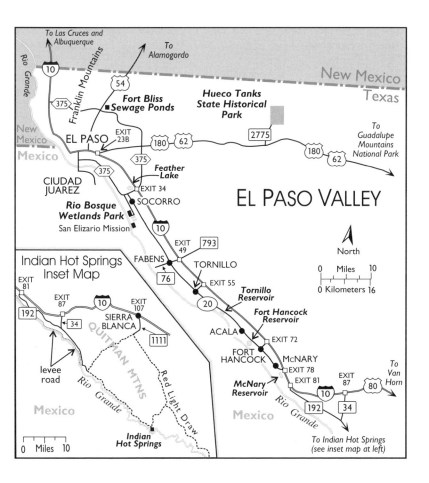

Black-throated Sparrow   Barry Zimmer

The Spaniards, on entering this area in the 16th century, found large and prosperous settlements occupied by the Tigua Indians, whose ancestors built the famous cliff houses of Mesa Verde, Colorado. They had developed a complex irrigation system, some of which is still in use today. Their principal crops were maize and squash.

INDIAN HOT SPRINGS

An interesting section of the Rio Grande, and the next readily accessible stretch of river west of Candelaria, can be reached by exiting I-10 at exit 87 (FM-34). Go south on FM-34 to the intersection with FM-192 (2.4 miles). Alternatively, this intersection can be reached from the west by leaving the freeway at exit 81 (FM-2217) and driving east for 7.9 miles. FM-2217 becomes FM-192 at 1.2 miles from the interstate.

Continue east on FM-192 from this intersection. The road is paved for the next 11.7 miles, but the birding here is not great. Look for Harris's Hawk, which is resident. Two miles before the pavement ends, look for the levee along the Rio Grande on the right. Signs will indicate "No Trespassing" and "Not Authorized for Public Use." Despite the signs, people frequently drive on the levee road and enforcement is generally lacking. You are highly unlikely to encounter any problems. Ultimately, however, you are responsible for your actions. This caveat applies to all sections of posted levee roads from here upriver to Las Cruces. This section is one of the most reliable areas near El Paso for Vermilion Flycatcher.

Once the pavement ends on FM-192, continue east on the dirt road. You will reach the **Indian Hot Springs** in roughly another 21 miles. This former cavalry post is now privately owned, and visits are by invitation only. The hot springs still flow, and a footbridge links the springs with a tiny Mexican village. The white buildings of the springs are visible from a hilltop to their west. Good birding starts when the road reaches the Rio Grande 6.2 miles after the pavement ends. The river is unleveed here and very narrow. It is surrounded by dense stands of tamarisk (salt cedar). From here until the hot springs come into view, the road meanders between the river and barren desert hills. The best spot is a large pond 19.6 miles from the end of the pavement. Because the river is unleveed here, water levels in this pond and several other smaller ones are unpredictable.

This area has been very lightly birded; it affords real opportunities for discovery. Great Blue Heron, Great Egret, Snowy Egret, Green Heron, and Black-crowned Night-Heron are found at the ponds, along with a variety of dabbling ducks in winter. Harris's Hawk might be seen throughout, and Gambel's Quail is fairly common. Breeding bird diversity is better here than anywhere else in the El Paso area. Regular breeders include Yellow-billed Cuckoo, Black Phoebe (resident), Vermilion Flycatcher (resident), Ash-throated Flycatcher, Bell's Vireo, Verdin (resident), Bewick's Wren (resident), Northern Mockingbird, Lucy's Warbler, Yellow-breasted Chat, Summer Tanager, Lark Sparrow, Blue Grosbeak, Painted Bunting, and Orchard and Bullock's Orioles. Rarer possibilities that have been seen include Black Vulture, Elf Owl, Common Ground-Dove, Brown-crested Flycatcher, and Northern Cardinal.

Although the dirt road is generally good, caution is necessary due to its isolation. Heavy rains could make the road impassable. Be sure to take water and to watch for loose livestock and Mule Deer. Car trouble could mean a long wait or a long hike. All land here is private, *so birding must be done from the road*. This is the general area where video was taken of people in Mexican military clothing on U.S. soil in 2006, a story that got some play in the media.

Another way to reach this area is to exit Interstate 10 at exit 107 (FM-1111) in Sierra Blanca. Go south on FM-1111 before turning right at the end of the pavement (4.8 miles). (A left turn here would follow Red Light Draw some 25 miles to a very poorly known area of the Rio Grande. This section of the Rio Grande is poorly vegetated and river access is very limited, so it is not worth a drive to the end of this road. However, Lucy's Warbler is quite reliable about ten miles down the road where it crosses thicker vegetation at the bottom of the draw.) After turning right and then veering left (3.0 miles), a passable dirt road crosses the Quitman Mountains to meet up with FM-192 near where the pavement ends. The Quitmans hold desert birds such as Ladder-backed Woodpecker, Verdin, Cactus and Rock Wrens, and Pyrrhuloxia. The U.S. Border Patrol is active throughout this area and may stop to see what you are doing. Sierra Blanca itself offers little in the way of birding, but Cassin's Kingbirds usually nest in town, and Bronzed Cowbird is reliable in spring and summer in the city park (in front of the Hudspeth County courthouse).

MCNARY RESERVOIR

The best birding location in the valley east of El Paso is **McNary Reservoir**. Exit Interstate 10 at exit 78 (TX-20). The overpass has a small colony of Cave Swallows, present here since at least 1984. There are numerous other colonies nearby, but this location is a convenient one. Cave Swallow, present from mid-February through October, is second only to Barn Swallow as the most common breeding swallow in the area and is a rare but increasing possibility in winter.

Continue west on TX-20 for 0.2 mile and turn left onto FM-192. Follow this road through desert scrub until you reach the McNary Reservoir dike on the left (1.7 miles). The quickest way to bird this fairly large body of water is to park along FM-192 about halfway down the dike, then walk onto the dike. *Absolutely do not drive onto the dike, even if the gates (at either end) are open.* The reservoir is posted "No Trespassing," but the El Paso/Trans-Pecos Audubon Society has permission to bring field trips here, and in hundreds of visits birders have not encountered problems. If you bird on foot on the dike parallel to FM-192, you are highly unlikely to have any problems. However, the inclusion of this site in the book should not be construed as blanket permission for visiting birders to trespass. Conditions can change and you alone are responsible for your actions. This caveat and disclaimer applies to the Fort Hancock and Tornillo Reservoirs as well.

The list of avian attractions here is long. Clark's and Western Grebes are resident, with multiple breeding records for each, starting in 1997. Hundreds of grebes are present in winter, with lesser numbers in summer. Breeding can occur at any season, though many years see no chicks. Since 1994 (the reservoir was created in the fall of 1993), the flooded trees on the north side have hosted a sizable rookery of Double-crested Cormorants, Snowy and Cattle Egrets, and Black-crowned Night-Herons. Neotropic Cormorant has bred since 1996, and at least a few individuals can be expected year-round (more common in summer). Yellow-crowned Night-Heron and Least Bittern are seen occasionally in summer and may be rare breeders.

Ross's and Snow Geese are regular in winter, with a combined flock of 500 or more in recent years. Even the rare blue morph of the Ross's Goose has been seen on a few occasions in recent years. All regularly occurring waterfowl can be found here. Common Mergansers generally winter in the hundreds; close scrutiny will typically reveal several Hooded and Red-breasted Mergansers as well. Look for Osprey in migration. The water levels are usually too high to provide much shorebird habitat, but Wilson's Phalaropes can dot the surface in migration. If there is any exposed mud to be found, it will be at the far west end. Ring-billed Gulls winter here in good numbers, usually with a Herring Gull or two. Franklin's and Bonaparte's Gulls are fairly common migrants, as are Forster's and Black Terns. A large Cave Swallow colony may be found near the west end of the reservoir under a bridge in front of a small

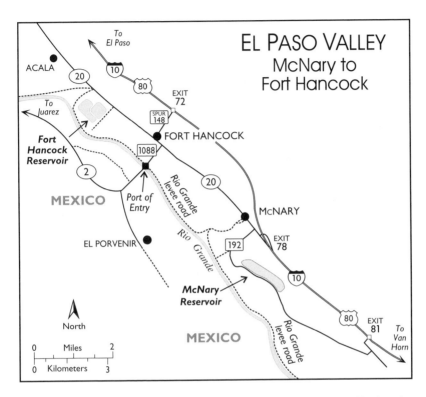

EL PASO VALLEY
McNary to
Fort Hancock

white house. Seven swallow species could be seen in migration. The brushy ditch parallel to FM-192 has breeding Common Yellowthroat and Red-winged Blackbird, with Marsh Wren and a few sparrows in winter.

McNary Reservoir has hosted a fascinating array of rarities in its brief history. These include Surf and White-winged Scoters, Long-tailed Duck, Red-throated and Pacific Loons, Anhinga, Reddish Egret, White Ibis, Roseate Spoonbill, Laughing, California, Lesser Black-backed, and Sabine's (May and July records plus many in fall) Gulls, Caspian Tern, Parasitic and Long-tailed Jaegers, and Purple Martin. Texas's first fully documented Arctic Tern was found here in June 1997, with another in June 2006.

RIO GRANDE LEVEE ROAD

The levee road of the Rio Grande offers some interesting birding. One of the most productive stretches of levee can be accessed at McNary. In downtown McNary just west of the TX-20/FM-192 junction, turn south from TX-20 onto a dirt road. Take this to the levee road (1.4 miles), which then can be traveled east about 20 miles to its eastern terminus with FM-192, or west about 6 miles to the Fort Hancock port of entry with Mexico. The levee is safe, and you are likely to encounter few others, aside from a dove hunter or two in season. Be aware that U.S. Border Patrol may find you interesting and stop to chat. Many birds can readily be seen in Mexico from the levee.

The levee goes past agricultural fields good for raptors in winter, including uncommon species such as Ferruginous Hawk, Merlin, and Prairie Falcon. Long-billed Curlew is a possibility in winter or migration; look for Upland Sandpipers in cut alfalfa fields in August and September. Burrowing Owl is possible at any season, but more likely in summer. The river will yield some dabbling ducks, and, with low water, shorebirds (such as Killdeer, Black-necked Stilt, American Avocet, both yellowlegs, and Least Sandpiper) on the sandbars. Any Mallard seen in summer will likely be a "Mexican Duck." Other birds to look for include Gambel's Quail, Greater Roadrunner, Black and Say's Phoebes, Vermilion Flycatcher (rare), Ash-throated Flycatcher (summer), Western Kingbird (summer), Loggerhead Shrike, Bell's Vireo (summer), Verdin, Crissal Thrasher, Yellow-breasted Chat (summer), Pyrrhuloxia, Painted Bunting (summer), Orchard and Bullock's Orioles (summer), and a variety of wintering sparrows. Farther west, breeding Bell's Vireo, Painted Bunting, and Orchard Oriole become scarce quickly.

FORT HANCOCK AREA

If you have chosen not to drive along the Rio Grande levee to Fort Hancock, continue west on TX-20 from Interstate 10 exit 78. After about 6 miles you will reach the TX-20/Spur 148 junction in Fort Hancock. Alternately, this corner can be reached by leaving I-10 at exit 72 (Fort Hancock/Spur 148) and going south through town. Fort Hancock has a small motel and several stores, gas stations, and cafes. Most of the other "towns" along TX-20—McNary, Acala, Alamo Alto—are practically deserted and offer no services.

Side roads branching out from residential Fort Hancock can be worth a brief exploration in winter. A small Pencil Cholla cactus grows in dense clumps here and, when laden with fruit, can be attractive to Sage (winter), Curve-billed, and Crissal Thrashers, Lark Bunting (winter), and Pyrrhuloxia. The best area is to the south of the cemetery, which is at the northwest corner of town. This is the most reliable spot near El Paso for Sage Thrasher. Numbers vary, but a few at least can usually be found. Northern Mockingbird is an abundant breeder in desert habitats, but in winter it retreats almost entirely into urban areas; it is common here in winter. If you don't find Sage Thrasher near the cemetery, there is also some scattered Pencil Cholla along dirt roads on the east side of town.

For those interested in birding in Mexico, there is a port of entry at the end of FM-1088, which intersects TX-20 just 0.8 mile east of the TX-20/Spur 148 junction. Traffic here is light, no car papers are needed, and hassles are unlikely. Once in Mexico, continue straight ahead on the paved road. Within several miles there will be a fork: left leads to the village of El Porvenir, right is Route 2 which takes you to the city of Juarez. This section of road gets crowded and slow, and aside from winter flocks of American Crows about 30 miles farther west, offers little notable birding. As you head from the port of entry to the fork mentioned above, watch on your right for a small "1 KM" post. Turn right here onto a dirt road; a concrete-lined channel will be on your left. This road, connecting with Route 2 in several miles, offers fairly good birding. Check any flooded fields for dabbling ducks and shorebirds. White-faced Ibis is likely in migration, and Long-billed Curlew is possible in winter. The birds here are similar to those on the Texas side, but, due to different agricultural practices, there are more trees and brush here. Return to Texas at the Fort Hancock port of entry.

The best birding near Fort Hancock is at **Fort Hancock Reservoir.** To reach it, go west from Fort Hancock on TX-20 for 2.2 miles. Park on the left at the west end of the dirt dike. Vehicle traffic is not permitted around the reservoir; do not drive in even if the gate happens to be open. Please remain on the levee parallel to TX-20.

Typically, there is more exposed mud here than at McNary Reservoir. As water levels drop, mudflats appear first at the northwest corner, occasionally extending over half of the reservoir. Often, however, there will be no exposed mud. Water levels fluctuate with irrigation needs and can change dramatically from day to day. When mudflats are present, look for Great Blue Heron, Great and Snowy Egrets, White-faced Ibis (migration), and a variety of shorebirds. Killdeer, Black-necked Stilt, American Avocet, both yellowlegs, Spotted, Western, Least, Baird's, and Stilt Sandpipers, Long-billed Dowitcher, Wilson's Snipe, and Wilson's Phalarope are the most common migrants. All but Baird's Sandpiper, Stilt Sandpiper, and Wilson's Phalarope might be seen in winter, but Lesser Yellowlegs and Western Sandpiper are rare at that season. Black-bellied, Snowy, and Semipalmated Plovers, Willet, Long-billed Curlew, Marbled Godwit, Pectoral Sandpiper, and Red-necked Phalarope migrate through in much smaller numbers.

Western and Clark's Grebes occur in low numbers and might be seen at any season. American White Pelican has been regular in recent winters. Ross's and Snow Geese may be seen in winter, along with many ducks, mostly dabblers. Common Merganser winters here in good numbers. Both Double-crested and Neotropic Cormorants usually are present; they like to loaf on an old dock and pilings in the southwest corner of the reservoir. Ring-billed Gull is common in winter; a wide assortment of other gulls has occurred here. Several Cave Swallow colonies breed nearby, with birds coming to hawk insects over the water. In recent years, the reservoir has attracted many rarities, including Eurasian Wigeon, Black Scoter, Brown Pelican, Hudsonian Godwit, Dunlin, Laughing, Mew, California, and Thayer's Gulls, Black-legged Kittiwake, and Arctic Tern. Be aware that light conditions, especially in the morning, can be frustratingly poor.

Continue driving west on TX-20. A left turn (0.8 mile) leads to the levee road, which can be taken east to the Fort Hancock port of entry; another left turn (0.1 mile farther along TX-20) also leads to the levee road. You could drive the levee road west about 20 miles to the Fabens port of entry; however, you are better off birding the levee around McNary.

The land here is heavily agricultural, with the principal crops being cotton, chiles, and alfalfa. Harris's Hawk is perhaps more reliable along the next ten miles of TX-20 than anywhere else around El Paso. In winter, look for Northern Harrier, Red-tailed and Ferruginous Hawks, American Kestrel, Say's Phoebe, Loggerhead Shrike, Lark Bunting (numbers variable), and Pyrrhuloxia. Brewer's and White-crowned are the most common wintering sparrows along the roadsides. Western Kingbird and Northern Mockingbird are conspicuous breeders.

A grove of ten or so mistletoe-infested cottonwoods at a roadside rest (7.8 miles) west of the Fort Hancock Reservoir is worth investigation. Breeding birds here may include Harris's Hawk (resident; look also in the row of trees extending westward on the north side of TX-20), Black-chinned Hummingbird, Ladder-backed Woodpecker (resident), Western Kingbird, Verdin (resident), Northern Mockingbird, Yellow-breasted Chat, Summer Tanager (rare), Pyrrhuloxia (resident), Painted Bunting, and Orchard (rare) and Bullock's Orioles. Western Bluebird occurs some winters, and Phainopepla is fairly reliable. This site takes only a few minutes to cover, and at times is not worth even that. As the largest grove for miles around, however, it has the potential to lure migrants, and numerous rarities have occurred here.

TORNILLO RESERVOIR

A short distance (1.1 miles) farther west on TX-20 is **Tornillo Reservoir**. Park on the left, and, as with the other reservoirs, bird on foot only. Another option is to bird from several pullouts along TX-20 and thus not be in violation of the "No Trespassing" signs. A large pullout near the west end allows scoping most of the reservoir from just one spot. In general, this is the least productive of the three reservoirs because the shores are made up of stone blocks, and only very rarely are water levels low enough to attract many shorebirds. Western and Clark's Grebes might be here in winter, but are not always present in summer. Eared Grebe should be seen in winter, and Pied-billed Grebe is a common non-breeding resident.

Tornillo Reservoir usually hosts large numbers of wintering waterfowl, perhaps including a few Ross's or Snow Geese. Very large numbers of wintering Green-winged and migrant Blue-winged and Cinnamon Teal can be present, along with all other regular waterfowl. Rarities recorded here include Eurasian Wigeon, Black Scoter, Barrow's Goldeneye, Pacific Loon, and Roseate Spoonbill.

The brushy ditch between the reservoir and TX-20 can produce Verdin, Cactus and Bewick's Wrens, Ruby-crowned Kinglet (winter), Crissal Thrasher, Green-tailed and Spotted Towhees (winter), wintering sparrows such as Brewer's, Song, Lincoln's, Swamp, and White-crowned, Pyrrhuloxia, and Painted Bunting (summer). Culverts here have a few pairs of Cave Swallows. Strong spring winds, mostly in March and April, can raise whitecaps and cause blowing dust. Birding the reservoirs under these conditions can be unpleasant.

At this point, the next good birding opportunities are in El Paso. Your best bet is to continue west on TX-20 to Tornillo, about 5 miles, before turning right onto O.T. Smith Road to connect in several miles with Interstate 10 at exit 55. The town of Fabens is about 12 miles west of the reservoir. A right turn here at the traffic light (FM-76, which soon becomes FM-793) will also take you north, in several miles, to Interstate 10 (exit 49). Fabens offers more services than does Tornillo.

EL PASO AREA

El Paso County is located at the western extremity of Texas. The city of El Paso lies in the valley of the Rio Grande at the base of the Franklin Mountains, in the heart of the Chihuahuan Desert. El Paso is a growing city of 700,000, offering the traveler a multitude of dining and lodging options. An average annual rainfall of about nine inches falls mostly in brief, intense thunderstorms between July and September. El Paso's birdfinding habitats are varied, though somewhat limited. Finding birds here means finding water first. Nevertheless, El Paso County boasts an impressive list of over 400 species of birds, about 90 of which are regular breeders. In addition, a stunning array of rarities has been found.

Some of the resident and nesting birds include "Mexican Duck" (Mexican Mallard), Scaled and Gambel's Quail, Swainson's Hawk (summer), Common Moorhen, White-winged and Inca Doves, Greater Roadrunner, Burrowing Owl, Lesser Nighthawk (summer), Common Poorwill (summer), White-throated Swift, Say's Phoebe, Ash-throated Flycatcher (summer), Chihuahuan Raven, Verdin, Cactus, Rock, and Canyon Wrens, Crissal Thrasher, Phainopepla, Black-throated Sparrow, and Scott's (summer) and Hooded (rare and local, summer) Orioles.

HUECO TANKS STATE HISTORIC SITE

Hueco (*WAY-co*) Tanks State Historic Site ($4/person, plus camping fee) is an excellent place to study the Chihuahuan Desert. To reach the park from downtown El Paso, take Interstate 10 exit 23B (Paisano/US-62/US-180) and drive east to FM-2775 (21.8 miles). Turn left here to the park (8.0 miles).

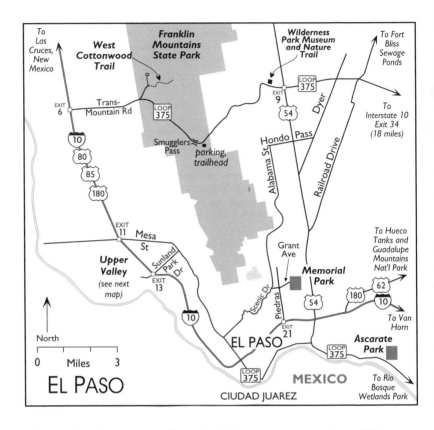

Alternately, exit Interstate 10 at exit 34 (Americas Avenue/Loop 375) and go north to US-62/US-180 (7.5 miles). Turn right and go east to FM-2775. (You can continue north on Loop 375 to cross US-54 [exit 9] on El Paso's northeast side before crossing the Franklin Mountains to reconnect with I-10 [exit 6] on El Paso's extreme northwest side. US-62/US-180 continues east to Guadalupe Mountains and Carlsbad Caverns National Parks.)

Hueco Tanks State Historic Site, created to preserve Native American rock art, is excellent for birds. There are six small ponds (or tanks) in wet winters, and some trees (mostly oak, willow, and hackberry, with a few cottonwoods) around the impressive rocky outcrops. The largest pond (but often dry) is over the dike behind the Old Ranch House, just down the road from the entrance station. Two other ponds are located in Mescalero Canyon, in the park's center between East Mountain and West Mountain. This is typically the best birding area. A small flock of Lawrence's Goldfinches was enjoyed here by many Texas birders in the winter of 1996–1997.

At any season, you should find Scaled Quail, Greater Roadrunner, White-throated Swift, Ladder-backed Woodpecker, Say's Phoebe, Loggerhead

Shrike, Verdin, Cactus, Rock, and Canyon Wrens, Crissal Thrasher, Canyon Towhee, Rufous-crowned and Black-throated Sparrows, and Pyrrhuloxia. In summer, watch for Swainson's Hawk, Lesser Nighthawk, Common Poorwill, Black-chinned Hummingbird, Ash-throated Flycatcher, Western Kingbird, Cliff and Barn Swallows, Northern Mockingbird, Cassin's Sparrow, Blue Grosbeak, Eastern Meadowlark, and Scott's Oriole. Winter is often the best time to visit the park. Not only is it cooler, but there may be water in the ponds. It is often a good site at this season for Black-chinned Sparrow. Also look for Northern Harrier, American Kestrel, Long-eared Owl (rare), Western Scrub-Jay, Western and Mountain Bluebirds (sporadic), Townsend's Solitaire (sporadic), Sage Thrasher (sporadic), Green-tailed and Spotted Towhees, Chipping, Brewer's, Vesper, Sage, Savannah, Song, Lincoln's, and White-crowned Sparrows, Dark-eyed Junco, Western Meadowlark, and American Goldfinch. In irruptive winters, the park can be good for Steller's Jay, Mountain Chickadee, and Red-breasted and White-breasted Nuthatches. Migration can be productive, with a variety of flycatchers, Warbling Vireo, swallows, warblers (including Orange-crowned, Virginia's, Black-throated Gray, Townsend's, MacGillivray's, and Wilson's), Western Tanager, Black-headed Grosbeak, and Lazuli Bunting.

If birding is slow during the warmer months, you can look for lizards: Southwestern Earless Lizard, Crevice Spiny Lizard, Fence Lizard, Big Bend Tree Lizard, Texas Horned Lizard, Round-tailed Horned Lizard, several whiptails, and Great Plains Skink. Rock Squirrel and Texas Antelope Squirrel frequent the rocks, and Gray Fox and Ringtail are common enough to sometimes be seen in the daytime. Be aware that Hueco Tanks is a renowned rock-climbing and bouldering destination, with the heaviest visitation from November through March. The park lets in only 70 visitors at a time and you may well find yourself shut out. Advance reservations are taken for the first 60 people each day (915-857-1135 or 800-792-1112), and 10 spots are held daily for first-come first-served. In addition, the entrance road is closed by a gate from dark until 8:00AM.

Due to continued vandalism of rock art, dramatic changes in visitation policies took effect in 1998. These include needing advance arrangements for camping and restricted access within the park. All first-time visitors need to obtain a pass. This is good for a year and visitors must first watch a 15-minute video on the park and its policies. Even with the pass, visitors can visit on their own only the areas of the park around North Mountain. Guides are available to take visitors to other parts of the park on all days except Monday and Tuesday. There is a bird tour offered on the third Sunday of every month.

RIO BOSQUE WETLANDS PARK

One of the best birding locations in El Paso is **Rio Bosque Wetlands Park** on the southeast corner of town. Formerly neglected, the 372-acre park has experienced a renaissance under the management of the University of Texas–El Paso Center for Environmental Resource Management. To reach Rio Bosque, exit I-10 at exit 34 (Loop 375/Americas Avenue/Joe Battle Boulevard) and head south to the Pan American Drive exit (1.9 miles). Continue south on the frontage road through lights for Alameda Avenue and Socorro Road to reach Pan American (0.9 mile). Turn left onto Pan American and drive through the industrial park and across the Riverside Canal (1.5 miles). Straight ahead is the Bustamante Wastewater Treatment Plant. Turn left here and drive along the dirt road with the canal on your left. Look for shorebirds on sandbars in the canal (though plans call for lining it with concrete). You will reach the park in 0.8 mile (trailhead and parking lot). The road may be gated just past this point. If the gate is open, the second parking lot is the best place to park. Another 0.4 mile east along the canal will bring you to the east end of the park and yet another parking area. The road to the park is generally passable, but can be very muddy after rains.

Three trails can be taken from the middle parking lot and trailhead. The kiosk here has a map of the park. The best trail is the Rio Trail, a 2.4-mile loop. Large areas have been cleared of salt cedar and many stands of Screwbean Mesquite have sprung up. Much work has been done to promote the growth of native vegetation. Canals crisscross the park and several wetland cells hold water when available. Water comes from the wastewater plant, primarily during the non-growing season (mid-October through February). In winter (assuming water), look for various ducks (especially dabblers), Pied-billed Grebe, and Great Blue Heron, as well as Northern Harrier, Red-tailed Hawk, Gambel's Quail, Greater Roadrunner, Black and Say's Phoebes, Loggerhead Shrike, American Crow (very local in the county), and a variety of sparrows. The park can be very good in migration. In summer, look for Mississippi Kite, Burrowing Owl, Lesser Nighthawk, Ash-throated Flycatcher, Bell's Vireo, Cliff, Cave, and Barn Swallows, Northern Mockingbird, Yellow-breasted Chat, Cassin's Sparrow, Blue Grosbeak, Painted Bunting, and Bullock's Oriole. Cave Swallow has occurred here regularly during winter in recent years; Cinnamon Teal also has been increasing in winter. Harris's Hawk is pretty reliable here but not farther upriver. The park has hosted many rarities, including Fulvous Whistling-Duck, Tundra Swan, Eurasian Wigeon, Reddish Egret, White-tailed Kite, Bald Eagle, and American Golden-Plover.

It is possible to continue east from the east end of the park along the dirt road, curving right along the park's eastern boundary to reach the levee of the Rio Grande. From the levee, you can overlook some of the park's wetland cells, as well as look into Mexico. This is an easy way to add American Crow to your Mexico list. The U.S. Border Patrol is very active in this area.

Two of the area's original Spanish missions are near Rio Bosque. Retrace your path to Loop 375 and head north to Socorro Road. The Socorro Mission lies along Socorro Road 1.5 miles east of Loop 375 (Americas Avenue). Founded in 1682 for Piro Indians fleeing the Pueblo Revolt in what is now New Mexico, this is the oldest active church building in the United States. The

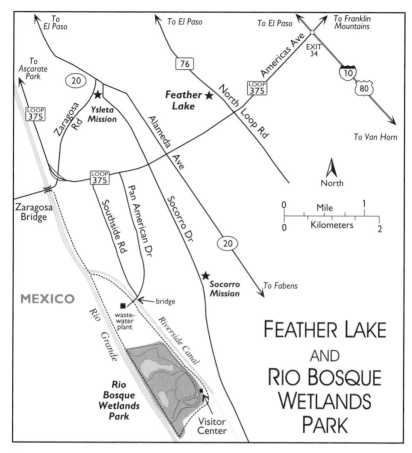

Ysleta Mission, also founded in 1682, can be reached by taking Socorro Road west from Americas Avenue for about a mile. These missions lie along the Camino Real, or Royal Road, which linked Chihuahua, Mexico, with Santa Fe.

Two other birding spots can be reached readily from Rio Bosque. **Feather Lake** is a storm-water retention basin protected and managed by the El Paso/Trans-Pecos Audubon Society. Since 2003, irrigation deliveries to the park have ceased and the park is wholly dependent on storm runoff. Consequently, the basin is often dry. A variety of ducks (mostly dabblers) and shorebirds is possible when water is present, and large flocks of White-faced Ibis can occur in migration. Cottonwoods surround part of the lake and may provide refuge to migrant passerines. The site is open October to April (water permitting) from 8:00AM to noon on Saturdays and from 2:00PM to dusk on Sundays; admission is free. To reach Feather Lake, exit I-10 at Loop 375/Americas Avenue (exit 34) and go south to North Loop Road (1.2 miles). Turn right, then left into the parking area (0.4 mile). **Ascarate Park**, a city park

Burrowing Owl   Barry Zimmer

with a lake, can be reached by continuing west on Loop 375 from Pan American. Watch for Burrowing Owl on the river levee along this stretch, particularly between the Zaragosa and Yarbrough exits. After 10 miles or so, exit at Fonseca Boulevard (see El Paso map on page 166). Head right to the traffic light (0.6 mile) and turn right to the park entrance on the right (0.6 mile, Manny Martinez Street). Once in the park ($1 entrance fee on weekends and holidays), continue straight. The lake will soon be visible on your right, with a smaller concrete-lined lake farther down on the left. Generally the variety of birds is poor, but a few ducks may be present and the lake has hosted a rarity or two. Neotropic Cormorant is regular in winter, and the lake often has a few diving ducks or grebes at that season as well. It is not worth a special trip, but it is easy to drop by and check if you are in the area. By returning to Loop 375 and continuing west, you will soon reach the I-10/US-54 junction just east of downtown.

MEMORIAL PARK

Memorial Park, located near downtown El Paso, is a favorite with local birders. To reach it from Interstate 10, drive north on Piedras Avenue (exit 21) for seven blocks before turning right onto Grant Avenue and going 0.3 mile to the park (see El Paso map on page 166). Resident and breeding birds include White-winged and Inca Doves, Black-chinned Hummingbird (summer), Ladder-backed Woodpecker, Western Kingbird (summer),

American Robin, Northern Mockingbird, Great-tailed Grackle, Bullock's Oriole (summer), and House Finch. Migration can be great for warblers, including Orange-crowned, Virginia's, Yellow, Yellow-rumped, Black-throated Gray, Townsend's, MacGillivray's, and Wilson's. Also look in migration for Western Wood-Pewee, Plumbeous, Cassin's, and Warbling Vireos, Western Tanager, and Black-headed Grosbeak. A variety of eastern warblers has been seen here. *Empidonax* flycatchers are present in spring and fall: Willow, Least (rare), Hammond's, Gray (rarer in spring), Dusky, and Cordilleran. Also look in fall and winter for possible Flammulated Owl (very rare, fall), along with Williamson's and Red-naped Sapsuckers, Steller's Jay, Western Scrub-Jay, Red-breasted, White-breasted, and Pygmy (very rare) Nuthatches, Mountain Chickadee, Golden-crowned Kinglet, and Red Crossbill. A few of these montane species can be expected most winters (Red-naped Sapsucker, Western Scrub-Jay, and Red-breasted Nuthatch are the most regular), but the others will be completely absent most years. Expect to see wintering Ruby-crowned Kinglet, Orange-crowned Warbler (uncommon), Yellow-rumped Warbler, White-crowned Sparrow, Dark-eyed Junco (mostly Oregon/Pink-sided types, plus a few Gray-headeds), and perhaps Pine Siskin, Lesser Goldfinch, or American Goldfinch.

FRANKLIN MOUNTAINS

The Franklin Mountains, towering above El Paso, look very dry and barren, but they do harbor some desert species such as Scaled Quail, Verdin, Cactus, Rock, and Canyon Wrens, Rufous-crowned and Black-throated Sparrows, and Scott's Oriole (summer). There is good birding in several of the canyons off TransMountain Road (Loop 375), which crosses the mountains (see El Paso map on page 166). To reach Loop 375, drive west on Interstate 10 from downtown for about 15 miles to exit 6, or go north on US-54 for 9 miles to exit 9. From I-10 exit 6, proceed east to **Franklin Mountains State Park** on the left (3.3 miles). This is a fee area ($4/day), with picnicking and primitive camping by permit and with advance reservations (915-566-6441). The gate is open daily from 8:00AM to 5:00PM. You can pay the fee at the self-pay station at the entrance or at the first building down the road (not always manned).

Drive the paved road in for 1.0 mile and turn right, following the signs for **West Cottonwood Spring.** Park at the end of this road and walk the wide, rocky path up the large canyon to the isolated clump of cottonwoods one-half mile to the east. This is West Cottonwood Spring, a great area in fall migration (mid-July through mid-September) for Calliope, Broad-tailed, and Rufous Hummingbirds. Warblers such as Orange-crowned, Virginia's, Black-throated Gray, Townsend's, and MacGillivray's, and even rare ones, including Hermit Warbler and Painted Redstart, have been found here. Western Scrub-Jays often occur in fall and winter, along with Black-chinned Sparrows, which may occasionally be found in summer. Resident birds include Scaled Quail,

White-throated Swift, Cactus, Rock, Canyon, and Bewick's Wrens, Curve-billed and Crissal Thrashers, Canyon Towhee, and Rufous-crowned and Black-throated Sparrows. Keep an eye out overhead for the resident pair of Golden Eagles. This canyon can be good for butterflies, and Collared Lizard is usually easy to find on the lower portion of the trail during the warmer months.

Return to the entrance of the park and continue driving east on Loop 375. Just after you go over the crest, notice the large gravel parking lot on your right. This is still in the state park and several trails (with self-service fee stations) can be taken from here and offer most of the same birds as West Cottonwood Spring. Continue east on Loop 375. Most of the eastern slope of the Franklins is U.S. Army property and access to the canyons here is prohibited. Common Poorwill can be heard at night from any pulloff along this road, but the challenge will be getting away from the traffic noise. At the bottom of the hill, note the Wilderness Park Museum on the left. The nature trail here is good for desert species (including both Scaled and Gambel's Quail), sparrows, and possibly both meadowlarks. After wet winters, Mexican Poppies can cover the ground in all directions, making for a fabulous display.

From the Wilderness Park Museum, continue east to US-54 (0.6 mile), which can be taken south about 10 miles to downtown. If you want to visit the **Fort Bliss Sewage Ponds**, actually named the Fred Hervey Water Reclamation Plant, continue east on Loop 375 to Railroad Drive (3.0 miles). Turn left on Railroad to the entrance road on your right (3.6 miles; Loop 375 continues east to connect with Interstate 10 at exit 34 in 18.2 miles.) Drive across the railroad tracks and follow the paved road to the east. As the road curves left toward the buildings, continue straight on the gravel road. This will put you at the south end of three large ponds (two are likely to be entirely dry) enclosed by dikes that can be driven or walked. Be aware that the roads can be a real mess when wet and that vegetation can be thick by late summer. The extensive trees at the south end are an excellent spot to search for passerines. Water levels, and thus shorebird and waterbird habitat, vary. Though still a worthwhile stop, a limited amount of water has reduced habitat at the ponds and they are just a shadow of their former glory.

The ponds are still birdy all year and can be exceptional during migration. Fully one-half (some 320 species) of the Texas state list has been seen here, making this one of the best vagrant traps in the Southwest. Resident birds include "Mexican Duck," Ruddy Duck, Pied-billed and Eared Grebes, American Kestrel, Scaled and Gambel's Quail, Common Moorhen, American Coot, Killdeer, Mourning Dove, Greater Roadrunner, Ladder-backed Woodpecker, Say's Phoebe, Loggerhead Shrike, Verdin, Cactus Wren, Crissal Thrasher (very reliable), Black-throated Sparrow, and Pyrrhuloxia. Additional summer nesters are Swainson's Hawk, Black-necked Stilt, American Avocet, Lesser Nighthawk, Western Kingbird, Blue Grosbeak, and Bullock's Oriole. Winter brings in a variety of waterfowl, raptors (Harris's Hawk is a rare possibility at any season), Northern Flicker, Marsh Wren, Green-tailed and Spotted Tow-hees, and an assortment of sparrows, including Swamp.

The ponds contain no fish, so although numerous gulls and herons have been seen, they generally do not linger. If mudflats are present, shorebirding can be exceptional. Over 35 shorebird species have been seen, including the first Red-necked Stint for Texas in July 1996. Anything is possible in migration, and up to 100 total species have been seen in a day. A partial list of the incredible assortment of rarities deserves mention: White-winged Scoter, Long-tailed Duck, Masked Duck, Brown Pelican, Reddish Egret, Glossy Ibis, Gray Hawk, Piping Plover, Red Knot, Ruff, Western Gull, Arctic Tern, Spotted Owl (specimen), Downy Woodpecker, Yellow-throated Vireo, Blue-winged, Golden-winged, Magnolia, Blackburnian, Prairie, Palm, and Mourning War-blers, Varied Bunting, Eastern Towhee, Bobolink, and Lawrence's Goldfinch.

In the warmer months, look for lizards, including Desert Side-blotched, Twin-spotted Spiny, Texas Horned, and several species of whiptails. Be careful if you decide to wander off the roads: Prairie Rattlesnakes are common in the brush. On another cautionary note, illegal shooting occurs here frequently and it is common to find spent shotgun shells along the roads.

UPPER VALLEY

The Rio Grande Valley on El Paso's northwest side is known locally as the Upper Valley, and it offers some of the most interesting and varied birding in the area. Established residential neighborhoods are a reasonable facsimile of woodland and are excellent in migration and winter. In addition to these neighborhoods and the Rio Grande itself, riparian thickets, ponds, canals, and agricultural fields intermix in this area. For the state lister, the geography is a bit baffling. The Texas/New Mexico state line does not follow the current course of the Rio Grande. There are areas of New Mexico to the east of the river, and portions of Texas to the west. A city map is the best way to sort out the situation.

Access is from Interstate 10 at exit 11 (Mesa Street) or exit 13 (Sunland Park Drive). From exit 13, go west on Sunland Park Drive for 0.85 mile to Gibson-Veck Road on your right. Turn left here into a short paved driveway. You are now in New Mexico, looking at the pond at the **Sunland Park Race-track**. The pond can be scoped from here over the rock wall. The primary attraction is the gull flock in winter. From late November into March, a flock of several hundred to a thousand Ring-billed Gulls roosts during the late afternoon (peaking just before dusk) after spending the day at a nearby landfill. A careful search will typically reveal a Herring Gull or two, and often a California Gull. Laughing, Mew, Thayer's, Iceland, Lesser Black-backed, and Glaucous Gulls have been seen in recent winters. Sabine's Gull has been found a handful of times in fall. There can be a decent assortment of waterfowl (Eurasian

Wigeon and Surf Scoter have been seen), and a small flock of Snow Geese (usually with a Ross's or two) winters in nearby fields and is sometimes seen at the pond. Eared Grebe is regular in winter. A few shorebirds and perhaps a Black Tern may be present in migration.

If the gull flock is not at the racetrack, check the nearby (and back inside Texas) **Keystone Heritage Park**, formerly known as Doniphan Marsh. Head north on Doniphan Drive from its intersection with Sunland Park Drive for 0.6 mile, turn right onto Kappa, and take an immediate left into the parking lot of the El Paso Desert Botanical Gardens. The marsh will be beyond the fence to the north. Expect the fence to be locked here, though future plans call for making it open at times for birding. You can readily scope the marsh from the parking lot.

The gull flock often spends much of the afternoon roosting and bathing in the water at the south end of the marsh, with birds coming and going much of the time. All of the rare winter species seen at Sunland Park Racetrack have also been seen here. Eventually, as dusk approaches, the gulls will head over to the racetrack, allowing you to perhaps add a rarity for both states. Resident species include Wood Duck, Ruddy Duck, Pied-billed Grebe, Common Moorhen, American Coot, and Killdeer. Summer brings nesting Black-necked Stilts (occasionally lingering into winter) and American Avocets. Although not a great area for shorebirds, a decent variety may be found in migration. Greater Yellowlegs is regular in winter, along with Least Sandpiper. Great Blue Heron, Great and Snowy Egrets, and Green Heron are usually present, although the latter three can be missing in winter. Hundreds of migrant White-faced Ibises roost at dusk. Immense numbers of Yellow-headed Black-birds, almost entirely males, winter in west El Paso. Thousands can be seen here at dusk, when they cover the utility lines and cattail beds. It makes for quite an impressive spectacle. Blackbird roost-sites do sometimes change from year to year. This site has not been great for non-gull rarities, but Surf Scoter and Little Blue and Tricolored Herons have been recorded.

There are two good spots for accessing the Rio Grande near here. Both are in New Mexico. The traffic light on Doniphan just south of Kappa is Frontera. Head west on Frontera about 1.5 miles until it dead-ends. You crossed into New Mexico when Frontera became dirt. Unless signs indicate otherwise you can park here, cross the small canal, and walk the levee of the Rio Grande for several miles in each direction. In winter, look for various ducks, Green Heron (rare), raptors, including Ferruginous Hawk, Greater Roadrunner, Belted Kingfisher, Black and Say's Phoebes, Verdin, Bewick's and Marsh Wrens, Ruby-crowned Kinglet, Crissal Thrasher, American Pipit, Phainopepla, Yellow-rumped Warbler, various sparrows, Pyrrhuloxia, and Western Meadowlark. The floodplain to the south has numerous trees which may hold some migrants. Evidence of American Beaver is easy to find here. To reach the other river access, head back east on Frontera to Gibson-Veck Road (0.8 mile). On the way, note Girl Scout Lane; a pond on the right about

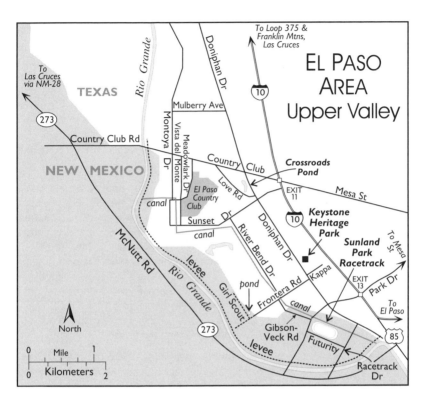

To Loop 375 &
Franklin Mtns,
Las Cruces

EL PASO
AREA
Upper Valley

To
Las Cruces
via NM-28

TEXAS

273

Rio Grande

Doniphan Dr

Mulberry Ave

10

Country Club Rd

NEW MEXICO

Montoya Dr

Meadowlark Dr

Vista del Monte

Country Club

Love Rd

Crossroads
Pond

EXIT
11

Mesa St

El Paso
Country
Club

canal

Sunset Dr

canal

Dr

River Bend Dr

Doniphan Dr

10

Keystone
Heritage
Park

Sunland
Park
Racetrack

To Mesa St.

McNutt Rd

Rio Grande

levee

Girl Scout

pond

Frontera Rd

Kappa

EXIT
13

Park Dr

To
El Paso

North

273

Gibson-
Veck Rd

canal

Futurity

85

Mile

levee

Racetrack
Dr

Kilometers

100 yards up is worth a quick peek and sometimes has shorebird habitat. Mississippi Kite, a local breeder, often can be seen overhead along Frontera from May to August. Turn right on Gibson-Veck and go to Sunland Park Drive (0.5 mile). Turn right here to Futurity Drive (0.4 mile), then go left to Racetrack Drive (0.5 mile). A right turn takes you to the Rio Grande in 0.3 mile. Just before the river, turn right into the gravel parking lot of the park. Once again, the levee can be walked in both directions from the bridge. The birds will be similar to those at the other access point; however, Black-necked Stilt is fairly regular in winter and the gull flock sometimes hangs out on sandbars downstream of the bridge.

Several excellent spots can be reached by exiting Interstate 10 at Mesa Street, exit 11. Go west on Mesa (after 0.6 mile it is called Country Club Road) for 1.05 miles and turn left onto Love Road. Park on the left by a fence (0.6 mile). The small pond here, known as Crossroads Pond, is reliable in winter for Wood Duck, Gadwall, American Wigeon, Mallard, Northern Shoveler, Green-winged Teal, Ruddy Duck, and Pied-billed Grebe. Diving ducks are more unlikely possibilities. Green Heron is usually present in summer and may be around in winter. Neotropic Cormorant is regular, and a Least Grebe spent three weeks here in the winter of 2005–2006.

Return to Country Club Road and head west toward the Rio Grande (1.0 mile). Notice cross streets such as Meadowlark, Vista del Monte, and Montoya. The richly wooded neighborhoods for a mile to the north and south offer good birding in migration and in winter. Unless otherwise posted, the dirt roads along the numerous irrigation canals can be walked. Once again, a city map will be helpful. Look between Doniphan Drive on the east, Sunset Drive to the south, Mulberry to the north, and the Rio Grande to the west. Although the residents here are accustomed to some birding activity, these are among El Paso's most exclusive neighborhoods; *respect the property and privacy of the homeowners, please.*

Resident and breeding birds to look for are Mississippi Kite (summer), American Kestrel, White-winged, Mourning, and Inca Doves, Yellow-billed Cuckoo (rare, summer), Lesser Nighthawk (summer), Black-chinned Hummingbird (summer), Ladder-backed Woodpecker, Black Phoebe, Western Kingbird (summer), American Robin, Northern Mockingbird, Phainopepla, and Bullock's Oriole (summer). Winter is often the best time to visit, with Sharp-shinned and Cooper's Hawks, Belted Kingfisher, Yellow-bellied (rare) and Red-naped Sapsuckers, Northern Flicker, Plumbeous and Cassin's Vireos (both rare), Ruby-crowned Kinglet, Cedar Waxwing (irregular), Orange-crowned and Yellow-rumped Warblers, Spotted Towhee, White-crowned Sparrow, Dark-eyed Junco, and American Goldfinch.

Irregular montane invaders in fall and winter add spice to the scene: Western Scrub-Jay, Red-breasted Nuthatch, Western Bluebird, and Pine Siskin are nearly annual and can be common some years. The following species are highly irregular and are completely absent most years, but are occasionally present: Steller's Jay, Mountain Chickadee, White-breasted and Pygmy Nuthatches, Eastern Bluebird, Townsend's Solitaire, Cassin's Finch, Red Crossbill, and Evening Grosbeak. Expect the unexpected in migration. Rarities from all directions have sought refuge in these "woodlands." These include Northern Goshawk, Band-tailed Pigeon, Ruddy Ground-Dove, Ruby-throated Hummingbird, Lewis's, Acorn, Downy, and Hairy Woodpeckers, Juniper Titmouse, Bushtit, Carolina Wren, Gray Silky-flycatcher (January–March 1995), a number of rare warblers (including Red-faced), Golden-crowned Sparrow, and Lawrence's Goldfinch. A particularly good spot is along a canal near the west end of Sunset Road. From Doniphan, head west on Sunset until you cross a canal (1.4 miles). Turn right and park. You can walk the canal to the north until it ends at the levee of the Rio Grande. The salt cedars along the canal can be very good in migration, especially for warblers. Lucy's Warbler has become somewhat regular in late summer and early fall. You may hear or see some Lilac-crowned Parrots from an escaped flock that frequents this area. Cave Swallows nest under the bridge at the parking spot.

Once you are at the Country Club bridge over the Rio Grande, it is possible to walk the west levee south for about ten minutes to a fairly extensive area of cottonwoods, canals, and brush. This spot is known locally as Randall's

Pool and is in New Mexico. Wood Duck is regular, and migrants can abound. Expect to see Gambel's Quail and Crissal Thrasher. In recent years, increased residential construction and its use as a campsite by transients have made this area less productive, and, at times, a bit creepy to bird alone.

The most direct route to Las Cruces, New Mexico, is to return to Interstate 10 via Country Club Road. Another possibility is to continue west for 1.0 mile to NM-273, McNutt Road. Turn right here. In about 6 miles, you will reach the intersection with NM-28, which can be followed north through agricultural fields and pecan orchards to Las Cruces. Cave Swallows breed under bridges at 5.1 and 5.5 miles north of this intersection. When discovered, this site was the species' first known breeding locale in New Mexico away from the Carlsbad Caverns area. Flooded fields can hold shorebirds; check the edges of the pecan groves (private and generally fenced) for migrants.

Before you reach NM-28, note a turn to Airport Road 1.7 miles after turning onto McNutt Road. Turn left here and go to the traffic light (2.3 miles). Turn left onto NM-136 and go 2.5 miles. A right turn here will take you west on good paved roads (NM-9) to Portal, Arizona, about 170 miles away. This road is the most direct and scenic route from El Paso to Arizona. Services are few and far between, but gas is available in Columbus and usually in Animas. Pancho Villa State Park in Columbus can be productive during migration and winter, and the nearby fields can host large wintering flocks of Snow Geese and Sandhill Cranes.

LAS CRUCES, NEW MEXICO

Las Cruces is a growing city of nearly 100,000 located in the valley of the Rio Grande some 40 miles north of El Paso. It is here that this book bids farewell to the Rio Grande, having followed the river some 1,300 miles from the Gulf of Mexico. For the birder traveling west on Interstate 10, the Arizona state line is only 140 miles distant. En route, a visit to the Gila River at Redrock, north of Lordsburg, can yield several species that occur only locally in New Mexico, such as Common Black-Hawk, Gila Woodpecker, and Abert's Towhee. If you are traveling north on Interstate 25, a side trip into the Black Range west of Hillsboro via NM-152 (exit 63) might yield Zone-tailed Hawk (uncommon), Band-tailed Pigeon, Flammulated Owl (summer), Steller's Jay, Mountain Chickadee, Bridled and Juniper Titmice, Pygmy Nuthatch, Olive Warbler (uncommon, summer), Grace's Warbler (summer), Red-faced Warbler (summer), and Painted Redstart (summer). Percha Dam State Park and Caballo Lake (exit 59), and Bosque del Apache National Wildlife Refuge (exit 139), are well worth visiting at any season. (See References for information on birdfinding guides covering all of these areas.)

As well as offering a wealth of restaurants and hotels, the Las Cruces area is close to some fine birding spots, including the nearest Ponderosa Pine

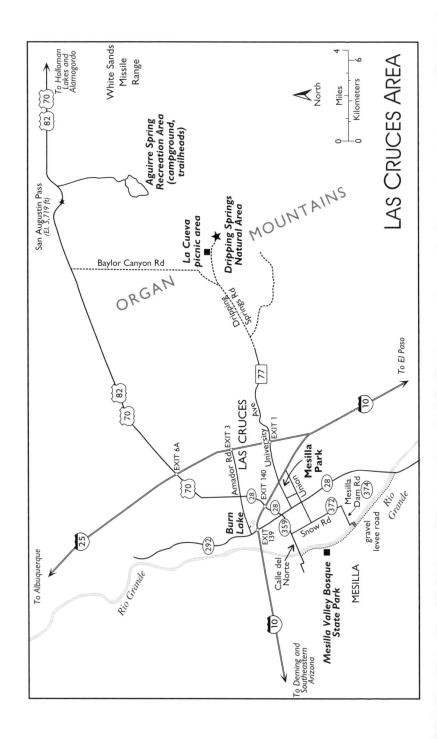

LAS CRUCES AREA

woods to El Paso. One of the best spots is the **Mesilla Valley Bosque State Park** (formerly known as the Old Refuge), a remnant of thickets and trees along this very heavily cultivated stretch of the Rio Grande. To reach the park, part of the New Mexico state park system, leave Interstate 10 at the Avenue de Mesilla/NM-28 exit (exit 140). Go south on NM-28 for 1.0 mile, then turn right onto NM-359 (Calle del Norte) at the north edge of Mesilla. Continue west for 2.0 miles over the Rio Grande and park on the left. Walk south along the levee about one mile to the park; the large field on the right can be good for raptors. At the park there are two small ponds, as well as a canal running to the south. Plans call for an entrance road from Calle del Norte, as well as a visitor center.

Look for residents such as Gambel's Quail, Great Blue Heron, American Kestrel, Common Moorhen, White-winged Dove, Barn Owl, Greater Road-runner, Ladder-backed Woodpecker, Black and Say's Phoebes, Loggerhead Shrike, Verdin, Bewick's Wren, Crissal Thrasher, Pyrrhuloxia, and House Finch. In winter, check mistletoe-infested cottonwoods for Eastern (rare) and Western Bluebirds; both are irregular. Long-eared Owls have wintered in dense thickets along the canal. A few dabbling ducks will be on the river. Look for Least Sandpiper and American Pipit on the sandbars. Other wintering birds are Northern Harrier, Sharp-shinned, Cooper's, and Ferruginous Hawks, Belted Kingfisher, Western Scrub-Jay (irregular), American Crow, Marsh Wren, Ruby-crowned Kinglet, Yellow-rumped Warbler, Green-tailed and Spotted Towhees, and Chipping, Brewer's, Vesper, Savannah, Song, Lincoln's, Swamp, White-throated (rare), and White-crowned Sparrows. Breeders include Yellow-billed Cuckoo, Lesser Nighthawk, Black-chinned Hummingbird, Western Kingbird, Ash-throated Flycatcher, Yellow-breasted Chat, Blue Grosbeak, and Bullock's Oriole. Migration can be very birdy. Note that areas like this along the river are popular for off-road vehicle use, illegal shooting, partying, and other activities that can detract from the birding.

Formerly, it was possible to cross the Rio Grande at the Mesilla Dam and approach the Old Refuge from the south. Though this is no longer an option, the area around the Mesilla Dam still offers good birding. To reach this spot, head back toward Mesilla on Calle del Norte from the Rio Grande. Turn right onto Snow Road (NM-372) (1.0 mile) and head south to NM-374 (2.6 miles). Turn right here and go to the Rio Grande (1.0 mile). It is possible to drive the levee to the north back to Calle del Norte (2.8 miles), though a gate may block the levee 1.1 miles north of NM-374 and force you to backtrack. This section of the levee, with the river on one side and a brushy canal and pecan groves on the other, can be productive birding. Ruddy Ground-Dove and Varied Thrush are among the rarities spotted in recent years. The pecan groves are all private and posted.

A different nearby habitat is the wooded residential neighborhoods of **Mesilla Park**. Like neighborhoods in El Paso, the trees attract an interesting assortment of wintering birds, especially montane species like corvids, nuthatches, and finches. In addition, the abundant vegetation, ornamental plantings, and relatively warm microclimates can hold lingerers into winter. The following rarities have been found in winter: Yellow-bellied Sapsucker, Hammond's Flycatcher, Hutton's Vireo, Mountain Chickadee, Pygmy Nuthatch, Olive Warbler, and Hepatic Tanager. A careful search in winter should turn up Plumbeous or Cassin's Vireo, along with Orange-crowned Warbler. Migration is also an excellent time to visit. The handful of winter Olive Warbler records, along with a few records from the Organ Mountains, suggests that a few pairs may nest in the Organ Mountains.

To reach Mesilla Park, go south on NM-28 from Interstate 10 for about 2 miles to NM-373 (Union Avenue). Turn left on Union to McDowell (0.5 mile); park here. The best areas can be canvassed by walking north on McDowell to Conway, east to Bowman, and then south back to Union. Mississippi Kite has bred here a time or two, and White-winged Dove cannot be missed at any season. Confine your birding to the roads, and respect the property and privacy of the residents.

Another local spot is worth a brief mention. **Burn Lake** is a small fishing lake with steep, sterile dirt banks. It can be reached by leaving I-10 at exit 139 (NM-292/Motel Boulevard) and going north to the first right, Amador Road. Turn right onto Amador, then make another right at the sign for Burn Lake (0.8 mile). The lake is not worth a special trip, but stop by if you are in the neighborhood. It can be thoroughly birded in ten minutes. Wintering waterfowl may include Canvasback, Redhead, Ring-necked Duck, Lesser Scaup, and Bufflehead. Expect Pied-billed and maybe Eared Grebes in winter; Western or Clark's Grebes are rarer possibilities. The domestic goose contingent may include a habituated Snow or Ross's Goose. Rare species such as White-winged Scoter, Pacific Loon, and Brown Pelican have been recorded, and the first Elegant Tern for New Mexico visited in May 2001.

ORGAN MOUNTAINS, NEW MEXICO

The dominant feature on the Las Cruces horizon is the imposing Organ Mountain range just east of town. This rugged range is crossed by only one road, and explorations must be made on foot. An excellent site is **Dripping Springs Natural Area** (entrance fee), jointly administered by the Bureau of Land Management and The Nature Conservancy. To reach Dripping Springs, exit Interstate 25 at exit 1 (University Avenue), and head east on University. Continue east after the road turns to gravel (4.9 miles) to the lot for the A. B. Cox Visitor Center (5.3 miles), open seven days a week year-round from 8:00AM to dusk. Sign in here, pick up a trail map, and check the chalkboard showing recent wildlife sightings. The desert en route is good for desert residents, including the local Black-tailed Gnatcatcher. Sage Sparrow is possible in winter. Hummingbird feeders at the visitor center could have Cal-

Pyrrhuloxia   Brad McKinney

liope, Broad-tailed, and Rufous Hummingbirds from mid-July through September.

Begin your easy 30-minute hike to Dripping Springs from the south end of the parking lot. The crumbling remains of several century-old ventures, a hotel, and a tuberculosis clinic are clustered in the oaks and hackberries near the springs. The trail follows a wash before passing through an open area with scattered junipers. Resident and breeding birds include Turkey Vulture (summer), Red-tailed Hawk, Golden Eagle, American Kestrel, Mourning Dove,

White-throated Swift, Black-chinned Hummingbird (summer), Ladder-backed Woodpecker, Ash-throated Flycatcher (summer), Violet-green Swallow (summer), Cactus, Rock, and Canyon Wrens, Curve-billed Thrasher, Phainopepla, Canyon Towhee, Rufous-crowned Sparrow, Blue Grosbeak (summer), and Scott's Oriole (summer). This is a very good place for Black-chinned Sparrow, which can be common in winter.

Winter birding can be slow. Much depends on the supply of hackberries, which can attract Eastern, Western, and Mountain Bluebirds, Townsend's Solitaire, Hermit Thrush, American Robin, and Sage Thrasher some years. Other montane species such as Steller's Jay, Western Scrub-Jay, Mountain Chickadee, Juniper Titmouse, Bushtit, nuthatches, Cassin's Finch, and Evening Grosbeak may be present during occasional winters, but are usually absent. Expect to see Ruby-crowned Kinglet, Green-tailed and Spotted Towhees, and various sparrows. Long-eared Owls sometimes flush from the dense trees.

On your drive back to Las Cruces, note the La Cueva picnic area on your right about one-half mile west of the visitor center. This, too, is part of the natural area, and a trail meanders between it and the visitor center. Long-eared Owls sometimes roost in winter in the brushy ravine. This can be a good spot for Black-tailed Gnatcatcher. The Fillmore Canyon trail, which loops around to the north of the rocks, also starts here. Expect similar birds to those on the Dripping Springs trail. Native Americans inhabited caves (*cuevas* in Spanish) at the base of the beautiful red cliffs. If you are headed to Aguirre Spring, you might want to turn right on Baylor Canyon Road (about 2 miles west of the visitor center) and take this road north to US-70/82 at a point about 10.6 miles east of Interstate 25. Desert birds can be found along Baylor Canyon Road.

AGUIRRE SPRING RECREATION AREA, NEW MEXICO

Aguirre **Spring Recreation Area** (entrance fee, additional fee for camping) on the east side of the Organ Mountains offers access to oak/juniper woodland, with Ponderosa Pines at higher elevations. This is the closest location to El Paso for a handful of montane breeding species. Leave I-25 in Las Cruces at exit 6A and take US-70/82 east to San Augustin Pass (elevation 5,719 ft) (13.7 miles). Continue east to the turn for Aguirre Spring (1.1 miles). Take the paved road south to the camping area and trailheads (5.5 miles). The gate opens daily at 8:00AM to non-campers.

The scenery here is beautiful. The broad Tularosa Basin to the east is home to the White Sands Missile Range and White Sands National Monument. Across the basin rise the Sacramento Mountains, with extensive areas of coniferous forest above 8,500 feet elevation. To the northeast is the towering cone of Sierra Blanca, southern New Mexico's highest peak at 12,003 feet. Collared Lizard is fairly common at Aguirre Spring, and Chihuahuan Spotted Whiptail is abundant along the trails in summer.

Park on the left across from the trailhead for the Pine Tree Trail. This 4.5-mile loop will take several hours at least and has considerable elevation gain. Pack water at any season and be prepared in winter for the potential of abrupt temperature changes or cold, snowy conditions. The trail passes through open Ponderosa Pine woodland at the top.

Resident and breeding birds around the trailhead are White-throated Swift (rare in winter), Black-chinned and Broad-tailed Hummingbirds (summer), Acorn Woodpecker, Western Wood-Pewee (summer), Cassin's Kingbird (summer), Gray Vireo (irregular, summer), Violet-green Swallow (summer), Juniper Titmouse, Bushtit, Rock, Canyon, and Bewick's Wrens, Hepatic Tanager (summer), Rufous-crowned and Black-chinned Sparrows, Black-headed Grosbeak (summer), Scott's Oriole (summer), and Lesser Goldfinch. Campers should listen for Western Screech-Owl and Common Poorwill. On the upper reaches of the trail look for breeding Cordilleran Flycatcher, Plumbeous and Hutton's Vireos, White-breasted Nuthatch (resident), Mountain Chickadee (rare resident), Virginia's Warbler (in thickets of Gambel Oak), Black-throated Gray Warbler (rare, in oaks), Grace's Warbler, and Hepatic Tanager. Northern Pygmy-Owl has been sighted here a couple of times, and there are a few records of Olive Warbler, perhaps a rare breeder on the highest slopes.

Winter birding is highly variable and often can be slow. Typically this is a good area for frugivores such as bluebirds, Townsend's Solitaire, and Sage Thrasher, but these species can be completely absent some winters. In some winters, jays, nuthatches, Cassin's Finch, Red Crossbill, and Evening Grosbeak (very rare) are present.

If you are heading east on US-70/82 toward Alamogordo, be sure to stop at Holloman Lakes, an excellent spot for shorebirds and waterbirds. Snowy Plovers breed there, and many rarities have turned up over the years. This site is reached by turning left onto a dirt road just past an alkali flat, 39 miles east on US-70/82 from the turnoff to Aguirre Spring.

GUADALUPE MOUNTAINS NATIONAL PARK

Birders who are trying to build up their Texas lists will find that a visit to the **Guadalupe Mountains** is a must. This is the only place in the state where some Rocky Mountain species can be found reliably. This is also one of the best sites in the state for Juniper Titmouse, Grace's Warbler, and Hepatic Tanager, and it is also very good for Gray Vireo and Black-chinned Sparrow.

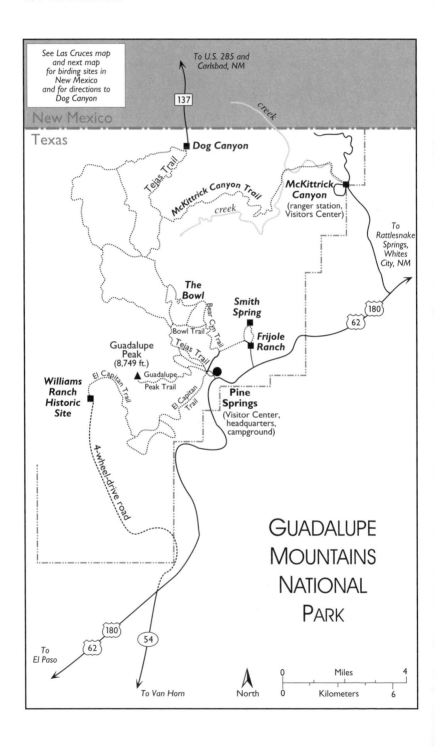

See Las Cruces map
and next map
for birding sites in
New Mexico
and for directions to
Dog Canyon

To U.S. 285 and
Carlsbad, NM

137

creek

New Mexico

Texas

■ Dog Canyon

Tejas Trail

McKittrick Canyon Trail

creek

McKittrick
Canyon
(ranger station,
Visitors Center)

To
Rattlesnake
Springs,
Whites
City, NM

The
Bowl

Bear Cyn Trail

Bowl Trail

Tejas Trail

Smith
Spring

Frijole
Ranch

Guadalupe
Peak
(8,749 ft.)

▲ Guadalupe
Peak Trail

El Capitan Trail

El Capitan
Trail

180

62

Williams
Ranch
Historic
Site

Pine
Springs
(Visitor Center,
headquarters,
campground)

4-wheel-drive road

GUADALUPE
MOUNTAINS
NATIONAL
PARK

180

62

To
El Paso

54

To Van Horn

North

0   Miles   4

0   Kilometers   6

To reach this interesting area, drive east from Hueco Tanks on US-62/180 for 88 miles (the park is 110 miles east of El Paso). Watch for Pronghorn along the middle sections of this drive. If you are coming from Van Horn, head north on US-54 for some 60 miles. This 76,293-acre park was created in 1972. It is intended to have only limited development; there is a primitive campground and a number of trails. Stop at the visitor center for more information. Pick up a bird checklist as well as maps, books, and other literature.

Approaching from the south, the most impressive view of the Guadalupe Mountains is the towering cliffs of El Capitan (elevation 8,085 feet), perhaps the most-photographed natural landmark in Texas. This majestic peak marks the southern end of Capitan Reef, an ancient limestone formation that was laid down beneath the oceans of long ago. From El Capitan the reef rises to the top of Guadalupe Peak (elevation 8,749 feet), the highest point in Texas, and then slopes downward into New Mexico like the prow of a colossal ship rising from the land. The edges of the reef have been eroded into deep canyons. The center has been partially dissolved to form huge caves such as those of Carlsbad Caverns, which are in the northern part of the reef.

The visitor center and headquarters is located at **Pine Springs**, the first road to the left as you drive north from the south park boundary sign (0.9 mile). The campground is located nearby at the trailhead for El Capitan and Guadalupe Peak. To really see Guadalupe Mountains National Park, one must be prepared to hike. There are 80 miles of hiking trails. Over 250 species of birds have been recorded in the park, and most are seen only by hiking, although some are found at the campground and several other places where one can drive. Resident birds around Pine Springs include Scaled Quail, Red-tailed Hawk, Golden Eagle, American Kestrel, Mourning Dove, Greater Roadrunner, Western Screech-Owl, Great Horned Owl, Common Poorwill (not in winter), Acorn and Ladder-backed Woodpeckers, Phainopepla, Green-tailed (rare in summer), Spotted, and Canyon Towhees, Rufous-crowned, Chipping, Black-chinned, Lark (summer), and Black-throated Sparrows, and Pyrrhuloxia. In winter, look also for Mountain Chickadee, Western Bluebird, Sage Thrasher, Dark-eyed Junco, and various sparrows.

Continuing north on US-62/180, turn left at the road (1.2 miles) leading to **Frijole Ranch** (0.7 mile). The old ranch house has a spring in the yard with pecans and Chinkapin Oaks. A trailhead to Smith and Manzanita Springs (2.3 miles round-trip) is also located here. In winter, rare woodpeckers, such as Red-headed, Lewis's, and Williamson's Sapsucker, have been found. All three bluebirds can be rather common some winters, both in the yard and in the surrounding junipers. Look also for Western Scrub-Jay, Townsend's Solitaire, Sage Thrasher, resident Juniper Titmouse, and, in some years, Cassin's Finch. Juniper-clad mountain slopes such as these are particularly attractive to wintering frugivores, but numbers vary annually.

McKittrick Canyon — Possibly the prettiest spot in the park is McKittrick Canyon, which is reached by continuing on US-62/180 for some 5 miles to the turnoff on the left, and then to the end of the road (4.4 miles). This is a day-use-only area. There is a small ranger station and visitor center here. The trail starts in the low desert, but as you gently climb higher, the canyon closes in and the walls get higher and higher, reaching over 2,000 feet in places. The canyon eventually forks. The north fork is rugged and much drier. The south fork has a permanent supply of water, which is first encountered as scattered puddles, then as a quiet brook, and finally as a rushing, rock-hopping stream.

In the desert brushland at the mouth of the canyon, you should find Scaled Quail, Greater Roadrunner, Ladder-backed Woodpecker, Verdin, Cactus and Rock Wrens, Curve-billed and Crissal Thrashers, Canyon Towhee, Rufous-crowned and Black-throated Sparrows, Pyrrhuloxia, and House Finch. In winter, look for Sage Thrasher, Spotted Towhee, and numerous sparrows, including Chipping, Brewer's, Song, Lincoln's, and White-crowned. You may also see Desert Cottontail, Black-tailed Jackrabbit, Texas Antelope Squirrel, Rock Squirrel, Porcupine, American Badger, Striped and Common Hog-nosed Skunks, Bobcat, and Mule Deer.

Farther up the canyon, the talus slopes become covered with dense brush, and the streamside forest of Alligator Juniper, Gray Oak, Black Walnut, Velvet Ash, and Texas Madrone gets thicker. The canyon is well known for the vivid fall colors of its Bigtooth Maples. Scattered throughout are huge Faxon Yuccas, an endemic species that may reach 20 feet in height. An unforgettable sight is to see Scott's Orioles feeding in the yucca's six-foot stalks of snowy-white flowers. The yucca in lower grassy flats with thinner, floppier leaves is Soaptree Yucca.

In spring, the canyon rings with the songs of Gray, Plumbeous, and Warbling Vireos and Black-headed Grosbeak. It is an excellent location for Black-chinned Sparrows. However, the one sound which dominates the canyon is the song of the Canyon Wren, tripping down from every ledge and cliff. Higher up, every pine may seem to have a Grace's Warbler singing from its tip, and you might see Wild Turkey, Zone-tailed Hawk, and Hepatic Tanager.

Other birds to look for in McKittrick Canyon are White-throated Swift, Blue-throated (rare) and Black-chinned Hummingbirds, Acorn and Ladder-backed Woodpeckers, Say's Phoebe, Ash-throated Flycatcher, Cassin's Kingbird, Western Scrub-Jay, Cliff Swallow, Bushtit, Bewick's Wren, Virginia's Warbler, Western Tanager, Spotted and Canyon Towhees, Rufous-crowned Sparrow, Blue Grosbeak, Hooded Oriole (rare), and Lesser Goldfinch. Many of these species are breeders only. In winter, look for Cooper's and Sharp-shinned Hawks, Golden Eagle, Steller's Jay, Mountain Chickadee, Golden-crowned Kinglet, and Hermit Thrush. There are two records of American Dipper, and one winter a Yellow-eyed Junco stayed the season.

El Capitan, Guadalupe Mountains National Park   Mark Lockwood

The upper reaches of the canyon have never been open to cattle, thanks to the far-sighted conservation attitude of its owners, J. C. Hunter, Jr. and Wallace Pratt. These men realized that the fragile habitats would have been destroyed by grazing. Because of their enlightened vision, the park has a canyon that is little changed from its pristine condition.

The high country along the top of McKittrick Ridge is well-forested with Douglas-fir, Limber and Ponderosa Pines, and even Quaking Aspen. In this forested area, you should find Band-tailed Pigeon, Hairy Woodpecker, Steller's Jay, Mountain Chickadee, White-breasted and Pygmy Nuthatches, Brown Creeper, Western Bluebird, Hermit Thrush, Dark-eyed Junco, Red Crossbill (irregular), and Pine Siskin. In summer, there may be Blue-throated (rare), Magnificent (rare), Black-chinned, and Broad-tailed Hummingbirds, Olive-sided and Cordilleran Flycatchers, Western Wood-Pewee, Violet-green Swallow, Blue-gray Gnatcatcher, Orange-crowned, Virginia's, and Yellow-rumped Warblers, Hepatic and Western Tanagers, and Black-headed Grosbeak. Also watch for Gray-footed Chipmunk, Porcupine, Mule Deer, and Elk.

The Bowl — North of Guadalupe Peak is a forested depression rimmed on three sides by the sharp edges of the reef. Fittingly, it is known as The Bowl. The only way to reach these highland forests is to hike. The 4-mile trail to the top of Guadalupe Peak is popular and offers an excellent view. The Bowl can be reached by a roundabout trail via Pine Canyon, or by the 2.5-mile trail up Bear Canyon. Each originates near the park's main visitor center.

Most birders use the Bear Canyon Trail, but it has one slight drawback: although relatively short, it goes almost straight up the side of the escarpment. Be sure to get an early start and take lots of water. As you rest at the top of each switchback, enjoy the magnificent view and scan the sky for Zone-tailed Hawk and Golden Eagle. Near the top of the trail, if you are very lucky, you may flush a Spotted Owl, but you will have to stay overnight to see or hear Flammulated Owl, Western Screech-Owl, Common Nighthawk, and Whip-poor-will. Most of the other birds found in The Bowl are similar to those listed above for McKittrick Ridge.

Hikes to The Bowl should not be taken lightly. Camping is primitive and one must carry in all supplies, including water. Strong winds in excess of 50 miles per hour are not unusual in the Guadalupes and are especially prevalent in spring. Strong thunderstorms with heavy lightning can materialize quickly in summer and early fall. In addition, sudden temperature swings are possible at any season.

Dog Canyon — A less physically challenging way to reach forested areas in the Guadalupe Mountains is to drive in from the north side via Dog Canyon. This means traveling into New Mexico. Drive north on US-62/180 to the New Mexico line and beyond about 16 miles to Whites City. Here is the entrance to Carlsbad Caverns National Park. Continue north for another 9.5 miles before turning left onto FR-408 (Dark Canyon Road). After 22.6 miles, turn left onto NM-137 and follow it into Dog Canyon. The road is paved all the way except for the last half-mile into Dog Canyon. By the way, Dog Canyon is back inside Texas, so you should keep your state lists properly shuffled. The campground here has water and modern restrooms, and there is a trailhead for several trails with relatively easy grades.

In this forested area of junipers, pines, maples, and oaks, look for Band-tailed Pigeon, Hairy Woodpecker, Steller's Jay, Mountain Chickadee, Pygmy Nuthatch, and Dark-eyed Junco. In summer, there should be Broad-tailed Hummingbird, Olive-sided and Cordilleran Flycatchers, Warbling Vireo, Violet-green Swallow, Western Bluebird, Hermit Thrush, Yellow-rumped Warbler, Hepatic and Western Tanagers, Black-headed Grosbeak, and Red Crossbill (irregular).

After exploring the Dog Canyon area, you may wish to bird the North Rim Road (FR-540) for wonderful views down into North McKittrick Canyon. Birds of this area include many of the same species seen in The Bowl and other higher park elevations. The North Rim trail eventually crosses back into Texas and ends at the escarpment overlooking the mouth of McKittrick Canyon. *Do not descend into the canyon.* This is an extremely fragile area and each hiker's passage carries the potential of increasing the damage that it has already sustained.

A detour to Sitting Bull Falls on FR-409 on the way out of the area is a wonderful way to spend an afternoon. The falls are impressive, and the climb into the cool caves behind them is worth the effort. Birding is excellent in the riparian area above the falls where the stream feeds the falls themselves. There are several deep pools for swimming. A rough trail to the top of the falls leaves from the parking area and follows switchbacks to the top. It is fairly easy and short, and promises many of the same species found in McKittrick Canyon.

CARLSBAD CAVERNS NATIONAL PARK, NEW MEXICO

On your way to and from Dog Canyon you will pass Carlsbad Caverns National Park. The spectacular caverns are worth a visit, and one site in the park, Rattlesnake Springs, offers excellent birding.

From Whites City, go south on US-62/180 for 5.4 miles to CR-418 (Washington Ranch Road). This intersection is 10.3 miles north of the Texas/New Mexico line. Head west on CR-418 for 2.3 miles to the stop sign. Turn right for 0.15 mile, then left into Rattlesnake Springs. Going straight ahead before this last turn will take you to Washington Ranch, a private facility that can be used for functions such as weddings and parties. It may even be possible to rent a room (505-785-2228). In recent years, a trickle of birders has birded the wooded grounds. If you ask permission at the office (often closed on weekends and holidays), park out of the way, and are quiet and unobtrusive, you will likely be able to bird the property. The birds here are similar to those at Rattlesnake Springs, and migration can be exciting. Please don't intrude on any functions, and do not do anything that would put birding privileges in jeopardy.

Rattlesnake Springs is a must during migration. The area is fairly small and can be thoroughly birded in several hours. The cottonwoods and dense brush surrounding the damp, grassy swales, all in the midst of arid surroundings, make it a fabulous migrant trap. Two of the best rarities ever seen here were a Piratic Flycatcher (September 1996) and a Yellow-green Vireo. Nearly every eastern warbler and passerine has been recorded. This is one of the best vagrant traps in the entire country. Expect to see an eastern warbler or two during any visit in the first half of May. Fall migration is more diffuse, but equally interesting. Expect the unexpected.

In summer, it's hard to miss breeders such as White-winged Dove, Yellow-billed Cuckoo, Vermilion Flycatcher, Cassin's and Western Kingbirds, Cliff and Barn Swallows, Common Yellowthroat, Yellow-breasted Chat, Summer Tanager, Blue Grosbeak, and Orchard and Bullock's Orioles. Be alert for more local and uncommon breeders, including Bell's Vireo, Northern Cardinal, Painted Bunting, and Hooded Oriole. Winter brings a variety of sparrows, as well as montane invaders some years. Brown Thrasher and Field Sparrow are rare but regular here at the western edge of their winter ranges. Resident Wild Turkeys are often seen, especially early in the morning, and Scaled Quail are common in adjacent arid areas.

You may have noticed signs for Slaughter Canyon Cave on your way in from US-62/180. The cave is reached by heading south on CR-418 (following signs and several road changes) for another 9.0 miles, and can be entered only by guided, prearranged tours. Although Cave Swallows can be seen at the mouth, it is not worth a special birding visit. The road ends before the trees appear in the canyon, and a lengthy hike is needed to reach the birdy areas.

Lastly, there are a few good birds to be had along the main road into Carlsbad Caverns. From Whites City head west on NM-7 toward the headquarters and caverns entrance (7.0 miles). Cave Swallows are abundant around the cave mouth. Along the road, check in brushy areas on the canyon floor for Varied Bunting, a rare and local breeder. It will be hard to miss Canyon Wren, Canyon Towhee, Rufous-crowned Sparrow, and other common desert birds. Just before reaching the headquarters, note the entrance on the right to the 9.5-mile wildlife drive. The one-way gravel loop passes through the arid brush typical of much of the park and is not especially birdy. Look for Green-tailed Towhee from fall through spring, along with numerous sparrows. Mountain Bluebird and Sage Thrasher are more sporadic, but they can be numerous at times. Gray Vireos nest along the road about 6 to 7 miles in; listen for their songs in areas of heavier juniper growth.

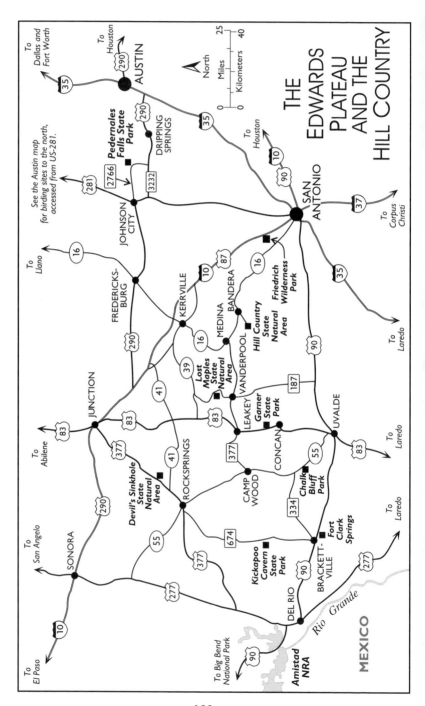

THE
EDWARDS
PLATEAU
AND THE
HILL COUNTRY

North

Miles
Kilometers

0   25
0   40

See the Austin map
for birding sites to the north,
accessed from US-281.

To Dallas and
Fort Worth

To Houston

AUSTIN

Pedernales
Falls State
Park

DRIPPING
SPRINGS

To Houston

SAN ANTONIO

To Corpus
Christi

JOHNSON CITY

To Llano

FREDERICKS-
BURG

KERRVILLE

MEDINA
BANDERA

Friedrich
Wilderness
Park

Hill Country
State Natural
Area

VANDERPOOL

Lost
Maples
State
Natural
Area

JUNCTION

To Abilene

LEAKEY

Garner
State
Park

CONCAN

UVALDE

To Laredo

To Laredo

ROCKSPRINGS

CAMP
WOOD

Chalk
Bluff
Park

Devil's Sinkhole
State Natural
Area

SONORA

To San Angelo

Kickapoo
Cavern
State Park

Fort Clark
Springs

BRACKETT-
VILLE

To Laredo

DEL RIO

Rio Grande

To Big Bend
National Park

Amistad
NRA

MEXICO

To El Paso

THE EDWARDS
PLATEAU

If you are generally following the route in this book, you might want to reach the Edwards Plateau by leaving the Rio Grande Valley at Laredo and traveling northward on Interstate 35. As an alternative, you might go as far northwest as Del Rio and travel eastward on US-90. Although there are birding opportunities to be enjoyed on the Edwards Plateau at any time of the year, spring and early summer is definitely the time most birders will want to visit this beautiful area.

The Edwards Plateau is the southernmost extension of the Great Plains and is characterized by its rolling terrain, which is honeycombed with caves and sinkholes. This distinct region is a well-defined formation of Cretaceous limestone that slopes from northwest to southeast. The northwestern and central regions of the plateau are characterized by broad, relatively level uplands between deep canyons. To the north, the plateau gradually grades into the Rolling Plains, but on the south it is bounded by the Balcones Escarpment (*ball-CO-nes*, Spanish for "balconies"). The escarpment is particularly steep along the southern boundary of the region. The deeply dissected portion adjacent to the escarpment is known as the Balcones Canyonlands and is the true "Hill Country" of Texas. In this region, it is not uncommon to see stream valleys that are over 200 feet below the surrounding ridges. To the west, the plateau is separated from the geologically similar Stockton Plateau by the Pecos/ Devils River divide.

The arid western end of the plateau (annual rainfall of 12 inches) still retains some of its original shortgrass prairies, but overgrazing has heavily modified many of them. The worst areas look like rocky wastelands. The eastern end of the plateau is much wetter (annual rainfall of 33 inches) and is characterized by wooded hills, valleys, and clear sparkling streams.

Historically, much of the plateau has been occupied by sheep and goat ranches, although some of the land is set aside for recreation sites such as parks, guest ranches, and hunting preserves. One of the most important functions of the plateau, however, is that of an aquifer. The limestone collects vast amounts of water, which is slowly released along its innumerable springs. Many of these springs are home to endemic species of fish, amphibians, and aquatic plants. The Aquarena Springs in San Marcos is home to the world's only site of Texas Wild-rice and of the Fountain Darter (a small fish). There are at least six species of aquatic salamanders endemic to the plateau. Each is found in only one, or sometimes a few, of the springs of the Edwards aquifer.

Because this is an overlap region—where many western species reach the eastern limits of their range and many eastern species reach their western limits—the plateau is an excellent birding area. Most birders visit the Edwards Plateau in search of just three birds, however: Golden-cheeked Warbler, Black-capped Vireo, and Cave Swallow.

GOLDEN-CHEEKED WARBLER

The entire breeding range of the Golden-cheeked Warbler is within the borders of Texas. This striking bird is federally listed as an Endangered Species. Golden-cheekeds are found exclusively in diverse juniper/oak woodlands. They are dependent on the presence of Ashe Juniper (*Juniperus ashei*), from which the birds use strips of bark from mature trees to construct their nests. The nest may be placed in any type of tree, but there must be mature junipers in the vicinity. It is because of this obligate relationship with the juniper, and the fact that habitat is being cleared for agriculture and, increasingly, urbanization, that this species is endangered.

Golden-cheeked Warbler   Mark Lockwood

To have the best chance of seeing Golden-cheeked Warbler, you must be in the right habitat at the right time. The birds arrive by mid-March and the males soon begin to actively defend territories. By late July and early August, most of the warblers have departed for southern Mexico and Guatemala. The best time to find them is from mid-March to early May, when the males are singing. Luckily, males often sing from conspicuous perches. From mid-March to mid-April, territorial males often sing through much of the day. In late April, the first broods of the season fledge, and from this time onward the adults become more difficult to locate. Being familiar with the bird's song is a must, but you should have no trouble locating a Golden-cheeked Warbler without using a tape. As with the endangered Black-capped Vireo, use of tapes to arouse and attract this species is inappropriate.

BLACK-CAPPED VIREO

The endangered Black-capped Vireo is considerably harder to see than the Golden-cheeked Warbler. Although widespread, this is not a common bird and it is rather shy. Trying to lure one out into the open for a good look is a very difficult task at best. It responds to *pishing* and squeaking, but it will often stay hidden in the middle of a bush. Being familiar with its song is almost required.

The best way to see this bird is to find a singing male and quietly wait for it to come into view. There are many colonies on publicly accessible lands. Many colonies are also found in preserves with strict access control or on private property. Trespassing on any of these sites or private lands without permission is a very serious transgression. Please pay special attention to directions and warnings given on sites for this species in the following pages.

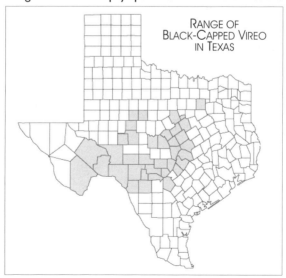

RANGE OF
BLACK-CAPPED VIREO
IN TEXAS

This vireo prefers ungrazed, fairly open shrublands where the foliage of the shrubs reaches the ground. The species composition of the habitat is not what is important. The structure, or profile, of the vegetation is what determines vireo habitat. On the eastern Edwards Plateau, habitat is often the result of disturbance (e.g., fire, removal of livestock after overgrazing). In the more arid western parts of the bird's range, this habitat type may be the normal climax community; this is the case on south- and west-facing slopes of the western plateau and in the Devils River drainage. Habitat may be found on alluvial flats, in canyons, or on hillsides. Black-caps are found from southwestern Oklahoma south across the Edwards Plateau to Big Bend and Coahuila, Mexico. Overbrowsing from sheep, goats, and the native White-tailed Deer have heavily impacted vireo habitat over much of the bird's range.

Vireos arrive on the southern parts of the plateau by the last week in March and depart in early September. Vireos are very active singers from the time they arrive until early July. Males frequently sing all day during most of this time period, even during the hottest times of the day.

CAVE SWALLOW

The Cave Swallow historically nested in just 16 limestone caves and sink-holes ranging from Kerrville to New Mexico's Carlsbad Caverns. Within the last 25 years, the species began utilizing highway bridges and other man-made structures. This has resulted in an incredible expansion of its range and numbers. Cave Swallows can now be found over much of the Edwards Plateau, southward across the South Texas Plains to the Lower Rio Grande Valley, and west through many parts of the Trans-Pecos. The Edwards Plateau remains a prime area for finding Cave Swallows.

Cave Swallows arrive very early at nest sites, often by the end of February. Most sites are occupied by the first of April. As Cave Swallows have expanded their breeding range, they also seem to be expanding their winter range into South Texas. It is now an expected wintering swallow south of the Balcones Escarpment.

The tour outlined below will give you a chance of finding all three of these specialties plus many other species. It also will lead you to some of the most beautiful scenery in Texas. The layout of this section is in four parts: birding sites near the three metropolitan areas and sites scattered throughout the rest of the plateau. These sites generally follow from east to west.

SAN ANTONIO

San Antonio is a great city in which to spend a day or so. In addition to the Alamo and other historic missions, the zoo, and the River Walk, you may also enjoy birding some of the city parks, especially **Friedrich Wilderness Park**. To reach these 232 acres of typical Hill Country habitat preserved by the San Antonio Department of Parks and Recreation, go west on Interstate

Cave Swallow   Shawneen Finnegan

10 for about 10 miles beyond Interstate 410. Exit onto Camp Bullis Road (exit 554), cross under the freeway, and drive north on the frontage road for 1.2 miles. Turn left (west) at the Friedrich Wilderness Park sign and drive one-half mile to the park entrance. The park (free) is open 9:00AM–5:00PM Wednesday through Sunday, with no admittance after 4:00PM. (See map on next page.)

Golden-cheeked Warblers can be found from around 15 March to the first of July along the north-facing slopes of the central ravine. The habitat is mature cedars (junipers) mixed with Texas Oak, Black Cherry, and Cedar Elm. After the singing slows down in June, the warblers can be difficult to find. Black-capped Vireos are no longer found at this location. Habitat for this species on the eastern plateau can be very transitory as the vegetation matures into woodland.

One of the better birding areas in the park is around the parking lot. Other nesting species include Northern Bobwhite, Greater Roadrunner, Black-chinned Hummingbird, Golden-fronted and Ladder-backed Woodpeckers, Ash-throated Flycatcher, White-eyed Vireo, Western Scrub-Jay, Verdin, Bewick's Wren, Blue-gray Gnatcatcher, Yellow-breasted Chat, Painted Bunting, Orchard and Bullock's Orioles, House Finch, and Lesser Goldfinch.

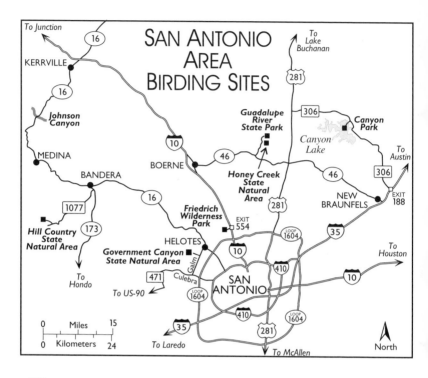

Government Canyon State Natural Area (8,622 acres; entrance fee $6 per person, additional fee for camping) is located on the west side of San Antonio near the town of Helotes. To reach the park from the intersection of I-10 and Loop 1604, travel south on Loop 1604 to Culebra Road (FM-471), turn right (west), and travel 3.5 miles to Galm Road. Turn north (right) onto Galm Road for another 1.6 miles to the gate located on the left.

The majority of Government Canyon State Natural Area is located to the north of the Balcones Escarpment and is dominated by Ashe Juniper/oak woodlands. Typical Hill Country birds are found here, including a small population of Golden-cheeked Warblers. This portion of the Natural Area is closed to vehicular traffic. The best birding area that is easily accessible is in Wildcat Canyon. Park at the visitor center and walk 0.8 mile up Government Canyon (on the Joe Johnson Trail) to the mouth of Wildcat Canyon. The 1.5-mile Wildcat Canyon Trail meanders through a diverse woodland where Golden-fronted Woodpecker, White-eyed Vireo, Carolina Chickadee, Black-crested Titmouse, Blue-gray Gnatcatcher, Golden-cheeked and Black-and-white Warblers, and Summer Tanager can be found in the spring and summer. The wintering avifauna includes Yellow-bellied Sapsucker, Ruby-crowned Kinglet, Hermit Thrush, and Spotted Towhee, among others. The area below the escarpment is a mix of brush country and savanna where a different suite of birds can be found, including Common Ground-Dove, Eastern Phoebe, Scissor-tailed Flycatcher, Painted Bunting, and Orchard Oriole.

Guadalupe River State Park (1,900 acres; entrance fee $6 per person, plus fee for camping) is located northwest of San Antonio. This park may be reached by traveling along I-10 to Boerne (21 miles from the intersection of I-10 and Loop 410) and turning right onto TX-46 (13 miles) to Park Road 31, which leads into the park (7 miles). Park Road 31 also can be reached by traveling north out of San Antonio on US-281 to TX-46 (21 miles from the intersection of US-281 and Loop 410) and then traveling west for 8 miles.

The primary birding area in the park is along the Guadalupe River. The river is lined with Bald Cypress, and Northern Parula and Yellow-throated Warbler (scarce) nest here. The trees and brushy areas along the river can be an excellent place to find migrant songbirds. Green Kingfishers often can be seen flying up and down the river. Other breeding birds along the river and in the tent-camping area include Eastern Wood-Pewee, Great Crested Flycatcher, Yellow-throated Vireo, and Summer Tanager. The remainder of the park is dominated by live oak savanna, with birds such as Western Scrub-Jay, Bewick's Wren, Lark Sparrow, and Painted Bunting. The neighboring **Honey Creek State Natural Area** (2,293 acres) is currently open only to scheduled guided tours at 9:00AM on Saturdays (fee; be sure to call in advance, 830-438-2656, to confirm the tour). Green Kingfisher, Acadian Flycatcher, Northern Parula, Yellow-throated Warbler, and Louisiana Waterthrush nest along this drainage. Golden-cheeked Warblers also are found in the juniper/oak woodland that overlooks the creek. The guided tours are not designed for birders, but it is worth the time to see this magnificent area and you may have the opportunity to see a few birds in the process.

A side trip from San Antonio (or Austin) that is worthwhile during the winter months is **Canyon Lake**. There are numerous parks around the lake and all charge a $4 fee; the best birding location, however, is along the entrance road to Canyon Park on the north side of the lake. From San Antonio, take I-35 north to New Braunfels (21 miles from Loop 410). At exit 188, turn left onto FM-306 to Canyon Park (19.5 miles). Immediately upon turning left into the park, you will see two "fingers" of the lake. Both of these should be checked. This is one of the most reliable places in central Texas for Greater Scaup. Watch for other ducks, including Lesser Scaup, Ring-necked Duck, and Red-breasted Merganser. Common Loon, Ring-billed and Bonaparte's Gulls, and Forster's Tern normally can be found as well. Pacific Loon has been found at this location at least twice, and during the winter of 1996–1997, there were three Red-throated and two Pacific Loons present. The willows along the shore of the lake and the oak woodlands on the hillsides are worth checking for passerines.

If you are going to Kerrville from San Antonio, take TX-16 through Bandera, a very pretty drive. About 12 miles north of Medina, you will come to

Johnson Canyon. Park near the highway sign marked "HILL" and walk down the slope. Black-capped Vireos and Golden-cheeked Warblers have been found in this area.

Upon reaching Bandera, turn left onto TX-16 on the south edge of town, and then make a right turn onto FM-1077 (11 miles) to **Hill Country State Natural Area** (5,369 acres; entrance fee $3 per person, plus fee for camping). The park is closed on Tuesdays and Wednesdays. There are few roads within this undeveloped park and hiking is required to reach most areas. A preliminary bird checklist and a trail map are available at the headquarters.

Steep hills and large canyons dominate the northwestern section of the park. These protected canyons contain deciduous hardwoods that are surrounded by open juniper/oak woodland. Golden-cheeked Warblers can be found in the canyons. The woodland habitats can be reached in the Twin Peaks area. From the park headquarters, proceed north to the trailhead parking area and follow the trail up the slope. White-eyed Vireo, Carolina Chickadee, Black-crested Titmouse, Blue-gray Gnatcatcher, Black-and-white Warbler, and Summer Tanager are some of the other breeding birds found in this habitat. The wintering avifauna is equally diverse, with Yellow-bellied Sapsucker, Ruby-crowned Kinglet, Hermit Thrush, and Spotted Towhee, among others.

Foothills dominate the landscape in the southern two-thirds of the park. There is a mixture of open grassland with live-oak mottes and mixed scrublands composed primarily of Texas Persimmon, Evergreen Sumac, and other dense shrubs. Black-capped Vireos are found in these habitats. There are two main areas in which to look for the vireo. The first is around the Wilderness Camp. Vireos nest on the escarpment above the camp area as well as on the small hills surrounding it. The other good area is the foothills across the road from "Nacho's House." To reach these spots, proceed eastward along the entrance road past the headquarters for 1.5 miles to the abandoned (Nacho's) house on the left side of the road and park here. To reach the Wilderness Camp, follow Trail 1, which begins directly across the road from the house. Follow this trail for 1.1 miles to reach the camp. During the breeding season, Common Poorwill, Eastern Phoebe, Vermilion Flycatcher, Bewick's Wren, Painted Bunting, and Scott's Oriole can be found in these areas.

West Verde Creek is a perennial stream that runs near the eastern boundary of the park. Remnant riparian woodland habitat can be found here, which attracts a wide variety of birds. Breeding birds include Red-shouldered Hawk, Yellow-billed Cuckoo, and Blue Grosbeak. Numerous other springs are scattered over the park and provide excellent birding opportunities, particularly in the summer.

AUSTIN

Austin is the capital of Texas and was named after Stephen F. Austin, colonizer of the first American settlement in Texas. The city of over 700,000 contains cultural, educational, and commercial features aplenty. Situated in the wooded hills at the eastern edge of the Edwards Plateau, the city overlooks the Colorado River. Austin has landscaped the banks of the Colorado with beautiful parks and paths. Many outdoor recreational activities also revolve around the nearby Highland Lakes, and even in the midst of the large urban population, there are such novelties as the colony of Brazilian Free-tailed Bats that resides beneath the Congress Avenue Bridge. Austin is also home to a population of Monk Parakeets. The parakeets build their large stick nests on the lights surrounding softball fields in the city parks along the Colorado River. One of the best locations can be found by traveling west from I-35 on Riverside Drive to where it ends at Lamar Avenue. Cross Lamar and park in the hike-and-bike trail parking lot. The parakeets can be seen around the softball fields. (See map on next page.)

Known simply as "City Park" to the locals, **Emma Long Metropolitan Park** is the closest place from downtown Austin to find Golden-cheeked Warblers. To reach the park, go north on I-35 from downtown and take the exit for US-290 (4.0 miles), which goes east to Houston, but turn west onto FM-2222 (Koenig Lane). Go under Loop-1 (3.3 miles) and proceed to Loop-360 Road (4.0 miles). After passing this, start watching for the small signs marking City Park Road (0.5 mile), which is on the left. Turn left and go to the top of the hill. From here to the end of the road (6.0 miles), you will see much prime habitat for the warbler. Unfortunately, the first five miles of this road traverse private property, and developments are consuming more of the habitat each year. Warblers are still frequently heard and seen at the several dirt pullouts as the road skirts the hillside. Perhaps the best location in the park for finding the warbler is near the little rock bridge at the only creek crossing on the road (4.5 miles). Small footpaths leading upstream and downstream from this bridge traverse prime warbler habitat.

Balcones Canyonlands National Wildlife Refuge encompasses a diversity of Hill Country habitats. The refuge covers over 16,000 acres and is located west and northwest of Austin in parts of Travis, Burnet, and Williamson Counties. The area hosts a substantial population of Golden-cheeked Warblers and a few colonies of Black-capped Vireos. Typical Hill Country birds can be observed on the refuge, including some of the easternmost populations of Canyon Towhee and Black-throated Sparrow. There are currently several primary access points to the refuge. Call the refuge office at 512-339-9432 for further information.

Perhaps the most popular destination on the refuge is the **Shin Oak Observation Deck**. From Austin, go west on TX-71 to US-281 (44 miles) and

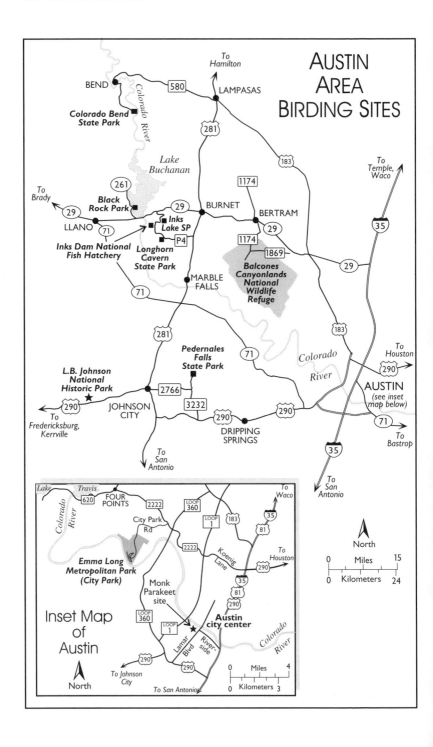

AUSTIN
AREA
BIRDING SITES

To Hamilton

BEND
580
LAMPASAS

Colorado Bend
State Park

Colorado River

281

183

Lake
Buchanan

To Temple, Waco

261

To Brady

Black
Rock Park

29
BURNET

1174

35

29

LLANO

71

BERTRAM

29

Inks
Lake SP

P4

1174

Inks Dam National
Fish Hatchery

Longhorn
Cavern
State Park

1869

29

MARBLE
FALLS

Balcones
Canyonlands
National
Wildlife
Refuge

183

71

Colorado

River

281

Pedernales
Falls
State Park

71

To Houston

290

L.B. Johnson
National
Historic Park

2766

AUSTIN
(see inset
map below)

290

JOHNSON
CITY

3232

71

To Fredericksburg, Kerrville

290

DRIPPING
SPRINGS

290

To Bastrop

To San Antonio

35

To San Antonio

Lake Travis

620

FOUR POINTS

2222

LOOP 360

To Waco

Colorado River

City Park Rd

LOOP 1

183

35

81

2222

Koenig Lane

To Houston

Emma Long
Metropolitan Park
(City Park)

290

35

Monk
Parakeet
site

81

290

Inset Map
of
Austin

LOOP 360

LOOP 1

Austin
city center

Lamar Blvd

River-side

Colorado River

290

North

To Johnson City

290

To San Antonio

North

0   Miles   15
0 Kilometers 24

0   Miles   4
0 Kilometers 3

turn north onto TX-281 to Burnet (17 miles) and the intersection with TX-29. Go east on TX-29 for 11.1 miles to the intersection with FM-1174 in Bertram. Turn south onto FM-1174 for 7.2 miles to the intersection with FM-1869. Turn left (east) onto FM-1869 and travel 1.3 miles to the observation deck (on the left). As the name implies, the deck overlooks a large area of Shin Oak that is home to Black-capped Vireos. This is the closest location to Austin where this bird may be seen. Other breeding species that are regularly observed from this location included Yellow-breasted Chat, Rufous-crowned Sparrow, and Painted Bunting. The deck is closed at the beginning of the vireo nesting season and normally is opened for viewing in mid- to late April.

The **Doeskin Ranch trailhead** is not far from the observation deck. Return west on FM-1869 for 1.3 miles to the intersection with FM-1174. Turn south (left) on FM-1174 and travel 2.4 miles to the trailhead. There are three trails that originate at this location. The Pond and Prairie Trail is a short, 0.4-mile trail that is primarily in open habitats where White-eyed Vireo, Field Sparrow, and Painted Bunting are found in spring and summer, and a variety of sparrows in winter. The Creek Trail is 0.6 mile long and includes some riparian habitats that can be particularly good during migration. During the spring and summer, look for Yellow-billed Cuckoo, Summer Tanager, and Blue Grosbeak in addition to the birds previously mentioned. The final trail is the 2.2-mile Rimrock Trail that climbs up through Ashe Juniper woodlands and offers the opportunity to see and hear Golden-cheeked Warbler.

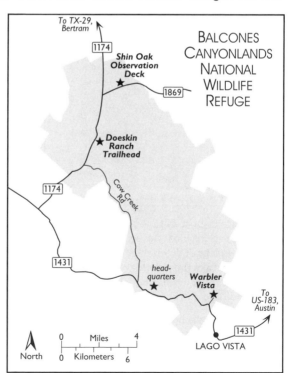

The final access point on the refuge is known as **Warbler Vista**. Continue south on FM-1174 for 4.6 miles to FM-1431. Turn left onto FM-1431 and head east 12.7 miles to a refuge road on the left. Follow this road for 0.7 mile to the parking area for the Cactus Rock Trail. This 0.6-mile trail leads through old-growth Ashe Juniper/oak woodland where Golden-cheeked and Black-and-white Warblers can be found.

Starting from Austin, go west on US-290 toward Fredricksburg. After passing Dripping Springs (24 miles), start watching on the right for FM-3232 (8 miles), which leads to **Pedernales Falls State Park** (6.3 miles) (entrance fee $5 per person, plus fee for camping). The 5,200-acre park stretches along both banks of the Pedernales River, although there is no need to cross the river. Bald Cypresses and sycamores line the riverbanks; Ashe Juniper and oaks cover the uplands. A seasonal checklist is available at the headquarters.

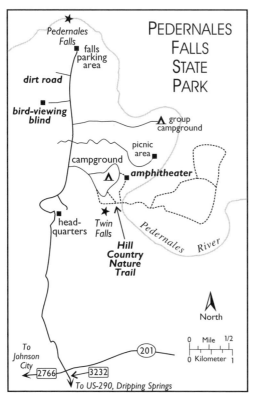

There is a large population of Golden-cheeked Warblers in this park. One of the best and most accessible places to find the bird is along the **Hill Country Nature Trail**. This trail starts between campsites 19 and 21. Warblers can normally be found between the trailhead and the overlook at Twin Falls. Also look for Golden-cheekeds in the area around the amphitheater (next to campsite 33). Another area where this species may be found is in the mixed woodlands west of the falls parking lot at the very north end of the park. Once you have parked your car, walk back down the main road about one-quarter mile to a dirt road on the right. Take the right fork of this dirt road and follow it another quarter-mile until it forks again. There are several pairs of warblers in the area between the road and the Pedernales River.

Other birds to be found in the park include Golden-fronted and Ladder-backed Woodpeckers, Western Kingbird, Great Crested and Ash-throated Flycatchers, Eastern Phoebe, White-eyed and Yellow-throated Vireos, Cliff Swallow, Carolina Chickadee, Black-crested Titmouse, Verdin, Bushtit,

Bewick's, Carolina, and Canyon Wrens, Summer Tanager, Canyon Towhee, Rufous-crowned and Black-throated Sparrows, Blue Grosbeak, Painted Bunting, and Lesser Goldfinch.

There is also a large bird-viewing blind at the north end of the park at the horse corral. This blind accommodates up to 25 people and attracts a large diversity of birds year-round, but is particularly good in the winter. It has a glass front and allows excellent viewing opportunities. As you leave the park, turn right onto FM-2766. At Johnson City (9 miles), either travel north on US-281 to the Lake Buchanan area or continue west on US-290 towards Kerrville.

LAKE BUCHANAN REGION

The Lake Buchanan region offers another opportunity to observe Golden-cheeked Warblers, but this area is better known for providing some of the best waterbirding on the Edwards Plateau. As a result, it is best visited from October to March.

From Johnson City, travel north on US-281, past Marble Falls (23 miles), to the Park Road 4 (9 miles; see map on page 202). Turn left onto Park Road 4 and proceed 6 miles to **Longhorn Cavern State Park**. The park is small (639 acres) and currently there is no fee to picnic or to walk the trails. There is a fee to enter the cavern, which has a long and interesting past, including having a dance floor installed in the cave during the 1930s. Birding at this site is limited to oak/juniper woodland and the diversity of birds is not high; however, Golden-cheeked Warblers can be found along the hiking trails between mid-March and early June. Resident birds include Ladder-backed Woodpecker, Canyon Wren, Bushtit, and Rufous-crowned Sparrow. Breeding species also include Ash-throated Flycatcher, Summer Tanager, and Painted Bunting.

Continue westward on Park Road 4 to **Inks Dam National Fish Hatchery** (4.2 miles). The hatchery is worth checking for migrant shorebirds and wintering ducks. The hatchery is open from 8:00AM to 4:00PM Monday through Friday. The brushy areas between the hatchery and the Colorado River are a good place to look for Eastern Phoebe, Carolina Chickadee, Carolina Wren, Hermit Thrush, Spotted Towhee, Northern Cardinal, and a variety of wintering sparrows. Return to Park Road 4 and continue 2.4 miles to **Inks Lake State Park** (1,201 acres; entrance fee $5 per person, additional fee for camping). The park sits on the shore of Inks Lake, which is an excellent place to find wintering Red-breasted Merganser, Common Loon, and Horned, Eared, and Pied-billed Grebes. There are over seven miles of hiking trails in the park. Golden-fronted Woodpecker, Western Scrub-Jay, Black-crested Titmouse, Bewick's Wren, among other typical Hill Country species, can be found in the park. A seasonal checklist (which includes Longhorn Cavern State Park) is available at the park headquarters.

Return to Park Road 4 and continue toward **Lake Buchanan**. Upon reaching the intersection with TX-29 (3.6 miles), turn left toward the dam (3 miles). The overlook from the dam can reveal many of the species listed for Inks Lake, particularly Common Loon. Another good vantage point is **Black Rock Park** ($3 per person). To reach the park, continue west on TX-29 (1.5 miles) to TX-261 and turn right to the park (2.7 miles). Black Rock Park sits on a point that offers an excellent vantage point for scoping the lake. Red-breasted Merganser, Common Loon, Horned Grebe, and Bonaparte's, Ring-billed, and Herring Gulls usually are visible from the point. The remainder of the park is small and primarily a picnic area with a few scattered live oaks and other trees. Black-crested Titmouse can be found in the park. There is little reason to visit this site during the breeding season. A Llano County park is located next to Black Rock Park and has no admission fee, but it is around a cove of the lake and only a small portion of the lake can be viewed.

Lake Buchanan is also the winter home to Bald Eagles. The best way to observe these birds is by taking the Vanishing Texas River Cruise (P.O. Box 901, Burnet, TX 78611; phone 512-756-6986) from late November to March. The cruise visits part of the lake and also goes up the Colorado River.

From Lake Buchanan, travel to Burnet via TX-29 (13 miles) and make a right turn onto US-281 to Lampasas (22 miles). Proceed through town until you see the sign for **Colorado Bend State Park** (5,328 acres: entrance fee $4 per person, additional fee for camping). Turn left onto North Street and follow it until it dead-ends at FM-580, turn right, and follow it to Bend. Upon reaching Bend, you will cross the Colorado River, where there is a large colony of Cliff Swallows nesting under the bridge. In Bend, follow the signs down a well-maintained gravel road to the park entrance (6 miles). The park office and the best birding are both found at the far end of the park at the Colorado River. There are hiking trails upstream from the upper end of the camping area and downstream from the boat-ramp parking area. Golden-cheeked Warblers can be found along both trails, and both are excellent places to look for migrants. The upstream trails follow the river and take the hiker through a mixed gallery forest where a wide variety of birds can be found. During spring and summer, look for Red-shouldered Hawk, Yellow-billed Cuckoo (after 1 May), Golden-fronted Woodpecker, Acadian Flycatcher (rare), Great Crested Flycatcher, White-eyed, Yellow-throated, and Red-eyed Vireos, Western Scrub-Jay, Carolina Chickadee, Canyon and Carolina Wrens, and Summer Tanager. This trail eventually enters an open grassland that is about 100 yards wide and a half-mile long. In winter, Savannah, Vesper, and Grasshopper Sparrows can be found here. Other wintering species found along the river corridor include Hermit Thrush, Spotted Towhee, and Chipping, Song, Lincoln's, White-throated, and White-crowned Sparrows.

The downstream trail turns up into Spicewood Canyon. This beautiful canyon is worth the trip. Golden-cheeked Warblers can be seen anywhere from the parking area to upper Spicewood Canyon. The species listed for the

White-winged Dove   Brad McKinney

previous trail can be observed here as well. There are a few large pecan trees next to the parking area that attract nesting Orchard Orioles and can be excellent for woodpeckers, including Downy and Golden-fronted year-round and Yellow-bellied Sapsucker and Northern Flicker in winter. There are usually a few nesting pairs of Indigo Buntings along the trail before it reaches Spicewood.

Upland areas of the park support a different avifauna. There is a nature tour that leads from the main park road down to the Colorado River. This trail traverses the drier uplands and can produce Ash-throated Flycatcher, Bushtit, Bewick's Wren, and Field, Rufous-crowned, and Black-throated Sparrows.

A seasonal checklist is available at the headquarters. The park provides guided tours to Gorman Falls on the weekends. The 60-foot-high falls are the highest on the Edwards Plateau and are well worth the $2/person tour fee.

KERRVILLE

From Johnson City (see Austin map on page 202), travel west on US-290 until you reach FM-1 (10.9 miles), which leads to the LBJ Ranch. To visit the ranch, park at the state park on the south side of the road and board one of the tour buses, which will take you to the birthplace, the cemetery, and for a short tour of the ranch.

At Fredericksburg (14 miles), which is famous for its German-style cooking, you can turn left onto TX-16 toward Kerrville (24 miles). Kerrville (population 22,000, elevation 1,645 feet) is the hub of the vacation area for the Hill Country. Motels, guest ranches, and campgrounds are numerous in the vicinity. After seeing this pretty little town on the beautiful Guadalupe River, you may not want to go any farther. Birding can be good almost anywhere in the area. **Louise Hayes Park**, which is just across the river from the downtown area, has some tall trees that can be good for warblers and other migrants.

Kerrville-Schreiner Park (517 acres; entrance fee, additional fee for camping), is just south of town. Take TX-16 to TX-173 (0.5 mile) and turn left to the park (2.5 miles). The best birding spot is usually on the hillside above the camping area. Wild Turkeys may be found here among the oaks. Some common resident species include Inca Dove, Greater Roadrunner, Belted Kingfisher, Golden-fronted and Ladder-backed Woodpeckers, Eastern Phoebe, Western Scrub-Jay, Carolina Chickadee, Black-crested Titmouse, Carolina and Bewick's Wrens, Eastern Bluebird, Northern Mockingbird, Northern Cardinal, Brown-headed Cowbird, and House Finch. Other summer nesters include Green Heron, Yellow-billed Cuckoo, Chimney Swift, White-eyed Vireo, Cliff and Barn Swallows, Summer Tanager, and Bronzed Cowbird. Yellow-throated Warbler is an uncommon breeder.

Johnson Canyon is good for Golden-cheeked Warbler. The canyon is along TX-16 some 12 miles south of Kerrville or 12 miles north of Medina. Park near the highway sign which reads "HILL" and walk down the highway. The birds may be found anywhere in the stands of oak. Of course, they are most active early in the morning.

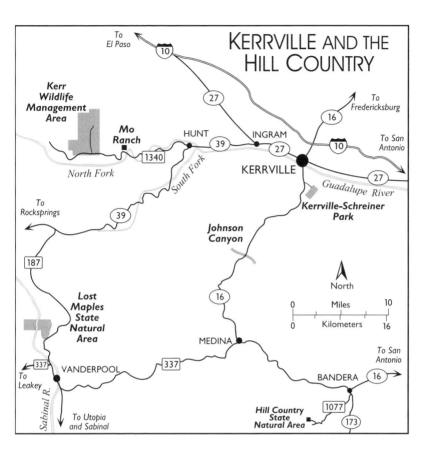

THE HILL COUNTRY

To reach the very heart of the Hill Country, go northwest from Kerrville on TX-27 to Ingram (7 miles). Turn west onto TX-39, which runs along the Guadalupe River. At Hunt, turn right onto FM-1340 to explore a beautiful stretch of the North Fork of the Guadalupe River. After a couple of blocks, watch on the left for a house with feeders, which swarm with Black-chinned Hummingbirds in summer.

The area along the river is great for Wood Duck, Eastern Phoebe, Yellow-throated Vireo, Cliff Swallow, Canyon Wren, and many other species. Green Kingfisher can be found here in summer if you look hard enough. This small, shy bird is easily overlooked because it perches close to the water on rocks or low overhanging limbs. Your best bet is to stop as often as possible and scan the river.

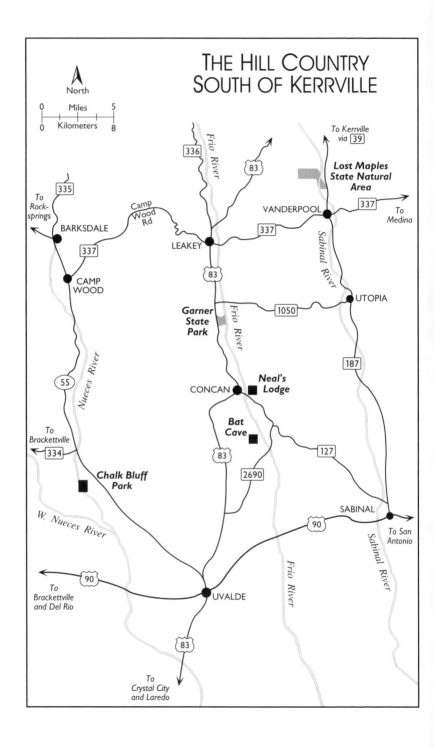

THE HILL COUNTRY
SOUTH OF KERRVILLE

North

Miles
0   5
Kilometers
0   8

Frio River

336

83

To Kerrville
via 39

Lost Maples
State Natural
Area

337

To
Medina

VANDERPOOL

335

Camp
Wood
Rd

337

To
Rock-
springs

BARKSDALE

Sabinal River

337

LEAKEY

83

CAMP
WOOD

Garner
State
Park

Frio River

1050

UTOPIA

187

Nueces River

55

Neal's
Lodge

CONCAN

Bat
Cave

To
Brackettville

334

Chalk Bluff
Park

83

2690

127

W. Nueces River

SABINAL

90

To San
Antonio

Sabinal River

To
Brackettville
and Del Rio

90

Frio River

UVALDE

83

To
Crystal City
and Laredo

The **Mo Ranch Church Camp** (10.7 miles) on the right is a delightful place to bird. Accommodations can be had during off seasons. The **Kerr Wildlife Management Area** (2.0 miles; 6,439 acres) is home to Golden-cheeked Warblers and Black-capped Vireos. There are approximately 20 pairs of the warbler and over 300 pairs of vireos within the area. The aggressive management activities that have produced vireo habitat have resulted in the species doing well and increasing in numbers here. Their preferred habitat is live-oak thickets that have a low, thick understory. There is a 4.5-mile interpretive driving tour. Pick up a copy of the WMA guide at the registration booth. Northern Bobwhites and Wild Turkeys are rather common here. To see the warbler and vireo requires a visit to the WMA office. All birders need to register at the bulletin board located at the office.

The best opportunities for viewing Golden-cheeked Warblers here is at the Spring Trap pasture. This area is accessed by foot only and is located approximately 0.6 mile east of the main entrance to the WMA on FM-1340. The gate is marked with a sign indicating the Spring Trap. Enter through the gate (close it behind you!) and continue up the dirt road approximately 100 yards. At this point, the road will intersect a footpath through the Ashe Juniper woodland that eventually ends up back at the dirt road. Golden-cheeked Warblers are frequently seen in this area.

Black-capped Vireos can be found throughout most of the WMA, and some of the best viewing opportunities are in the Doe and Fawn Pastures. From the headquarters, go north on the main paved road approximately 1.2 miles to where there is an intersection with another paved road to the left, which is closed to the public. Park at this location and walk into the pasture a short distance. Another ideal location is down the main road another 0.3 mile, where you will notice a shelter on your right.

More detailed information and other suggestions for birding areas can be obtained at the WMA office, which is open from 8:00AM to 5:00PM weekdays.

Beyond this point, the road leaves the river and crosses open ranchland. Turn around, go back to Hunt, and continue west on TX-39, which follows the South Fork of the Guadalupe River. This stretch is just as pretty and birdy as the North Fork.

Eventually, the road leaves the river and crosses grasslands dotted with Shin Oak. Watch for Wild Turkey, Greater Roadrunner, Great Horned Owl, Golden-fronted Woodpecker, Western Scrub-Jay, Common Raven, Carolina Chickadee, Black-crested Titmouse, Verdin, Bushtit, Bewick's, Carolina, Canyon, and Rock Wrens, Eastern Bluebird, Canyon Towhee, Lark, Rufous-crowned, Cassin's, Black-throated, Chipping, and Field Sparrows, Eastern Meadowlark, House Finch, and Lesser Goldfinch. In summer, look for Common Poorwill, Chuck-will's-widow, Common Nighthawk, Western Kingbird, Scissor-tailed, Great Crested, Ash-throated, and Vermilion Flycatchers, Eastern Phoebe, White-eyed, Bell's, and Red-eyed Vireos, Grasshopper Sparrow,

Blue Grosbeak, Painted Bunting, and Orchard and Scott's Orioles. In migration, you may see large concentrations of Mississippi Kites and Broad-winged and Swainson's Hawks, and in winter there should be Lark Buntings and Savannah, Vesper, Lincoln's, Fox, White-crowned, and White-throated Sparrows. Also keep an eye out for the black race of the Rock Squirrel.

At FM-187 (20 miles) turn left. For the next few miles, watch the telephone wires for Cave Swallows, particularly in late afternoon. On the right, there is a windmill with a water trough (1.5 miles), where the swallows often come to drink. If you do not see them here, check the utility wires at the buildings of the former Bonnie Hills Ranch (2.8 miles) on the right.

LOST MAPLES STATE NATURAL AREA

One of the favorite spots for Texans to view fall colors is Sabinal Canyon, where an isolated stand of Big-toothed Maples turns a brilliant red. This remote area is in **Lost Maples State Natural Area** (9.8 miles; 2,174 acres: entrance fee $5 per person, $6 during October and November; additional fee for camping). Not only is this a very scenic spot, it is also a good birding area. A seasonal bird checklist is available at the park headquarters.

Lost Maples has one of the largest populations of Golden-cheeked Warblers on publicly accessible lands. Black-capped Vireos can also be found at this location. Golden-cheeks can be seen from any of the main trails. East Trail makes a long loop covering the eastern section of the natural area. The trail can be accessed from the picnic area or the overflow parking lot. Many warbler territories are located along the trail between the picnic area and primitive camping area (1.7 miles). The other end of the loop, starting at the overflow parking area and heading to the pond, is also an excellent area (1.1 miles). This section of the trail is better for Black-capped Vireos. The vireos are found on brushy west- and south-facing hillsides. These areas are not very accessible and seeing the birds here can be particularly difficult. The lower slope next to the pond is one of the best places to look. The park staff is very knowledgeable about these birds and can usually direct visitors to places where the two species have been observed recently.

Keep an eye out for Zone-tailed Hawk while in the park and surrounding area. There are scattered breeding pairs in the area and they can sometimes be seen flying up and down the canyons or over the surrounding hills. Other nesting species include Greater Roadrunner, Green Kingfisher, Ladder-backed Woodpecker, Acadian Flycatcher, Black Phoebe, Great Crested and Ash-throated Flycatchers, White-eyed, Yellow-throated, and Red-eyed Vireos, Common Raven, Western Scrub-Jay, Bushtit, Black-and-white Warbler, Louisiana Waterthrush, Canyon Towhee, Northern Cardinal, Painted Bunting, Orchard Oriole, and Lesser Goldfinch. The waterthrush is normally

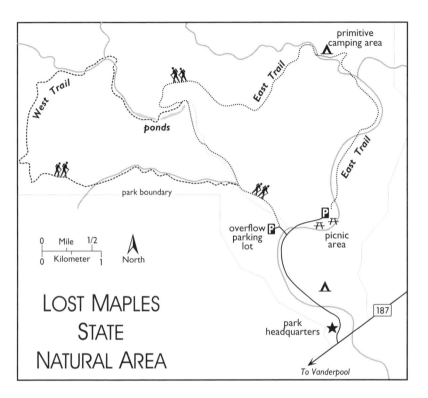

LOST MAPLES STATE NATURAL AREA

found along the many small streams in the park. West Trail is a more strenuous walk but a good place look for these birds.

In the summer and fall, take some time to see what is coming to the hummingbird feeder at the park headquarters. Normally there are just Black-chinned Hummingbirds, but there also may be Ruby-throateds and Rufous in the fall. There also have been such rarities as Green Violetear (1995 and 2000) and Blue-throated (1996) documented at this feeder.

GARNER STATE PARK

Continue south on FM-187 through Vanderpool (4.7 miles) to Utopia (10.5 miles; see map on page 210). Turn right (west) onto the very scenic FM-1050 to US-83 (15.0 miles). Turn left after about a mile to **Garner State Park** (1,419 acres; entrance fee $6 per person, additional fee for camping). Birding is often good along the Frio River and along the six miles of hiking trails. The park can be very crowded on weekends in the spring and anytime during the summer.

The clear, spring-fed Frio River has large Bald Cypress lining its banks. Birding along the river can produce Green Kingfisher, Black Phoebe, and Yellow-throated Warbler (in the Bald Cypress). Golden-cheeked Warblers can be found in the oak/juniper woodlands in the southwest portion of the park. The hillsides are very steep, and leaving the trail is strongly discouraged. The steepness of the hillsides makes finding the warblers difficult. One segment of the trail is the old entrance road to the park and is paved. This is probably the best place to see these birds. There is a small parking area on the right at the top of the hill where the main park road goes to the extreme southern camping area. If you see the pavilion and miniature golf course, you have passed the trailhead.

Resident birds in this area include Western Scrub-Jay, Common Raven, Verdin, Bushtit, Cactus, Canyon, Carolina, and Bewick's Wrens, Canyon Towhee, Rufous-crowned Sparrow, and Pyrrhuloxia. Additional nesting species include White-winged Dove, Vermilion Flycatcher, Black-and-white Warbler, and Scott's Oriole.

NEAL'S LODGE

From Garner State Park, continue south on US-83 and turn left onto TX-127 at Concan (7.3 miles). **Neal's Lodge** (0.6 mile) (P.O. Box 165, Concan, TX 78838; phone 830-232-6118) is on the left on the beautiful Frio River. This attractive vacation spot, operating since 1927, has rooms and many housekeeping cabins available year-round. The cafe serves home-cooked meals every day from Memorial Day to Labor Day, and weekends only from Easter to Memorial Day and Labor Day through December. During January, February, and March, arrangements can be made for large groups. A grocery store is available on the property.

Birds are abundant about the 300-acre grounds. White-winged and Inca Doves, Eastern Phoebe, Carolina, Canyon, and Bewick's Wrens, Rufous-crowned Sparrow, and Hooded Oriole can be found right around the buildings. At night, you may hear Common Nighthawk, Common Poorwill, and Chuck-will's-widow. By walking up the road and across the cattle-guard behind the store, you can reach a dry hillside covered with cacti and thorny brush. This is the area in which to find Vermilion and Ash-throated Flycatchers, Say's Phoebe, Cactus Wren, Verdin, Curve-billed Thrasher, Canyon Towhee, Black-throated Sparrow, and Pyrrhuloxia. Unless there are lots of campers, a hike along the river will produce Black Phoebe and possibly a Green Kingfisher or a Yellow-throated Warbler. There is even a chance for Black-capped Vireo on the hill behind the store. Several Valley specialties such as Long-billed Thrasher and Olive Sparrow may be seen, and rarities found include Tropical Parula and Rufous-capped Warbler. The trail going up the hill starts behind cabin #15; or take the road behind the store. If this area is crowded, try the trail on the other side of the river. It can be reached from the highway. Ask at the office for directions.

CONCAN BAT CAVE

If you are staying at Neal's Lodge, or are in the area in late evening, you may want to see bats. Drive east on TX-127 to FM-2690 (4.4 miles; see map on page 210). Turn right and start checking the swallows, especially at the low-water crossing on the Frio River (0.1 mile). In the hills off to the right, there is a cave that harbors some 500 to 600 Cave Swallows and about 17,000,000 Brazilian Free-tailed Bats. The cave is not open to the public, but the swallows can usually be seen flying around, particularly in the evening. If you set up a scope at the wooden gate (1.6 miles) on the right, you can see the bats come swirling up at dark like a stream of smoke.

CAMP WOOD ROAD

Return to US-83 and drive north past Garner State Park to the little town of Leakey (17 miles from Concan), where you will find restaurants, stores, and cabins (see map on page 210). Turn left in the heart of town onto the Camp Wood Road (FM-337), which runs along a ridge through stands of scrub oak. Over the years, this has been one of the better spots for Zone-tailed Hawk, and the best way to find one is to check all of the vultures. In flight, even at close range, the Zone-tailed can look similar to a Turkey Vulture.

At Camp Wood (20.7 miles), you have a choice of routes. The shortest one is to turn south onto TX-55 toward Uvalde; the birding can be good along this stretch. At the Nueces River (3.6 miles), check the area below the dam for Green Kingfisher. For several years, a pair nested on the east side of the road in a small bank on the north side of the stream. Cave Swallows have attempted to nest in the road culverts (12 miles), but the nests are usually wiped out by high water. At FM-334 (2.5 miles), you can either turn right toward Brackettville (30 miles) to continue your trip up the Rio Grande, or continue south on TX-55 to Chalk Bluff Park (22.6 miles). A longer route is to turn north at Camp Wood onto TX-55 toward Rocksprings (29 miles). **Devil's Sinkhole State Natural Area** (1,860 acres) is located on US-377, 8 miles northeast of Rocksprings. The park is currently open to bat-flight tours through the Devil's Sinkhole Society (830-683-2287; $12 for adults, $6 for children). There are plans to be open for day use in the near future. The Devil's Sinkhole is a spectacular vertical cavern with a drop to the main cavern of about 140 feet. The main cavern is circular and reaches a total depth of 350–400 feet. There is a very large population of Brazilian Free-tailed Bats resident in the cave from mid-March through mid-November. There is also a large population of Cave Swallows nesting in the cave. Small numbers of Black-capped and Gray Vireos nest in the oak woodlands.

From Rocksprings, go south on TX-377 to FM-674 (3 miles), where a very scenic road along the West Nueces River leads to Kickapoo Cavern State Park (34 miles; see map on page 192). The entrance to the park faces to the south and is marked with a sign. It is located one-half mile north of the Edwards/Kinney County line.

KICKAPOO CAVERN STATE PARK

Kickapoo Cavern State Park (6,400 acres; entrance fee $3 per person, additional fee for camping) is an undeveloped park currently open only by reservation (830-563-2342). There are plans to have the park fully open for camping by 2010. Currently, it is recommended that reservations be made at least two weeks prior to the date you wish to visit the site, although last-minute visits often can be arranged. The park is located 22.5 miles north of Brackettville on FM-674. Kickapoo Cavern is a great place to spend a day or two. Spring and early summer offer the best birding, but this scenic park offers good birding opportunities at all seasons. Its location on the southwestern corner of the plateau provides for a unique assemblage of birds. Species normally associated with the Edwards Plateau, the Trans-Pecos, and the South Texas Plains can all be found here. The starting point for all birding begins at the center of the park at the old hunting lodge. The park staff will lead you to this point, and all of the birds found in the park can be located by walking the roads that radiate out from this point. A bird checklist is available upon request. The area surrounding the lodge is one of the best places in the park to find Vermilion Flycatcher and Hooded Oriole. During dry periods or in midsummer, the water troughs around the lodge attract many birds, including Varied Buntings.

Kickapoo's claim to fame is a large population of Black-capped Vireos. Censuses have recorded more than 100 pairs within the boundaries of the park. Other breeding species include Wild Turkey, Common Ground-Dove (scarce), Common Poorwill, Vermilion Flycatcher, Bell's and Gray Vireos, Cave Swallow, Yellow-breasted Chat, Cassin's, Grasshopper, and Black-throated Sparrows, Pyrrhuloxia, Varied and Painted Buntings, and Hooded and Scott's Orioles.

The Black-capped and Gray Vireos arrive and are on territory by the first of April. Black-caps are easily heard and, with some patience, seen in the clumps of Texas Persimmon along the roads leading from the lodge. The park staff conducts surveys of these birds and can point you to areas where territorial individuals are present. *It is important to remain on the roads so that the vireos are not disturbed.* Some of the best places to look are along the roads leading directly north and south from the lodge. It is not uncommon to hear singing males from the parking area at the lodge.

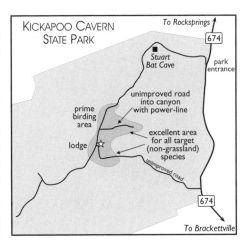

KICKAPOO CAVERN STATE PARK

To Rocksprings

674

Stuart Bat Cave

park entrance

unimproved road into canyon with power-line

prime birding area

excellent area for all target (non-grassland) species

lodge ☆

unimproved road

674

To Brackettville

The Gray Vireo is far more difficult to locate. As with the Black-cap, being familiar with the bird's song is the key to finding it. Gray Vireos defend large territories, so locating one takes a little bit of luck. Fortunately, as with most vireos, the males sing almost constantly through the spring and early summer. Be sure to ask the park staff if they have seen any recently.

One of the best birding spots in the park is within easy walking distance from the lodge. Walk north along the entrance road past the first creek crossing (dry except after heavy rains) to an old two-track road leading off to the right. This road leads into a canyon with a power line running down it. This is one of the best places in the park for Varied Bunting and Scott's Oriole. The songs of Painted and Varied Buntings are very similar, so check every bunting you hear. Black-capped and Gray Vireos are also found in this canyon. While at Kickapoo during the spring and summer, watch for Zone-tailed Hawks; there are at least three pairs in the area and they are frequently seen in the park.

A sight not to be missed is the emergence of Brazilian Free-tailed Bats from Stuart Bat Cave. There are frequent tours to see this spectacular bat flight between early April and September. Before the bats begin to emerge, there is ample time to study the colony of Cave Swallows at the entrance to the cave. After watching the bat flight, drive slowly around the park roads to see Common Poorwills. Eastern Screech- and Great Horned Owls are common in the park. There are usually a few Elf Owls in spring and summer, but these birds are more often heard than seen.

Fall and winter are a great time to study sparrows at Kickapoo. Look for Rufous-crowned, Chipping, Field, Vesper, Black-throated, Savannah, Song, Lincoln's, and White-crowned. Check the old cleared pastures that are now grass-covered for Grasshopper and Le Conte's Sparrows among the numerous Savannah and Vesper Sparrows.

Upon leaving the park, turn right (south) toward Brackettville (22.5 miles). Before reaching Brackettville, the road crosses the escarpment and heads

Crested Caracara   Brad McKinney

down onto the South Texas Plains, where the habitat changes dramatically. Watch for Scaled Quail, Harris's Hawk, and Crested Caracara along the roadsides. At dusk this road, as well as US-90, is a good place to see Common and Lesser Nighthawks. After dark, if there is not much traffic, nighthawks and Common Poorwills land on the pavement.

FORT CLARK SPRINGS

Fort Clark Springs (1,600 acres) is located on the south side of US-90 at Brackettville (see map on page 192) and is a gated private community that offers excellent birding opportunities along Las Moras Creek. There are specific procedures needed to visit this area. The entrance to Fort Clark is located approximately 100 yards east of the intersection of US-90 and FM-674. Check in at the entrance station for the Fort and you will be directed to park at the primitive camping area. This area is reached by continuing south on Fort Clark Road 0.8 mile to the intersection with Scales Road. Turn left onto Scales Road and continue another 0.7 mile to the camping area, which is marked with brown signs. The campground is located on the bank of Las Moras Creek and there are trails leading along the creek to the south and north (across Scales Road). There is a motel, RV park, and restaurant at Fort Clark Springs (800-937-1590).

The woodland along Las Moras Creek is dominated by large Plateau Live Oaks and other smaller trees. The birds found here are typical of those found in South Texas. Year-round residents include Red-shouldered and Harris's Hawks, Inca and White-winged Doves, Barred Owl, Green Kingfisher, Golden-fronted Woodpecker, Vermilion Flycatcher, Great Kiskadee, White-eyed Vireo, Black-crested Titmouse, Blue-gray Gnatcatcher, Long-billed Thrasher, and Olive Sparrow. During the spring and summer, look for Yellow-billed Cuckoo (after 1 May), Black-chinned Hummingbird, Ash-throated and Brown-crested Flycatchers, Couch's Kingbird, Bell's Vireo, Yellow-breasted Chat, Summer Tanager, Blue Grosbeak, and Painted Bunting. Migration can be very good along this woodland, as it is stands out as an oasis in this widespread brush country. Ringed Kingfishers have been a regular winter resident in the area over the past decade, and Green Jays have been a very irregular visitor as well. Some of the more unexpected birds found in this woodland over the years include American Woodcock, Lewis's and Red-headed Woodpeckers, Tropical Parula, and Painted Redstart.

CHALK BLUFF PARK

Chalk Bluff Park (entrance fee $3 per person during the winter, $5 per person during the remainder of the year) is a private park along the bank of the Nueces River. To reach the park from Uvalde (see map on page 210), travel north from the center of town on US-83 approximately 2 miles to the intersection with TX-55. Turn left (west) onto TX-55 and travel 15 miles to the park entrance on the left side of the road. Many species that are usually found farther south on the South Texas Plains can be seen here. The river is lined with sycamores and Bald Cypress; this has been a reliable location in recent years to find Ringed and Green Kingfishers. Green is resident and Ringed

Zone-tailed Hawk   Mark Lockwood

has been seen year-round, although winter is the best time to find that species. The park contains some remnant riparian habitat as well as live-oak mottes above the floodplain. Year-round residents include Golden-fronted Woodpecker, Western Scrub-Jay, Cactus, Canyon, Carolina, and Bewick's Wrens, Long-billed Thrasher, Olive Sparrow, Rufous-crowned, Black-throated, and Field Sparrows, Northern Cardinal, and Pyrrhuloxia. During the spring and summer, look for Common Ground-Dove, Ash-hroated and Brown-crested Flycatchers, Black Phoebe, Couch's Kingbird, Yellow-breasted Chat, Indigo and Painted Buntings, Hooded Oriole, and Lesser Goldfinch. Zone-tailed Hawks nest in the area. A Rufous-capped Warbler spent the entire summer here in 1995.

During the winter, the park is home to an impressive array of sparrows, including the resident species listed above as well as Chipping, Vesper, Savannah, Song, Lincoln's, Swamp, White-throated, White-crowned, and Dark-eyed Junco. Other wintering species found frequently here include Yellow-bellied Sapsucker, Ruby-crowned Kinglet, Hermit Thrush, Orange-crowned and Yellow-rumped Warblers, Spotted Towhee, and American Goldfinch.

ANNOTATED CHECKLIST:
THE BIRDS
OF THE REGION

In *A Birder's Guide to the Rio Grande Valley*, an annotated checklist replaces the standard bar-graph checklist used in many of the guides in this ABA birdfinding series. The avifaunas of the three major regions covered in this guide obviously have common components, but they are more different than they are similar. The differences in latitude and longitude between El Paso and Brownsville strongly affect the average arrival times of migrants, winter residents, and breeding species. In order to produce a valuable and accurate component of the book, three or four lines of bars would be needed for many species. An annotated checklist is the best way to overcome this obstacle. The checklist includes every species that has been documented within the area covered by this guide through spring 2008.

For each species, there are three components to the checklist. The relative abundance of each species is included. The seven terms used to describe abundance are:

COMMON: Found in moderate to large numbers, and easily found in appropriate habitat at the right time of year.

FAIRLY COMMON: Found in small to moderate numbers, and usually easy to find in appropriate habitat at the right time of year.

UNCOMMON: Found in small numbers, and usually—but not always—found with some effort in appropriate habitat at the right time of year.

RARE: Occurs annually in very small numbers. Not to be expected on any given day, but may be found with extended effort over the course of the appropriate season(s).

CASUAL: Occurs less than annually, but there tends to be a pattern over time at the right time of year in appropriate habitat.

ACCIDENTAL: Represents an exceptional occurrence that might not be repeated again for decades; there are usually fewer than five records.

IRREGULAR: Represents an irruptive species whose numbers are highly variable from year to year. There may be small to even large numbers present in any one year, while in another year it may be absent altogether.

The normal range for each species in the annotated checklist is described. The proper habitat is included for many species, primarily permanent residents, breeding species, and a few winter residents. Migrants often are found in a variety of habitat types, and for that reason, no specific habitats are included for them.

This checklist is a brief overview. Locally produced checklists for specific sites will provide you with more locally accurate (usually!) information.

Nomenclature and taxonomic sequence follow the American Ornithologists' Union *Check-list of North American Birds*, 7th edition, and supplements through July 2008. Records of rarities are summarized through spring 2008.

ABBREVIATIONS

Ave: Avenue	NWR: National Wildlife Refuge
Blvd: Boulevard	SNA: State Natural Area
Co: County	SP: State Park
Dr: Drive	St: Street
Mtns: Mountains	WBC: World Birding Center
NP: National Park	

Black-bellied Whistling-Duck (*Dendrocygna autumnalis*) — Common resident throughout most of the Lower Valley from about La Joya to the coast, becoming uncommon in the Falcon Dam area and on the immediate coast; locally uncommon resident on the southern Edwards Plateau; accidental in the Trans-Pecos. Most common from Brownsville to Mission in oxbow lakes and ponds. Easy to find along the banks of many of Brownsville's resacas. Also fairly easy to see at City Lake in Harlingen, the Weslaco sewage treatment plant (Airport Dr), Estero Llano Grande SP, Willow and Pintail Lakes at Santa Ana NWR, McAllen Sewage Ponds, and Edinburg WBC.

Fulvous Whistling-Duck (*Dendrocygna bicolor*) — Uncommon spring migrant and summer resident in the Lower Valley from the coast to about Santa Ana NWR; rarely found in winter. Rare post-breeding wanderer inland to Travis and Bexar Cos. Accidental in the Trans-Pecos. Easiest to find in late spring and early summer at Willow and Pintail Lakes at Santa Ana NWR and on Brownsville's Old Port Isabel Rd. Although difficult to find in winter, occasionally turns up in large Black-bellied Whistling-Duck flocks in the Brownsville area, for example, at the resaca on Central Blvd south of FM-802. Also to be looked for at Estero Llano Grande SP and Edinburg WBC.

Greater White-fronted Goose *(Anser albifrons)* — Fairly common winter resident (November–March) in agricultural areas of the Lower Valley. Locally uncommon winter resident in agricultural areas east of Uvalde in the northern South Texas Brush Country. Rarely encountered migrant over the eastern Edwards Plateau. Rare winter visitor and migrant (especially September–October) to reservoirs in the Trans-Pecos.

Snow Goose *(Chen caerulescens)* — Rare to uncommon migrant and winter resident (October–early April) throughout. Most numerous along coast (where locally common) and in the vicinity of El Paso and Las Cruces. Regular at Balmorhea Lake as well. Scarce on the Edwards Plateau and in the Big Bend region. Rare stragglers in summer.

Ross's Goose *(Chen rossii)* — Rare to very uncommon winter visitor and migrant in the Trans-Pecos. Most likely to be found at reservoirs southeast of El Paso (especially McNary) and at Balmorhea Lake, where the species seems to be increasing in recent years. Rare winter visitor coastally in the Lower Valley, though perhaps regular in Snow Goose flocks north of Edinburg (e.g., Sal del Rey) and near the coast (e.g., Laguna Atascosa NWR). Two recent winter records of blue-morph individuals from McNary Reservoir below El Paso.

Brant *(Branta bernicla)* — Very rare migrant and winter visitor to Texas; one Lower Valley record near Vernon (Willacy Co) 28 December 1956.

Cackling Goose *(Branta hutchinsii)* — Status somewhat uncertain due to difficulties in identification and its being split only recently from Canada Goose. Casual to rare winter visitor, possibly annual, to coastal areas. Casual in far western Trans-Pecos.

Canada Goose *(Branta canadensis)* — Rare to uncommon migrant and winter resident (October–April) throughout. Presumed escapees thought to be responsible for recent breeding at Feather Lake near El Paso.

Trumpeter Swan *(Cygnus buccinator)* — Accidental. One just north of Las Cruces 14–21 December 1985 and another along the Rio Grande below Falcon Dam 28 December 1989–14 January 1990.

Tundra Swan *(Cygnus columbianus)* — Accidental to casual winter visitor (November–March) throughout, with perhaps more records for the Trans-Pecos than elsewhere. Generally found singly or, less regularly, in small groups.

Muscovy Duck (*Cairina moschata*) — This duck has been present along the lower Rio Grande since 1984, where it is a rare to uncommon resident in the Falcon Dam area (from Fronton to San Ygnacio), becoming very rare east to Santa Ana NWR. Most often seen flying up and down the river at Santa Margarita Ranch, Chapeño, Salineño, and below Falcon Dam from April through September; rarer during winter months. Apparently this species increased recently in northeastern Mexico, responding to a Ducks Unlimited of Mexico nest-box program. First nesting evidence was at Bentsen SP in July 1994. *Caution:* Muscovy Ducks of recent domestic origin are found throughout the Lower Valley. Birds in the middle section (e.g., Hidalgo Co) may be of either wild or domestic origin. Birds should be checked for extra white in the greater coverts and red in the bare facial skin, found on domestic adult birds.

Wood Duck (*Aix sponsa*) — Uncommon and local resident along portions of the Rio Grande and on the Edwards Plateau. Breeds regularly along the river below Falcon Dam, around El Paso and Las Cruces, and in the Hill Country. Irregular elsewhere, with more records for winter than for other seasons. Appears to be on the increase in portions of its range.

Gadwall (*Anas strepera*) — Fairly common to common migrant and winter resident (September–April) throughout. Rare summer visitor.

Eurasian Wigeon (*Anas penelope*) — Very rare migrant and winter visitor (November–early May) throughout, with about 20 records overall. Interestingly, 12 of these records are from El Paso and Hudspeth Cos in the far western Trans-Pecos. Should be looked for wherever large concentrations of American Wigeons occur.

American Wigeon (*Anas americana*) — Fairly common to common migrant and winter resident (September–April) throughout. Rare straggler in summer, with no evidence of breeding.

Mallard (*Anas platyrhynchos*) — Genuine Mallards (wild birds not of the "Mexican Duck" race) are uncommon to common winter birds (September–April) and somewhat rare breeders in the Trans-Pecos. They are generally uncommon in winter on the Edwards Plateau. Basically absent altogether from the Lower Valley, where birds that appear to be Mallards are likely of domestic origin.

"Mexican Duck" ("Mexican Mallard") (*Anas platyrhynchos novimexicanus*) — Considered conspecific with Mallard. Uncommon to fairly common permanent resident of rivers, ponds, and irrigation canals from Balmorhea Lake and Big Bend NP westward. Most numerous along the river southeast and north of El Paso, but is fairly widespread. Regular in the Falcon Dam area in winter and migration, where numbers seem to be increasing and where it is occasionally seen side-by-side with Mottled Ducks for comparison.

Mottled Duck (*Anas fulvigula*) — Locally common resident along the Lower Valley coast and west along the Rio Grande to about Falcon Dam. Regular post-breeding wanderer inland to Travis and Bexar Cos. Often seen at the Sabal Palm Audubon Center resaca, at Willow and Pintail Lakes at Santa Ana NWR, in freshwater coastal wetlands, and along the Rio Grande in the Falcon Dam area.

Blue-winged Teal *(Anas discors)* — Fairly common to common migrant (mid-March–May, August–October) throughout, decreasing in numbers westward. Fairly common in winter in the Lower Valley, but casual in the Trans-Pecos at that season. Summer lingerers are rare to very uncommon throughout, with documented breeding only in El Paso Co.

Cinnamon Teal *(Anas cyanoptera)* — Uncommon to common migrant (late February–May, August–October) in the Trans-Pecos. Generally less numerous or absent in mid-winter. Rare and localized to uncommon breeder in the western Trans-Pecos. Non-breeding summer lingerers are occasionally seen throughout. Locally uncommon in the Lower Valley in winter; some years mostly absent except at Santa Ana NWR, where there are usually small numbers present.

Northern Shoveler *(Anas clypeata)* — Common migrant and winter resident (September–May) throughout. Rare and local to very uncommon as a nesting species in the Trans-Pecos. Non-breeding summer lingerers are rare to uncommon throughout.

White-cheeked Pintail *(Anas bahamensis)* — Accidental. One documented record for Texas: Laguna Atascosa NWR 20 November 1978–15 April 1979.

Northern Pintail *(Anas acuta)* — Fairly common to common fall migrant and winter resident (September–early March) throughout. Less numerous in spring, as most tend to depart northward by March. Rare summer visitor, with verified breeding only at El Paso.

Garganey *(Anas querquedula)* — Accidental in spring. A male was found in Presidio Co 29 April–6 May 1994. It eventually died of undetermined causes and the specimen is now at Texas A&M University.

Green-winged Teal *(Anas crecca)* — Fairly common to very common migrant and winter resident (September–early May) throughout. Rare summer visitor, with no evidence of breeding.

Canvasback *(Aythya valisineria)* — Uncommon to fairly common winter resident (October–March) throughout. Scarce later in spring and earlier in fall migration (April/September). Casual summer visitor.

Redhead *(Aythya americana)* — Uncommon to fairly common migrant and winter resident (October–March) throughout. Most numerous along the coast. An uncommon and local breeding species mostly in the vicinity of El Paso. A rare straggler to other areas in summer.

Ring-necked Duck *(Aythya collaris)* — Uncommon to fairly common migrant and winter resident (late September–April) throughout. Casual summer visitor.

Greater Scaup *(Aythya marila)* — Rare winter visitor (November–March). Perhaps more numerous along the coast than elsewhere. Accidental in summer in the Trans-Pecos.

Lesser Scaup *(Aythya affinis)* — Uncommon to common migrant and winter resident (late September–April) throughout. Casual summer visitor.

Harlequin Duck *(Histrionicus histrionicus)* — Accidental in winter. One was at South Padre Island 30 January–4 February 1990.

Surf Scoter *(Melanitta perspicillata)* — Rare migrant and winter visitor along the Lower Coast, on the Edwards Plateau, and in the Trans-Pecos (where the vast majority of records are from October/November). Best spots are in the Laguna Madre between Port Isabel and South Padre Island, and in the Brownsville Ship Channel.

White-winged Scoter *(Melanitta fusca)* — Casual fall migrant and winter visitor along the Lower Coast, on the Edwards Plateau, and in the Trans-Pecos. Look for on both the immediate coast and in the waters of the Laguna Madre.

Black Scoter *(Melanitta nigra)* — Rare winter visitor along the central and upper coasts (not yet recorded in the Lower Valley). Accidental in fall and winter in the Trans-Pecos.

Long-tailed Duck *(Clangula hyemalis)* — Casual to rare migrant and winter visitor throughout.

Bufflehead *(Bucephala albeola)* — Uncommon to fairly common winter resident throughout (late October–March). Rare later in spring or earlier in fall migration. Much less numerous downriver of Salineño. Casual summer visitor.

Common Goldeneye *(Bucephala clangula)* — Rare to uncommon winter resident (November–March) throughout, except for the Lower Coast, where accidental. More numerous in western Trans-Pecos than elsewhere.

Barrow's Goldeneye *(Bucephala islandica)* — Accidental winter visitor to the Trans-Pecos: a male photographed at Tornillo 20 December 1995.

Hooded Merganser *(Lophodytes cucullatus)* — Rare winter visitor throughout (November–March). Somewhat regular in very small numbers on larger Trans-Pecos reservoirs.

Common Merganser *(Mergus merganser)* — Uncommon winter resident (November–March) on larger reservoirs in much of the Trans-Pecos. Generally rare to absent elsewhere. Some years large flocks of several hundred grace reservoirs such as McNary, Fort Hancock, and Red Bluff. Accidental summer visitor around El Paso.

Red-breasted Merganser *(Mergus serrator)* — Fairly common winter resident (November–March) along the coast. Rare inland, although somewhat regular in small numbers on Trans-Pecos reservoirs and reservoirs of the eastern Edwards Plateau (e.g., Lake Buchanan and Canyon Lake) in late fall and early winter.

Masked Duck *(Nomonyx dominicus)* — Rare and irregular on the Lower Valley coastal plain northward beyond our region to Brazos Bend SP and Anahuac NWR. Absent in most years; however, some years they may be widespread in small numbers. Masked Ducks are often secretive, seldom venturing far from cover. This species has been recorded at Willow and Cattail Lakes at Santa Ana NWR, the resaca at Sabal Palm Audubon Center, on Alligator Pond at Laguna Atascosa NWR, and north of our coverage area along US-77 on the King Ranch. Accidental in El Paso.

Ruddy Duck *(Oxyura jamaicensis)* — Uncommon to common migrant and winter resident (September–April) throughout, a few remaining to June. Very uncommon and localized breeding species in portions of the Trans-Pecos, most easily found at the Fort Bliss Sewage Ponds.

Plain Chachalaca *(Ortalis vetula)* — Locally common resident of the Lower Valley; found in thorn scrub and riparian habitats from Falcon Dam to the Gulf of Mexico. This species is easily seen at bird-feeding stations at Bentsen SP, Santa Ana NWR, Frontera Audubon Thicket, and Sabal Palm Audubon Center.

Ring-necked Pheasant *(Phasianus colchicus)* — Rare resident around Rattlesnake Springs, NM. Formerly an uncommon resident in the agricultural areas near Balmorhea northward toward Pecos, but apparently no longer present.

Wild Turkey *(Meleagris gallopavo)* — Fairly common resident on the Edwards Plateau and in the central mountains of the Trans-Pecos. This species is fairly common just north of the Lower Valley on the King Ranch. Often seen from highways.

Scaled Quail *(Callipepla squamata)* — Fairly common to common resident of arid brushlands from the Falcon Dam area westward. Perhaps easiest to find at Big Bend NP and Balmorhea Lake, but look also in desert areas above Salineño and Santa Margarita Ranch, at Hueco Tanks, and on the lower slopes of the Franklin Mtns in El Paso.

Gambel's Quail *(Callipepla gambelii)* — Fairly common to common resident along the Rio Grande from Las Cruces south to Presidio. Less numerous in desert arroyos and brushy canyons of the western Trans-Pecos away from the river, but seems to be increasing in some of those areas. Accidental as far south as Big Bend NP.

Northern Bobwhite *(Colinus virginianus)* — Common, but declining, resident in the Lower Valley northward to the Edwards Plateau. Uncommon in the eastern Trans-Pecos, becoming rare and local as far west as Balmorhea.

Montezuma Quail *(Cyrtonyx montezumae)* — Fairly common but secretive resident in the Davis Mtns and surrounding mountain ranges (including the Chinatis). Uncommon and local on the southwestern Edwards Plateau. Easiest to see at Davis Mtns SP and along the scenic loop up to the Lawrence E. Wood Picnic Area. Recently (2005) rediscovered in the Chisos Mtns of Big Bend NP, where it appears to be very rare.

Red-throated Loon *(Gavia stellata)* — Casual fall and winter visitor to reservoirs in the Trans-Pecos and the eastern Edwards Plateau. Most records are from Balmorhea Lake, but also documented in El Paso, Hudspeth, Pecos, Comal, and Bexar Cos.

Pacific Loon *(Gavia pacifica)* — Casual fall and winter visitor to reservoirs of the Trans-Pecos and the eastern Edwards Plateau. Accidental along the Lower Coast. About 15 records overall, with the majority being in late fall and early winter, plus a June 2006 record from Balmorhea Lake.

Common Loon *(Gavia immer)* — Uncommon winter resident (late October–April) on large reservoirs of the eastern Edwards Plateau and on Falcon Reservoir, as well as along the coast; easier to find along the coast. Rare migrant and winter visitor at reservoirs in the Trans-Pecos.

Yellow-billed Loon *(Gavia adamsii)* — Accidental winter visitor. Two documented records from Balmorhea Lake (25 November–10 December 1993, 21 December 1996–2 January 1997), and another from South Padre Island 22 December 2000–mid-May 2001.

Least Grebe *(Tachybaptus dominicus)* — Uncommon to locally common resident of freshwater ponds in South Texas; irregular from Del Rio to the coast. To be looked for at the resaca at Sabal Palm Audubon Center and at both Willow and Pintail Lakes at Santa Ana NWR. This species is known to wander in fall and winter, when it is accidental to casual in the Trans-Pecos (especially along the Rio Grande near Big Bend NP) west to El Paso. Rare breeder in the Austin area.

Pied-billed Grebe *(Podilymbus podiceps)* — Common winter resident (September–April) throughout. Uncommon as a breeding species over much of the region, but may be locally common.

Horned Grebe *(Podiceps auritus)* — Rare migrant and winter visitor (October–March) to larger reservoirs throughout. Casual along the Lower Laguna Madre. More records from late fall than other seasons.

Eared Grebe *(Podiceps nigricollis)* — Fairly common to common migrant and winter resident (October–April) throughout. Most often seen on larger reservoirs or along the coast. Breeds locally in the El Paso area, especially at Fort Bliss Sewage Ponds.

Western Grebe *(Aechmophorus occidentalis)* — Uncommon to fairly common migrant and winter resident (October–April) at larger bodies of water throughout the Trans-Pecos. Look for it at Balmorhea Lake, McNary Reservoir, and Fort Hancock Reservoir. Casual in the Lower Valley. Increasingly regular in summer in Reeves, Hudspeth, and El Paso Cos, where breeding has occurred at McNary Reservoir and Balmorhea Lake. Has interbred with Clark's Grebe on at least two occasions in the region.

Clark's Grebe *(Aechmophorus clarkii)* — Uncommon to fairly common migrant and winter resident (October–April) to larger bodies of water in the western Trans-Pecos. Rare to uncommon but increasing, in summer, with documented breeding at McNary Reservoir and Balmorhea Lake.

American Flamingo *(Phoenicopterus ruber)* — Accidental; about seven Texas records. There are two Lower Valley records from coastal Cameron Co: Bahía Grande (a U.S. Fish & Wildlife Service wetland near Port Isabel) 24 June–29 July 2004 and Laguna Madre near Green Island 28 May 2007.

Yellow-nosed Albatross *(Thalassarche chlororhyncos)* — Accidental. There are four accepted records of this species for Texas, three from the Lower Coast: Port Isabel 14 May 1972, South Padre Island 28 October 1976, and offshore from South Padre Island 26 September 2003. The 1976 bird was held in Gladys Porter Zoo, Brownsville, until its death on 19 April 1977. The specimen is located at the University of Texas–Pan American in Edinburg. The 2003 bird was discovered near a shrimp boat on a pelagic trip in relatively shallow (340 feet) offshore waters about 40 miles east-northeast of South Padre Island.

Cory's Shearwater *(Calonectris diomedea)* — Rare to uncommon in offshore Gulf of Mexico waters in summer and fall. Although both subspecies, *C. d. borealis* (Atlantic Cory's) and *C. d. diomedea* ("Scopoli's" Shearwater) have been documented off the Lower Coast, the *borealis* race is much more likely in Gulf of Mexico waters. Best months are August through October; very rare at other seasons. Casually seen from land at South Padre Island or Boca Chica.

Greater Shearwater *(Puffinus gravis)* — Accidental in fall. The majority of state sightings have come from the Upper and Central Texas coasts. Just two records for the Lower Coast: both off South Padre Island, 1 October 2004 and 19 July 2008.

Sooty Shearwater *(Puffinus griseus)* — Casual offshore and along the coast; most state records in spring and summer. Only one record from the Lower Coast, at Boca Chica on the surprising date of 6 January 1992.

Manx Shearwater (*Puffinus puffinus*) — Accidental in fall. The lone record from the Lower Coast occurred along bayshore waters of South Padre Island on 13 September 2002.

Audubon's Shearwater (*Puffinus lherminieri*) — Rare to uncommon in offshore Gulf of Mexico waters in summer and fall (August–September). Less common than Cory's Shearwater. Audubon's is normally found in pelagic waters where the depth is greater than 100 fathoms (600 feet), and, unlike Cory's, is seen very rarely in the relatively shallow waters over the continental shelf.

Leach's Storm-Petrel (*Oceanodroma leucorhoa*) — Rare to very rare summer and fall visitor to the deep offshore waters of the Gulf of Mexico. Most state records come from pelagic trips off Port O'Connor and South Padre Island.

Band-rumped Storm-Petrel (*Oceanodroma castro*) — Rare to uncommon but regular in offshore Texas waters from spring through early fall (June and July are the best months). After tropical storms, this species has been found along the coast and inland. There are two inland records occurring far from the coast: Lower Valley at Edinburg 25 June 1954 and San Antonio 14 June 1984.

Red-billed Tropicbird (*Phaethon aethereus*) — Accidental to casual in summer and fall in offshore Gulf of Mexico waters. Between 2001–2008, this species has been recorded six times off South Padre Island (May through September). There is also a very unusual record of a specimen along the Rio Grande at Zapata 29 April 1989.

Masked Booby (*Sula dactylatra*) — Rare to uncommon migrant and non-breeding summer resident off the Lower Coast. Seen fairly regularly on offshore trips from San Padre Island; very rare to rare offshore in winter. Rarely seen along the immediate coast, mostly in summer.

Blue-footed Booby (*Sula nebouxii*) — Accidental; one record for Texas. An immature bird was found on the Edwards Plateau at Granite Shoals, Burnet Co (Lake L. B. Johnson) from 2 June 1993–6 October 1994. This bird was refound 80 miles downstream at Lake Bastrop 10 December 1994–12 April 1995. (An immature *Sulid* on 5 October 1976 from South Padre Island that was first reported as a Blue-footed Booby has been determined to be a Masked Booby upon reexamination of photographs.)

Brown Booby (*Sula leucogaster*) — Casual to very rare along the Texas coast in all seasons. Most of the Lower Coast records are from summer and fall. Although this species is to be looked for on pelagic birding trips, it is most often seen sitting on solid structures along the immediate coast. In recent years, this species has been observed at the South Padre Island and Boca Chica jetties and on offshore buoys and channel markers along the Laguna Madre/Brownsville Ship Channel.

Northern Gannet (*Morus bassanus*) — Uncommon migrant and winter visitor along the Lower Coast and offshore, occasionally seen in large numbers. Often seen from South Padre Island and Boca Chica. Rare in summer.

American White Pelican (*Pelecanus erythrorhynchos*) — Common migrant and winter resident along the Lower Coast, on many inland lakes and reservoirs, and along the Rio Grande to Falcon Reservoir; less common farther west. Non-breeding birds are very rare to locally uncommon in summer along the coast and on some inland reservoirs.

Brown Pelican (*Pelecanus occidentalis*) — Locally common resident along the Lower Coast; rare along the Rio Grande west to the Trans-Pecos (where the majority of records are from May–October) and at inland reservoirs.

Neotropic Cormorant (*Phalacrocorax brasilianus*) — Uncommon to fairly common permanent resident (though more numerous in summer) along the Rio Grande from Del Rio south. Easiest to find in the Falcon Dam area, at Santa Ana NWR, Llano Grande Lake, and resacas in Brownsville. Less numerous north along the river. Irregularly rare to uncommon through much of the Trans-Pecos, most numerous in summer. Increasing in El Paso and Hudspeth Cos, where it has bred in recent years at Fort Hancock and McNary Reservoirs, and in El Paso Co.

Double-crested Cormorant (*Phalacrocorax auritus*) — Common winter resident (late September–April) in the Lower Valley and on the eastern Edwards Plateau. Year-round resident in the El Paso area, with a breeding colony at McNary Reservoir.

Anhinga (*Anhinga anhinga*) — Fairly common spring migrant and locally uncommon winter resident along the Lower Coast and most of the Lower Valley, becoming rare around Falcon Dam; uncommon summer resident on the coastal plain and rare inland to the Edwards Plateau. Accidental in the Trans-Pecos. Often seen at both Willow and Pintail Lakes at Santa Ana NWR, the resaca at Sabal Palm Audubon Center, and along vegetated resacas in the Brownsville area.

Magnificent Frigatebird (*Fregata magnificens*) — Uncommon summer visitor along the Lower Coast and offshore, becoming rare inland to about Brownsville and accidental farther west to the Falcon Dam area; very rare along the coast in winter. Accidental to Austin and San Antonio.

American Bittern (*Botaurus lentiginosus*) — Rare to uncommon in winter and migration (late September–April) in the eastern Lower Valley; casual to rare in the remainder of the region.

Least Bittern (*Ixobrychus exilis*) — Uncommon resident in coastal areas and cattail-lined resacas (e.g., Brownsville) in the Lower Valley. Uncommon summer resident west to Santa Ana NWR; rare as far west as Falcon Dam. Irregular breeder along the Rio Grande in Presidio Co. Rare in summer around

El Paso, where it may breed as well. This secretive species may be more wide-spread along the Rio Grande than is currently known.

Great Blue Heron *(Ardea herodias)* — Common resident on the Ed-wards Plateau and in South Texas in appropriate habitat. Uncommon summer visitor in the Trans-Pecos, where there are very few breeding records, be-coming more common in migration and winter.

Great Egret *(Ardea alba)* — Fairly common to common at all seasons in the Lower Valley. Nests locally along the coast. Less numerous upriver, where the species is an uncommon to fairly common and local visitor through much of the Trans-Pecos and the Edwards Plateau. Recent breeding at McNary Reservoir and Rio Bosque Wetlands Park provides the only nesting records for the Trans-Pecos.

Snowy Egret *(Egretta thula)* — Fairly common to common at all seasons in the Lower Valley. Nests locally along the coast. Less numerous and more localized upriver. Breeds locally around El Paso and Las Cruces. A fairly com-mon migrant elsewhere in the Trans-Pecos and on the Edwards Plateau; rare to very uncommon there in winter.

Little Blue Heron *(Egretta caerulea)* — Uncommon resident in the Lower Valley; very rare and irregular post-breeding wanderer as far west as El Paso.

Tricolored Heron *(Egretta tricolor)* — Common resident of the Lower Valley, becoming uncommon in the Falcon Dam area; casual to rare visitor in-land, mostly in summer and fall.

Reddish Egret *(Egretta rufescens)* — Locally common resident along the Lower Coast, where it is found almost exclusively in saltwater habitats. Often seen in the Laguna Madre, especially along the bayshore of South Padre Island. Two good spots are the South Padre Island Convention Center boardwalk and where the causeway first meets South Padre Island. Also look near the end of TX-4 at Boca Chica and along Bayside Dr at Laguna Atascosa NWR. Casual to rare visitor inland, mostly in summer and fall.

Cattle Egret *(Bubulcus ibis)* — Uncommon to common migrant through-out. Breeds locally along the coast in the Lower Valley and around El Paso and Las Cruces. Rare to uncommon in winter along western stretches of the Rio Grande, uncommon in the Lower Valley.

Green Heron *(Butorides virescens)* — Fairly common migrant and sum-mer resident along most of river and on the Edwards Plateau. Less numerous in winter, when it may be quite difficult to find in much of the Trans-Pecos. Of-ten found along vegetated canals, small ponds, and along the banks of the Rio Grande.

Black-crowned Night-Heron *(Nycticorax nycticorax)* — Locally com-mon resident along the Lower Coast. Rare to locally common migrant and summer resident in the rest of the region, with breeding reported west to El Paso Co. Rare to locally uncommon winter resident inland. Black-crowned Night-Herons roost in large numbers in the Black Mangrove trees at the mouth of the Rio Grande at Boca Chica. McNary Reservoir (Hudspeth Co) has a fairly large rookery.

Yellow-crowned Night-Heron (*Nycticorax violacea*) — Uncommon resident in the Lower Valley and on the eastern Edwards Plateau. More common along the immediate coast and along the Rio Grande, becoming much more local in the western Lower Valley. Casual to rare post-breeding wanderer as far west as El Paso.

White Ibis (*Eudocimus albus*) — Locally common resident along the Lower Coast; nesting reported at several inland locales. Regular post-breeding wanderer inland to Travis and Bexar Cos just off the Edwards Plateau. Accidental in the Trans-Pecos.

Glossy Ibis (*Plegadis falcinellus*) — Rare visitor in many parts of the state; most sightings are concentrated along the upper and central coasts. In the Lower Valley, there are records from Brownsville, Estero Llano Grande SP, Santa Ana NWR, and McAllen. Also records from El Paso and Doña Ana Co. Although Glossy Ibises have been seen in all months, reports have been concentrated between March and June, when adults are in breeding plumage.

White-faced Ibis (*Plegadis chihi*) — Fairly common to common migrant and winter resident in the Lower Valley. Some local breeding along the coast, with birds present throughout summer at various Lower Valley locations. Uncommon to fairly common migrant (March–May, August–October) through the Trans-Pecos and the eastern Edwards Plateau; rare in winter. A few scattered breeding records from the El Paso/Las Cruces area.

Roseate Spoonbill (*Platalea ajaja*) — Locally common resident along the Lower Coast, becoming somewhat less common in winter; wanders rarely inland to Falcon Dam. Regular post-breeding wanderer inland to Travis and Bexar Cos. Casual in the Trans-Pecos.

Jabiru (*Jabiru mycteria*) — Accidental in late summer and fall. Of the seven Texas records, three come from the Lower Valley: La Sal de Vieja, Hidalgo Co September 1972, near Bentsen SP 5–8 August 1985, and Laguna Atascosa NWR 11 August 1997. There is also another record from just outside our coverage area near Encino, north of McAllen, 29 October 1979.

Wood Stork (*Mycteria americana*) — Uncommon post-breeding visitor in the Lower Valley during summer and fall, becoming rare to the west in the Falcon Dam area; no recent records in the Trans-Pecos. Very rare along the Lower Coast in winter.

Black Vulture (*Coragyps atratus*) — Common resident on the Edwards Plateau southward to the Lower Valley. Uncommon and local along the Rio

Grande in the Big Bend region west to northern Presidio Co; casual in Hudspeth Co.

Turkey Vulture *(Cathartes aura)* — Common summer resident and migrant (mid-March–October) throughout. Absent from much of the Trans-Pecos in winter (November–February), but still common at that season in the Lower Valley and on the Edwards Plateau

Osprey *(Pandion haliaetus)* — Fairly common migrant and winter visitor (August–May) to the Lower Valley. Rare to uncommon migrant in the remainder of the region. Rare in summer in Lower Valley, except along the immediate coast where it is locally uncommon. Casual in summer and winter in the Trans-Pecos.

Hook-billed Kite *(Chondrohierax uncinatus)* — Rare resident in the Lower Valley from Santa Ana NWR to the Falcon Dam area. The species is most often seen at Santa Ana NWR, Anzalduas County Park, Bentsen SP, and along the Rio Grande at Salineño and Chapeño. Although this raptor is occasionally seen flying to and from roost sites at dawn and dusk, it is more often seen soaring during late morning and mid-day hours. Pairs may be spotted soaring over breeding territories in spring and early summer.

Swallow-tailed Kite *(Elanoides forficatus)* — Rare to uncommon migrant in the Lower Valley, very rare on the eastern Edwards Plateau, and accidental in the Trans-Pecos. This species is most numerous on the coastal plain, with one of the better spots being along the Rio Grande at Sabal Palm Audubon Center during March. Seen nearly annually at hawkwatches at Bentsen SP and Santa Ana NWR, and at Laguna Atascosa NWR. On the Edwards Plateau, Swallow-tailed Kite is more regular during fall migration.

White-tailed Kite *(Elanus leucurus)* — Uncommon to fairly common resident of coastal prairies and farmlands of the Lower Valley; good spots are along TX-4 toward Boca Chica Beach, along FM-511 between US-77 and the Port of Brownsville, and along Old Port Isabel Rd. Also may be seen along the entrance road to the Sabal Palm Audubon Center and at Estero Llano Grande SP. Rare visitor to the southwestern Edwards Plateau and the Trans-Pecos. Recently bred just southeast of El Paso.

Snail Kite *(Rostrhamus sociabilis)* — Accidental. Only three state records, two of which are from the Lower Valley: one along the Rio Grande in Hidalgo Co 17–29 May 1998 and the other near Laguna Vista, Cameron Co 14 July 2007.

Mississippi Kite *(Ictinia mississippiensis)* — Uncommon to fairly common migrant along the Rio Grande and on the Edwards Plateau. Less numerous as one moves westward. A fairly common but extremely localized nesting species in older established neighborhoods of El Paso and occasionally Las Cruces. Should be looked for in migration at Santa Ana NWR or Bentsen SP (often with migrant Broad-winged Hawks) or in breeding season (May–August) in wooded neighborhoods of west El Paso.

Bald Eagle *(Haliaeetus leucocephalus)* — Casual to rare winter visitor (November–March) at larger reservoirs and rivers in the Trans-Pecos and on the Edwards Plateau. Most regular at Lake Buchanan, where uncommon. Accidental in winter in the Lower Valley. In February 2002, an active nest was discovered in Llano Co for the only known nesting on the Edwards Plateau.

Northern Harrier *(Circus cyaneus)* — Fairly common to common migrant and winter resident (September–April) in open country throughout. Rare summer visitor, with one historical nesting record in the Trans-Pecos and a recent breeding record from near El Paso.

Sharp-shinned Hawk *(Accipiter striatus)* — Uncommon to fairly common migrant and winter resident (September–April) to all areas. Very rare in summer, with nesting recently documented in the Davis Mtns and historical nesting in Big Bend, the Edwards Plateau, Hidalgo Co, and possibly the Guadalupe Mtns.

Cooper's Hawk *(Accipiter cooperii)* — Fairly common winter resident (September–April) throughout. Local breeder in the Lower Valley, on the Edwards Plateau, and in the mountains of the Trans-Pecos.

Northern Goshawk *(Accipiter gentilis)* — Casual winter visitor (most from November–January) to the Trans-Pecos; accidental on the eastern Edwards Plateau. Many other unverified reports from scattered localities.

Crane Hawk *(Geranospiza caerulescens)* Accidental. One documented record for Texas and the U.S.: at Santa Ana NWR 20 December 1987–9 April 1988.

Common Black-Hawk *(Buteogallus anthracinus)* — Local summer resident (March–August) in the Davis Mtns, where best observed along Limpia Creek near Davis Mtns SP; also along the Rio Grande in Big Bend NP. Very rare migrant in the El Paso area. There are scattered summer records from other areas of the Trans-Pecos and the Edwards Plateau. Casual winter visitor to Lower Valley, primarily along the Rio Grande in the Falcon Dam and Salineño area.

Harris's Hawk *(Parabuteo unicinctus)* — Fairly common to common resident of brushlands of South Texas as far north as the Edwards Plateau. Especially common from Rio Grande City to Laredo along US-83. Also seen regularly at Santa Ana NWR. Often seen perched atop utility poles, especially along FM-511 (Brownsville) from US-77 to the Port of Brownsville. Rarely found on the Edwards Plateau proper. Generally uncommon and localized in the Trans-Pecos, with known nesting near El Paso and in the Big Bend region. Also look for this species along US-90 east of Del Rio and along US-20 between Fort Hancock and Tornillo.

Roadside Hawk *(Buteo magnirostris)* — Accidental in winter. Some seven accepted records for the state, all from along the Rio Grande between San

Ygnacio east to Cameron Co. Probably the best areas would be the riparian woodlands at Santa Ana NWR and Bentsen SP, where there are three records between them. Be careful not to confuse this vagrant with Red-shouldered or Broad-winged Hawks.

Red-shouldered Hawk *(Buteo lineatus)* — Common resident in riparian and other mixed-hardwood woodlands on the Edwards Plateau. Uncommon winter resident and rare in summer in the Lower Valley (not known to breed). Casual winter visitor to the eastern Trans-Pecos. Two records for Doña Ana Co, NM.

Broad-winged Hawk *(Buteo platypterus)* — Common migrant in the Lower Valley and on the Edwards Plateau (late March– April, October); rare in the Trans-Pecos. Rare in winter in riparian woodlands in the Lower Valley.

Gray Hawk *(Buteo nitidus)* — Local summer resident (March–August) along the Rio Grande in Big Bend NP and in the Lower Valley. Very local summer resident (two or three pairs) in the Davis Mtns. More common in winter (October–March) in the Lower Valley. Good Lower Valley spots include Bentsen SP, Santa Ana NWR, and Anzalduas County Park.

Short-tailed Hawk *(Buteo brachyurus)* — Rare summer visitor to the Lower Valley and accidental northward to the Edwards Plateau and west to the Trans-Pecos. The first record was from Santa Margarita Ranch in Starr Co in July 1989. Since then, there has been a flurry of sightings, and there are currently some 30 records for Texas. Most of the sightings are along the Rio Grande corridor between Bentsen SP and Santa Ana NWR, but there are also recent records from Sabal Palm Audubon Center and Santa Margarita Ranch. In addition to the Lower Valley sightings, there are also records from the Edwards Plateau (mostly at Lost Maples SP), from the Trans-Pecos (Chisos and Davis Mtns), and along the coast north of our coverage area in Corpus Christi. Most sightings occur between March and October, with the greatest concentration between April and June.

Swainson's Hawk *(Buteo swainsoni)* — Fairly common to common migrant (mid-March–May, August–October) throughout. Often seen in large concentrations around recently plowed fields. A common breeder in grasslands and mesquite brushlands throughout much of the Trans-Pecos (except for Big Bend country) and open areas bordering the Edwards Plateau south to about Falcon Dam. Rare and local (probably annual) in the Lower Valley in winter.

White-tailed Hawk *(Buteo albicaudatus)* — Uncommon local resident of the coastal plain of the Lower Valley; fairly common just north of the Lower Valley along US-77 on the King Ranch (south of Kingsville to Raymondville). Uncommon but regular near Brownsville along FM-511 between US-77 and the Port of Brownsville. Occasionally seen at other coastal areas such as along

TX-4 and near Laguna Atascosa NWR. Accidental on the Edwards Plateau and in the Trans-Pecos.

Zone-tailed Hawk *(Buteo albonotatus)* — Uncommon summer resident (April–September) in the mountains of the Trans-Pecos and southern Edwards Plateau; irregular migrant and rare winter visitor to the Lower Valley. This species is accidental in the extreme western end of the Trans-Pecos. Look for it at Kickapoo Cavern SP, Big Bend NP, and the Davis Mtns. Best spot in the Lower Valley is Anzalduas County Park.

Red-tailed Hawk *(Buteo jamaicensis)* — Fairly common to common permanent resident throughout. Generally more numerous in winter, in some areas markedly, with an influx of wintering birds from the north. Breeding birds in west and South Texas usually lack the belly band often associated with this species. The "Harlan's" subspecies of Red-tailed is a rare winter visitor to the Trans-Pecos region and casual in the Lower Valley.

Ferruginous Hawk *(Buteo regalis)* — Uncommon and declining winter resident through much of the Trans-Pecos and areas surrounding the Edwards Plateau. Casual to rare in the Lower Valley. Best looked for from late October through early March in grasslands around the Davis Mtns or along the Rio Grande from Fort Hancock to Las Cruces.

Rough-legged Hawk *(Buteo lagopus)* — Casual to rare winter visitor (November–March) to grasslands of the Trans-Pecos and perhaps elsewhere.

Golden Eagle *(Aquila chrysaetos)* — Uncommon permanent resident of the mountains of the Trans-Pecos. More common and widespread in winter (October–March), when it reaches the Edwards Plateau and elsewhere. Your best bet for finding this bird in summer is probably either in Big Bend NP or in the Franklin Mtns (especially TransMountain Rd) of El Paso, where a couple of pairs breed annually. In winter, good locations include the Davis Mtns and along US-90 west of Alpine. Accidental in the Lower Valley.

Collared Forest-Falcon *(Micrastur semitorquatus)* — Accidental. One accepted record for Texas and the U.S.: Bentsen SP 22 January–24 February 1994.

Crested Caracara *(Caracara cheriway)* — Fairly common permanent resident in the ranch country and coastal savanna of South Texas. Although this species is fairly common on the coastal plain and less common in the drier regions of Starr Co, it is much scarcer in between (mid-Valley). Often seen roadside with vultures feeding on carrion. Crested Caracara is easily seen at the Brownsville Sanitary Landfill and just north of the Valley along US-77 between Raymondville and Kingsville. Also seen regularly along the road to Boca Chica, Sabal Palm Audubon Center, Laguna Atascosa NWR, and the area around Falcon Dam. Accidental in the central and western Trans-Pecos.

American Kestrel *(Falco sparverius)* — Common winter resident and migrant (September–April) throughout. An uncommon to fairly common breeding species in the Trans-Pecos and perhaps portions of the Edwards Plateau.

Merlin *(Falco columbarius)* — Rare to uncommon migrant (March–April, September–mid-November) throughout. Less numerous in mid-winter. Probably more numerous along the coast than elsewhere.

Aplomado Falcon *(Falco femoralis)* — Formerly a rare summer resident of the Lower Valley and the Trans-Pecos. A record from the Trans-Pecos in 1992 was accepted as pertaining to a wild bird. Small (and threatened) populations occur in Chihuahua, Mexico, within 100–150 miles of El Paso, principally near the villages of Coyame and Villa Ahumada. These are likely the source of the handful of recent records near Las Cruces, NM, and Valentine, TX. The Peregrine Fund and the U.S. Fish & Wildlife Service began an Aplomado Falcon reintroduction program in the Lower Valley at Laguna Atascosa NWR in 1985 and releases were completed in 2005. A pair from this program successfully nested near the Port of Brownsville in 1995, and several pairs have nested each year since. Banded birds are seen regularly in lands adjacent to Laguna Atascosa NWR, including Old Port Isabel Road, at the Brownsville Sanitary Landfill, along TX-100 west of Laguna Vista, and along TX-4 toward Boca Chica. Reintroduction of Aplomado Falcons began near Valentine in the Trans-Pecos in 2002. These birds often can be seen along US-90 near Valentine and along the western stretches of RR-505. As of the date of this book's publication (2008), however, these populations were not yet treated as established and "countable."

Peregrine Falcon *(Falco peregrinus)* — Rare summer resident in Big Bend NP and in the Guadalupe Mtns. Possible breeding in the Davis Mtns and Franklin Mtns in recent years. Most common as a migrant along the coast, especially in fall (October–November), but may be encountered anywhere in the region as a rare to uncommon migrant and winter visitor.

Prairie Falcon *(Falco mexicanus)* — Rare to very uncommon permanent resident of the mountains of western Texas. Nests in Big Bend NP, the Davis Mtns, and at least formerly at Hueco Tanks. More numerous and widespread in winter, when often found in grasslands or agricultural areas. At that season, check especially in grasslands surrounding the Davis Mtns (the Valentine area along US-90 seems particularly good) or along the river levees southeast of El Paso. Rare winter visitor to the Lower Valley.

Yellow Rail *(Coturnicops noveboracensis)* — Accidental migrant and winter visitor along the Lower Coast and on the Edwards Plateau.

Black Rail *(Laterallus jamaicensis)* — Very rare migrant and winter resident along the Lower Coast; best spot is the South Padre Island Convention

Center boardwalk, where at least two birds have been heard calling sporadically since the mid-1990s.

Clapper Rail *(Rallus longirostris)* — Common resident in salt marshes along the Lower Coast; accidental inland. May be seen anywhere along the South Padre Island bayshore where *Spartina* and mangrove vegetation exists. The best way to see this species is to walk the South Padre Island Convention Center boardwalk at dawn or dusk. Also often seen in mangrove habitat at the base of the Queen Isabella Memorial Causeway (on the South Padre Island side) and other bayshore access points. Also found in Black Mangroves at the mouth of the Rio Grande at Boca Chica.

King Rail *(Rallus elegans)* — Uncommon resident in freshwater marshes of the Lower Valley; rare to uncommon migrant on the Edwards Plateau and in the eastern Trans-Pecos. One of the better spots is Pintail Lake at Santa Ana NWR. Rare summer records from the eastern Trans-Pecos (Balmorhea Lake) suggest sporadic breeding. This species is largely absent from saltwater wetlands.

Virginia Rail *(Rallus limicola)* — Rare to fairly common migrant (April–mid-May, August–October) throughout. Rare and localized to uncommon in winter. Breeding sporadic and very localized in the El Paso area.

Sora *(Porzana carolina)* — Uncommon to fairly common migrant (April–mid-May, mid-August–mid-October) throughout. An uncommon winter resident at least in the Lower Valley and El Paso. Has bred sporadically in the El Paso area.

Purple Gallinule *(Porphyrio martinica)* — Rare to uncommon migrant in the Lower Valley from the coast to about Bentsen SP (April and August). One of the best spots is the South Padre Island Convention Center boardwalk in spring. Rare to uncommon summer resident and very rare in winter in the Lower Valley. Rare post-breeding wanderer inland to Travis and Bexar Cos. Accidental in the Trans-Pecos.

Common Moorhen *(Gallinula chloropus)* — Fairly common permanent resident in the Lower Valley and the El Paso/Las Cruces area. Rare and local on the Edwards Plateau. Prefers reed-choked ponds or drainage canals near the river. A rare migrant in most other areas.

American Coot *(Fulica americana)* — Common winter resident throughout. Somewhat less common and more localized as a breeding species in the Lower Valley, the eastern Edwards Plateau, around El Paso and Las Cruces, and occasionally in the Big Bend region.

Sandhill Crane *(Grus canadensis)* — Rare to uncommon migrant and winter resident (late September–mid-March). Most likely to be seen near the coast or in the El Paso area; Dell City (Hudspeth Co) also hosts a large population.

Whooping Crane *(Grus americana)* — Endangered. Wintering range of natural population restricted to central Texas Coast, where approximately 270 individuals wintered in 2007–2008. One recent record for the Lower Valley: a single bird was seen sporadically north of Edinburg near the Rudman Tract (La Sal Vieja) 18 November 2005–25 February 2006.

Black-bellied Plover *(Pluvialis squatarola)* — Common migrant and winter resident along the Lower Coast; uncommon migrant farther inland. Regularly seen along the bayshore at South Padre Island and along the beach at Boca Chica. Rare migrant in the Trans-Pecos.

American Golden-Plover *(Pluvialis dominica)* — Common spring migrant and rare fall migrant in the eastern portions of the Lower Valley (March–April, August–October). This species can be found in a range of coastal habitats, including farmland, wet fields, and mudflats. Best spots include the bayshore on South Padre Island, agricultural fields on FM-510 near Laguna Atascosa NWR, short grassy fields at Brownsville Airport near the Nexrad radar tower, and the La Feria Sod Farms. Accidental spring migrant and very rare fall migrant in the Trans-Pecos.

Collared Plover *(Charadrius collaris)* — Accidental. One documented record for Texas and the U.S.: the Edwards Plateau at Uvalde 9–12 May 1992.

Snowy Plover *(Charadrius alexandrinus)* — Uncommon summer resident along the Lower Coast (April–August); rare to uncommon in winter. Rare to uncommon in migration on the Edwards Plateau and the Trans-Pecos. Breeds in most years in the Trans-Pecos at Balmorhea Lake and Imperial Reservoir. Good spots include Boca Chica beach, north of the South Padre Island Convention Center along the bayshore, and at inland salt lakes at La Sal Vieja and La Sal del Rey.

Wilson's Plover *(Charadrius wilsonia)* — Uncommon to locally common summer and rare winter resident along the Lower Coast. Can be found on South Padre Island bayshore mudflats and higher sand flats. Frequently seen above the high-tide mark at the base of the Queen Isabella Memorial Causeway (on the South Padre Island side).

Semipalmated Plover *(Charadrius semipalmatus)* — Uncommon to fairly common migrant and winter resident (August–early May) to coastal portions of the Lower Valley. Rare to uncommon migrant (April–mid-May, August–September) in remainder of region.

Piping Plover *(Charadrius melodus)* — Locally common winter resident along the Lower Coast (September–April). Fairly easily found along bayshore mudflats of South Padre Island (at and north of the convention center); also seen along Boca Chica beach and along the bayshore at Laguna Atascosa NWR (Bayside Drive). Uncommon migrant on the Edwards Plateau. Accidental in the Trans-Pecos.

Mountain Plover *(Charadrius montanus)* — Rare and local migrant and winter resident in some portions of the Lower Valley (for exact directions to a site in Willacy Co, see the end of the Harlingen section titled "Mountain Plovers north of Harlingen"), the eastern Edwards Plateau, and recently in the vicinity of Dell City in Hudspeth Co. A very rare breeder in small numbers in grasslands of the Davis Mtns. A casual migrant at sod farms in the El Paso/Las Cruces area.

American Oystercatcher *(Haematopus palliatus)* — Uncommon to locally common resident along the Lower Coast. Most common along the bayshore of the Laguna Madre at South Padre Island. A good spot on South Padre Island is the bayshore mudflat at the base of the Queen Isabella Memorial Causeway.

Black-necked Stilt *(Himantopus mexicanus)* — Uncommon to common breeding bird in the Lower Valley and the El Paso area. Uncommon to fairly common in winter in the Lower Valley; rare and localized but seemingly increasing at that season in El Paso. An uncommon to fairly common migrant to other areas.

American Avocet *(Recurvirostra americana)* — Fairly common to common migrant (March–May, August–October) throughout. Common in winter along the coast, becoming much less numerous inland; a casual winter visitor to the El Paso area. A fairly common breeding bird around El Paso; scarce as a breeding species along the coast.

Northern Jacana *(Jacana spinosa)* — Casual visitor in the Lower Valley, with records from Brownsville to Falcon Dam; more than half of the 30-plus Texas records are from the Lower Valley. Check any ponds with emergent vegetation from July through November, although jacanas have been recorded in all months. Most sightings have come from Santa Ana NWR, although this species could turn up anywhere in the Lower Valley. Accidental to the Edwards Plateau and the Trans-Pecos. The only documented sightings between 1994 and 2008 were from a mini-invasion during the latter half of 2006.

Spotted Sandpiper *(Actitis macularius)* — Fairly common to common migrant (March–May, July–October) throughout. Less numerous in winter, when it ranges from very uncommon and local in the Trans-Pecos to fairly common in Lower Valley.

Solitary Sandpiper *(Tringa solitaria)* — Uncommon to fairly common migrant (April–May, July–mid-October) throughout. Uncommon but regular in winter in the Lower Valley. Accidental in winter in the El Paso area.

Greater Yellowlegs *(Tringa melanoleuca)* — Fairly common migrant (March–early May, mid-July–October) throughout. Fairly common in winter in the Lower Valley, but becoming less numerous as one moves farther inland. An uncommon wintering species in El Paso.

Willet *(Tringa semipalmata)* — Common year-round along the coast in Lower Valley, although locally breeding birds ("Eastern" Willet) thought to fully vacate the U.S. in winter, replaced by wintering birds from Great Plains and interior West ("Western" Willet). "Western" Willet also a very uncommon to fairly common migrant (April–May, July–September) through the rest of the region, decreasing in abundance westward.

Lesser Yellowlegs *(Tringa flavipes)* — Fairly common to common migrant (mid-March–early May, mid-July–October) throughout. Fairly common in the Lower Valley in winter, but rare to very uncommon inland at that season.

Upland Sandpiper *(Bartramia longicauda)* — Uncommon to fairly common migrant (late March–early May, late July–September) on the Edwards Plateau southward to the Lower Valley. Uncommon and primarily a fall migrant (mostly August) over much of the Trans-Pecos.

Eskimo Curlew *(Numenius borealis)* — Possibly extinct. Nine specimen records from the Lower Valley at Brownsville between 1889–1894. All records are from between 13 March and 2 April. One specimen from the Edwards Plateau at Boerne 17 March 1880.

Whimbrel *(Numenius phaeopus)* — Uncommon migrant in the Lower Valley, more common on the coast (April, September). Best spots are at the South Padre Island tidal mudflat just south of the base of the Queen Isabella Memorial Causeway and on the mangrove bayshore near the South Padre Island Coast Guard Station. Casual winter resident (October–March) and rare straggler in summer on the coast. Casual to rare migrant on the Edwards Plateau and in the Trans-Pecos

Long-billed Curlew *(Numenius americanus)* — Common migrant and winter resident (August–April) in the Lower Valley. Uncommon to fairly common migrant in remainder of region. A rare and local breeder along the coast in Cameron Co. One historical nest record for the Trans-Pecos, otherwise a rare visitor at that season and in winter.

Hudsonian Godwit *(Limosa haemastica)* — Rare spring migrant along the Lower Coast (April), becoming very rare farther inland to about the McAllen Sewage Ponds. To be looked for along the South Padre Island bayshore access points. Very rare spring migrant on the Edwards Plateau; accidental to the Trans-Pecos.

Marbled Godwit *(Limosa fedoa)* — Fairly common winter resident and migrant (August–April) along the coast in the Lower Valley. Rare to uncommon migrant (April–May, July–September) in rest of the region. Accidental in El Paso in winter.

Ruddy Turnstone *(Arenaria interpres)* — Common migrant and winter resident along the Lower Coast; uncommon visitor during summer. Easily seen in winter on the South Padre Island and Boca Chica jetties, as well as on open beaches and bayshore mudflats. Accidental to rare migrant inland.

Red Knot *(Caladris canutus)* — Common migrant along the Lower Coast (April, September), accidental to rare inland. Rare and local winter resident along the coast. Look for this species at Boca Chica beach and bayshore mudflats just north of the South Padre Island Convention Center.

Sanderling *(Caladris alba)* — Common migrant and winter resident along the Lower Coast, uncommon in summer. Rare to uncommon migrant inland. Casual spring migrant and rare fall migrant in the Trans-Pecos. Most abundant shorebird along the beach during most months of the year.

Semipalmated Sandpiper *(Calidris pusilla)* — Uncommon migrant (April–May, July–October) through the eastern Lower Valley northward to the Edwards Plateau. Rare fall migrant and casual spring migrant in the Trans-Pecos.

Western Sandpiper *(Calidris mauri)* — Fairly common to common migrant (late March–mid-May, July–October) throughout. Common along the coast in winter, but decreasingly numerous as one moves inland at that season. Casual in mid-winter anywhere in the Trans-Pecos.

Red-necked Stint *(Calidris ruficollis)* — Accidental fall migrant. One adult at the Fort Bliss Sewage Ponds 17–22 July 1996 represents the only Texas record.

Least Sandpiper *(Calidris minutilla)* — Common migrant (March–early May, mid-July–October) throughout. Fairly common to common wintering bird in most of the region.

White-rumped Sandpiper *(Calidris fuscicollis)* — Rare to uncommon spring migrant (May) over the eastern Edwards Plateau and the Lower Valley. Very rare spring migrant in the Trans-Pecos.

Baird's Sandpiper *(Calidris bairdii)* — Rare to fairly common spring (mid-March–May) and uncommon to fairly common fall (July–mid-October) migrant. In the Trans-Pecos, seen far more often in fall. Often seen away from water on sod farms and golf courses.

Pectoral Sandpiper *(Calidris melanotos)* — Rare to fairly common migrant (mid-March–mid-May, late July–October) throughout the region. Most numerous in the Lower Valley, rarest in the Trans-Pecos (where the majority of records are in fall). One winter record from Hidalgo Co in late January 2004.

Purple Sandpiper *(Caladris maritima)* — Accidental in winter in the Lower Valley and on the Edwards Plateau. Most of the Texas records are from the Upper Texas coast. There are two records from opposite ends of the Lower Valley: Falcon Dam 15–16 December 1975 and Boca Chica 28 February–10 March 1991. One record from Austin 29–30 March 1976. This species prefers man-made structures and should be looked for on rock jetties along the coast.

Dunlin *(Calidris alpina)* — Common migrant and wintering species (August–April) along the coast at South Padre Island and Boca Chica. Uncommon migrant inland; rare in the Trans-Pecos.

Curlew Sandpiper *(Calidris ferruginea)* — Accidental. Three records from the Lower Valley: Santa Ana NWR 3–7 May 1994 and 22 May 1996, and South Padre Island 16 May 2007.

Stilt Sandpiper *(Calidris himantopus)* — Fairly common migrant (April–May, mid-July–October) and uncommon winter resident in the Lower Valley. Rare to uncommon migrant in the rest of the region. Near El Paso, this species is fairly common in fall, but is rare to uncommon in spring.

Buff-breasted Sandpiper *(Tryngites subruficollis)* — Rare to uncommon migrant in the Lower Valley, becoming very rare on the Edwards Plateau (April, August–September). This grassland species is found in the eastern Lower Valley, where it prefers coastal fields and farmland. One of the better spots is the La Feria Sod Farms. Also may be found in appropriate habitat adjacent to the McAllen Sewage Ponds.

Ruff *(Philomachus pugnax)* — Casual fall migrant and winter visitor (July–March). Most records from Travis and Bexar Cos just off the Edwards Plateau. One Trans-Pecos record from El Paso Co, one Willacy Co record, and one coastal record in Cameron Co.

Short-billed Dowitcher *(Limnodromus griseus)* — Common migrant and wintering species (August–April) along the coast at South Padre Island and Boca Chica. Rare to uncommon migrant inland; accidental spring migrant and rare fall migrant in the Trans-Pecos.

Long-billed Dowitcher *(Limnodromus scolopaceus)* — Fairly common to common migrant (March–May, July–October) throughout. Common in winter in Lower Valley; rare to uncommon elsewhere at that season.

Wilson's Snipe *(Gallinago delicata)* — Uncommon to fairly common migrant and winter resident (September–early May) throughout the region.

American Woodcock *(Scolopax minor)* — Local and difficult-to-find winter resident (November–February) on the eastern Edwards Plateau. Casually found as far west as Del Rio; accidental farther west, and south to the Lower Valley.

Wilson's Phalarope *(Phalaropus tricolor)* — Uncommon to common migrant (April–May, July–mid-October). Most numerous in the western Trans-Pecos, where groups of many hundreds, if not thousands, can be found in migration. Less numerous in the Lower Valley and on the eastern Edwards Plateau. Migrants in late spring and early "fall" result in sightings from virtually throughout the summer. In winter, very rare in the Lower Valley (except at La Sal del Rey, where over 100 individuals have wintered some years) and accidental in El Paso.

Red-necked Phalarope *(Phalaropus lobatus)* — Rare spring (April–May) and rare to uncommon fall (mid-August–October) migrant throughout. Most common around El Paso and Las Cruces in September and October, when the species is at times found in numbers. Casual stragglers into November. Scarcest in the Lower Valley.

Red Phalarope *(Phalaropus fulicarius)* — Casual fall (mid-September–early November) and accidental spring (May) migrant. One winter record. Most records from the El Paso area and Travis and Bexar Cos just off the Edwards Plateau. Two Lower Valley records: 15 July 1978 and 20 May 2002.

Black-legged Kittiwake *(Rissa tridactyla)* — Casual to rare winter visitor throughout (November–March). About 20 records widely scattered over the region.

Sabine's Gull *(Xema sabini)* — Very rare to rare fall migrant (September–October) throughout, with a few birds into November. Over 30 records for the region, the majority from the western Trans-Pecos. Two exceptional records at McNary on 6 May 1995 and 13–15 July 1996.

Bonaparte's Gull *(Chroicocephalus philadelphia)* — Uncommon to fairly common migrant and locally uncommon winter resident along the coast. Less numerous inland, but still regular on the eastern Edwards Plateau and in the Trans-Pecos (where most numerous in fall). June records for McNary and Fort Hancock.

Black-headed Gull *(Chroicocephalus ridibundus)* — Accidental in winter. One record from the region: an adult was photographed from the South Padre Island Convention Center boardwalk on 12 December 2004.

Little Gull *(Hydrocoloeus minutus)* — Although casual during winter in the northern part of the state, this species is accidental in this region. A first-winter bird was photographed from the Boca Chica jetties on 3 January 2006.

Laughing Gull *(Leucophaeus atricilla)* — Very common resident along the Lower Coast, becoming rare to uncommon inland to Falcon Dam; recent breeding records at Lake Amistad. Very rare to rare on the Edwards Plateau and in the Trans-Pecos, mostly in late summer and fall.

Franklin's Gull *(Leucophaeus pipixcan)* — Uncommon to common migrant (late March-May, September–mid-November) throughout. Probably most numerous along the coast in the Lower Valley, but readily found on the eastern Edwards Plateau and in the Trans-Pecos as well. The Brownsville Sanitary Landfill can be an excellent place for seeing numbers of this species. Casual mid-winter and mid-summer straggler throughout.

Black-tailed Gull (*Larus crassirostris*) — Accidental. Two records for Texas. One adult was present at the Brownsville Sanitary Landfill from 11–13 February and 5–16 March 1999. A second-winter bird was photographed north of our coverage area at a Corpus Christi landfill on 6 March 2006.

Heermann's Gull (*Larus heermanni*) — Accidental. One photographed on 1 April 1984 south of Las Cruces. Another report from Tornillo Reservoir (El Paso Co) 5 Apr 1997 seemed credible but was ultimately rejected by the TBRC. A third record is from Big Lake (Reagan Co) 24 December 1975, just outside of the coverage area of this guide.

Mew Gull (*Larus canus*) — Casual winter visitor (late November–early March) with about 15 total records. All records to date from either Travis or Bexar Cos just off the Edwards Plateau or the far western Trans-Pecos. This species has become nearly annual in the El Paso area in the past decade.

Ring-billed Gull (*Larus delawarensis*) — Fairly common to common migrant and winter resident throughout. Most numerous coastally and least numerous in the Trans-Pecos. Non-breeders regularly oversummer along the coast or at large reservoirs.

Western Gull (*Larus occidentalis*) — Accidental. One at Fort Bliss Sewage Ponds 14 May 1985, one at Boca Chica 6 April 1995, and one at La Sal del Rey 14–16 November 2004.

California Gull (*Larus californicus*) — Rare visitor, mostly in winter, in the far western Trans-Pecos. Casual farther east to Travis and Bexar Cos (just off the Edwards Plateau) and the Lower Valley. Most often found on large reservoirs or at dumps. Records concentrated between November and March, but every month represented. Seems to be increasing in the far west Trans-Pecos.

Herring Gull (*Larus argentatus*) — Common migrant and winter resident along the Lower Coast, locally uncommon farther inland; rare to uncommon winter visitor to reservoirs throughout. Uncommon summer visitor along the coast and inland lakes and reservoirs; absent in summer in the Trans-Pecos. One breeding record from the Lower Laguna Madre in 1990.

Thayer's Gull (*Larus thayeri*) — Casual winter visitor (December–March) to the coastal Lower Valley, Travis and Bexar Cos just off the Edwards Plateau, and the far western Trans-Pecos. About a dozen overall records, most from large reservoirs, dumps, or coastal beaches. Nearly all are of first-winter birds.

Iceland Gull (*Larus glaucoides*) — Accidental. Only five Texas records, and two are from our region. The first was documented from South Padre Island 15 January–12 February 1977; another from El Paso 26 December 2006–10 February 2007.

Lesser Black-backed Gull (*Larus fuscus*) — Rare but regular winter resident along the Lower Coast, less common inland. There are several documented records in the Trans-Pecos from Balmorhea Lake and El Paso. The species seems to be increasing in numbers in Texas.

Slaty-backed Gull (*Larus schistisagus*) — Accidental in winter. The first state record was documented at Brownsville Sanitary Landfill from 7–22 February 1992. A second record from Balmorhea Lake on 1–10 December 2003. Two records from north of the region, at Corpus Christi and Houston landfills.

Glaucous Gull (*Larus hyperboreus*) — Rare migrant and winter resident along the Lower Coast; very rare inland at landfills and reservoirs. Accidental in the Trans-Pecos (El Paso).

Great Black-backed Gull (*Larus marinus*) — Accidental in winter. Look for this species at South Padre Island, Boca Chica, and the Brownsville Sanitary Landfill.

Brown Noddy (*Anous stolidus*) — Accidental. Several records from the Lower Coast (June–September). Birds have been found in pelagic waters off South Padre Island and in coastal waters near the South Padre Island and Boca Chica jetties.

Sooty Tern (*Onychoprion fuscata*) — Rare to uncommon summer visitor to pelagic waters off the Texas coast. Often found near deepwater tuna schools. Very local breeding species along the Lower Laguna Madre near Arroyo City (April–June). Rarely seen along the coast at South Padre Island and Boca Chica from April–September, casually to November. There are many records along the coast and at scattered inland locations, including the Trans-Pecos, following tropical storms.

Bridled Tern (*Onychoprion anaethetus*) — Uncommon but regular summer visitor (May–September) to offshore waters. Pelagic birding trips since the 1990s have turned up numerous birds during the summer season. May be found singly, in small flocks, or in large feeding congregations, sometimes with Sooty Terns. Very rare along the coast following tropical storms.

Least Tern (*Sternula antillarum*) — Common summer resident (April–September) along the coast at South Padre Island and Boca Chica. Uncommon breeding species at Falcon Reservoir and Lake Amistad. Rare migrant and summer visitor to lakes in the Trans-Pecos; may casually breed at some of these locations.

Gull-billed Tern (*Gelochelidon nilotica*) — Common resident along the Lower Coast, becoming rare inland, less numerous in winter. A small population breeds on Falcon Reservoir. Often seen hawking insects over shortgrass prairies a few miles inland from the Gulf coast and the Laguna Madre. Best spots are at Laguna Atascosa NWR and along TX-4 toward Boca Chica.

Caspian Tern *(Hydroprogne caspia)* — Common resident along the coast; uncommon to locally common on freshwater oxbow lakes in the Lower Valley. Rare migrant and winter visitor on Edwards Plateau. Rare in the Trans-Pecos in summer and fall.

Black Tern *(Chlidonias niger)* — Uncommon to fairly common migrant (mid-April–early June, July–mid-October) throughout. Rare stragglers in mid-summer and early winter.

Common Tern *(Sterna hirundo)* — Fairly common migrant (April–May, August–October) along the coast; some seen through November in fall and into early June in spring. Increasingly rare westward. Only a casual spring and rare fall migrant in the Trans-Pecos. Formerly bred along the coast in Lower Valley. Non-breeding stragglers casually seen in summer throughout.

Arctic Tern *(Sterna paradisaea)* — Accidental. The first documented state record was from McNary Reservoir (Hudspeth Co) 5–6 June 1997. Since then, seen at Fort Bliss Sewage Ponds 27 May 2002, Balmorhea Lake 1–11 June 2006, and Fort Hancock/McNary Reservoirs 9 June 2006.

Forster's Tern *(Sterna forsteri)* — Common resident along the coast at South Padre Island and Boca Chica. Uncommon migrant (April–May, August–October) inland throughout the region. Uncommon to locally common winter resident along inland watercourses throughout the Lower Valley. Regular in small numbers during winter (December–February) on the highland lakes on the Edwards Plateau; accidental in winter in the Trans-Pecos.

Royal Tern *(Thalasseus maximus)* — Common resident along the Lower Coast. Accidental as far west as Zapata and the Edwards Plateau, usually after tropical storms.

Sandwich Tern *(Thalasseus sandvicensis)* — Common summer resident and uncommon winter resident along the Lower Coast. Reported casually as far west as Zapata and the Edwards Plateau, usually after tropical storms.

Elegant Tern *(Thalasseus elegans)* — Accidental. One photographed at Balmorhea Lake 23 December 1985 represents one of only several accepted Texas records. Another in Las Cruces 7–8 May 2001 provided a first for New Mexico.

Black Skimmer *(Rynchops niger)* — Locally common resident along the Lower Coast; rare inland to Falcon Dam area, especially in summer and fall. Accidental to the Trans-Pecos (Balmorhea Lake), mostly following tropical storms.

South Polar Skua *(Stercorarius maccormicki)* — Accidental. One documented record for Texas. A bird was photographed near a shrimp boat in relatively shallow continental shelf waters about 30 miles off South Padre Island on 1 October 2004.

Pomarine Jaeger (*Stercorarius pomarinus*) — Rare migrant and winter visitor along Lower Coast and to offshore waters; very rare in summer. To be looked for on pelagic trips as well as from the South Padre Island and Boca Chica jetties. Very rare inland, usually after tropical storms. Accidental in the Trans-Pecos.

Parasitic Jaeger (*Stercorarius parasiticus*) — Rare migrant and winter visitor along Lower Coast and to nearshore waters; very rare in summer. Accidental in the Trans-Pecos. To be looked for on fall pelagic birding trips as well as from the South Padre Island or Boca Chica jetties.

Long-tailed Jaeger (*Stercorarius longicaudus*) — Casual to accidental June–early November, with about 10 records, including from Austin, El Paso, McNary, and off South Padre Island.

Rock Pigeon (*Columba livia*) — Common permanent resident of cities and larger towns. Less numerous in smaller towns and rural areas.

White-crowned Pigeon (*Patagioenas leucocephala*) — Accidental. One sight record for Texas on the Lower Coast at Green Island 24 June and 2 July 1989. Not included in the official Texas bird list, as all first Texas records require either a specimen or an unequivocal photograph or audio recording.

Red-billed Pigeon (*Patagioenas flavirostris*) — Rare to uncommon summer resident in the Lower Valley from Santa Ana NWR upriver to San Ygnacio; very rare farther west along the Rio Grande to near Del Rio. Best spots are along the Rio Grande at Santa Margarita Ranch, Salineño, Chapeño, and Falcon Dam area. Also seen at times at Starr County Park near Falcon SP and from the Roma Bluffs. Rare winter resident in many of these same areas; accidental along the coast in winter.

Band-tailed Pigeon (*Patagioenas fasciata*) — Fairly common summer resident of the higher, forested mountains of the Trans-Pecos. Easiest to see along the Boot Spring Trail in Big Bend NP, at The Bowl in Guadalupe Mtns NP, or along the scenic loop in the Davis Mtns. In late spring when the mulberries are ripe, it may be seen in Fort Davis. Casual to rare in winter. Casual in migration away from breeding areas in migration.

Eurasian Collared-Dove (*Streptopelia decaocto*) — This species has rapidly expanded across Texas since the 1990s. It can now be found in virtually every town from Brownsville to Las Cruces. It is commonly found in much of the Lower Valley and the Trans-Pecos, as well as on the Edwards Plateau.

White-winged Dove (*Zenaida asiatica*) — Common summer resident of brushlands and towns along the entire river and on the Edwards Plateau. Away from urban areas the majority seem to depart in winter, but they still can be found at that season (in some cities abundantly so) in Brownsville, McAllen, San Antonio, Austin, El Paso, and Las Cruces.

Mourning Dove *(Zenaida macroura)* — Common permanent resident throughout. Somewhat less numerous in the Trans-Pecos in winter.

Inca Dove *(Columbina inca)* — Fairly common to common resident in larger towns and cities throughout, less frequently in smaller towns and around farms.

Common Ground-Dove *(Columbina passerina)* — Fairly common resident of brushlands and farmlands of the Lower Rio Grande Valley northward to the southern edge of the Edwards Plateau west to the lower Pecos River drainage. Becoming more localized in the Trans-Pecos, where it is most often found in close proximity to the Rio Grande in Big Bend NP, with scattered spring and fall records elsewhere.

Ruddy Ground-Dove *(Columbina talpacoti)* — Very rare visitor (almost 20 records overall) along the entire length of the river from Brownsville to Las Cruces. Most records are between mid-October and March, with a few to early May. This species has been documented south of Las Cruces, in El Paso, in Big Bend NP, and in the Lower Valley. *Caution:* confusion with brightly colored male Common Ground-Doves in South Texas has led to many misidentifications.

White-tipped Dove *(Leptotila verreauxi)* — Common resident in the Lower Valley; accidental in the eastern Trans-Pecos and the southwestern Edwards Plateau. Easy to find at Sabal Palm Audubon Center, Santa Ana NWR, Bentsen SP, and in the riparian woodlands in the Falcon Dam area.

Ruddy Quail-Dove *(Geotrygon montana)* — Accidental. One record for Texas: Bentsen SP 2–6 March 1996.

Monk Parakeet *(Myiopsitta monachus)* — A large population of this exotic parakeet is present in Austin. They can be found nesting in the light standards at softball fields all along the Colorado River. Usually easy to see at the city park at the intersection of Lamar and Riverside Aves.

Green Parakeet *(Aratinga holochlora)* — Although the origin of both Green Parakeet and Red-crowned Parrot flocks is indeterminable, their populations appear to be stable in the Lower Valley, due in part to successful nesting. Green Parakeets are year-round residents centered principally (but not exclusively) in urban areas, including Brownsville, Weslaco, McAllen, and Mission. Over 200 individuals have been reported recently in Weslaco (near Fairfield Inn in Weslaco), McAllen (at 10th St and Dove St), and Brownsville (at Fort Brown).

Red-crowned Parrot *(Amazona viridigenalis)* — This species has been reported in the Lower Valley for decades. In recent years, flocks of several dozen to a hundred or more are seen in Brownsville, San Benito, Harlingen, Weslaco, and McAllen. Nesting is occurring in each of these cities. Best spots to look are at the intersection of Coria and Los Ebanos Streets in Brownsville, at the K-Mart near the intersection of Morgan and Grimes Streets in Harlingen, near the Frontera Audubon Thicket in Weslaco, and on the east end of Dallas Ave (in the vicinity of Mockingbird St) in McAllen. Best times are at dusk and dawn. Because of fruit availability, parrots can be quite nomadic, changing roosts from year to year, and sometimes within a given season. Therefore, finding parrots can prove challenging at times. It is best to check with local sanctuaries, such as the Valley Nature Center in Weslaco, to find the birds' latest whereabouts. Both Red-crowned Parrots and Green Parakeets are fairly common in adjacent northeast Mexico, where habitat loss has been extensive, suggesting that some of the birds may be displaced wild birds. Severe freezes in the late 1980s that reached into northern Mexico may have induced a natural dispersal of some birds, as large numbers of parrots appeared in the wake of these hard freezes. However, the origin of any individual or flock is uncertain. There are also scattered reports of Red-crowned Parrots in central Texas (Austin and San Marcos). (Red-crowned Parrots are threatened in Mexico, and it is possible that there are now more individuals in South Texas than there are south of the border.)

Exotic Parrots of the Lower Rio Grande Valley — Red-crowned Parrots are by far the most likely *Amazona* parrot species encountered while birding the Lower Valley, although other species may be seen as well. Both Yellow-headed (*A. oratrix*) and Red-lored (*A. autumnalis*) Parrots are occasionally mixed in with the large Red-crowned flocks in Brownsville, Harlingen, and McAllen. Although these species are found just 200 miles to the south of the Valley, their origin is at best uncertain due to the illicit parrot trade along the Texas/Mexico border. Because both species are popular cage birds and have been released (up to 30 at a time along the Rio Grande), Yellow-headed and Red-lored Parrots seen in South Texas are presumed escapees. Other exotics include Lilac-crowned (*A. finschi*) (a small but stable population exists in west El Paso) and White-fronted (*A. albifrons*) Parrots, which are native to western and southern Mexico, and White-crowned Parrot (*Pionus senilis*), a smaller parrot from east Mexico and Central America.

Black-billed Cuckoo (*Coccyzus erythropthalmus*) — Uncommon migrant (mid-April–mid-May, August–September) in the eastern Lower Valley. Rare to very rare on the eastern Edwards Plateau and accidental to casual farther west in the region.

Yellow-billed Cuckoo (*Coccyzus americanus*) — Common migrant and summer resident in the Lower Valley (mid-April–September) and Edwards Plateau (late April–September), becoming a more uncommon and local summer resident of riparian woodlands in the Trans-Pecos (May–September), particularly in the El Paso region (arriving in late May).

Dark-billed Cuckoo (*Coccyzus melacoryphus*) — Accidental. One state record (specimen): the bird was delivered alive (and unidentified) to a bird rehabilitation center near Weslaco on 10 February 1986. It died shortly thereafter and was sent to Louisiana State University, where it was subsequently identified as a Dark-billed Cuckoo. This South American species is a long-distance migrant, having also been recorded in Panama and Mexico.

Mangrove Cuckoo (*Coccyzus minor*) — Accidental. Four records from the Lower Valley (April–August): from Laguna Atascosa NWR, Frontera Audubon Thicket, and Santa Ana NWR.

Greater Roadrunner (*Geococcyx californianus*) — Fairly common to common permanent resident of brushlands, desert, farmlands, and foothills (up to about 5,500 feet) throughout. Fairly easy to find at Falcon SP and Big Bend NP, among other areas.

Groove-billed Ani (*Crotophaga sulcirostris*) — Common summer resident (late April–September) in the Lower Valley west to Laredo. Good spots in late spring and summer include near the "old manager's residence" at Santa Ana NWR and at Hidalgo Pumphouse. Anis can be found anywhere along the Rio Grande at this season. Sometimes seen in migration in the bayshore woodlots on South Padre Island. In winter, anis are rather rare and could turn up anywhere in the Lower Valley, but they are more often encountered at Sabal Palm Audubon Center, Laguna Atascosa NWR, Estero Llano Grande SP, Santa Ana NWR, and Roma Bluffs. Rare on the southwestern Edwards Plateau and in the eastern Trans-Pecos; accidental in the western Trans-Pecos.

Barn Owl (*Tyto alba*) — Uncommon to fairly common permanent resident throughout. Prefers open country and brushlands rather than densely wooded areas. Utilizes old buildings, holes in embankments, and palm trees as roost and nest sites.

Flammulated Owl (*Otus flammeolus*) — Uncommon to fairly common summer resident at upper elevations of the Chisos, Davis, and Guadalupe Mtns. A rare migrant, mostly in fall, away from breeding areas in the western Trans-Pecos.

Western Screech-Owl (*Megascops kennicottii*) — Fairly common permanent resident of riparian habitat and the oak zone of mountains in West Texas. A rare and local resident on the western Edwards Plateau, east to Kerrville. Occasionally in other habitats. Easiest to find in Big Bend NP and the Davis Mtns.

Eastern Screech-Owl (*Megascops asio*) — Common resident in the Lower Valley and on the Edwards Plateau west to the Pecos River. Rare and local in the central and southern Trans-Pecos. Can be found in both natural and artificial cavities throughout the Lower Valley, including at Laguna Atascosa NWR, Estero Llano Grande SP, Santa Ana NWR, Quinta Mazatlan (McAllen), Bentsen SP, and Salineño.

Great Horned Owl *(Bubo virginianus)* — Uncommon to common permanent resident throughout. Uses a wide variety of habitats and elevations from coastal plain to desert to forested areas.

Northern Pygmy-Owl *(Glaucidium gnoma)* — Accidental in mountains of the Trans-Pecos and Doña Ana Co in New Mexico. Three accepted records from Big Bend NP: 12 August 1982, 25 April 1993, and 17 August–7 October 2007. Three sightings at Aguirre Springs in the Organ Mtns near Las Cruces. A specimen listed as taken in El Paso in 1918 cannot be located. Various other undocumented and insufficiently documented sightings from Big Bend and the Guadalupe Mtns.

Ferruginous Pygmy-Owl *(Glaucidium brasilianum)* — Rare and local resident in the Lower Valley; formerly found in the riparian woodlands of the Falcon Dam area, but no longer reported at this location. A pair of birds has taken up residence at Bentsen SP from about 2003 through the time of this printing (2008). Locally fairly common just north of the Lower Valley in Kenedy Co (El Canelo, Kenedy, and King Ranches).

Elf Owl *(Micrathene whitneyi)* — Uncommon to fairly common summer resident (mid-March–September) in the Lower Valley and the Big Bend Region; less numerous in the Davis Mtns; rare to locally uncommon summer resident on the southwestern Edwards Plateau and the Guadalupe Mtns. Accidental in the El Paso area.

Burrowing Owl *(Athene cunicularia)* — Uncommon and local to fairly common summer resident (mid-March–August) through much of the Trans-Pecos. Most depart in winter, but a few can be found then around El Paso and Las Cruces. A rare to very uncommon migrant and winter visitor to the eastern Edwards Plateau and the Lower Valley.

Mottled Owl *(Ciccaba virgata)* — Accidental. Two documented records for Texas and the U.S.: a photograph of a road-kill near Bentsen SP 23 February 1983 and a sight record at Frontera Audubon Thicket in Weslaco 5–11 July 2006.

Spotted Owl *(Strix occidentalis)* — Rare and extremely local permanent resident in the Guadalupe and Davis Mtns. Seldom encountered. Accidental visitor around El Paso, with three winter/spring records.

Barred Owl *(Strix varia)* — Uncommon resident in riparian woodlands on the Edwards Plateau west to the Nueces River. Also a local resident along drainages into the Rio Grande between Eagle Pass and Del Rio.

Long-eared Owl *(Asio otus)* — Irregular and difficult-to-find winter visitor to much of the region, including the Lower Valley. Rare to uncommon migrant and winter visitor (mid-October–mid-April) throughout El Paso/Las Cruces area. Nesting documented southeast of El Paso in the summer of 2007.

Stygian Owl (*Asio stygius*) — Accidental. Two documented records for Texas and the U.S. Both sightings came from Bentsen SP, 9 December 1994 and 26 December 1996.

Short-eared Owl (*Asio flammeus*) — A casual to rare winter visitor (November–March) throughout. This species is probably annual in the Lower Valley yet is very local and typically overlooked. It has declined substantially in the western Trans-Pecos over the past two decades. Interesting were two road-killed birds found 26 May 2005 in Jeff Davis Co (Trans-Pecos).

Northern Saw-whet Owl (*Aegolius acadicus*) — Casual migrant and winter visitor throughout the Trans-Pecos. Apparently a very rare summer resident at upper elevations of the Guadalupe and Davis Mtns.

Lesser Nighthawk (*Chordeiles acutipennis*) — Common summer resident (April–September) from the Falcon Dam area northward to the Balcones Escarpment and westward to El Paso. Less common in the remainder of the Lower Valley, but numerous at Laguna Atascosa NWR. Uncommon to fairly common migrant along the Lower Valley coast. Fall migrants may linger in some areas through early November. Casual to very rare in winter in the western South Texas Brush Country and the Lower Valley.

Common Nighthawk (*Chordeiles minor*) — Fairly common but local and decreasing breeder (May–September) on the Edwards Plateau, in the Lower Valley, and in the Trans-Pecos mountain ranges except those in El Paso Co. Very uncommon to fairly common migrant throughout. Common Nighthawks may linger in urban areas (such as Austin and San Antonio) and in the Lower Valley into at least the early winter, with reports as late as mid-January.

Common Pauraque (*Nyctidromus albicollis*) — Common resident in South Texas. Best found on night walks at Bentsen SP. May also be seen on forest trails at dusk at Sabal Palm Audubon Center, Laguna Atascosa NWR, and Santa Ana NWR, as well as along the entrance roads to these sanctuaries. Look for the red eye-shine in the car headlights. Its song, a plaintive *purwhEEer,* is often heard on late winter and early spring nights throughout the Lower Valley.

Common Poorwill (*Phalaenoptilus nuttallii*) — Fairly common breeder (March–October) in dry, rocky habitats in the Trans-Pecos and on the Edwards Plateau; uncommon in the Lower Valley east to the Falcon Dam/Santa Margarita Ranch area. A few winter records; regular at that season on the southwestern Edwards Plateau, as at Kickapoo Cavern. Look for it in Big Bend, the Franklin Mtns, and state parks on the Edwards Plateau.

Chuck-will's-widow (*Caprimulgus carolinensis*) — Common summer resident (April–September) of the eastern Edwards Plateau, becoming rare to uncommon on the western plateau. Uncommon migrant through the Lower Valley, mostly in the eastern half. Can be heard easily at the state parks on the eastern half of the plateau as far west as Garner SP. Accidental in Davis Mtns.

Whip-poor-will *(Caprimulgus vociferus)* — Common summer resident (April–September) at upper elevations of the Guadalupe, Davis, and Chisos Mtns. Regular but seldom detected migrant on the extreme eastern portions of the Edwards Plateau and in the Lower Valley. Casual migrant in El Paso.

Black Swift *(Cypseloides niger)* — Accidental. There is an accepted sight record from El Paso 22 August 1985.

White-collared Swift *(Streptoprocne zonaris)* — Accidental. Four accepted records for the state, all of them from along or near the coast; one bird photographed at Brownsville 18 May 1997.

Chimney Swift *(Chaetura pelagica)* — Common migrant through the Lower Valley and the Edwards Plateau. Rare and local summer resident in the Lower Valley, particularly around Edinburg, Harlingen, and Brownsville. Common summer resident (April–October) in urban areas on the eastern Edwards Plateau. This species becomes less common westward to Pecos. A casual migrant west to El Paso. (Vaux's Swift has not been documented in Texas; however, it is a potential migrant through the western Trans-Pecos and should be looked for and carefully documented.)

White-throated Swift *(Aeronautes saxatalis)* — Common summer resident of cliffs and mountain peaks in West Texas east to the Devils River. Less numerous but still present throughout the winter in most areas. On warm winter days, often seen feeding over the Rio Grande from at least Big Bend westward. Easy to find in Boquillas and Santa Elena Canyons and around the Pinnacles in Big Bend NP, McKittrick Canyon in the Guadalupe Mtns, and at Hueco Tanks.

Green Violetear *(Colibri thalassinus)* — There are over 50 documented Texas records since 1961 (April–September) of this tropical hummer. An almost annual visitor to the Hill Country (May–September). There are also numerous records from the Lower Valley, several from the coast, and two from the Davis Mtns.

Green-breasted Mango *(Anthracothorax prevostii)* — Casual visitor to the Lower Valley. Most Texas records are concentrated between Brownsville and McAllen during summer and fall, and most of these involve immature birds.

Broad-billed Hummingbird *(Cynanthus latirostris)* — Very rare but increasing visitor in all seasons throughout. The majority of records are from the Trans-Pecos, but there are several Lower Valley and a few Edwards Plateau records as well.

White-eared Hummingbird *(Hylocharis leucotis)* — Casual summer and fall visitor to the Chisos Mtns and El Paso. In recent years, has become a rare but regular summer visitor very locally in the Davis Mtns, with breeding at least suspected. One Starr Co record 14–16 July 1990. The summer of 2005 yielded an amazing 14 records in the Trans-Pecos.

Berylline Hummingbird *(Amazilia beryllina)* — Accidental late spring to late summer visitor, with single records from Big Bend NP 18 August 1991 and four from the Davis Mtns: 17 August–4 September 1997, 3–8 August 1999, 25 May–July 2000, and 25–28 August 2007.

Buff-bellied Hummingbird *(Amazilia yucatanensis)* — Uncommon to locally common summer resident of the Lower Valley, becoming rare to very rare inland to the Edwards Plateau. Locally rare to uncommon in winter in the Lower Valley, primarily from Brownsville to Mission, where it may be found at hummingbird feeders, native flowers, including Turk's Cap *(Malvaviscus arboreus)*, and ornamental plantings. Good spots year-round include the Sabal Palm Audubon Center, Valley Nature Center and Frontera Audubon Thicket in Weslaco, Quinta Mazatlan (McAllen), Edinburg Wetlands, and Santa Ana NWR. This species ranges north of our region along the coast to about Victoria Co.

Cinnamon Hummingbird *(Amazilia rutila)* — Accidental. One west of El Paso in southern Doña Ana Co, NM 18–21 September 1993. This bird established only the second U.S. record.

Violet-crowned Hummingbird *(Amazilia violiceps)* — Casual visitor to the Trans-Pecos, with records from El Paso, Anthony NM, Big Bend NP, Presidio Co, Alpine, and the Davis Mtns. Accidental in the Lower Valley, with one record from Weslaco 10–11 May 1999 and another record from farther north in Val Verde Co 31 October 1996.

Blue-throated Hummingbird *(Lampornis clemenciae)* — Uncommon to fairly common breeder in the Chisos Mtns; rare in the Davis Mtns and Guadalupes. Accidental to casual visitor to lowlands throughout, including the Lower Valley.

Magnificent Hummingbird *(Eugenes fulgens)* — Rare to uncommon breeder in the Chisos, Davis, and Guadalupe Mtns. Accidental visitor elsewhere, mostly in the Trans-Pecos. Exceptionally late was a 28 November 2001 record for the Davis Mtns.

Lucifer Hummingbird *(Calothorax lucifer)* — Uncommon summer resident (mid-March–October) in Big Bend NP and a regular post-breeding wanderer north to the Davis Mtns in summer and early fall. Look for it at blooming agaves at all elevations in the spring and summer. The Window Trail (especially at blooming *Anisacanthus* on lower portions of the trail), Laguna Meadows, and Blue Creek Canyon are usually good places to look. In late summer and fall, the large patches of flowers along the South Rim Trail are worth checking. Accidental west to El Paso and in the Lower Valley.

Ruby-throated Hummingbird *(Archilochus colubris)* — Common migrant (late March–early May, July–early October) on the Edwards Plateau southward to the Lower Valley. Casual spring and rare (to occasionally uncommon) fall migrant in the Davis and Chisos Mtns. Accidental in El Paso. Rare and local in winter in the Lower Valley.

Black-chinned Hummingbird *(Archilochus alexandri)* — Common summer resident (mid-March–September) on the Edwards Plateau and in the Trans-Pecos. Rare to uncommon migrant and breeder in the Lower Valley, more common westward. Rare and local in winter in the Lower Valley.

Anna's Hummingbird *(Calypte anna)* — Rare to uncommon winter resident (late September–March) in the Trans-Pecos; very rare farther east. Rare in fall in the western Lower Valley (Falcon Dam area) and accidental in the eastern Lower Valley in winter. Accidental in summer in the Davis Mtns and El Paso, where it has bred a few times.

Costa's Hummingbird *(Calypte costae)* — Casual visitor to extreme West Texas and the Las Cruces area. Four records for El Paso Co from March–December. Accidental east to Big Bend NP, Alpine, and the Davis Mtns.

Calliope Hummingbird *(Stellula calliope)* — Rare to uncommon fall migrant (mid-July–September) in the western half of the Trans-Pecos. Casual farther east to the Edwards Plateau. Easiest to find at feeders in El Paso and the Davis Mtns or in canyons of the Franklin Mtns. Also seen with some regularity in late summer in Big Bend NP. There are several winter records from El Paso.

Broad-tailed Hummingbird *(Selasphorus platycercus)* — Uncommon summer resident in the Davis, Chisos, Guadalupe, and Organ Mtns. Uncommon to fairly common elsewhere in West Texas in migration, particularly in El Paso. Can be found along the Boot Spring Trail in Big Bend NP, at The Bowl in the Guadalupe Mtns, and along the Pine Tree Trail in the Organ Mtns. A rare migrant on the western Edwards Plateau, and a very rare migrant and winter resident in the Lower Valley. In winter, it is almost annual in small numbers at feeders in El Paso.

Rufous Hummingbird *(Selasphorus rufus)* — Common fall migrant (mid-July–mid-October) in the Trans-Pecos; rare to uncommon eastward. Casual spring migrant in the Trans-Pecos (most records in March), and rare to uncommon (Brownsville area) winter visitor throughout.

Allen's Hummingbird *(Selasphorus sasin)* — Casual fall migrant and winter visitor throughout. Perhaps most regular in the Davis Mtns. Numerous reports, but relatively few are acceptably documented. Some of the unaccepted records are of fully green-backed adult males and are likely valid.

Elegant Trogon *(Trogon elegans)* — Accidental. Three documented records from the Lower Valley: 14 September 1977, 25–31 January 1990, and 14 January–12 May 2005. Three from the Chisos Mtns in Big Bend NP: 29 April 1993, 28 November–8 January 1996, and 16 June 1996.

Ringed Kingfisher *(Megaceryle torquata)* Locally common resident along the Lower Rio Grande west to about Laredo; rare to Del Rio and the southern Edwards Plateau. Often seen along the Rio Grande at Santa Margarita Ranch, Saliñeno, and Chapeño. Can also be found at Sabal Palm Audubon Center, Santa Ana NWR, Anzalduas County Park, Bentsen SP, and occasionally on utility lines near roadside ponds. Rare to accidental elsewhere on the Edwards Plateau and along the lower Pecos River.

Belted Kingfisher *(Megaceryle alcyon)* — Fairly common to common winter resident (September–April) throughout. Local summer resident on the eastern Edwards Plateau; rare straggler to the Lower Valley and the El Paso area at that season.

Green Kingfisher *(Chloroceryle americana)* — Uncommon resident along the Rio Grande from the Lower Valley northward, becoming very rare west of the mouth of the Pecos River, although reported annually from Rio Grande Village in Big Bend NP. Uncommon resident on the Edwards Plateau. Look for this species particularly at Salineño, Bentsen SP, Edinburg Scenic Wetlands, Estero Llano Grande SP, Harlingen Arroyo Colorado, Lost Maples SNA, and Garner SP.

Lewis's Woodpecker *(Melanerpes lewis)* — Casual winter visitor (September–May) to the Trans-Pecos and the western Edwards Plateau. Not seen every year.

Red-headed Woodpecker *(Melanerpes erythrocephalus)* — Rare, primarily winter (October–April) visitor to the eastern edge of the Edwards Plateau, casually wandering as far west as El Paso and Las Cruces. Accidental in the Lower Valley.

Acorn Woodpecker *(Melanerpes formicivorus)* — Fairly common permanent resident of oak woodlands in the Chisos, Davis, Guadalupe, and Organ Mtns. Can be found anywhere in the Chisos Mtns in Big Bend NP and at the Lawrence E. Wood Picnic Grounds in the Davis Mtns. Very local and rare resident near Kerrville on the western Edwards Plateau. Casual in fall and winter away from breeding areas. Accidental in the Lower Valley.

Golden-fronted Woodpecker *(Melanerpes aurifrons)* — Common resident from the Rio Grande north to the Edwards Plateau. Easily found in both natural and residential areas throughout the Lower Valley. In the Trans-Pecos, best found along Calamity Creek in the Del Norte (Davis) Mtns, at Rio Grande Village and Cottonwood Campground in Big Bend NP, along Alamito Creek (between Big Bend NP and Presidio), and at Cibolo Creek at the eastern base of the Chinati Mtns (west of Big Bend).

Red-bellied Woodpecker *(Melanerpes carolinus)* — Rare resident along the Colorado River on the eastern Edwards Plateau. Common in urban habitats in the extreme eastern Hill Country, such as in Austin, but generally replaced by Golden-fronted Woodpecker on the plateau. Also an accidental straggler to the Lower Valley west to about Santa Ana NWR

Williamson's Sapsucker *(Sphyrapicus thyroideus)* — Rare but probably overlooked migrant and winter resident (September–April) of the Trans-Pecos, especially in montane conifers. Most regular in the Davis Mtns. Accidental to casual elsewhere.

Yellow-bellied Sapsucker *(Sphyrapicus varius)* — Uncommon to locally common migrant and winter resident in the region, except in the western Trans-Pecos, where rare.

Red-naped Sapsucker *(Sphyrapicus nuchalis)* — Uncommon migrant and rare to uncommon winter resident in the Trans-Pecos (late September–April); very rare on the Edwards Plateau and in the Lower Valley. May breed in the Guadalupes.

Red-breasted Sapsucker *(Sphyrapicus ruber)* — Accidental winter visitor. Records from Big Bend Ranch SP 3 December 2000 and the Davis Mtns 11–28 March 2005. Care should be taken to rule out possible hybrids—which are more likely to occur.

Ladder-backed Woodpecker *(Picoides scalaris)* — Fairly common to common resident throughout, except for the highest Trans-Pecos elevations.

Downy Woodpecker *(Picoides pubescens)* Local resident in riparian woodlands along the Colorado and Medina Rivers on the eastern Edwards Plateau. Very rare in winter in the Guadalupe Mtns and the western Edwards Plateau, accidental to casual elsewhere in the region.

Hairy Woodpecker *(Picoides villosus)* — Fairly common resident in the Guadalupe Mtns and casual winter visitor to the Davis and Organ Mtns. Accidental on the Edwards Plateau and at El Paso.

Northern Flicker *(Colaptes auratus)* — Common migrant and winter resident (October–March) and rare to locally uncommon breeder in the Trans-Pecos and the Edwards Plateau. Very rare to rare migrant and winter visitor in the Lower Valley. ("Red-shafted" forms predominate in the Trans-Pecos.)

Pileated Woodpecker *(Dryocopus pileatus)* — Accidental visitor to riparian woodlands in the eastern Hill Country.

Northern Beardless-Tyrannulet *(Camptostoma imberbe)* — Rare to locally uncommon resident in the Lower Valley. Most often seen at Bentsen SP, Santa Ana NWR, and Anzalduas County Park. Very rare on the Lower Coast and in the Falcon Dam area. In winter, it can be found moving with mixed-species flocks. Best located by voice, usually a slightly nasal *peeEEt* or a short plaintive *dee-dee-dee*. Best found in spring (mid-March–April), when males are on territory and most vocal. Accidental in the Trans-Pecos.

White-crested Elaenia (*Elaenia albiceps*) — Accidental. One record for Texas and the U.S. This highly migratory South American species was present on South Padre Island 9–10 February 2008.

Tufted Flycatcher (*Mitrephanes phaeocercus*) — Accidental visitor to West Texas. One record from Rio Grande Village in Big Bend NP (3 November 1991–17 January 1992) and another from a rest-stop in Pecos Co (2–5 April 1993).

Olive-sided Flycatcher (*Contopus cooperi*) — Uncommon migrant (late April–early June, late July–September) throughout. Uncommon breeder in the Guadalupes and rare in the Davis Mtns.

Greater Pewee (*Contopus pertinax*) — Casual visitor to the Trans-Pecos. The majority of the records (about seven) are from May and June in the Davis Mtns, where nesting was documented in the summer of 2002. Also recorded in Big Bend NP, the Guadalupe Mtns, and El Paso. Accidental on the Edwards Plateau. Two recent winter records from the Lower Valley.

Western Wood-Pewee (*Contopus sordidulus*) — Common migrant (May–early June, late July–October) in the Trans-Pecos; very rare to uncommon eastward (western Edwards Plateau). Fairly common to common breeder in the Davis, Guadalupe, and Organ Mtns. Accidental migrant in the Lower Valley (Hidalgo Co).

Eastern Wood-Pewee (*Contopus virens*) — Fairly common summer resident (late April–September) in riparian woodlands on the Edwards Plateau west to the Pecos River. Uncommon to fairly common migrant (late April–May, late August–October) through the Lower Valley (more common along the coast) and Edwards Plateau. Accidental as far west as Big Bend Ranch SP.

Yellow-bellied Flycatcher (*Empidonax flaviventris*) — Uncommon migrant in the Lower Valley and the eastern Edwards Plateau (May, September–October); accidental in the Trans-Pecos.

Acadian Flycatcher (*Empidonax virescens*) — Common migrant (mid-April–May, September–early October) in the Lower Valley. Locally uncommon summer resident on the Edwards Plateau west to the Devils River drainage, where it is rare. Look for it at Lost Maples SNA. One breeding record for the Lower Valley at Santa Ana NWR.

Alder Flycatcher (*Empidonax alnorum*) — Uncommon migrant in the Lower Valley and on the eastern Edwards Plateau (May, mid-August–September).

Willow Flycatcher (*Empidonax trailii*) — Rare to uncommon migrant throughout the region (May, August–September). Formerly bred in the western Trans-Pecos.

Least Flycatcher *(Empidonax minimus)* — Common migrant (late April–May, late August–mid-October) through the Lower Valley northward through the Edwards Plateau and the eastern Trans-Pecos. Rare to very uncommon as far west as El Paso; more numerous in the Trans-Pecos during the fall. Rare winter resident in the Lower Valley.

Hammond's Flycatcher *(Empidonax hammondii)* — Rare to uncommon migrant (April–May, August–September), and casual to rare winter resident in the Trans-Pecos. One winter record for Cameron Co in the Lower Valley.

Gray Flycatcher *(Empidonax wrightii)* — Rare to uncommon migrant (April–May, August–September) in the Trans-Pecos. Rare to very uncommon in winter around Big Bend. Uncommon and local breeder in the Davis Mtns. Some suggestion of breeding in the Guadalupes, with at least one territorial bird in June 2003.

Dusky Flycatcher *(Empidonax oberholseri)* — Uncommon to fairly common migrant (April–May, August–October) in the Trans-Pecos. Discovered breeding at upper elevations of the Davis Mtns since 2001, with up to 11 pairs present. Rare suspected breeder in the Guadalupe Mtns. Casual to rare in winter around Big Bend; two winter records for El Paso.

Pacific-slope Flycatcher *(Empidonax difficilis)* — Accidental. One calling bird was identified by sonogram 17–23 December 1995 at Old Refuge, Las Cruces, NM. Not on the official Texas list, though at least two late fall and winter records in the Big Bend area may pertain to this species. Any aseasonal "Western" Flycatcher should be scrutinized carefully and audio-recorded if possible.

Cordilleran Flycatcher *(Empidonax occidentalis)* — Uncommon summer resident of the higher forests of the Chisos, Davis, Guadalupe, and Organ Mtns. An uncommon to fairly common migrant (mid-April–May, August–mid-October) at lower elevations elsewhere in West Texas. Easiest to find near Boot Spring in Big Bend NP or at The Bowl in the Guadalupe Mtns. Two documented (by recordings) winter records for Doña Ana Co, NM. Winter records for "Western" Flycatchers from Cameron, Hidalgo, Hudspeth, and Frio Cos.

Buff-breasted Flycatcher *(Empidonax fulvifrons)* — Rare and local summer resident (April–September) in Ponderosa Pine woodlands at higher elevations of the central Davis Mtns.

Black Phoebe *(Sayornis nigricans)* — Uncommon permanent resident near water from the western Edwards Plateau through West Texas. Can often be found along the Rio Frio at Neal's Lodge or anywhere along the Rio

Grande from Big Bend NP to Las Cruces. More localized during the breeding season. Breeding birds spreading along the Rio Grande downriver to the Falcon Dam area, where known to winter; probably nests as far east as Roma, sometimes to Anzalduas County Park. Winters regularly east to Anzalduas County Park, very rarely east of Weslaco.

Eastern Phoebe *(Sayornis phoebe)* — Fairly common migrant and winter resident (late September–April) throughout South Texas. Uncommon resident on the Edwards Plateau, becoming less common in winter. Rare to uncommon migrant and winter visitor in the Trans-Pecos, decreasing westward.

Say's Phoebe *(Sayornis saya)* — Uncommon to fairly common permanent resident of the Trans-Pecos. More widespread in winter and migration, when small numbers reach the Lower Valley and the Edwards Plateau. Often nests about old buildings or rocky cliff faces. Look for it around the Chisos Lodge in Big Bend NP and at Hueco Tanks.

Vermilion Flycatcher *(Pyrocephalus rubinus)* — Common but somewhat local summer resident over much of the Trans-Pecos and the Edwards Plateau. Rare around El Paso and Las Cruces. Generally withdraws from the Edwards Plateau and northern Trans-Pecos in winter, but winter range appears to be moving northward through these regions. Uncommon migrant and winter resident in the Lower Valley.

Dusky-capped Flycatcher *(Myiarchus tuberculifer)* — Casual to rare spring and summer visitor (April–September) to the Trans-Pecos. Recent confirmed nesting in both Big Bend NP and the Davis Mtns, with up to eight pairs present at the latter location. Historical record for El Paso. Several recent winter records of the brighter, east Mexican subspecies *lawrencei* from the Lower Valley (Cameron and Hidalgo Cos).

Ash-throated Flycatcher *(Myiarchus cinerascens)* — Fairly common to common summer resident (late March–August) from the Falcon Dam area to El Paso and on the Edwards Plateau. Rare but regular migrant along the Lower Coast. Occurs in a variety of habitats from desert scrub to lower oak foothills. Easy to find at Big Bend NP, the Davis Mountains, Hueco Tanks, and Aguirre Springs. Casual in winter in the Big Bend region; accidental at that season near El Paso.

Great Crested Flycatcher *(Myiarchus crinitus)* — Uncommon to fairly common migrant through South Texas. Fairly common migrant and summer resident (April–September) in riparian woodlands on the Edwards Plateau. A casual to rare migrant (mostly fall) through the Trans-Pecos. Found in more mesic habitats than Ash-throated Flycatcher.

Brown-crested Flycatcher *(Myiarchus tyrannulus)* — Common summer resident in the Lower Valley, becoming rare to uncommon north to the southern Edwards Plateau (April–August); rare in the Trans-Pecos. Locally uncommon at Big Bend along the Rio Grande at Rio Grande Village and Cottonwood Campground. Very rare in the Lower Valley in winter.

Great Kiskadee *(Pitangus sulphuratus)* — Common resident in the Lower Valley, becoming locally common in counties just north and west of the Lower Valley. Accidental in the Trans-Pecos and southern New Mexico. Usually noisy and conspicuous. Found in both residential and natural areas near water.

Social Flycatcher *(Myiozetetes similis)* — Accidental. Two records for Texas and the U.S.: a sight record from Anzalduas County Park 17 March–5 April 1990 and a photographic record from Bentsen SP 7–14 January 2005.

Sulphur-bellied Flycatcher *(Myiodynastes luteiventris)* — Accidental. One to two birds were present at Santa Margarita Ranch in spring and/or summer of 1975–1977, with other records from Falcon Dam (spring), Big Bend (spring and summer), South Padre Island (spring), and Quinta Mazatlan.

Piratic Flycatcher *(Legatus leucophaius)* — Accidental. One was photographed 2–7 September 1996 at Rattlesnake Springs, NM. A well-documented record from Rio Grande Village in Big Bend NP 4 April 1998 represented the first for Texas. One was at Bentsen SP 20–28 March 2006.

Tropical Kingbird *(Tyrannus melancholicus)* — Uncommon to fairly common resident of Cameron and Hidalgo Cos in the Lower Valley. The status of this species in Texas has changed dramatically in recent years. Before 1991, there was just one record documented by specimen: Brownsville 5 December 1909. Since 1991, the Tropical Kingbird population in the Lower Valley has grown to the extent that it was removed from the Texas Review List in 1998. Extensive breeding has been documented from the coast at Port Isabel inland to about Mission. In general, Tropical Kingbirds prefer disturbed habitats such as urban parks, golf courses, neighborhoods, and woodland edges. Although the nearly identical Couch's Kingbird prefers more wooded habitats, both species are often found in the same areas. Best identified by voice. Rare and local in the Trans-Pecos, with breeding documented at Cottonwood Campground in Big Bend NP

Couch's Kingbird *(Tyrannus couchii)* — Common summer resident in the Lower Valley to Del Rio, uncommon and irregular in winter; rare in summer in the eastern Trans-Pecos. Can be found in forest areas and disturbed habitats throughout the Lower Valley. Frequently seen on utility lines and other perches in residential areas and along highways. Generally nests in more wooded areas than Tropical or Western Kingbirds. Probably bred in 2007 at Big Bend NP. Accidental on the southwestern Edwards Plateau. Accidental in winter at El Paso and southern Doña Ana Co (NM).

Cassin's Kingbird *(Tyrannus vociferans)* — Fairly common summer resident (mid-April–August) of woodlands of the Davis Mtns and at Rattlesnake Springs (NM). Less regular in other areas of the Trans-Pecos. An uncommon migrant (mid-April–May, August–September) through most of West Texas. Accidental in fall and winter in the Lower Valley.

Thick-billed Kingbird *(Tyrannus crassirostris)* — Casual summer visitor along the Rio Grande in Big Bend NP and accidental in the Davis Mtns. Nested at Cottonwood Campground, Big Bend NP, from 1988–1991.

Western Kingbird *(Tyrannus verticalis)* — Fairly common to common, though somewhat local, summer resident in open areas of the Trans-Pecos, the Edwards Plateau, and portions of the Lower Valley (locally common in Brownsville). Easiest to find around El Paso and Las Cruces, where almost impossible to miss from mid-April through August.

Eastern Kingbird *(Tyrannus tyrannus)* — Common migrant (April–May, August–September) throughout the Lower Valley northward through the Edwards Plateau. A very rare migrant through most of the Trans-Pecos. Local summer resident on the northeastern Edwards Plateau.

Gray Kingbird *(Tyrannus dominicensis)* — Accidental in spring and fall. All Texas records from coastal locales. The lone record for the Lower Coast occurred at South Padre Island 18 May 2002.

Scissor-tailed Flycatcher *(Tyrannus forficatus)* — Common migrant and summer resident (March–October) from the Lower Valley northward through the Edwards Plateau. Uncommon and somewhat local in the Trans-Pecos as far west as Marathon and Pecos. A casual migrant to El Paso. Rare in winter in South Texas, especially near the coast and in western Hidalgo Co near La Joya.

Fork-tailed Flycatcher *(Tyrannus savana)* — Accidental. Three records from the Lower Valley: 4 February 1961 at Edinburg, 17 December–16 January 1985 near Rio Hondo, and 16–30 March 2008 near Brownsville, and one from the Trans-Pecos: 14–15 October 2004 at El Paso.

Rose-throated Becard *(Pachyramphus aglaiae)* — Casual visitor to the Lower Valley, primarily in Hidalgo and Cameron Cos. Recent sightings have come from Sabal Palm Audubon Center, Laguna Atascosa NWR, Santa Ana NWR, Anzalduas County Park, and Bentsen SP; also a record from Salineño December 1987–January 1988. To be looked for particularly at Santa Ana NWR. Accidental in the Trans-Pecos near Fort Davis 18 July 1973.

Masked Tityra *(Tityra semifasciata)* — Accidental. One documented record for Texas and the U.S.: Bentsen SP 17 February–10 March 1990.

Loggerhead Shrike *(Lanius ludovicianus)* — Common resident (less numerous and more localized in summer) throughout; in the Lower Valley, it is rare and local during summer in the western half east to about San Benito, and is absent from Brownsville to the coast.

Northern Shrike *(Lanius excubitor)* — Accidental winter visitor to the Trans-Pecos. Most birds seen this far south are immatures.

White-eyed Vireo *(Vireo griseus)* — Common migrant and summer resident (mid-March–October) on the Edwards Plateau and in South Texas, including the Lower Valley. Most withdraw from the plateau in winter. Accidental in the Trans-Pecos west to El Paso.

Bell's Vireo *(Vireo bellii)* — Fairly common and somewhat local summer resident (April–September) of dense mesquite brushland, foothills, and riparian edge in the Trans-Pecos and Edwards Plateau. Most numerous in Big Bend and the Hill Country. In the Trans-Pecos, found mostly along the Rio Grande and adjacent drainages. Rare migrant in the Lower Valley, and rare and irregular summer resident in the Falcon Dam area. Accidental in winter, with two records from the Lower Valley, one from Big Bend, and one from El Paso.

Black-capped Vireo *(Vireo atricapilla)* — Uncommon and often difficult-to-see summer resident (mid-March–August) of shrublands on the Edwards Plateau ranging westward locally to Big Bend NP. This species is very sensitive to overbrowsing by White-tailed Deer and domestic goats. Most common on the western and central Edwards Plateau. Some of the better locations to find this species include the vireo observation platform at Balcones Canyonlands NWR (usually opens in mid-April), Kickapoo Cavern SP, Devils River SNA, and the Chandler Ranch/Independence Creek Preserve.

Gray Vireo *(Vireo vicinior)* — Rare to uncommon summer resident (late March–September) in brushy canyons of the Chisos, Chinati, Guadalupe, and Organ Mtns and the western Edwards Plateau. Very localized, with much seemingly suitable habitat unoccupied. Best found at Kickapoo Cavern SP, along the Window Trail or in Blue Creek Canyon in Big Bend NP, in McKittrick Canyon in the Guadalupe Mtns, or at Aguirre Springs in the Organ Mtns. Rare in winter in southern Big Bend region. Virtually unknown as a migrant.

Yellow-throated Vireo *(Vireo flavifrons)* — Uncommon migrant in the Lower Valley northward to the Edwards Plateau. Uncommon and local summer resident (late March–August) in riparian woodlands on the Edwards Plateau west to the Pecos River. Rare migrant in the Trans-Pecos west to the Davis Mtns. Casual to El Paso.

Plumbeous Vireo *(Vireo plumbeus)* — Uncommon to fairly common nesting species in the Davis, Guadalupe, and Organ Mtns. Rare nester at Big Bend. A fairly common migrant throughout the Trans-Pecos. A rare winter visitor, particularly to lower elevation riparian areas.

Cassin's Vireo *(Vireo cassinii)* — Uncommon migrant to at least the western portions of the Trans-Pecos. Somewhat more numerous in fall than in spring. Migrant traps in the vicinity of El Paso and Las Cruces would probably be your best bet for finding this species. A few winter records from the El Paso and Las Cruces areas, Big Bend NP, and the Guadalupe Mtns. Recent winter sightings from the Lower Valley as well, though many are undocumented.

Blue-headed Vireo *(Vireo solitarius)* — Common migrant (April–early May, late September–October) throughout the Edwards Plateau southward through the Lower Valley. Common winter resident south of the plateau, rarely occurring on the plateau during mild winters. Rare migrant and casual wintering species in the Trans-Pecos.

Hutton's Vireo *(Vireo huttoni)* — Uncommon to common summer resident of oak woodlands in the Chisos, Davis, and Organ Mtns. Less numerous in winter. Casual in migration and winter at lower elevations. Scattered records for the Guadalupe Mtns, where breeding has not been substantiated. Increasing number of records from the southwestern Edwards Plateau suggests the species could be a very low-density resident there.

Warbling Vireo *(Vireo gilvus)* — Uncommon to fairly common migrant (April–May, August–September) in the Lower Valley, the eastern Edwards Plateau, and the Trans-Pecos. Rare migrant over the western plateau. Uncommon summer resident (April–August) in riparian and pine/oak woodlands in the Guadalupe and Davis Mtns.

Philadelphia Vireo *(Vireo philadelphicus)* — Uncommon spring and rare fall migrant in the Lower Valley and on the Edwards Plateau, more common on the coast (mid-April–mid-May, September–early October). Casual spring and very rare fall migrant in the Trans-Pecos.

Red-eyed Vireo *(Vireo olivaceus)* — Fairly common summer resident (April–September) in riparian woodlands on the Edwards Plateau locally westward to the Pecos River. Fairly common migrant on the plateau and in South Texas, becoming increasingly rare westward.

Yellow-green Vireo *(Vireo flavoviridis)* — Rare summer resident in the Lower Valley, with most records being concentrated in Cameron and Hidalgo Cos. Records fall between mid-April and mid-September, with the best bet being after the first week in May. Best spots are Sabal Palm Audubon Center, Laguna Atascosa NWR, Frontera Audubon Thicket, Santa Ana NWR, Bentsen SP, and tree-lined residential areas from Brownsville to Mission. Proven nesting records come from Laguna Atascosa NWR in 1988 and 1989. Accidental in the Trans-Pecos at Big Bend (two records) and on the Edwards Plateau in Austin (three records).

Black-whiskered Vireo *(Vireo altiloquus)* — Accidental in the Lower Valley, becoming casual north of our region along the central and upper Texas coast. The three local records are from Brownsville 25 May 1991, South Padre Island 23 April 2006, and South Padre Island 11–12 May 2006.

Steller's Jay *(Cyanocitta stelleri)* — Uncommon to locally fairly common resident in the higher parts of the Guadalupe and Davis Mtns. Best found at

The Bowl in the Guadalupe Mtns. In some winters, may move into lowlands throughout the western portion of the Trans-Pecos.

Blue Jay *(Cyanocitta cristata)* — Uncommon resident, primarily in urban areas, on the Edwards Plateau west to Rocksprings. Somewhat irruptive into woodland habitats throughout the plateau and occasionally wandering to the Lower Valley and the Trans-Pecos, where the species is accidental to casual. There is a small, isolated resident population in Edinburg in the Lower Valley.

Green Jay *(Cyanocorax yncas)* — Common resident in the Lower Valley west to about Laredo. Uncommon and local winter visitor as far north as Del Rio and Uvalde; a flock was at Concan in April 2008. Easily found in wooded areas throughout the Lower Valley, including bird feeders at Bentsen SP, Santa Ana NWR, Sabal Palm Audubon Center, and Laguna Atascosa NWR.

Brown Jay *(Cyanocorax morio)* — Casual in Starr Co along the Rio Grande at Salineño and Chapeño. This species has declined in recent years to the point where, in 2007, its entire U.S. population was comprised of three individuals. Virtually no sightings beginning in the fall of 2007 in areas accessible to the public. Formerly found from Rio Grande City to the woodlands below Falcon Dam and upriver to San Ygnacio in Zapata Co. The best spot in recent years has been at the feeders at Salineño; also at the feeders in Chapeño. Brown Jay was placed on the Texas Review List in 2007 in an effort to better understand its current status in the state.

Western Scrub-Jay *(Aphelocoma californica)* — Common permanent resident of brushlands on the Edwards Plateau. Fairly common to common resident in parts of the Trans-Pecos such as the Davis and Guadalupe Mtns. Look for it at Edwards Plateau state parks and Davis Mtns SP. Largely absent from the Big Bend region. In the El Paso area, present most winters in varying numbers depending on the intensity of the montane invasion in a given year.

Mexican Jay *(Aphelocoma ultramarina)* — Common resident in oak woodlands at middle and upper elevations of the Chisos Mtns. Accidental in El Paso involving individual of the *arizonae* race.

Pinyon Jay *(Gymnorhinus cyanocephalus)* — Irregular, casual to rare visitor (September–May) in the Trans-Pecos. Absent most years, but may be more regular around Dog Canyon in the Guadalupes.

Clark's Nutcracker *(Nucifraga columbiana)* — Accidental to casual visitor (mostly from September–January) to the Trans-Pecos. In the invasion winter of 2002–2003, some lingered in the Davis Mtns until June.

Black-billed Magpie *(Pica hudsonia)* — Accidental visitor to the Trans-Pecos (September–May). Most of the handful of reports are from the El Paso area; there is one accepted record from there (4–6 and 17 February 1990). It nests south to about Albuquerque in New Mexico.

American Crow *(Corvus brachyrhynchos)* — Irregular in occurrence on the eastern edge of the Edwards Plateau, though common just to the east of the plateau and within the city of Austin. Winters (October–March) from Fabens north to Las Cruces near large pecan groves; numbers vary annually, but at times there may be thousands of birds.

Tamaulipas Crow *(Corvus imparatus)* — Casual in spring and summer in southernmost Cameron Co near the Brownsville International Airport, where sporadic breeding has been documented. This species has declined dramatically during the past two decades and is no longer found in winter at the Brownsville Sanitary Landfill, and it no longer nests at the NOAA Nexrad weather station near the Brownsville International Airport. During spring, Tamaulipas Crows are sometimes seen flying in the general vicinity of the NOAA Nexrad weather station, but be cautious not to confuse one with the larger (and relatively common) Chihuahuan Raven. Tamaulipas Crow was placed on the Texas Review List in 2000 in an effort to better understand its presence in the state.

Chihuahuan Raven *(Corvus cryptoleucus)* — Fairly common to common resident in grasslands, mesquite brushlands, and other desert habitats through much of the Trans-Pecos and South Texas. Numbers decline in winter in much of the Trans-Pecos. Generally absent from the Big Bend region except as a migrant. Replaced by Common Raven on the Edwards Plateau and in montane habitats in the Trans-Pecos.

Common Raven *(Corvus corax)* — Fairly common in montane habitats in the central Trans-Pecos; uncommon on the Edwards Plateau. Largely absent from the El Paso/Las Cruces area. Some birds descend to lower elevations in the Trans-Pecos in winter.

Horned Lark *(Eremophila alpestris)* — Fairly common to common winter resident (October–March), and an uncommon and local breeder throughout.

Purple Martin *(Progne subis)* — Common migrant and summer resident (February–mid-September) from the Lower Valley northward through the Edwards Plateau as far west as Del Rio. Casual to rare migrant through the Trans-Pecos.

Gray-breasted Martin *(Progne chalybea)* — Accidental. Two documented records by specimen, both at Lower Valley locales: Rio Grande City 25 April 1880 and Hidalgo Co 18 May 1889.

Tree Swallow *(Tachycineta bicolor)* — Common migrant (February–May, August–October) throughout. Very rare to uncommon in winter throughout, though occasionally seen in large flocks.

Violet-green Swallow *(Tachycineta thalassina)* — Uncommon to fairly common summer resident of higher elevations of the Chisos, Davis, Guadalupe, Franklin, and Organ Mtns. Often seen along the Window Trail or near the Pinnacles in Big Bend NP, in the Davis Mtns, along Trans-Mountain Drive in the Franklin Mtns, and at Aguirre Springs. A fairly common migrant through at least the western half of the Trans-Pecos, becoming scarce farther east. Accidental as a migrant to the Lower Valley.

Northern Rough-winged Swallow *(Stelgidopteryx serripennis)* — Fairly common to common migrant (February–May, August–October) throughout; also an uncommon and local breeder. Rare to uncommon in winter upstream to Big Bend, and casual elsewhere.

Bank Swallow *(Riparia riparia)* — Uncommon migrant (April–May, August– early October) over entire region. Local and irregular breeding species over much of the region. Casual in winter in the Lower Valley.

Cliff Swallow *(Petrochelidon pyrrhonota)* — Common migrant and summer resident (March–early October) over the entire region. Cave Swallows are now nesting on man-made structures and may be in competition for nesting areas with Cliff Swallows. The effect, if there is one, this will have on the Cliff Swallow population is not clear.

Cave Swallow *(Petrochelidon fulva)* — Fairly common to common summer resident (late February–early October) throughout much of the Trans-Pecos, the Edwards Plateau, and south into the Lower Valley. Winters in some numbers in the Lower Valley and beginning to winter regularly in parts of the Trans-Pecos as well (Balmorhea Lake and El Paso and Hudspeth Cos). Largely absent from the Big Bend region and the Davis Mtns. Though virtually unknown from West Texas and the Lower Valley 30 years ago, this species has undergone an amazing expansion by using culverts, bridges, and overpasses as nesting sites. Historically, Cave Swallows nested only in limestone caves and sinkholes on the Edwards Plateau and at Carlsbad Caverns.

Barn Swallow *(Hirundo rustica)* — Common migrant and breeder throughout (March–October). Regular late stragglers through November. Rare in the Lower Valley in winter, casual elsewhere.

Carolina Chickadee *(Poecile carolinensis)* — Common resident in mixed woodland on the Edwards Plateau west to the Nueces River drainage. Accidental in the Lower Valley.

Black-capped Chickadee *(Poecile atricapillus)* — Accidental. One old El Paso specimen (10 April 1881) represents the only accepted Texas record. It nests south along the Rio Grande in New Mexico to below Albuquerque.

Mountain Chickadee *(Poecile gambeli)* — Uncommon to fairly common resident in the higher elevations of the Davis and Guadalupe Mountains. Rare to uncommon resident in the Organ Mts. During the fall and winter (October–March), some move to lower elevations, including into desert scrublands around the Guadalupe Mountains. Rare to uncommon, and irregular, in winter elsewhere in Trans-Pecos lowlands, though absent most years.

Juniper Titmouse *(Baeolophus ridgwayi)* — Uncommon permanent resident in the oak/juniper zone of the Guadalupe and Organ Mtns. Accidental in the El Paso area and the Davis Mtns. Look for it in Dog Canyon and at Frijole Ranch in Guadalupe Mtns NP, or at Aguirre Springs in the Organ Mtns

Black-crested Titmouse *(Baeolophus atricristatus)* — Common resident throughout South Texas, the Edwards Plateau, and the Davis and Chisos Mtns. Accidental in the Guadalupe Mtns..

Verdin *(Auriparus flaviceps)* — Uncommon to common resident of desert and lower woodlands throughout.

Bushtit *(Psaltriparus minimus)* — Fairly common resident in oak/juniper habitats over much of the Edwards Plateau and the mountains of the Trans-Pecos. Casual in fall and winter away from breeding areas. Most populations contain "black-eared" individuals, at least in late summer and fall.

Red-breasted Nuthatch *(Sitta canadensis)* — Rare to common, but highly irregular, winter visitor to the Trans-Pecos and the Edwards Plateau (September–May). Locally or completely absent some years. Casual in the Lower Valley. A rare resident (has bred) in the Guadalupe Mtns.

White-breasted Nuthatch *(Sitta carolinensis)* — Fairly common resident in pine/oak and riparian woodlands in the mountains of the Trans-Pecos. Rare and irregular in winter away from resident range.

Pygmy Nuthatch *(Sitta pygmaea)* — Fairly common permanent resident of mature pine forests at higher elevations in the Davis and Guadalupe Mtns. Can be found at The Bowl in the Guadalupe Mtns. Casual visitor elsewhere in West Texas in fall and winter.

Brown Creeper *(Certhia americana)* — Rare to uncommon winter resident and migrant throughout much of the region (October–April), except in the Lower Valley, where it is very rare. A rare to uncommon resident in the Guadalupe Mtns and likely the Davis Mtns.

Montane invaders: In the Trans-Pecos, each winter brings a different cast of characters in terms of invading montane species. Most years species such as Red-breasted Nuthatch and Western Scrub-Jay invade lower elevations in varying numbers. Some years, these species are joined by less-regular invaders such as Acorn Woodpecker, Steller's and Pinyon Jays, Clark's Nutcracker, Mountain Chickadee, Pygmy and White-breasted Nuthatches, Cassin's Finch, and Red Crossbill. Occasionally, no montane species invade at all. On the average, it seems that a major montane invasion (probably brought on by massive food crop failures in the mountains to the north) occurs about once every five years. Frugivores such as bluebirds, solitaires, and Sage Thrashers are also irregular and sporadic in their winter movements in West Texas. One year may bring hundreds of Mountain Bluebirds to widespread parts of the region, and then there may be two or three years without any at all.

Cactus Wren *(Campylorhynchus brunneicapillus)* — Fairly common permanent resident of desert habitats, brushlands, and lower foothills throughout. Noisy and conspicuous. Easy to find in Falcon SP, Big Bend NP, and Hueco Tanks, among other places.

Rock Wren *(Salpinctes obsoletus)* — Fairly common permanent resident of dry rocky areas from West Texas to the Edwards Plateau. Some movement to lower elevations in winter, including sporadically south to the Falcon Dam area, very rarely to the dam at Anzalduas County Park. Easy to find at Hueco Tanks, in the Franklin Mtns, and in Big Bend NP.

Canyon Wren *(Catherpes mexicanus)* — Fairly common resident of the Trans-Pecos and the Edwards Plateau. Easily found, and heard, in rocky canyons such as in Big Bend NP, Franklin Mtns, Hueco Tanks, McKittrick Canyon, and many other places.

Carolina Wren *(Thryothorus ludovicianus)* — Common resident from the Lower Valley northward through the Edwards Plateau and westward to the Devils River. Local resident along the Rio Grande as far west as the Big Bend region. Accidental west to El Paso.

Bewick's Wren *(Thryomanes bewickii)* — Fairly common to common resident of woodlands throughout. May be local in breeding season, more numerous and widespread in winter.

House Wren *(Troglodytes aedon)* — Uncommon to fairly common migrant throughout. Uncommon in winter in South Texas. A somewhat uncommon and local winter resident to most of the Edwards Plateau and the Trans-Pecos. Local summer resident in the Davis and Guadalupe Mtns in pine/oak woodlands.

Winter Wren *(Troglodytes troglodytes)* — Irregular winter visitor (October–March) to the eastern Edwards Plateau. Very rare in South Texas and the eastern Trans-Pecos. Casual to El Paso.

Sedge Wren *(Cistothorus platensis)* — Uncommon migrant and winter resident (September–late April) along the coast to extreme South Texas. Accidental to very rare throughout the remainder of the region.

Marsh Wren *(Cistothorus palustris)* — Uncommon to common migrant and winter visitor (September–May) throughout. One documented breeding record from El Paso Co in 1938.

American Dipper *(Cinclus mexicanus)* — Accidental. Five documented records: Franklin Mtns 8–16 November 1984, Big Bend 12 March 1986, Austin 5 March 1994, and two Guadalupe Mtns records from the winters of 1987–1988 and 1988–1989.

Golden-crowned Kinglet *(Regulus satrapa)* — Irregular, rare to fairly common winter resident (October–March) throughout. Most numerous on the Edwards Plateau, rare in much of the Trans-Pecos, and casual to rare in the Lower Valley.

Ruby-crowned Kinglet *(Regulus calendula)* — Fairly common to common winter resident (October–March) throughout. Less common in September and April–early May.

Blue-gray Gnatcatcher *(Polioptila caerulea)* — Common migrant (mid-March–April, late August–September) from the Lower Valley and the Edwards Plateau west to the central Trans-Pecos. Rare migrant farther west. Uncommon in winter in the Lower Valley, the southern Trans-Pecos, and along the river in Hudspeth Co, rarely in other areas. Fairly common to common summer resident on the Edwards Plateau and in the Chisos Mtns.

Black-tailed Gnatcatcher *(Polioptila melanura)* — Fairly common permanent resident of mesquite brushlands and desert scrub in the Big Bend region. Uncommon and local throughout the remainder of the Trans-Pecos, the western edge of the Edwards Plateau, and south along the river to about Rio Grande City. Seems to be increasing and expanding in some areas. Look for it in desert margins around Rio Grande Village, at Dugout Wells, and at Sam Nail Ranch in Big Bend NP.

Northern Wheatear *(Oenanthe oenanthe)* — Accidental. One documented record for Texas: at Laguna Atascosa NWR 1–6 November 1994.

Eastern Bluebird *(Sialia sialis)* — Uncommon and local summer resident (April–September) on the Edwards Plateau. Very local nester just north of the Lower Valley at El Canelo Ranch. More common and widespread from the central mountains of the Trans-Pecos eastward in winter, when rare but annual in parts of the Lower Valley and in El Paso.

Western Bluebird *(Sialia mexicana)* — Irregular, uncommon to fairly common winter resident (October–April) in the Trans-Pecos. Prefers mistletoe-infected cottonwoods and the pinyon/juniper belt of mountains, such as at Aguirre Spring in the Organ Mtns or Frijole Ranch in the Guadalupes. Uncommon to fairly common breeder in the Davis and Guadalupe Mtns. Casual eastward.

Mountain Bluebird *(Sialia currucoides)* — Highly irregular, rare to fairly common winter resident (November–March) in the Trans-Pecos and western Edwards Plateau. May be numerous and widespread some winters. Very rare in the Lower Valley. There is a nesting record from the Davis Mtns.

Townsend's Solitaire *(Myadestes townsendi)* — Irregular, rare to uncommon winter resident (late September–April) in the Trans-Pecos and Edwards Plateau. Very rare in the Lower Valley. Look especially in areas with junipers.

Orange-billed Nightingale-Thrush (*Catharus aurantiirostris*) — Accidental. Two documented records for Texas and the U.S.: one mist-netted at Laguna Atascosa NWR 8 April 1996 and one specimen from Edinburg 28 May 2004.

Black-headed Nightingale-Thrush (*Catharus mexicanus*) — Accidental. One record for Texas and the U.S.: at Pharr 28 May–29 October 2004.

Veery (*Catharus fuscescens*) — Uncommon migrant (mid-April–May, mid-September–October) in the Lower Valley, becoming rare on the Edwards Plateau and west to the Pecos River. Accidental in the Trans-Pecos.

Gray-cheeked Thrush (*Catharus minimus*) — Rare to uncommon migrant (mid-April–May, October) in the Lower Valley and the eastern Edwards Plateau; most common along the coast. Accidental in the Trans-Pecos.

Swainson's Thrush (*Catharus ustulatus*) — Common, primarily spring, migrant (mid-April–May, October) from the Lower Valley north to the Edwards Plateau. Rare migrant in the eastern Trans-Pecos, very rare west to El Paso.

Hermit Thrush (*Catharus guttatus*) — Uncommon to common migrant and winter resident (late September–May) throughout. Fairly common breeder at high elevations of the Guadalupe and Davis Mtns. Two July records for Big Bend NP.

Wood Thrush (*Hylocichla mustelina*) — Uncommon, primarily spring, migrant (April–May, October) in the eastern half of the Lower Valley. Rare migrant on the eastern Edwards Plateau. Very rare on the western plateau and the Trans-Pecos. Accidental in winter in the Lower Valley.

Clay-colored Thrush (*Turdus grayi*) — Locally rare to uncommon resident in the Lower Valley, primarily in Hidalgo and Starr Cos; casual in Cameron Co. Increasing. Most reports are from feeders and water drips at Bentsen SP, Quinta Mazatlan in McAllen, Santa Ana NWR; may also be found at Salineño, Santa Margarita Ranch, Roma Bluffs, and other forested regions upriver on the Rio Grande to about San Ygnacio. Some years this species is more numerous and also can be found in residential areas from along the coast near Laguna Vista inland to McAllen.

White-throated Thrush (*Turdus assimilis*) — Casual in the Lower Valley in winter. Prior to an influx of nine individuals during the winter of 2004–2005, there were only three records for the state, the first coming from Laguna Vista 18–25 February 1990. Cameron Co locales include Laguna Vista, Sabal Palm Audubon Center, Los Fresnos, and Rangerville; Hidalgo Co sightings are from Frontera Audubon Thicket, Pharr, Santa Ana NWR, Bentsen SP, and Mission.

Rufous-backed Robin *(Turdus rufopalliatus)* — Casual late fall and winter visitor (mid-October–mid-February). Most records from the Trans-Pecos, including three from Big Bend NP, two from El Paso, and one from the Davis Mtns. Several Lower Valley records and at least two from Doña Ana Co, NM.

American Robin *(Turdus migratorius)* — Uncommon to common migrant and winter resident (November–March) over virtually the entire region. Numbers of wintering individuals vary greatly from year to year, and it may be entirely absent some years in the Lower Valley. Local breeder, primarily in urban areas, on the Edwards Plateau and in El Paso/Las Cruces. Also a summer resident at upper elevations in the Davis and Guadalupe Mtns.

Varied Thrush *(Ixoreus naevius)* — Casual to very rare visitor (October–May) in the Trans-Pecos and accidental in the Lower Valley.

Aztec Thrush *(Ridgwayia pinicola)* — Accidental. Three accepted records, all from Boot Spring in Big Bend NP: 21–25 August 1977 (the first U.S. record), 31 July–7 August 1982, and 18 April 2003. There are other Big Bend reports, most likely valid, and it should be looked for in moist canyons in Big Bend in late summer. Also two coastal records from north of the Lower Valley: Port Aransas 30 January 1979 and Corpus Christi 16–20 May 1996.

Gray Catbird *(Dumetella carolinensis)* — Fairly common migrant (mid-April–May, mid-September–early November) in the Lower Valley and on the eastern Edwards Plateau. Increasingly rare farther west. Rare winter visitor in the Lower Valley, with scattered records of overwintering birds at many other locations throughout.

Black Catbird *(Melanoptila glabirostris)* — Accidental. One documented record for Texas: a specimen collected at Brownsville 21 June 1892.

Blue Mockingbird *(Melanotis caerulescens)* — Accidental. Three accepted Texas records, likely of just two birds, all from the Lower Valley: one in Weslaco 9 May 1999–27 February 2002 and another in Pharr 28 September 2002–26 May 2003, returning in mid-September 2003 and then seen sporadically to at least March 2005. One videotaped 7–8 August 1995 in Las Cruces, NM, was in good condition, suggesting a wild bird.

Northern Mockingbird *(Mimus polyglottos)* — Common resident throughout. Trans-Pecos populations are reduced in winter, when most birds either migrate south or retreat into urban areas or places with abundant fruit.

Sage Thrasher *(Oreoscoptes montanus)* — Uncommon to fairly common migrant (March–April, September–November) to desert habitats, mesquite grasslands, and juniper foothills throughout the Trans-Pecos, and to a lesser extent the western Edwards Plateau (rare in eastern portion) and the Lower Valley (where rare and irregular; absent along the coast). Less numerous in mid-winter. Numbers fluctuate from year to year, with large numbers often coinciding with good bluebird years. Easiest to find at Guadalupe Mtns NP,

Carlsbad Caverns NP, Aguirre Springs, and around fruiting cactus in Fort Hancock.

Brown Thrasher *(Toxostoma rufum)* — Uncommon migrant (April–May, September–early November) over the eastern Edwards Plateau; rare farther west. Rare in winter on the Edwards Plateau and in the Trans-Pecos. Casually wanders as far south as the Lower Valley in late fall and winter.

Long-billed Thrasher *(Toxostoma longirostre)* — Uncommon to common resident in South Texas from the Rio Grande north to the southern edge of the Edwards Plateau (where it is rare and local, although common around Concan in northern Uvalde Co); rare and local in the eastern Trans-Pecos. Prefers dense woodlands along the Rio Grande and brushlands throughout South Texas. Good spots include the bird feeders at Sabal Palm Audubon Center, Laguna Atascosa NWR, Santa Ana NWR, Bentsen SP, and Salineño/ Falcon Dam area.

Bendire's Thrasher *(Toxostoma bendirei)* — Accidental. One accepted record from the Old Refuge, Las Cruces, NM, on 5 June 1993. Not on the official Texas list. This species is a regular breeder to within 100 miles west of Las Cruces.

Curve-billed Thrasher *(Toxostoma curvirostre)* — Uncommon to common permanent resident of brushlands throughout. Somewhat localized in the Trans-Pecos, where it prefers yucca/cholla/grassland associations and not the floodplain and low-desert habitats favored by Crissal Thrasher. Occurs in many residential areas of the Lower Valley. Look for it at Falcon SP, around Panther Junction in Big Bend NP, and in residential areas of El Paso around the base of the Franklin Mtns.

Crissal Thrasher *(Toxostoma crissale)* — Fairly common but shy permanent resident of brushy arroyos, salt-cedar thickets, and lower mountain canyons in the western third of the Trans-Pecos. Less numerous in other portions of the Trans-Pecos from Big Bend NP east to the Pecos River. Best found in February and March when singing. Center of abundance is in the El Paso and Las Cruces areas. Look for it at Hueco Tanks, the Fort Bliss Sewage Ponds, and any brushy areas of the floodplain or low desert between Presidio and Las Cruces.

European Starling *(Sturnus vulgaris)* — Common resident in urban areas throughout, though it actually may be uncommon in large parts of the Lower Valley.

American Pipit *(Anthus rubescens)* — Fairly common to common winter resident and migrant (October–early April) throughout.

Sprague's Pipit *(Anthus spragueii)* — Uncommon and local winter resident (mid-October–early April) of agricultural areas in the Lower Valley; rare in grasslands and alfalfa fields of the Trans-Pecos as far west as El Paso. Rare migrant on Edwards Plateau.

Cedar Waxwing *(Bombycilla cedrorum)* — Irregular, uncommon to common winter resident and migrant (October–May) throughout. May be virtually absent some years in the Lower Valley.

Gray Silky-flycatcher *(Ptilogonys cinereus)* — Accidental fall and winter visitor. Observed at Laguna Atascosa NWR 31 October–11 November 1985 and in west El Paso 12 January–5 March 1995. These represent the only accepted U.S. records, the others thought to involve possible escapees. This species is largely fruit-eating and may be prone to seasonal wanderings.

Phainopepla *(Phainopepla nitens)* — Uncommon and local permanent resident of oak woodlands and riparian areas of the Trans-Pecos. Generally associated with mistletoe-infected trees. Some seasonal movement. Can usually be found in the Davis Mountains and in residential areas along the river in El Paso and Las Cruces. Rare in Big Bend and eastern portions of the Trans-Pecos. A casual visitor to the Edwards Plateau and accidental in the Lower Valley.

Olive Warbler *(Peucedramus taeniatus)* — Accidental. Six documented Trans-Pecos records (three spring and three fall), plus a handful of documented records from the Las Cruces, NM, area. Several of these are from December. Breeds uncommonly in the Black Range (60 miles northwest of Las Cruces), and the number of Las Cruces records suggests it may be a rare breeder in the upper Organ Mtns.

Blue-winged Warbler *(Vermivora pinus)* — Rare to uncommon migrant (April–early May, late August–early October) through the Lower Valley (fairly common near the coast) and Edwards Plateau. Accidental in the Trans-Pecos.

Golden-winged Warbler *(Vermivora chrysoptera)* — Rare to uncommon migrant (April–early May, September–early October) through the Lower Valley and the Edwards Plateau. Accidental to casual in the Trans-Pecos.

Tennessee Warbler *(Vermivora peregrina)* — Common migrant (April–May, mid-September–October) through the Lower Valley, particularly near the coast. Much less numerous, but regular, migrant on the eastern Edwards Plateau, becoming increasingly rare westward. Casual in El Paso.

Orange-crowned Warbler *(Vermivora celata)* — Fairly common to common migrant throughout. Fairly common to common (Lower Valley) in winter, except in the Trans-Pecos, where it is increasingly local and less common north and west. An uncommon breeder in high-elevation deciduous thickets in the Guadalupes, and rare in the Davis Mtns.

Nashville Warbler *(Vermivora ruficapilla)* — Uncommon migrant (April–early May, September–October) through the Lower Valley west to the El

Paso area, where rare. Probably the most common through-migrant wood-warbler on the Edwards Plateau. Uncommon winter resident in the Lower Valley.

Virginia's Warbler *(Vermivora virginiae)* — Uncommon to fairly common summer resident of higher elevations of the Guadalupe, Organ, and Davis Mtns. Prefers brushy slopes and areas with Gambel Oaks. An uncommon migrant through the western portions of the Trans-Pecos. A casual winter visitor to the Lower Valley.

Colima Warbler *(Vermivora crissalis)* — Fairly common summer resident in the oak woodlands at upper elevations of the Chisos Mtns in Big Bend NP. They arrive in mid-April and depart by mid-September. Males are normally easy to find from late April to early June, when they are most vocal. The Pinnacles Trail, Boot Springs, the Colima Trail, and Laguna Meadows are among the best places to search. Pine Canyon in late summer is also a possibility. Casual spring migrant and summer visitor to the Davis Mtns.

Lucy's Warbler *(Vermivora luciae)* — Rare to uncommon summer resident along the Rio Grande from Big Bend NP (Cottonwood Campground) westward to about McNary. Prefers dense mesquite, tornillo, and salt-cedar thickets adjacent to the river or around desert tanks. Very rare as a migrant away from breeding areas.

Crescent-chested Warbler *(Parula superciliosa)* — Accidental; an accepted sight record from the Chisos Mtns (2 June 1993).

Northern Parula *(Parula americana)* — Fairly common migrant (March–April, September–October) over the eastern Edwards Plateau and the Lower Valley. Casual to rare migrant in the Trans-Pecos. Local summer resident in riparian woodlands on the southeastern Edwards Plateau; look for it at Guadalupe River SP. Rare winter visitor in the Lower Valley.

Tropical Parula *(Parula pitiayumi)* — Rare to uncommon resident in the Lower Valley along the Rio Grande corridor between Santa Ana NWR and Bentsen SP; rare but more widespread in winter. This species is a locally uncommon breeder just north of the Lower Valley, primarily in live-oak woodlands on the King Ranch (north to Kingsville). It is most easily found in spring when males are singing. To be looked for at all seasons at Bentsen SP and at Santa Ana NWR. In winter, Tropical Parula should be searched for in mixed-species flocks at Sabal Palm Audubon Center, Frontera Audubon Thicket in Weslaco, Santa Ana NWR, Quinta Mazatlan, and Bentsen SP, as well as in residential Brownsville, Harlingen, Weslaco, and McAllen. This species prefers the moss-covered canopy of large Cedar Elm, Sugar Hackberry, and Texas Ebony trees. Rare and local along the Devils River on the extreme western Edwards Plateau and accidental in the Trans-Pecos (Big Bend NP and Davis Mtns SP).

Yellow Warbler *(Dendroica petechia)* — Fairly common to common migrant (April–May, late July–mid-October) throughout. Rare to locally uncommon in winter in the Lower Valley, casual elsewhere. Nested historically on the Edwards Plateau and along the Rio Grande in West Texas.

"Mangrove" Yellow Warbler *(Dendroica petechia erithachorides)* — Locally rare to uncommon resident of coastal Black Mangrove habitat. Formerly thought to be accidental in Texas, this distinctive subspecies has become well established in the southernmost Laguna Madre since 2004; surveys have estimated that there are at least 15 territorial males in the immediate area. Prior to 2004, there were just two Texas records: north of the Lower Valley at Rockport 26 May 1978 and at Boca Chica 20 March–6 April 1990.

Chestnut-sided Warbler *(Dendroica pensylvanica)* — Uncommon to fairly common spring migrant (mid-April–mid-May) and rare fall migrant (September–October) through the Lower Valley and rare on the eastern Edwards Plateau. Scarcer in fall. Casual to rare westward.

Magnolia Warbler *(Dendroica magnolia)* — Fairly common migrant (mid-April–mid-May, September–October) through the Lower Valley and uncommon on the eastern Edwards Plateau. Casual to rare westward. Very rare in winter in the Lower Valley.

Cape May Warbler *(Dendroida tigrina)* — Rare spring migrant (late April–early May) in the Lower Valley and accidental during spring west to El Paso.

Black-throated Blue Warbler *(Dendroica caerulescens)* — Rare migrant, mostly through the Lower Valley. Casual to very rare migrant in the Trans-Pecos (mostly in fall), and in the Lower Valley in winter. One El Paso winter record.

Yellow-rumped Warbler *(Dendroica coronata)* — Common winter resident and migrant throughout (mid-September–mid-May). Rare to uncommon breeder in the Davis and Guadalupe Mtns. "Audubon's" is rare to the east, "Myrtle" is rare to the west.

Black-throated Gray Warbler *(Dendroica nigrescens)* — Uncommon migrant (April–mid-May, August–October) in the Trans-Pecos. Locally rare to uncommon migrant elsewhere, and winter visitor in the Lower Valley. Accidental in winter in the Trans-Pecos. A few may breed on dry pine/oak slopes in the Organ and Guadalupe Mtns; one summer record in Davis Mtns.

Golden-cheeked Warbler *(Dendroica chrysoparia)* — Uncommon and local summer resident in Ashe Juniper/oak woodlands on the Edwards Plateau. Males normally arrive by 10 March and most of the population has departed by 1 August. At present, the best places to find them are Pedernales Falls SP, Colorado Bend SP, and Lost Maples SNA.

Black-throated Green Warbler *(Dendroica virens)* — Fairly common to common migrant (mid-April–mid-May, mid-September–late October) in the Lower Valley, and uncommon on the eastern Edwards Plateau. Casual to rare westward. Uncommon to fairly common in the Lower Valley in winter.

Townsend's Warbler *(Dendroica townsendi)* — Uncommon to fairly common Trans-Pecos migrant (April–mid-May, late August–mid-October); more numerous in fall; rare migrant elsewhere. Casual to rare winter visitor along the Rio Grande throughout.

Hermit Warbler *(Dendroica occidentalis)* — Casual to rare migrant (much more regular in fall, especially September) in the Trans-Pecos; mostly in mountains. Casual in winter in the Lower Valley.

Blackburnian Warbler *(Dendroica fusca)* — Uncommon spring (late April–early May) and rare fall (September–October) migrant in the Lower Valley. Rare migrant on the eastern Edwards Plateau and accidental in the Trans-Pecos.

Yellow-throated Warbler *(Dendroica dominica)* — Uncommon migrant on the eastern Edwards Plateau and in the Lower Valley. Accidental west to El Paso and Las Cruces. Locally common summer resident (March–August) in riparian woodlands on the southeastern Edwards Plateau. Look for it at Guadalupe River SP, Garner SP, and around Neal's Lodge. Fairly common winter resident, primarily in palms, in the Lower Valley.

Grace's Warbler *(Dendroica graciae)* — Fairly common summer resident of pine forests in the Davis, Guadalupe, and Organ Mtns. Very rare migrant at lower elevations. Easy to find in McKittrick Canyon in late April and May when the males are singing.

Pine Warbler *(Dendroica pinus)* — Locally rare to uncommon migrant and winter visitor (October–March) to the eastern Edwards Plateau and South Texas. In the Lower Valley, most often seen at Andalzuas County Park and at Bentsen SP. Accidental west to El Paso.

Prairie Warbler *(Dendroica discolor)* — Rare migrant in the Lower Valley, accidental elsewhere in the region.

Palm Warbler *(Dendroica palmarum)* — Rare to uncommon migrant and winter visitor in the Lower Valley, very rare elsewhere in the region.

Bay-breasted Warbler *(Dendroica castanea)* — Fairly common spring migrant and uncommon fall migrant in the Lower Valley, more numerous along the coast (late April–May, September–early October). Casual migrant on the eastern Edwards Plateau. Accidental in the Trans-Pecos.

Blackpoll Warbler *(Dendroica striata)* — Uncommon spring migrant (mid-April–mid-May) and rare fall migrant in the Lower Valley, mostly along the coast. Accidental to casual migrant on the Edwards Plateau and in the Trans-Pecos.

Cerulean Warbler *(Dendroica cerulea)* — Uncommon migrant (mid-April–early May, September) in the Lower Valley, accidental elsewhere in the region.

Black-and-white Warbler *(Mniotilta varia)* — Common migrant from the Lower Valley northward to the Edwards Plateau. Increasingly scarce westward, where this species is a rare migrant in the El Paso area. Fairly common summer resident (March–September) in mixed woodlands on the Edwards Plateau. Regular in winter in the Lower Valley, rarely found farther north.

American Redstart *(Setophaga ruticilla)* — Fairly common to common migrant (April–mid-May, late August–early October) in the Lower Valley and rare to uncommon on the eastern Edwards Plateau. Rare migrant in the Trans-Pecos (more numerous in fall). Rare in winter in the Lower Valley, accidental elsewhere.

Prothonotary Warbler *(Protonotaria citrea)* — Uncommon migrant (April–early May, September–mid-October) in the eastern Lower Valley. Rare to very rare migrant on the Edwards Plateau and casual in the Trans-Pecos.

Worm-eating Warbler *(Helmitheros vermivorum)* — Uncommon migrant (April–early May, mid-August–September) in the eastern Lower Valley. Rare to very rare migrant on the Edwards Plateau and accidental in the Trans-Pecos.

Swainson's Warbler *(Limnothlypis swainsonii)* — Uncommon migrant (mostly early–mid-April) in the Lower Valley, and mostly along the coast. Very rare migrant over the eastern Edwards Plateau.

Ovenbird *(Seiurus aurocapilla)* — Uncommon to fairly common migrant (mid-April–mid-May, September–October) in the Lower Valley and rare to uncommon on the eastern Edwards Plateau. Casual to rare in the Trans-Pecos. Rare in winter in the Lower Valley, casual elsewhere.

Northern Waterthrush *(Seiurus noveboracensis)* — Fairly common migrant (April–early May, late August–October) in the Lower Valley and on the Edwards Plateau. Rare to uncommon migrant in the Trans-Pecos. Rare in winter in the Lower Valley.

Louisiana Waterthrush *(Seiurus motacilla)* — Uncommon migrant (late March–mid-April, July–August) from the Lower Valley northward to the Edwards Plateau. Accidental in the Trans-Pecos. Local summer resident in mesic canyons on the Edwards Plateau, such as at Lost Maples SNA.

Kentucky Warbler *(Oporornis formosus)* — Uncommon spring (late March–early May) and rare fall (September) migrant in the eastern Lower Valley. Rare to very rare migrant on the Edwards Plateau and accidental in the Trans-Pecos.

Connecticut Warbler *(Oporornis agilis)* — Accidental; two records from the Edwards Plateau, one repeatedly mist-netted near Driftwood, Hays Co (3–14 May 1986) and a sight record from Utopia (19 May 2005).

Mourning Warbler *(Oporornis philadelphia)* — Uncommon, but secretive, migrant (May, September–early October) in the eastern Lower Valley and on the Edwards Plateau. Accidental in the Trans-Pecos.

MacGillivray's Warbler *(Oporornis tolmiei)* — Fairly common migrant (mid-April–May, mid-August–mid-October) in the Trans-Pecos; rare to uncommon in the Lower Valley and on the Edwards Plateau. One confirmed nesting record from the Davis Mtns in July 2002.

Common Yellowthroat *(Geothlypis trichas)* — Fairly common to common migrant throughout. Common in winter in the Lower Valley, becoming rare to uncommon in the western Trans-Pecos. Fairly common (El Paso area/ Lower Valley) to rare and local breeder along the Rio Grande throughout.

Gray-crowned Yellowthroat *(Geothlypis poliocephala)* — Accidental. Formerly a rare to uncommon resident in the Lower Valley near Brownsville. There are nine Texas records since 1988 from Cameron and Hidalgo Cos, most occurring at Sabal Palm Audubon Center and Santa Ana NWR.

Cautionary note about yellowthroats: Because of the variability among immature male Common Yellowthroats, there is potential confusion with Gray-crowned Yellowthroat. In a nutshell, Gray-crowned Yellowthroats are bulky, large-headed, and long-tailed birds, with thick, chat-like bicolored bills, often showing a distinctive gray forehead and crown, black lores, and eye crescents, and having a habit of swinging their tails from side to side. They prefer grassy areas rather than marshes. Also, Common Yellowthroats breeding in the Lower Valley have a more melodic and warbling song than do other subspecies. Don't be fooled!

Hooded Warbler *(Wilsonia citrina)* — Common migrant (late March–April, late August–early October) in the eastern Lower Valley. Very rare migrant on the Edwards Plateau and casual in the Trans-Pecos.

Wilson's Warbler *(Wilsonia pusilla)* — Common migrant (April–May, mid-August–October) throughout, especially westward. Uncommon in winter in the Lower Valley, and casual elsewhere.

Canada Warbler *(Wilsonia canadensis)* — Uncommon migrant (late April–early May, mid-August–mid-September) in the eastern Lower Valley. Rare to very rare migrant on the Edwards Plateau and accidental in the Trans-Pecos.

Red-faced Warbler *(Cardellina rubrifrons)* — Very rare migrant in the Trans-Pecos, with about 30 records for this region. Almost annual in recent years, with most records from August and from Big Bend, with a handful also from the El Paso area. Also recorded in the Davis and Guadalupe Mtns. This species breeds in numbers northwest of El Paso in the Black Range of south-central New Mexico. One Lower Valley record: 18 August 1985 at Laguna Atascosa NWR.

Painted Redstart *(Myioborus pictus)* — Irregular rare summer resident at upper elevations of the Chisos Mtns, absent some years and most numerous in wet years. Most often encountered around Boot Spring. Accidental breeder in the upper Davis Mtns (two records). Very rare migrant in the Trans-Pecos, especially late March–early April. Accidental in the Lower Valley, mostly in late fall and winter.

Slate-throated Redstart *(Myioborus miniatus)* — Accidental to casual. Four Big Bend records, all from Boot Canyon (late April–early May), two records from the upper Davis Mtns (June and August), and a lone record from the Lower Valley (Pharr 12–13 March 2003).

Fan-tailed Warbler *(Euthlypis lachrymosa)* Accidenal. One in Pine Canyon, Big Bend NP 13 August–24 September 2007 provided a first state record.

Golden-crowned Warbler *(Basileuterus culicivorus)* — Very rare winter visitor to the Lower Valley, with records ranging from August–April. Most records are from Brownsville and Santa Ana NWR; however, this species also has shown up at Sabal Palm Audubon Center, the Los Ebanos Preserve (north of Brownsville), Harlingen, Bentsen SP, and Edinburg. One notable spring record north of our region at Packery Channel near Corpus Christi.

Rufous-capped Warbler *(Basileuterus rufifrons)* — Casual to very rare. This species was first documented in the U.S. at Falcon Dam in 1973. Since then, there have been almost 25 additional documented records for Texas, mostly from the southwestern Edwards Plateau and Big Bend NP. May occur more regularly than previously thought, particularly on the southwestern Edwards Plateau, where there have been multiple records over the past decade.

Yellow-breasted Chat *(Icteria virens)* — Fairly common migrant throughout. An uncommon to locally common breeder in the Trans-Pecos and on the western Edwards Plateau, almost entirely in dense riparian thickets. Very rare in winter in the Lower Valley, casual elsewhere.

Hepatic Tanager *(Piranga flava)* — Fairly common summer resident of pine/oak forests of the Chisos, Davis, Guadalupe, and Organ Mtns. Very rare as a migrant away from breeding sites. Accidental in the Lower Valley in fall and early winter. Best found just above the Chisos Basin Lodge, at the Lawrence E. Wood Picnic Grounds (Davis Mtns), or at Aguirre Springs (Organ Mtns).

Summer Tanager *(Piranga rubra)* — Uncommon to common migrant and breeder (April–October) throughout, but absent as a breeder in the Lower Valley. Restricted primarily to cottonwoods in the Trans-Pecos. Rare in winter in the Lower Valley.

Scarlet Tanager *(Piranga olivacea)* — Uncommon, primarily spring, migrant (April–early May, September) in the eastern Lower Valley. Very rare migrant on the Edwards Plateau and accidental in the Trans-Pecos.

Western Tanager *(Piranga ludoviciana)* — Uncommon to fairly common summer resident (May–August) of the coniferous forests of the Davis and Guadalupe Mtns. Widespread and fairly common to common as a migrant (late April–May, mid-July–October) in the western half of the Trans-Pecos, when it may be found at any elevation. Rare in migration and winter south to the Lower Valley. Accidental in winter at El Paso.

Flame-colored Tanager *(Piranga bidentata)* — Accidental visitor to the Trans-Pecos and the Lower Valley. Four records from Big Bend NP (three records in April and one at Boot Spring 12–28 June 2008), one from the Davis Mtns (1–5 October 2001), and two from the Lower Valley (South Padre Island 11–14 April 2002 and Pharr 28 February 2005).

White-collared Seedeater *(Sporophila torqueola)* — Locally rare to uncommon resident along the Rio Grande from the Falcon Dam area to Laredo, slightly more numerous in winter. For the past decade, the two spots where seedeaters have been somewhat reliable are at Zapata library (check all areas around the pond) and at the San Ygnacio Bird and Butterfly Park at the end of Washington St. White-collared Seedeaters prefer weedy edges and second growth as well as tall cane (reeds) along the river. The subspecies in South Texas is *hoopesi,* with the males nearly collarless, though variable.

Yellow-faced Grassquit *(Tiaris olivaceus)* — Accidental. Three documented records for Texas: Santa Ana NWR 22–24 January 1990, Bentsen SP 11–29 June 2002, and Santa Ana NWR 28 September 2003. All three birds were males of the darker subspecies *pusilla,* which ranges from NE Mexico southward through Central America.

Olive Sparrow *(Arremonops rufivirgatus)* — Common resident in southern Texas west to Del Rio; rare at southern edge of the Edwards Plateau, although uncommon but very regular at Concan in northern Uvalde Co. Although shy, Olive Sparrows usually can be coaxed out of the brush with squeaking. They are fairly easy to see at Sabal Palm Audubon Center, Laguna Atascosa NWR, Santa Ana NWR, Bentsen SP, and Falcon Dam area.

Green-tailed Towhee *(Pipilo chlorurus)* — Rare to fairly common winter resident and migrant to riparian areas, desert thickets, and lower brushy canyons throughout the Trans-Pecos and south along the river to at least the Falcon Dam area (occasionally farther east to Brownsville), generally decreasing in abundance eastward. A sporadic winter visitor to the Edwards Plateau. A rare nester at high elevations in the Guadalupe and Davis Mtns

Spotted Towhee *(Pipilo maculatus)* — A fairly common to common breeder in the Chisos, Davis, and Guadalupe Mtns. Uncommon to common migrant and winter resident (October–April) throughout, but rare in the Lower Valley.

Eastern Towhee *(Pipilo erythrophthalmus)* — Rare winter visitor (November–March) to the eastern Edwards Plateau and South Texas. Accidental in the Trans-Pecos.

Canyon Towhee *(Pipilo fuscus)* — Fairly common to common resident of canyons, foothills, and arroyos throughout the Trans-Pecos and the Edwards Plateau. Some irregular movement to lower elevations in winter. Easy to find along the Window Trail in Big Bend NP, the Franklin Mtns, Aguirre Springs in the Organ Mtns, and Hueco Tanks, among other places.

Cassin's Sparrow *(Aimophila cassinii)* — Fairly common, though somewhat local, summer resident to grasslands, brushlands, and scrub desert throughout the Trans-Pecos, edges of the Edwards Plateau, and the Lower Valley. Watch for skylarking birds in appropriate habitat. In the Trans-Pecos, most vocal in late summer (July–August) during monsoonal rains, but may start singing as early as March (as they do in the Lower Valley). Less numerous and harder to see in winter, but still present, through much of the breeding range.

Botteri's Sparrow *(Aimophila botterii)* — Uncommon to locally fairly common summer resident on wthe Lower Valley coastal plain (April–September); prefers bunchgrass/mesquite/Prickly Pear habitat from east Brownsville north to Port Mansfield in Willacy Co. Best spots are along Old Port Isabel Rd (Brownsville), along TX-4 toward Boca Chica, in the vicinity of Laguna Atascosa NWR, and east of Raymondville on TX-186 toward Port Mansfield. Best searched for early and late in the day when males are singing. One documented breeding record in the Trans-Pecos (south of Marfa) in summer of 1997.

Rufous-crowned Sparrow *(Aimophila ruficeps)* — Fairly common permanent resident of lower slopes and canyons throughout the Trans-Pecos mountain ranges and on the Edwards Plateau. Very rare and local around Falcon Dam area. Often on boulder-strewn slopes with scattered oaks or junipers. Easy to find along the Window Trail in Big Bend NP, in Franklin Mtns SP, Lost Maples SP, and at Aguirre Springs in the Organ Mtns.

American Tree Sparrow *(Spizella arborea)* — Accidental to casual winter visitor to the Trans-Pecos. No recent records.

Chipping Sparrow *(Spizella passerina)* — Fairly common to common migrant and winter resident (August–May) throughout. More common in migration than in winter in the Trans-Pecos. Fairly common to common breeder on the Edwards Plateau and in the Davis and Guadalupe Mtns.

Clay-colored Sparrow *(Spizella pallida)* — Uncommon to fairly common migrant (April–early May, September–early November) over entire region. Increasingly scarce westward; in the Trans-Pecos, it is decidedly more numerous in fall. Rare in winter in South Texas and the eastern Trans-Pecos.

Brewer's Sparrow *(Spizella breweri)* — Uncommon to common migrant and winter resident (September–early May) to grasslands and desert brushlands throughout the Trans-Pecos. At times may be abundant. Increasingly numerous westward. Casual to rare as a winter visitor and migrant east to the Edwards Plateau and upper portions of the Lower Valley. Easiest to find around El Paso, including at Hueco Tanks and Franklin Mtns SP.

Field Sparrow *(Spizella pusilla)* — Common permanent resident in brushy habitats on the Edwards Plateau. More widespread in winter, when it can be found rarely as far south as Brownsville. It is a locally uncommon winter resident in the eastern Trans-Pecos, becoming accidental to casual farther west.

Black-chinned Sparrow *(Spizella atrogularis)* — Uncommon to fairly common permanent resident of brushy mountain slopes in the Chisos, Davis, Guadalupe, Franklin, and Organ Mtns. Some movement to lower elevations in winter. Males sing from April to well into the rainy season in August. Best locations include the Basin and Laguna Meadows in Big Bend NP, McKittrick Canyon in the Guadalupe Mtns, and Aguirre Springs in the Organ Mtns.

Vesper Sparrow *(Pooecetes gramineus)* — Fairly common to common migrant and winter resident (September–April) throughout.

Lark Sparrow *(Chondestes grammacus)* — Fairly common to common resident throughout much of the region, except absent November–March from much of the Trans-Pecos and less common then on the Edwards Plateau. Local as a breeder throughout.

Black-throated Sparrow *(Amphispiza bilineata)* — Common resident of desert habitats east to about Falcon Dam and La Joya in the Lower Valley. More local on the Edwards Plateau. Hard to miss in desert areas.

Sage Sparrow *(Amphispiza belli)* — Uncommon and local winter resident (November–March) in western portions of the Trans-Pecos. Prefers areas with sagebrush and scattered grass, but can be found in creosote flats as well. A particularly good area is east of El Paso: take Interstate 10, exit 37, and head north and east several miles east of Horizon; look here in the desert flats. Also possible near Hueco Tanks and below the Organ Mtns.

Lark Bunting *(Calamospiza melanocorys)* — Fairly common to common migrant and winter resident (late July–late April) to open country throughout. Numbers fluctuate from one year to the next. Can be found in grasslands, pastures, and desert brushlands. Often seen along roadsides in large flocks. Probably more numerous in the Trans-Pecos than other regions.

Savannah Sparrow *(Passerculus sandwichensis)* — Common winter resident (late September–April) in grasslands and weedy habitats throughout the region.

Grasshopper Sparrow *(Ammodramus savannarum)* — Rare to fairly common migrant and winter resident (October–April) throughout most of region. Casual in El Paso and Las Cruces. An uncommon and local breeder on the Edwards Plateau and in grasslands surrounding the Davis Mtns.

Baird's Sparrow *(Ammodramus bairdii)* — Casual to rare migrant and local winter resident (October–early May) in grasslands of the Trans-Pecos. Good areas are along US-90 near Valentine and Marfa, FM-505 near US-90, and Ranch Road 2810 several miles southwest of Marfa. Several records of migrants from Rio Grande Village in early May; a 30 August 2003 record from El Paso Co was notably early. Accidental migrant on the Edwards Plateau; historical records for the Lower Valley.

Le Conte's Sparrow *(Ammodramus leconteii)* — Rare to uncommon winter resident (mid-October–April) in grassy fields and marshy edges on the eastern Edwards Plateau. Fairly rare in South Texas and on the western Edwards Plateau. Accidental in the Trans-Pecos, although there are several records from the Balmorhea area.

Nelson's Sharp-tailed Sparrow *(Ammodramus nelsoni)* — Rare migrant and winter resident along the Lower Coast; favored habitat is *Spartina* marshes on the central and upper Texas coasts. Very rare west in the Trans-Pecos to Balmorhea Lake.

Seaside Sparrow *(Ammodramus maritimus)* — Rare to uncommon resident of Lower Valley coastal marshes, more numerous in winter. With patience, may be found in Black Mangrove habitats along the Laguna Madre bayshore from the South Padre Island Convention Center south to the mouth of the Rio Grande at Boca Chica.

Fox Sparrow *(Passerella iliaca)* — Eastern, or "Red," Fox Sparrow is a fairly common, but somewhat local, winter resident (November–February) on the eastern Edwards Plateau; very rare to rare on the western plateau and in the Trans-Pecos. The Intermountain, or "Slate-colored," Fox Sparrow is a very rare winter visitor to the Organ Mtns east of Las Cruces; it has yet to be documented in Texas.

Song Sparrow *(Melospiza melodia)* — Fairly common to common migrant and winter resident (late September–April) throughout, except for the Lower Valley, where very rare.

Lincoln's Sparrow *(Melospiza lincolnii)* — Fairly common migrant and winter resident (September–early May) throughout.

Swamp Sparrow *(Melospiza georgiana)* — Fairly common winter resident (mid-October–April) in appropriate habitat on the Edwards Plateau and in the eastern Trans-Pecos. Locally uncommon in coastal marshes and swamps in South Texas. Uncommon winter resident in the El Paso area along the river and in pond areas.

White-throated Sparrow *(Zonotrichia albicollis)* — Common winter resident (late October–April) on the Edwards Plateau. Rare in winter in the Trans-Pecos and the Lower Valley.

Harris's Sparrow *(Zonotrichia querula)* — Common winter resident (November–March) on the eastern Edwards Plateau. Rare on the western plateau and casual in the Trans-Pecos as far west as El Paso. Accidental in the Lower Valley.

White-crowned Sparrow *(Zonotrichia leucophrys)* — Common migrant and winter resident (September–May) throughout, but rare to uncommon in the Lower Valley east to about La Joya.

Golden-crowned Sparrow *(Zonotrichia atricapilla)* — Casual visitor (November–April) in the Trans-Pecos and, even more rarely, on the western Edwards Plateau. Typically found as a single bird, often immature, in a flock of White-crowned Sparrows.

Dark-eyed Junco *(Junco hyemalis)* — Fairly common to common migrant and winter resident (October–April) throughout, except in the Lower Valley, where accidental. "Slate-colored" birds dominate on the Edwards Plateau and are rare to uncommon westward. "Oregon" and "Gray-headed" (less common) birds dominate in the Trans-Pecos. "Gray-headed" is a fairly common breeder in the Guadalupe Mtns. Three Trans-Pecos records of "White-winged" Junco.

Yellow-eyed Junco *(Junco phaeonotus)* — Accidental. Seven accepted records, four from the Guadalupe Mtns, two from Big Bend NP, and one from El Paso. Six of the records are from November–early May, one is from June. No records since 1997.

McCown's Longspur *(Calcarius mccownii)* — Rare to very uncommon migrant and winter visitor (late October–March) to grasslands and agricultural areas of the Trans-Pecos and the Edwards Plateau. Prefers shortgrass pastures or plowed fields. Often in association with Horned Larks. Not reliable anywhere, but grasslands west of the Davis Mtns and sod farms and agricultural fields near El Paso or Dell City (Hudspeth Co) may be your best shots.

Lapland Longspur *(Calcarius lapponicus)* — Very rare winter visitor (late November–early February) to the grasslands of the Trans-Pecos.

Smith's Longspur *(Calcarius pictus)* — Accidental visitor (November) to the grasslands of the Trans-Pecos, plus one April record from Big Bend.

Chestnut-collared Longspur *(Calcarius ornatus)* — Rare to uncommon migrant and winter resident (early October–late March) to grasslands and agricultural areas in the Trans-Pecos and on the Edwards Plateau. Numbers may fluctuate from year to year, with flocks of several hundred occasionally encountered. Typically prefers taller grassland than does McCown's. Grasslands west of the Davis Mtns are often good for this species.

Snow Bunting *(Plectrophenax nivalis)* — Accidental. Three accepted records: 9 May 1988 in Big Bend, 27 November 1993 at Balmorhea Lake, and 24 December 2005–6 January 2006 at South Padre Island.

Crimson-collared Grosbeak *(Rhodothraupis celaeno)* — Casual winter visitor to the Lower Valley. Most of the state records have come from Cameron and Hidalgo Cos in winter. This species can be irruptive, as evidenced by the 17 individuals documented during the winter of 2004–2005. There are also isolated records from Laredo and coastal areas north of our region at Aransas NWR, Rockport, and Galveston. To be looked for at Sabal Palm Audubon Center, Frontera Audubon Thicket, Santa Ana NWR, McAllen, and Bentsen SP. This northeast Mexico endemic prefers a variety of habitats within its native range, including semi-arid woodland and second growth, which is similar to the thorn-scrub forest found in much of South Texas.

Northern Cardinal *(Cardinalis cardinalis)* — Common resident throughout, except in the Trans-Pecos, where it is locally common in the eastern part, but only casual in the Guadalupe Mtns and the El Paso area.

Pyrrhuloxia *(Cardinalis sinuatus)* — Fairly common to common resident of brushlands and desert in the Trans-Pecos and the Lower Valley. Fairly easy to see in the Falcon Dam area, especially at Falcon SP. Less numerous on southwestern portions of the Edwards Plateau; rare and local in eastern portions. May be more widespread in winter, when flocks are often encountered. Fairly easy to find in Big Bend NP, Falcon SP, at the base of the Franklin Mtns, and among fruiting cactus at Fort Hancock in winter.

Rose-breasted Grosbeak *(Pheucticus ludovicianus)* — Uncommon to fairly common migrant (April–early May, mid-September–October) in the Lower Valley. Rare migrant on the Edwards Plateau and in the Trans-Pecos. Rare in winter in the Lower Valley.

Black-headed Grosbeak *(Pheucticus melanocephalus)* — Fairly common to common migrant in the Trans-Pecos, and as a breeder in the Chisos, Davis, Guadalupe, and Organ Mtns. Rare migrant elsewhere. Casual in winter in the Lower Valley.

Blue Bunting *(Cyanocompsa parellina)* — Irregular and very rare winter visitor to the Lower Valley. Although this species has been recorded along the Rio Grande from Sabal Palm Audubon Center to Laredo, most sightings have occurred around the bird feeders and water features at Bentsen SP. Although male Blue Buntings are unmistakable, the identification of females should be made with caution because bright female Indigos are somewhat similar and occur in winter, when Blue Buntings are also most likely to occur.

Blue Grosbeak *(Passerina caerulea)* — Uncommon to common migrant over entire region. Common summer resident (mid-April–September) on the Edwards Plateau and throughout much of the Trans-Pecos (May–September). Less numerous in South Texas.

Lazuli Bunting *(Passerina amoena)* — Uncommon to fairly common migrant (late April–May, August–October) in the Trans-Pecos; rare to the east. Rare in winter from Big Bend NP downstream.

Indigo Bunting *(Passerina cyanea)* — Common migrant (late March–May, mid-September–early November) from the Lower Valley north to the Edwards Plateau. Rare to uncommon in the Trans-Pecos. Local summer resident on the Edwards Plateau in mesic habitats. Rare and very local breeder in the Trans-Pecos. Regular in winter in the Lower Valley.

Varied Bunting *(Passerina versicolor)* — Uncommon and local to fairly common resident (late April–August) in brushy canyons and dense thickets in southern half of the Trans-Pecos, including at Big Bend NP and Big Bend Ranch SP, and on the southwestern Edwards Plateau east to Kimble and Bandera Cos. Fairly common at Kickapoo Cavern SP and at Sam Nail Ranch, Blue Creek Canyon, and along the Window Trail in Big Bend NP. Rare in the vicinity of Carlsbad Caverns NP. Casual west to El Paso and Las Cruces. Local resident as far south as the western Lower Valley. Appears to be a rare migrant at South Padre Island and other coastal locations. Casual in winter in the Big Bend region.

Painted Bunting *(Passerina ciris)* — Uncommon to locally common summer resident in portions of the Trans-Pecos (rather spottily distributed away from the river), the Edwards Plateau, and the Lower Valley; arrives mid-April in the Lower Valley and the Hill Country, but not until May in most of the Trans-Pecos. Most often encountered in thickets and riparian edge along the Rio Grande or in the Hill Country. Fairly easy to see at Rio Grande Village in Big Bend NP west along the river to Hudspeth Co and throughout proper habitat in the Hill Country (Kickapoo Cavern SP is especially good). Migrants, especially in fall, are seen away from breeding areas. It is a fairly common migrant in the coastal Lower Valley.

Dickcissel *(Spiza americana)* — Uncommon to common summer resident (mid-April–mid-September) of pastures, farmlands, and thickets on the Edwards Plateau and in parts of South Texas. Common migrant along the Lower Coast. An uncommon to rare and somewhat sporadic fall (late August–mid-October) and accidental spring (May) migrant throughout the Trans-Pecos. Accidental in winter in the Lower Valley.

Bobolink *(Dolichonyx oryzivorus)* — Rare migrant (late April–early May, September–early October) along the coast. Accidental in the Trans-Pecos.

Red-winged Blackbird *(Agelaius phoeniceus)* — Common resident throughout, though less numerous and more local as a breeder.

Eastern Meadowlark *(Sturnella magna)* — Uncommon to common, but often local, resident throughout. The *lilianae* race breeds in the Trans-Pecos, *hoopesi* in South Texas, and *magna* on the eastern Edwards Plateau. Identification difficulties may shroud our knowledge of the winter distribution of both meadowlark species; assumptions that most winter meadowlarks in desert grassland and coastal prairie are Easterns, and those in agricultural and disturbed roadside areas are Westerns, are broadly but not absolutely correct.

Western Meadowlark *(Sturnella neglecta)* — Fairly common to common breeder in the northwestern Trans-Pecos and on the western Edwards Plateau; throughout the entire region in winter. Often breeds in agricultural habitats as opposed to the native grassland and coastal prairie preferred by Easterns.

Yellow-headed Blackbird *(Xanthocephalus xanthocephalus)* — Fairly common to common migrant and local winter resident (September–April) in the Trans-Pecos. Thousands winter around El Paso. Less numerous on the Edwards Plateau and in the Lower Valley, where it is locally rare to uncommon. Rare in summer (nonbreeding) in the Trans-Pecos.

Rusty Blackbird *(Euphagus carolinus)* — Rare winter visitor (December–February) on the eastern Edwards Plateau; casual elsewhere.

Brewer's Blackbird *(Euphagus cyanocephalus)* — Fairly common to common migrant and winter resident (September–April) throughout, except only rare to uncommon in the Lower Valley. Accidental breeder in the Davis Mtns.

Common Grackle *(Quiscalus quiscula)* — Common resident, primarily in urban areas, on the Edwards Plateau. A casual to rare winter visitor in El Paso and Las Cruces. Accidental in the Lower Valley in winter and spring.

Boat-tailed Grackle *(Quiscalus major)* — Accidental south to Willacy Co on the coastal northern edge of the Lower Valley. Locally common resident on the central and upper Texas coast.

Great-tailed Grackle *(Quiscalus mexicanus)* — Very common permanent resident in the Lower Valley and on the eastern Edwards Plateau. Very common summer resident and fairly common and more localized winter resident in cities and towns throughout the Trans-Pecos. Seldom found far from urban or agricultural areas in West Texas.

Bronzed Cowbird *(Molothrus aeneus)* — Common summer resident in the Lower Valley and on the Edwards Plateau; uncommon and often highly localized in migration and winter. Rare to fairly common summer resident thoughout the Trans-Pecos; casual in winter. Most often found in agricultural fields and at feedlots. Bronzed Cowbirds may be found in large Red-winged Blackbird flocks and in mixed-blackbird roosts in McAllen, Harlingen, and Brownsville.

Brown-headed Cowbird *(Molothrus ater)* — Fairly common to common resident throughout. Trans-Pecos populations smaller and more localized in winter.

Black-vented Oriole *(Icterus wagleri)* — Accidental. Two records from Rio Grande Village, Big Bend NP: the first involved a bird found 27 February 1967 that returned for the next two summers; the second was seen there on 6 October 2006.

Orchard Oriole *(Icterus spurius)* — Uncommon to fairly common migrant throughout, except in extreme West Texas (El Paso Co), where casual to rare. Uncommon to locally common breeder in much of the region, but absent from much of the Lower Valley, and local in the Trans-Pecos, mostly along the Pecos River and the Rio Grande west through eastern Hudspeth Co. The *fuertesi* race—a distinct subspecies breeding in northeastern Mexico—is accidental in the Lower Valley in spring and summer: Brownsville 3 April 1894 and Arroyo City (Cameron Co) 15 April–17 July 1998 and again 11 April–17 July 1999.

Hooded Oriole *(Icterus cucullatus)* — Uncommon to locally fairly common summer resident (late March–September) in South Texas; found along the Rio Grande from the Lower Valley west to El Paso. Uncommon to fairly common from Sabal Palm Audubon Center to San Ygnacio, where it prefers to nest in palms; rare at El Paso. Often found at hummingbird feeders throughout the Rio Grande corridor and adjacent counties. Locally common on the southwestern Edwards Plateau, rare elsewhere on the plateau. Rare in the Lower Valley during winter.

Streak-backed Oriole *(Icterus pustulatus)* — Accidental. One Trans-Pecos record: El Paso 16 Sep 2005. One photographed at Radium Springs, just north of Las Cruces 20 December 2003.

Bullock's Oriole *(Icterus bullockii)* — Fairly common to common migrant and local breeder (April–September) in the Trans-Pecos and on the Edwards Plateau; rare to uncommon in the western Lower Valley (Falcon Dam area). Rare but regular in migration near the coast. Casual in winter throughout.

Altamira Oriole *(Icterus gularis)* — Uncommon resident in the Lower Valley from southeast Brownsville upriver to Zapata, rarely to San Ygnacio. Good spots include Resaca de la Palma SP in Brownsville, Estero Llano Grande SP in Weslaco, Santa Ana NWR, Bentsen SP, and Salineño and Chapeño . Also found in wooded residential areas throughout the Lower Valley, where it is local.

Audubon's Oriole (*Icterus graduacauda*) — Rare to uncommon resident in South Texas west to Del Rio, most common along the Rio Grande between Fronton and Falcon Dam. To be looked for at Roma Bluffs, Salineño feeders (November–March), and Chapeño. Vagrant to the southern Edwards Plateau.

Baltimore Oriole (*Icterus galbula*) — Fairly common migrant in the Lower Valley and on the Edwards Plateau (April–May, August–early October). Casual migrant in the Trans-Pecos. Casual to rare in the Lower Valley in winter.

Scott's Oriole (*Icterus parisorum*) — Fairly common summer resident (April–October) of oak/juniper woodlands and yucca grasslands in the Trans-Pecos and the western and central Edwards Plateau. Can usually be found along the Window Trail in Big Bend NP, at Davis Mtns SP, Franklin Mtns SP, Aguirre Springs in the Organ Mtns, McKittrick Canyon, and in Lost Maples SNA. Accidental visitor to the Lower Valley.

Pine Grosbeak (*Pinicola enucleator*) — Accidental. One photographed in the Guadalupe Mtns 24 November 2000.

Purple Finch (*Carpodacus purpureus*) — Very rare winter visitor (December–February) to the eastern Edwards Plateau. Accidental in the Davis Mtns and the El Paso area.

Cassin's Finch (*Carpodacus cassinii*) — Irregular, rare to uncommon winter visitor (November–April) in the Trans-Pecos. Absent many years. Accidental on the western Edwards Plateau and in the Lower Valley.

House Finch (*Carpodacus mexicanus*) — Common resident in the Trans-Pecos and on the Edwards Plateau south to Laredo. Casual in the Lower Valley.

Red Crossbill (*Loxia curvirostra*) — Highly irregular, rare to fairly common winter visitor (October–May) in the Trans-Pecos, and, more rarely, on the Edwards Plateau. A rare to uncommon and irregular breeder in the Davis and Guadalupe Mtns. May breed at odd localities after major invasion winters, such as that of 1996–1997 and 2000–2001. Accidental in the Lower Valley.

Pine Siskin (*Carduelis pinus*) — Irregular, uncommon to common migrant and winter visitor (October–May) throughout, though absent most years in the Lower Valley. Sporadic breeding records from the Davis and Guadalupe Mtns.

Lesser Goldfinch (*Carduelis psaltria*) — Uncommon to fairly common permanent resident throughout the Edwards Plateau and much of the Trans-Pecos. Local breeder in the Trans-Pecos. Decidedly less numerous in winter in most areas. Locally uncommon to fairly common summer resident in the Lower Valley, becoming less numerous in winter.

Lawrence's Goldfinch *(Carduelis lawrencei)* — Accidental to casual and highly irregular winter visitor (October–April) in the Trans-Pecos. Prior to October 1996, there were only two accepted Texas records, along with numerous undocumented reports from earlier invasions. A major incursion during the winter of 1996–1997 brought hundreds of birds to the El Paso/Las Cruces area, as well as scattered records throughout the western Trans-Pecos. Absent the great majority of years.

American Goldfinch *(Carduelis tristis)* — Common winter resident (November–May) throughout most of the region. Uncommon to fairly common but irregular in parts of the Trans-Pecos, including El Paso. A few birds often remain into May.

Evening Grosbeak *(Coccothraustes vespertinus)* — Highly irregular, casual to rare and decreasing winter visitor to the Trans-Pecos and the Edwards Plateau. Not to be expected most years.

House Sparrow *(Passer domesticus)* — Common resident around human habitations throughout.

OTHER VERTEBRATES EXCLUSIVE OF FISH

Allan H. Chaney

ALLIGATORS

American Alligator—Ponds, resacas, streams; South Texas except coastal.

TURTLES

Common Snapping Turtle—Some permanent waters; Edwards Plateau.
Yellow Mud Turtle—Permanent waters with mud bottoms; throughout
Big Bend Mud Turtle—Rare, cattle tanks; Presidio County.
Desert and Ornate Box Turtle—Sandy plains, prairies, bottomlands; throughout.
Texas Map Turtle—Clear vegetated streams; central Colorado River basin only, Edwards Plateau.
Cagle's Map Turtle—Clear streams; Guadalupe River Basin only, Edwards Plateau.
Big Bend Slider Turtle—Muddy bottom ponds and streams; Brewster, Presidio, and Hudspeth Counties.
Red-eared Slider Turtle—Muddy streams and ponds; throughout except Big Bend.
Zug's River Cooter—Clear streams and ponds; Pecos and Rio Grande drainages
Texas River Cooter—Clear streams; Guadalupe and Colorado River basins, Edwards Plateau.
Western Painted Turtle—Clear streams; Culberson and El Paso Counties.
Texas Tortoise—Dry brushlands and sandy areas; South Texas to Val Verde County.
Spiny Softshells (2)—Rivers, lakes, ponds; throughout.
Stinkpot—Muddy bottom streams and ponds; eastern Edwards Plateau.

LIZARDS

Mediterranean Gecko—Introduced, commensal with man in buildings; South Texas, Val Verde, Brewster, and El Paso Counties.
Texas Banded Gecko—Rocky areas; throughout except eastern Edwards Plateau and eastern South Texas.
Reticulated Gecko—Dry rocky areas; Presidio and Brewster Counties.
Western Spiny-tailed Iguana—Escapees; Brownsville area.
Green Anole—Commensal with man, spreading; eastern and lower South Texas and Del Rio.
Collared Lizards (3)—Rocky areas; Balcones Escarpment to El Paso.
Reticulate Collared Lizard—Sandstone rock outcrops; Eagle Pass to McAllen.

Longnose Leopard Lizard—Desert flats; Big Bend to El Paso.
Texas and Southwestern Earless Lizard—Rocky areas; throughout to Cameron County.
Speckled Earless Lizard—Desert washes; Trans-Pecos.
Plateau and Southern Earless Lizard—Brushlands and road margins; Edwards Plateau to upper South Texas.
Keeled Earless Lizard—Sandy savannahs and dry brushlands; Laredo east to the Gulf.
Rosebelly Lizard—Brushlands and rocky areas; South Texas.
Mesquite Lizard—Commensal with man, in mesquite trees; South Texas.
Crevice Spiny Lizard—Rocky areas; Edwards Plateau to El Paso.
Blue Spiny Lizard—Rocky areas; Del Rio to McAllen.
Twin-spotted Spiny Lizard—Dry areas; Trans-Pecos.
Texas Spiny Lizard—Woodlands; throughout, Big Bend to Brownsville.
Prairie and Fence Lizards—Many habitats; throughout.
Canyon Lizards (3)—Rocky canyon walls; Del Rio through Big Bend.
Eastern and Big Bend Tree Lizards—Trees and rocky areas; Trans-Pecos, Edwards Plateau, and along Rio Grande to Brownsville.
Desert Side-blotched Lizard—Desert flats; Trans-Pecos.
Texas Horned Lizard—Open terrain; throughout.
Mountain Short-horned Lizard—Forests; Davis and Guadalupe mountains.
Round-tailed Horned Lizard—Dry, open, rocky terrain; Trans-Pecos, western Edwards Plateau, Zapata County.
Texas Spotted Whiptail—Rocky grasslands; throughout except Hudspeth and El Paso Counties.
New Mexico Whiptail—Sandy washes; El Paso Valley.
Gray-checkered Whiptail—Dry rocky areas; Presidio County.
Chihuahuan Spotted Whiptail—Open area habitats; Big Bend to El Paso.
Desert Grassland Whiptail—Open grasslands; El Paso Valley.
Plateau Spotted Whiptail—Dry rocky flats; Big Bend.
Trans-Pecos Striped Whiptail—Dry rocky foothills; Trans-Pecos.
Prairie-lined and Yellow-headed Race Runners—Open sandy areas; South Texas to Del Rio.
Colorado Checkered Whiptail—Rocky flats; Trans-Pecos.
Marbled Whiptail—Desert flats; Laredo to El Paso.
Laredo Striped Whiptail—Open dry areas; Rio Grande basin, Laredo to McAllen.
Ground Skink—Oak woodlands; Edwards Plateau and eastern South Texas to Willacy County.
Short-lined and Four-lined Skinks—Many variable habitats; throughout except Guadalupe Mountains.
Great Plains Skink—Sandy and loamy soils; throughout.
Variable Skink—Debris piles; Davis and Guadalupe mountains.
Western Slender Glass Lizard—Sandy coastal soils near water; coastal South Texas.
Texas Alligator Lizard—Rocky woodlands; Edwards Plateau and Brewster County.

SNAKES

New Mexico and Plains Blind Snakes—Variable moist habitats; throughout.
Trans-Pecos Blind Snake—Rocky areas near water; Del Rio to El Paso.
Diamondback Water Snake—Ponds, tanks, and streams; throughout from Big Bend east.
Blotched Water Snake—Ponds and streams; Davis Mountains, Big Bend, Edwards Plateau, Starr County, NE South Texas.
Texas Brown Snake—Variable habitats; South Texas.
New Mexico Garter Snake—Near water; El Paso.
Eastern Checkered Garter Snake—Near water; throughout.
Blackneck Garter Snakes (2)—Near water; Trans-Pecos and Edwards Plateau.
Ribbon Snakes (4)—Near water; throughout from Big Bend east.

Texas Lined Snake—Under debris; Edwards Plateau and Duval, McMullen, and LaSalle Counties.

Eastern Hognose Snake—Variable habitats; eastern Edwards Plateau and northern SouthTexas.

Mexican and Dusky Hognose Snakes—Variable habitats; throughout.

Regal and Prairie Ringneck Snakes—Woodland; Trans-Pecos and Edwards Plateau.

Racers (3)—Variable habitats, open areas; Davis Mountains, eastern South Texas, and eastern Edwards Plateau.

Western Coachwhip—Open areas; throughout.

Whipsnakes (2)—Variable habitats; throughout

Western Rough Green Snake—River thickets; throughout except Big Bend to El Paso.

Speckled Racer—Resaca and river thickets; Cameron County.

Texas Indigo Snake—Variable habitats; South Texas from Del Rio east.

Big Bend Patchnose Snake—Rocky lowlands; Big Bend to El Paso.

Texas and Mountain Patchnose Snakes—Rocky areas; throughout.

Trans-Pecos Rat Snake—Rocky areas; El Paso to Uvalde.

Great Plains Rat Snake—Variable habitats; throughout.

Texas Rat Snake—Variable habitats; South Texas and eastern Edwards Plateau.

Baird's Rat Snake—Rocky outcrops; Big Bend and western Edwards Plateau.

Glossy Snakes (3)—Sandy and dry open habitats; throughout except Edwards Plateau.

Sonoran Gopher and Bull Snakes—Variable dry habitats; throughout.

Gray-banded Kingsnake—Dry rocky areas; Trans-Pecos east to Edwards County.

Prairie Kingsnake—Coastal brushland and open pasture; eastern South Texas to Willacy County.

Desert Kingsnake—Variable habitats; throughout.

Texas Longnose Snake—Friable and sandy soils; throughout except central Edwards Plateau.

Texas Scarlet Snake—Sandy areas of South Texas.

Milk Snakes (2)—Variable habitats; throughout.

Ground Snake—Open terrain under rocks and debris; throughout.

Black-striped Snake—Under debris; Lower Rio Grande Valley.

Western Hooknose Snake—Under debris in arid open regions; Trans-Pecos and Edwards Plateau.

Mexican Hooknose Snake—Under debris in arid open regions; South Texas.

Texas Night Snake—Under debris in various habitats; throughout.

Northern Cat-eyed Snake—Near water; coastal South Texas and Hidalgo County.

Big Bend Blackhead and Devils River Blackhead Snakes—variable habitats; Val Verde, Brewster, Presidio, Pecos, and Jeff Davis Counties.

Flathead Snake—Under debris and rocks; Brewster County, Edwards Plateau south to McAllen.

Texas Blackhead Snake—Under debris and rocks, variable habitats; throughout.

Southwestern Blackhead Snake—Under rocks and debris in dry areas; Webb County, Trans-Pecos, Edwards Plateau.

Rough Earth Snake—Under rocks and debris; Coastal South Texas to Willacy County.

Trans-Pecos and Broad-banded Copperhead—Woodland and rocky habitat; absent from South Texas and west of Davis Mountains.

Western Cottonmouth—Near ponds and rivers; eastern Edwards Plateau.

Texas Coral Snake—Variable habitats; Pecos County east and south throughout.

Massasaugas (2)—Dry and sandy grasslands; Trans-Pecos except Big Bend, South Texas.

Western Diamondback Rattlesnake—Various habitats; throughout.

Mojave Rattlesnake—Desert and foothills; Big Bend to El Paso.

Prairie Rattlesnake—Prairies and rocky areas; Trans-Pecos.

Blacktail Rattlesnake—Rocky desert areas; Edwards Plateau and Trans-Pecos.

Banded and Mottled Rock Rattlesnakes—Rocky cliffs of higher elevations; Edwards Plateau and Trans-Pecos.

SALAMANDERS

Lesser Sirens (2)—Isolated ponds and resacas; South Texas.
Barred Tiger Salamander—Isolated ponds; South Texas and Trans-Pecos.
Black-spotted Newt—Isolated ponds; coastal counties of South Texas.
Whitethroat Slimy Salamander—around springs and caves; Balcones Escarpment.
Texas Salamander—Helotes Creek Spring; Balcones Escarpment.
Texas Blind Salamander—Springs and caves; extreme eastern Balcones Escarpment.
Blanco Blind Salamander—Springs and caves; extreme eastern Balcones Escarpment.
Comal Blind Salamander—Springs and caves; extreme eastern Balcones Escarpment.
Barton Springs Salamander—Springs; Hays County, Balcones Escarpment.
San Marcos Salamander—Springs; Hays County, Balcones Escarpment.
Fern Bank Salamander—Springs; Hays County, Balcones Escarpment.
Cascade Cave Salamander—Cave; Kendall County, Balcones Escarpment.
Unnamed, several new species—Springs; Kerr, Bandera, Real, Medina, Gillespie, Uvalde, Val Verde Counties.
Valdina Farms Salamander—Sinkhole; Medina County, Balcones Escarpment.
Unnamed, a new species—Springs; Bell, Travis, Williamson Counties.

TOADS AND FROGS

Mexican Burrowing Toad—Rare around Falcon Lake; Starr and Zapata Counties.
Hurter's Spadefoot—Temporary water on sandy plains; South Texas.
Couch's Spadefoot—Temporary water in variable habitat; throughout.
Plains Spadefoot—Temporary water in variable habitat; South Texas and Trans-Pecos except Big Bend.
New Mexico Spadefoot—Temporary water in grasslands; Trans-Pecos and western Edwards Plateau.
White-lipped Frog—Near water; Hidalgo and Starr Counties, South Texas.
Eastern Barking Frog—In crevices and under limestone rocks; Edwards Plateau.
Cliff Chirping Frog—Cracks and crevices in limestone cliffs; Edwards Plateau.
Spotted Chirping Frog—Wet rocky areas; Big Bend.
Rio Grande Chirping Frog—Moist areas; Cameron and Hidalgo Counties, South Texas.
Woodhouse's Toads (2)—Lowland ponds; Trans-Pecos and coastal Lower Rio Grande Valley.
Gulf Coast Toad—Various habitats near water; throughout from Brewster County, south and east.
Great Plains Toad—Temporary water; Brewster County north and west to border.
Texas Toad—Temporary water in lowlands; throughout.
Red-spotted Toad—Under stones near water; throughout except eastern South Texas.
Green Toads (2)—Under debris and rocks in various habitats; throughout.
Giant Toad—Ponds, lakes, resacas; Lower Rio Grande Valley.
Blanchard's Cricket Frog—Edges of streams and lakes; throughout except west of Big Bend.
Green Tree Frog—Pond and lake shores; coastal South Texas.
Canyon Tree Frog—Rocky canyons and streams; Big Bend and Davis Mountains.
Mexican Tree Frog—Cities and near woodland ponds; Cameron and Hidalgo Counties.
Gray Tree Frog—Trees near temporary water; eastern Edwards Plateau.
Spotted Chorus Frog—Ditches and temporary pools in grasslands; eastern Edwards Plateau and South Texas.
Strecker's Chorus Frog—Near water in various habitats; eastern Edwards Plateau and Kenedy, Brooks, and Willacy Counties in South Texas.
Great Plains Narrowmouth Toad—Ditches and pools, grasslands; throughout except El Paso Valley.
Sheep Frog—Sandy brushlands and coastal plains; eastern South Texas.
Bullfrog—Permanent waters; throughout except Presidio and Counties north.
Rio Grande Leopard Frog—Near water in various habitats; throughout.

MARSUPIALS

Opossum—Woodlands, cities and farms; South Texas and Edwards Plateau.

SHREWS AND MOLES

Desert Shrew—Brushlands and deserts; throughout.
Least Shrew—Grasslands; South Texas.
Eastern Mole—Sandy soils; eastern South Texas.

BATS

Ghost-faced Bat—Caves; Big Bend, Edwards Plateau, South Texas.
Mexican Long-nosed Bat—Cave; Chisos Mountains.
Hairy-legged Vampire Bat—Caves; Val Verde County.
Little Brown Myotis—Rare, elevated areas; Hudspeth County.
Yuma Myotis—Caves and crevices; Trans-Pecos.
Cave Myotis—Caves; Trans-Pecos and Edwards Plateau.
Fringed Myotis—Caves and crevices; Trans-Pecos.
Long-legged Myotis—Caves, crevices, buildings; Trans-Pecos.
California Myotis—Wooded canyons, caves, buildings; Trans-Pecos.
Western Small-footed Myotis—Deserts, caves, buildings; Trans-Pecos.
Silver-haired Bat—Caves and buildings; Davis Mountains; Edwards Plateau.
Western Pipistrel—Caves and crevices; Trans-Pecos.
Eastern Pipistrel—Caves and crevices; Edwards Plateau, South Texas.
Big Brown Bat—Woodlands, caves, buildings; Trans-Pecos.
Eastern Red Bat—Woodlands; throughout.
Seminole Bat—Woodlands; Edward's Plateau, South Texas.
Hoary Bat—Woodlands; throughout.
Northern and Southern Yellow Bats—Palm trees; Lower Rio grande Valley.
Evening Bat—Woodlands; Edwards Plateau, South Texas.
Spotted Bat—Crevices; Big Bend, El Paso Valley.
Townsend's Big-eared Bat—Caves and crevices; Trans-Pecos.
Pallid Bat—Crevices and buildings; Trans-Pecos, Edwards Plateau.
Brazilian Free-tailed Bat—Caves and buildings; throughout.
Pocketed Free-tailed Bat—Caves and crevices; Trans-Pecos.
Big Free-tailed Bat—Caves and crevices; Trans-Pecos.
Western Mastiff Bat—Caves and buildings; Trans-Pecos.

CARNIVORES

Black Bear—Rare, forests; mountains of Trans-Pecos.
Raccoon—Variable habitats except deserts; throughout.
White-nosed Coati—Rare, woodlands along Rio Grande; throughout.
Ringtail—Brushlands and rocky areas; throughout except South Texas.
Long-tailed Weasel—Rare, variable habitats; throughout.
American Badger—Grasslands and deserts; throughout.
Eastern and Western Spotted Skunks—Variable habitats; throughout.
Striped Skunk—Variable habitats; throughout.
Hooded Skunk—Rare, woodlands and rocky areas; Trans-Pecos.
Common Hog-nosed Skunk—Varied habitats; throughout.
Coyote—Varied habitats; throughout.
Kit Fox—Deserts; Trans-Pecos.
Common Gray Fox—Woodland, brushland, rocky areas; throughout.
Mountain Lion—Rare, canyons and brushlands; throughout.
Ocelot—Rare, thick brush; South Texas.
Jaguarundi—Very rare, thick brush; South Texas.
Bobcat—Brushlands and rocky areas; throughout.

RODENTS

Rock Squirrel—Rocky areas; Trans-Pecos, Edwards Plateau.
Mexican Ground Squirrel—Sandy grasslands and brushlands; throughout.
Spotted Ground Squirrel—Sandy grasslands and deserts; throughout except Edwards Plateau.
Texas Antelope Squirrel—Rocky areas of deserts; Trans-Pecos.
Gray-footed Chipmunk—Forests; Guadalupe Mountains.
Eastern Fox Squirrel—Woodlands and cities; Edwards Plateau, South Texas.
Black-tailed Prairie Dog—Prairies; Trans-Pecos.
Desert Pocket Gopher—Friable and sandy soils; Trans-Pecos.
Plains Pocket Gopher—Grasslands; eastern Edwards Plateau.
Botta's Pocket Gopher—Varied soils desert to montane; Trans-Pecos and western Edwards Plateau.
Yellow-faced Pocket Gopher—Alluvial soils along streams; Trans-Pecos and Lower Rio Grande Valley.
Texas Pocket Gopher—Sandy soils; South Texas.
Mexican Spiny Pocket Mouse—Palm and brush thickets; Lower Rio Grande Valley.
Silky Pocket Mouse—Varied dry habitats; throughout.
Desert Pocket Mouse—Sandy deserts; Trans-Pecos.
Rock Pocket Mouse—Rocky areas; western Trans-Pecos.
Nelson's Pocket Mouse—Rocky slopes; Trans-Pecos.
Hispid Pocket Mouse—Varied habitats; throughout except western Trans-Pecos.
Banner-tailed Kangaroo Rat—Grasslands; northern and western Trans-Pecos.
Ord's Kangaroo Rat—Sandy deserts and grasslands; Trans-Pecos and western South Texas.
Padre Island Kangaroo Rat—Sandy grasslands; eastern South Texas.
Merriam's Kangaroo Rat—Deserts and grasslands; Trans-Pecos.
American Beaver—Wooded streams; throughout.
Plains Harvest Mouse—Grasslands; Trans-Pecos, Edwards Plateau.
Western Harvest Mouse—Grasslands and deserts; Trans-Pecos.
Fulvous Harvest Mouse—Grasslands; throughout except western Trans-Pecos.
Cactus Mouse—Low rocky deserts; Del Rio to El Paso.
Deer Mouse—Varied habitats; Trans-Pecos, eastern Edwards Plateau.
White-ankled Mouse—Rocky woodlands and brushlands; Trans-Pecos and Balcones Escarpment.
Northern Pygmy Mouse—Short grasslands, sandy soil; South Texas.
Brush Mouse—Rocky montane slopes; Trans-Pecos.
Pinyon Mouse—Rocky pinyon-juniper slopes; Guadalupe Mountains.
Rock Mouse—Rocky peaks of mountains; Trans-Pecos.
Texas Mouse—Rocky juniper associations; eastern Edwards Plateau.
Northern Grasshopper Mouse—Grasslands; throughout except Big Bend.
Mearn's Grasshopper Mouse—Grasslands and deserts; Trans-Pecos.
Southern Plains Woodrat—Deserts and brushlands; throughout.
White-throated Woodrat—Desert brushlands; Trans-Pecos.
Mexican Woodrat—Rocky elevated areas; Trans-Pecos.
Marsh Rice Rat—marshlands; coastal northern South Texas.
Coues' Rice Rat—marshlands; Lower Rio Grande Valley.
Hispid Cotton Rat—Tall grasslands and fields; throughout.
Yellow-nosed Cotton Rat—Tall grasslands; Big Bend and Davis Mountains.
Tawny-bellied Cotton Rat—Tall grasslands; Davis Mountains.
Mexican Vole—Open forests; Guadalupe Mountains.
Muskrat—Drainage ditches; El Paso.
Roof Rat—Cities; Lower Rio Grande Valley.
Norway Rat—Cities; throughout.
House Mouse—Cities and farms; throughout.

Porcupine—Woodlands in rocky areas; Trans-Pecos, Edwards Plateau.
Nutria—Marshes, ponds and streams; South Texas, Edwards Plateau.

RABBITS

Black-tailed Jack Rabbit—Open areas in varied habitats; throughout.
Eastern Cottontail—Open brushlands and woodlands; throughout except western Trans-Pecos.
Desert Cottontail—Open plains and deserts; throughout except coastal South Texas.

EVEN-TOED UNGULATES

Collared Peccary—Brushlands and desert; throughout.
Elk—Forests; Guadalupe Mountains.
Mule Deer—Deserts, brushlands, forests; Trans-Pecos.
White-tailed Deer—Varied wooded habitats; throughout.
Pronghorn—Prairies; Trans-Pecos.
Mountain Sheep—Rare, rocky terrain; Big Bend and adjacent areas.
Bison—Reintroduced to prairies; Trans-Pecos.

EDENTATES

Nine-banded Armadillo—Woodlands and brushlands; Edwards Plateau and South Texas.

INTRODUCED EXOTICS THAT HAVE ESCAPED AND ESTABLISHED WILD POPULATIONS

Axis Deer
Fallow Deer
Sika Deer
Nilgai
Barbary Sheep
Blackbuck
Aoudad

Selected References

Ajilvsgi, G. 1984. *Wildflowers of Texas*. Shearer Publishing, Bryan, Texas.

Benson, L. 1982. *Cacti of the United States and Canada*. Stanford University Press, Stanford, California.

Bomar, G. W. 1983. *Texas Weather*. University of Texas Press, Austin.

Brock, J. P., and K. Kaufman. 2003. *Butterflies of North America*. Houghton Mifflin, Boston.

Brush, T. 2005. *Nesting Birds of a Tropical Frontier: The Lower Rio Grande Valley of Texas*. Texas A&M University Press, College Station.

Bryan, K., T. Gallucci, G. Lasley, M. Lockwood, and D. H. Riskind. 2006. *A Checklist of Texas Birds*. Texas Parks and Wildlife Press, Austin.

Chaney, A. H. 1982 rev. 1996. *Keys to the Vertebrates of Texas Exclusive of Birds*. Biology Department, Texas A&I University, Kingsville.

Cooksey, M., and R. Weeks. 2006. *A Birder's Guide to the Texas Coast*. Fifth ed. American Birding Association, Colorado Springs, Colorado.

Cox, P., and P. Leslie. 1988. *Texas Trees: A Friendly Guide*. Corona Press, San Antonios.

Davis, W. B., and D. J. Schmidly. 1994. *The Mammals of Texas*. Texas Parks and Wildlife Press, Austin.

Dixon, J. R. 1987. *Amphibians and Reptiles of Texas, with keys, taxonomic synopses, bibliography, and distribution maps*. Texas A&M University Press, College Station.

Enquist, M. 1987. *Wildflowers of the Texas Hill Country*. Lone Star Botanical, Austin.

Everitt, J. H., and D. L. Drawe. 1993. *Trees, Shrubs & Cacti of South Texas*. Texas Tech University Press, Lubbock.

Garrett, J. M., and D. G. Baker. 1987. *A Field Guide to Reptiles and Amphibians of Texas*. Texas Monthly Press, Austin.

Howell, S. N. G., and S. Webb. 1995. *A Guide to the Birds of Mexico and Northern Central America.* Oxford University Press, New York.

Lellinger, D. B. 1985. *Field Manual of the Ferns and Fern-allies of the United States and Canada.* Smithsonian Press, Washington, D.C.

Lockwood, M. W. 2001. *Birds of the Texas Hill Country.* University of Texas Press, Austin.

Lockwood, M. W., and B. Freeman. 2004. *The TOS Handbook of Texas Birds.* Texas A&M University Press, College Station.

Lonard, R. I., J. H. Everitt, and F. W. Judd. 1991. *Woody Plants of the Lower Rio Grande Valley, Texas.* Misc. Paper #7. Texas Memorial Museum, University of Texas at Austin.

Loughmiller, C., and L. Loughmiller. 1984. *Texas Wildflowers: A Field Guide.* University of Texas Press, Austin.

Kutac, E. A. 1998. *Birder's Guide to Texas.* Lone Star Books, Houston.

Kutac, E., and S. C. Caran. 1993. *Birds and Other Wildlife of South Central Texas.* University of Texas Press, Austin.

McKinney, B. 2002. *A Checklist of Lower Rio Grande Valley Birds.* Valley Nature Center, Weslaco, Texas.

Neihaus, T. F. 1984. *A Field Guide to the Southwestern and Texas Wildflowers.* Houghton Mifflin, Boston.

Oberholser, H. C. 1974. *The Bird Life of Texas.* University of Texas Press, Austin.

Overton, M. D. 2003. Rev. 2007. *Butterflies of Uvalde County, Texas – Field Checklist.* Texas Hill Country River Region, Uvalde, Texas.

Overton, M. D., and S. King. 2006. *Frontera Audubon's Butterfly Checklist – Cameron, Hidalgo and Starr Counties, Texas.* Frontera Audubon, Weslaco, Texas.

Pelham, J. P. 2006. Checklist of the Butterflies of the United States and Canada. From: Pelham, J. P. (in press). *Catalogue of the Butterflies of the United States and Canada.* Vol 40. Journal of Research on the Lepidoptera.

Peterson, J. J., and B. R. Zimmer. 1998. *Birds of the Trans-Pecos.* University of Texas Press, Austin.

Peterson, R. T. 1963. *A Field Guide to the Birds of Texas.* Houghton Mifflin Company, Boston.

Powell, A. M. 1998. *Trees and Shrubs of Trans-Pecos Texas, including Big Bend and Guadalupe Mountains National Park.* University of Texas Press, Austin.

————. 1994. *Grasses of the Trans-Pecos and Adjacent Areas.* University of Texas Press, Austin.

Richardson, A. 1990. *Plants of Southernmost Texas.* University of Texas at Brownsville, Brownsville.

Schmidley, David J., 1977. *The Mammals of Trans-Pecos Texas.* Texas A&M University Press.

————. 1991. *The Bats of Texas.* Texas A&M University Press, College Station.

Scott, J. A. 1986. *Butterflies of North America, a natural history and field guide.* Stanford University Press, Stanford, Calif.

Taylor, R. B., J. Rutledge, and J. G. Herrera. 1994. *A Field Guide to Common South Texas Shrubs.* Texas Parks and Wildlife Press, Austin.

Tennant, A. 1984. *The Snakes of Texas.* Texas Monthly Press, Austin.

Texas Ornithological Society. 1995. *Checklist of the Birds of Texas.* Printed by Capital Printing Inc., Austin.

Vines, R. 1960. *Trees, Shrubs, and Woody Vines of the Southwest.* University of Texas Press, Austin.

Warnock, B. H. 1970. *Wildflowers of the Big Bend Country, Texas.* Sul Ross University Press, Alpine, Texas.

————. 1974. *Wildflowers of the Guadalupe Mountains and the Sand Dune Country, Texas.* Sul Ross University Press, Alpine, Texas.

————. 1977. *Wildflowers of the Davis Mountains and the Marathon Basin, Texas.* Sul Ross University Press, Alpine, Texas.

Wauer, R. H. 1980. *Naturalist's Big Bend.* Texas A & M University Press, College Station.

————. 1996. *A Field Guide to Birds of the Big Bend.* Gulf Publishing, Houston.

West, S. 2000. *Northern Chihuahuan Desert Wildflowers.* Falcon Publishing, Helena, Montana.

TEXAS BIRD RECORDS COMMITTEE'S LIST OF REVIEW SPECIES

REVIEW LIST A — RARITIES

These species, in general, include birds that have occurred four or fewer times per year anywhere in Texas over a ten-year average. The TBRC requests documentation for review for any new or any previously unsubmitted record of the below species, no matter how long ago the record occurred. The TBRC also requests details on any record of a species not yet accepted on the Texas State List.

Brant
Trumpeter Swan
Eurasian Wigeon
American Black Duck
White-cheeked Pintail
Garganey
King Eider
Common Eider
Harlequin Duck
Barrow's Goldeneye
Masked Duck
Yellow-billed Loon
Red-necked Grebe
American Flamingo
Yellow-nosed Albatross
White-chinned Petrel
Black-capped Petrel
Stejneger's Petrel
Greater Shearwater
Sooty Shearwater
Manx Shearwater

Wilson's Storm-Petrel
Leach's Storm-Petrel
Red-billed Tropicbird
Blue-footed Booby
Brown Booby
Red-footed Booby
Jabiru
Snail Kite
Northern Goshawk
Crane Hawk
Roadside Hawk
Short-tailed Hawk
Collared Forest-Falcon
Gyrfalcon
Paint-billed Crake
Spotted Rail
Double-striped Thick-knee
Pacific Golden-Plover
Collared Plover
Northern Jacana
Wandering Tattler

Spotted Redshank
Eskimo Curlew
Surfbird
Red-necked Stint
Sharp-tailed Sandpiper
Purple Sandpiper
Curlew Sandpiper
Ruff
Red Phalarope
Black-legged Kittiwake
Black-headed Gull
Little Gull
Black-tailed Gull
Heermann's Gull
Mew Gull
Western Gull
Iceland Gull
Slaty-backed Gull
Glaucous-winged Gull
Great Black-backed Gull
Kelp Gull
Brown Noddy
Black Noddy
Roseate Tern
Arctic Tern
Elegant Tern
South Polar Skua
Long-tailed Jaeger
Ruddy Ground-Dove
Ruddy Quail-Dove
Dark-billed Cuckoo
Mangrove Cuckoo
Snowy Owl
Northern Pygmy-Owl
Mottled Owl
Stygian Owl
Northern Saw-whet Owl
White-collared Swift
Green Violetear
Green-breasted Mango
White-eared Hummingbird
Berylline Hummingbird

Violet-crowned Hummingbird
Costa's Hummingbird
Elegant Trogon
Red-breasted Sapsucker
Ivory-billed Woodpecker (presumed
    extirpated in Texas)
Barred Antshrike
Greenish Elaenia
Tufted Flycatcher
Greater Pewee
Buff-breasted Flycatcher
Dusky-capped Flycatcher
Social Flycatcher
Sulphur-bellied Flycatcher
Piratic Flycatcher
Thick-billed Kingbird
Gray Kingbird
Fork-tailed Flycatcher
Rose-throated Becard
Masked Tityra
Black-whiskered Vireo
Yucatan Vireo
Brown Jay
Clark's Nutcracker
Black-billed Magpie
Tamaulipas Crow
Gray-breasted Martin
Black-capped Chickadee
American Dipper
Northern Wheatear
Orange-billed Nightingale-Thrush
Black-headed Nightingale-Thrush
White-throated Thrush
Rufous-backed Robin
Varied Thrush
Aztec Thrush
Black Catbird
Blue Mockingbird
Bohemian Waxwing
Gray Silky-flycatcher
Olive Warbler
Connecticut Warbler

Gray-crowned Yellowthroat
Slate-throated Redstart
Fan-tailed Warbler
Golden-crowned Warbler
Rufous-capped Warbler
Flame-colored Tanager
Yellow-faced Grassquit
Baird's Sparrow
Golden-crowned Sparrow
Yellow-eyed Junco

Snow Bunting
Crimson-collared Grosbeak
Blue Bunting
Shiny Cowbird
Black-vented Oriole
Streak-backed Oriole
Pine Grosbeak
White-winged Crossbill
Common Redpoll
Lawrence's Goldfinch

REVIEW LIST B —
SUBSPECIES OF SPECIAL INTEREST

List of recognizable subspecies which, if they were elevated to full species status, would qualify for placement under Review List A. Reports of these subspecies will always be solicited and formally reviewed.

Green-winged (Common) Teal
Dark-eyed (White-winged) Junco
Orchard (Fuertes's) Oriole

PRESUMPTIVE SPECIES LIST

The following is the official TBRC list of species for which written descriptions of sight records have been accepted by the TBRC, although the descriptions have not met the requirements for full acceptance onto the Texas list (specimen, photo, or tape recording for at least one record).

Murre species
White-crowned Pigeon
Black Swift
Crescent-chested Warbler

TEXAS ORNITHOLOGICAL SOCIETY
Texas Bird Records Committee
Report Form

This form is intended as a convenience in reporting observations of rare or unusual birds. The form is also available on the TOS website at: *www. texasbirds.org/tbrc/forms.htm.* It may be used flexibly and need not be used at all except as a guideline. Attach additional sheets as necessary. PLEASE PRINT IN BLACK INK OR TYPE. Attach original field notes, drawings, photos, etc., if possible. When complete, mail to: Mark Lockwood, Secretary, Texas Bird Records Committee, 402 E. Harriet Ave., Alpine, Texas 79830. Thank you!

1. Common and scientific name:

2. Number of individuals, sexes, ages, general plumage (e.g., 2 adults in breeding plumage):

3. Location (include specific County in Texas):

4. Date and time observed:

5. Reporting observer and address:

6. Other observers:

7. Light conditions:

8. Optical equipment:

9. Distance to bird:

10. Duration of observation:

11. Habitat (be specific):

12. Description: (Include only what was actually seen, not what "should" have been seen. Include, if possible, size and shape of the bird, the bill, the eye

color, other characters. Include plumage patterns and colors. Try to describe voice, behavior, or anything else that might help to confirm the identification.)

13. How were similar species eliminated?

14. Was it photographed? By whom? Attached?

15. Previous experience with this and similar species:

16. List any books or references used in identification:
a. at time of observation:

b. after observation:

17. This description was written from: _____notes made during observation; _____notes made after observation; _____memory.

18. Are you positive of your identification?_____ If not, explain:

19. Signature of reporter along with date and time of writing this account:

Please attach additional sheets if necessary.

NEW MEXICO BIRD RECORDS COMMITTEE LIST OF REVIEW SPECIES

The Committee maintains a Review List of bird species for which it requests documentation of New Mexico records. In addition, the Committee requests documentation of all New Mexico reports of species not currently on the official State List and, hence, potentially new to the state. The Committee provides a standardized Rare/Unusual Bird Report Form – PDF version and Word version – available at *www.nmbirds.org/nmbrc.html*.

Black-bellied Whistling-Duck
Fulvous Whistling-Duck
Brant
Trumpeter Swan
Garganey
Harlequin Duck
Surf Scoter
White-winged Scoter
Black Scoter
Barrow's Goldeneye (outside San Juan Co.)
Gunnison Sage-Grouse
Sharp-tailed Grouse
Red-throated Loon
Yellow-billed Loon
Red-necked Grebe
Least Storm-Petrel
Anhinga
Magnificent Frigatebird
Reddish Egret
Yellow-crowned Night-Heron
White Ibis
Glossy Ibis
Roseate Spoonbill
Wood Stork
Black Vulture
Swallow-tailed Kite
Red-shouldered Hawk
Gray Hawk
Short-tailed Hawk
Crested Caracara
Aplomado Falcon
Yellow Rail
King Rail

Purple Gallinule
American Golden-Plover
Piping Plover
Wandering Tattler
Whimbrel
Hudsonian Godwit
Ruddy Turnstone
Red Knot
Little Stint
Sharp-tailed Sandpiper
Curlew Sandpiper
Buff-breasted Sandpiper
Ruff
Short-billed Dowitcher
American Woodcock
Red Phalarope
Black-legged Kittiwake
Little Gull
Laughing Gull
Heermann's Gull
Mew Gull
Western Gull
Thayer's Gull
Lesser Black-backed Gull
Glaucous-winged Gull
Glaucous Gull
Royal Tern
Elegant Tern
Arctic Tern
Black Skimmer
Pomarine Jaeger
Parasitic Jaeger
Long-tailed Jaeger

Ancient Murrelet
Ruddy Ground-Dove
Black-billed Cuckoo
Groove-billed Ani
Eastern Screech-Owl
Whiskered Screech-Owl (outside
  Peloncillo Mts.)
Barred Owl
Chuck-will's-widow
Buff-collared Nightjar
Green Violetear
White-eared Hummingbird
Berylline Hummingbird
Cinnamon Hummingbird
Blue-throated Hummingbird
  (outside Catron, Grant, and
  Hidalgo Cos.)
Lucifer Hummingbird (outside
  Peloncillo Mts.)
Ruby-throated Hummingbird
Costa's Hummingbird (outside
  Grant and Hidalgo Cos.)
Allen's Hummingbird
Elegant Trogon (outside Hidalgo
  Co.)
Red-bellied Woodpecker
Eastern Wood-Pewee
Yellow-bellied Flycatcher
Acadian Flycatcher
Pacific-slope Flycatcher
Buff-breasted Flycatcher
Great Crested Flycatcher (west of
  Pecos Valley)
Great Kiskadee
Sulphur-bellied Flycatcher
Piratic Flycatcher
Couch's Kingbird
White-eyed Vireo
Black-capped Vireo
Yellow-throated Vireo
Blue-headed Vireo
Philadelphia Vireo
Yellow-green Vireo
Carolina Wren
Sedge Wren
Veery (outside San Juan and Sangre
  de Cristo Mts.)

Gray-cheeked Thrush
Wood Thrush
Clay-colored Thrush
Rufous-backed Robin
Varied Thrush
Long-billed Thrasher
White Wagtail
Bohemian Waxwing
Blue-winged Warbler
Golden-winged Warbler
Tennessee Warbler
Magnolia Warbler
Cape May Warbler
Black-throated Green Warbler
Blackburnian Warbler
Yellow-throated Warbler
Pine Warbler
Prairie Warbler
Palm Warbler
Bay-breasted Warbler
Blackpoll Warbler
Cerulean Warbler
Worm-eating Warbler
Swainson's Warbler
Louisiana Waterthrush
Kentucky Warbler
Mourning Warbler
Canada Warbler
Slate-throated Redstart
Golden-crowned Warbler
Scarlet Tanager
Eastern Towhee
Botteri's Sparrow (outside Hidalgo
  Co.)
Worthen's Sparrow
Henslow's Sparrow
Le Conte's Sparrow
Nelson's Sharp-tailed Sparrow
Snow Bunting
Yellow Grosbeak
Bobolink
Streak-backed Oriole
Baltimore Oriole
Purple Finch
White-winged Crossbill
Lawrence's Goldfinch

AMERICAN BIRDING ASSOCIATION
PRINCIPLES OF BIRDING ETHICS

Everyone who enjoys birds and birding must always respect wildlife, its environment, and the rights of others. In any conflict of interest between birds and birders, the welfare of the birds and their environment comes first.

CODE OF BIRDING ETHICS

1. Promote the welfare of birds and their environment.

1(a) Support the protection of important bird habitat.

1(b) To avoid stressing birds or exposing them to danger, exercise restraint and caution during observation, photography, sound recording, or filming.

Limit the use of recordings and other methods of attracting birds, and never use such methods in heavily birded areas or for attracting any species that is Threatened, Endangered, or of Special Concern, or is rare in your local area.

Keep well back from nests and nesting colonies, roosts, display areas, and important feeding sites. In such sensitive areas, if there is a need for extended observation, photography, filming, or recording, try to use a blind or hide, and take advantage of natural cover.

Use artificial light sparingly for filming or photography, especially for close-ups.

1(c) Before advertising the presence of a rare bird, evaluate the potential for disturbance to the bird, its surroundings, and other people in the area, and proceed only if access can be controlled, disturbance can be minimized, and permission has been obtained from private land-owners. The sites of rare nesting birds should be divulged only to the proper conservation authorities.

1(d) Stay on roads, trails, and paths where they exist; otherwise keep habitat disturbance to a minimum.

Respect the law and the rights of others.

2(a) Do not enter private property without the owner's explicit permission.

2(b) Follow all laws, rules, and regulations governing use of roads and public areas, both at home and abroad.

2(c) Practice common courtesy in contacts with other people. Your exemplary behavior will generate goodwill with birders and non-birders alike.

Ensure that feeders, nest structures, and other artificial bird environments are safe.

3(a) Keep dispensers, water, and food clean and free of decay or disease. It is important to feed birds continually during harsh weather.

3(b) Maintain and clean nest structures regularly.

3(c) If you are attracting birds to an area, ensure the birds are not exposed to predation from cats and other domestic animals, or dangers posed by artificial hazards.

Group birding, whether organized or impromptu, requires special care.

- Each individual in the group, in addition to the obligations spelled out in Items #1 and #2, has responsibilities as a Group Member.

4(a) Respect the interests, rights, and skills of fellow birders, as well as those of people participating in other legitimate outdoor activities. Freely share your knowledge and experience, except where code 1(c) applies. Be especially helpful to beginning birders.

4(b) If you witness unethical birding behavior, assess the situation and intervene if you think it prudent. When interceding, inform the person(s) of the inappropriate action and attempt, within reason, to have it stopped. If the behavior continues, document it and notify appropriate individuals or organizations.

- Group Leader Responsibilities [amateur and professional trips and tours].

4(c) Be an exemplary ethical role model for the group. Teach through word and example.

4(d) Keep groups to a size that limits impact on the environment and does not interfere with others using the same area.

4(e) Ensure everyone in the group knows of and practices this code.

4(f) Learn and inform the group of any special circumstances applicable to the areas being visited (e.g., no tape recorders allowed).

4(g) Acknowledge that professional tour companies bear a special responsibility to place the welfare of birds and the benefits of public knowledge ahead of the company's commercial interests. Ideally, leaders should keep track of tour sightings, document unusual occurrences, and submit records to appropriate organizations.

PLEASE FOLLOW THIS CODE— DISTRIBUTE IT AND TEACH IT TO OTHERS.

American Birding Association
4945 N 30th Street, Suite 200
Colorado Springs, CO 80919
(800) 850-2473 or (719) 578-9703 or (719) 578-1480
e-mail: member@aba.org; website: www.americanbirding.org

This ABA Code of Birding Ethics may be reprinted, reproduced, and distributed without restriction. Please acknowledge the role of ABA in developing and promoting this code.

7/1/96

Join Today!

AmericanBirding

A S S O C I A T I O N

Name _____

Address _____

_____

City _____ State _____ Zip _____

Country _____ Phone _____

Email _____

Each level entitles members to certain benefits.
Visit <www.americanbirding.org/memgen.htm> or call 800-850-2473 to find out more.

O Individual. . . . . US $45

O Joint . . . . US $52

O Student[a] . . . . US $25

O International / Canada Individual[b] . . . US $55

O International / Canada Joint[b] . . . . . . US $63

O International / Canada Student[ab] . . . . US $35

[a] Please include your birth date, school name, and graduation date
[b] Canadian dues include GST, which is paid to the Canadian government
All membership dues include $30 for **Birding** magazine and

Sent this form to:

ABA Membership
4945 N. 30th Street
Colorado Springs, CO
80910

You may also join by phone fax, or web:
Phone 800-850-2473
Fax 719-578-1480
www.americanbirding.org/join.html

Membership: $ _____

Additional Contribution: $ _____ for: O Unrestricted O Conservation O Education

Total: $ _____

U.S. dollars; check or money order payable to American Birding Association, or charge to:

O VISA   O Mastercard   O Discover

Card # _____ Exp Date _____

Signature _____

Index

Frontera Thicket (Weslaco) 54-55

G

Gadwall 92, 147, 175, 224
Gallinule, Purple 29, 39, 53, 64-65, 239
Gannet, Northern 30, 33, 35, 40-41, 231
Garganey 225
Garner State Park (Kerrville) 213
Gladys Porter Zoo (Brownsville) 22
Gnatcatcher
  Black-tailed 79, 81, 90-91, 94-95, 106,
    127, 129, 131, 137, 141, 180, 182, 272
  Blue-gray 21, 28, 61, 79, 104, 111, 127,
    129, 141, 187, 197-198, 200, 219, 272
Godwit
  Hudsonian 38, 69, 121, 163, 242
  Marbled 35, 38, 163, 242
Golden-Plover, American 51, 69, 84, 121
Goldeneye
  Barrow's 164, 226
  Common 226
Goldfinch
  American 93, 127, 167, 171, 176, 220, 293
  Lawrence's 125, 166, 173, 176, 293
  Lesser 26, 28, 43, 46, 53, 55, 67, 70-72,
    82, 89, 93-94, 96, 108, 127, 138, 141,
    143, 153, 171, 183, 186, 197, 205,
    211-212, 220, 292
Goose
  Cackling 223
  Canada 223
  Greater White-fronted 92, 95, 223
  Ross's 84-85, 156, 160, 163-164, 174, 180,
    223
  Snow 85, 92, 145, 160, 163-164, 174, 180,
    223
Goshawk, Northern 176, 235
Government Canyon State Natural Area
  (San Antonio) 198
Government Spring, Big Bend NP 135
Grackle
  Boat-tailed 290
  Common 139, 155, 290
  Great-tailed 143, 155, 171, 290
Grassquit, Yellow-faced 16, 58, 65, 81, 283
Grassy Banks, Big Bend Ranch SP 139
Grebe
  Clark's 121, 156, 160, 163-164, 180, 229
  Eared 31, 33, 35, 38-39, 84, 164, 172,
    174, 180, 205, 229
  Horned 38, 111, 205-206, 228
  Least 13, 15, 23, 26, 28-29, 41-43, 50-51,
    53-54, 57-58, 61, 64-65, 67, 69, 76, 82,
    92, 95, 111, 128, 175, 228
  Pied-billed 38, 51, 79, 82, 92, 111, 128,
    164, 168, 172, 174-175, 180, 205, 228
  Western 38, 121, 156, 160, 163-164, 180,
    229

Green Gulch, Big Bend NP 131

Grosbeak
  Black-headed 20, 39, 70, 124, 129, 131,
    147, 150-152, 167, 171, 183, 186-187, 189,
    288
  Blue 38, 84, 91, 96, 111-112, 119, 127, 132,
    136-137, 141, 147, 155, 159, 167-168, 172,
    179, 182, 186, 190, 200, 203, 205, 212,
    219, 289
  Crimson-collared 26, 42, 55, 58, 72, 288
  Evening 176, 182-183, 293
  Pine 292
  Rose-breasted 38, 288
Ground-Dove
  Common 35, 43, 45, 53, 61, 73, 79, 81, 86,
    96, 118, 127, 153, 159, 199, 216, 220, 250
  Ruddy 58, 75, 127, 138, 176, 179, 250
Guadalupe Mountains National Park 183-189
Guadalupe River 199, 209, 211
Guadalupe River State Park (San Antonio)
  199
Gull
  Black-headed 245
  Black-tailed 30, 246
  Bonaparte's 40, 49, 110, 160, 199, 206, 245
  California 29, 161, 163, 173, 246
  Franklin's 29, 39, 160, 245
  Glaucous 30, 33, 96, 173, 247
  Great Black-backed 30, 33, 247
  Heermann's 246
  Herring 29, 33, 38, 40, 160, 173, 206, 246
  Iceland 173, 246
  Laughing 29, 33, 38, 40, 48, 111, 121, 161,
    163, 173, 245
  Lesser Black-backed 29, 33, 40, 101, 161,
    173, 247
  Little 13, 33, 245
  Mew 163, 173, 246
  Ring-billed 29, 33, 38, 40, 110, 160, 163,
    173, 199, 206, 246
  Sabine's 33, 40, 121, 156, 161, 173, 245
  Slaty-backed 30, 247
  Thayer's 29, 96, 163, 173, 246
  Western 85, 173, 246

H

Harlingen 45-49
Harlingen Arroyo Colorado 45
Harlingen Thicket 47

Dark-eyed 127, 141, 150-151, 155, 167, 171, 176, 185, 187, 189, 220, 287
Yellow-eyed 132, 186, 287
Juniper Canyon, Big Bend NP 131

K

Kerr Wildlife Management Area (Kerrville) 211
Kerrville 208
Kerrville-Schreiner Park 208
Kestrel, American 26, 31, 50, 88, 96, 114, 145, 156, 164, 167, 172, 176, 179, 181, 185, 238
Keystone Heritage Park (El Paso) 174
Kickapoo Cavern State Park (Brackettville) 216-217
Killdeer 162-163, 172, 174
Kingbird
  Cassin's 143, 149-150, 155, 159, 183, 186, 190, 263
  Couch's 13, 15, 18, 20-21, 23, 26-29, 31, 39, 41-45, 50, 54-55, 57-58, 61, 63-64, 67, 69, 71-72, 74, 76, 79, 82, 84-85, 89, 91, 93, 95, 100, 108-109, 119, 137, 219-220, 263
  Eastern 38, 264
  Gray 39, 264
  Thick-billed 127, 137, 264
  Tropical 13, 18, 21, 23, 25, 29, 37, 39, 42, 45, 48, 50, 54-55, 57, 70, 82, 100, 125, 137, 263
  Western 38, 50, 85, 108, 127, 137, 141, 153, 155, 162, 164, 167, 170, 172, 176, 179, 190, 204, 211, 264
Kingfisher
  Belted 54, 88, 92, 104, 128, 174, 176, 179, 208, 258
  Green 20, 22-23, 25, 29, 45, 54-55, 58, 61-62, 64, 72, 79, 82, 84, 88-90, 92, 94, 97-98, 104, 108, 111, 116, 118, 199, 209, 212, 214-215, 219, 258
  Ringed 13, 15, 18, 20, 22-23, 29, 41-42, 44, 50-51, 54, 58, 61, 72, 79, 82, 88-90, 92, 98-99, 104, 108, 111, 114, 119, 219, 258
Kinglet
  Golden-crowned 62, 171, 186, 272
  Ruby-crowned 21, 28, 61, 79, 104, 127, 141, 155, 165, 171, 174, 176, 179, 182, 198, 200, 220, 272
Kiskadee, Great 13, 15, 18, 20, 22-23, 25-26, 29, 42-45, 47, 49, 54-55, 57-58, 60, 64, 69, 71-72, 76, 79, 81-82, 85, 89-90, 93, 95, 108-109, 115, 219, 263
Kite
  Hook-billed 13, 15, 57-58, 62-66, 75-76, 79-81, 88, 90, 93-95, 99, 234
  Mississippi 31, 39, 62-63, 73, 75, 84, 88, 111, 168, 175-176, 180, 212, 234
  Snail 35, 234

Swallow-tailed 26, 29, 39, 62, 84, 139, 234
White-tailed 26, 29, 31, 34, 50, 64, 82, 85, 108, 168, 234
Kittiwake, Black-legged 33, 40, 96, 121, 163, 245
Knot, Red 33, 40, 173, 243

L

La Feria Sod Farm 51
La Joya 86
La Lomita Mission 75
La Paloma Reservoir (Brownsville) 49
La Sal del Rey Tract, Lower Rio Grande Valley NWR 84
Lajitas 138
Lake
  Amistad 109
  Balmorhea 155
  Buchanan (Austin) 205-206
  Burn (Las Cruces, NM) 180
  Canyon (San Antonio) 199
  Cattail, Santa Ana NWR 65
  City (Harlingen) 48
  Delta (Edinburg) 85
  Edinburg (Retama Reservoir 84
  Feather (El Paso) 169
  Llano Grande (Weslaco) 51
  Loma Alta (Brownsville) 34
  Red Bluff (Pecos Valley) 121
  Willow (Santa Ana NWR) 61
Lamar Bruni Vergara Environmental Science Center (Laredo) 105
Langtry 117
Laredo 104
Lark, Horned 51, 145, 149, 268
Las Cruces, NM 177-183
Lawrence E. Wood Picnic Grounds, Davis Mtns. SP 151
Limpia Creek, Davis Mtns. 153
Llano Grande Lake (Weslaco) 51
Llano Pasture, Big Bend Ranch SP 143
Loma Alta Lake (Brownsville) 34
Longhorn Cavern State Park (Austin) 205
Longspur
  Chestnut-collared 143, 145-146, 152-153, 288
  Lapland 287
  McCown's 143, 145-146, 152-153, 287
  Smith's 287

ABBREVIATED TABLE OF CONTENTS	

NOTES